N. M. KARAMZIN

A STUDY

OF HIS LITERARY CAREER

1783-1803

A. G. Cross

SOUTHERN ILLINOIS UNIVERSITY PRESS

Carbondale and Edwardsville

FEFFER & SIMONS, INC.

London and Amsterdam

for my mother

CONTENTS

List of Illustrations *ix*

Acknowledgments *xi*

Introduction *xiii*

ONE
The Formative Years (1766–1790) 1

TWO
The *Moscow Journal* (1791–1792) 35

THREE
Letters of a Russian Traveler (1791–1801) 66

FOUR
Sentimental Fiction (1789–1803) 96

FIVE
From *Aglaia* to
The Pantheon of Russian Authors (1793–1801) 143

SIX
Karamzin's Verse and *Aonides* (1796–1799) 172

SEVEN
The *Messenger of Europe* (1802–1803) 193

EIGHT
Into the Temple of History 218

Checklist of Original and Translated Reviews in the
Moscow Journal 233

Notes 243

Selected Bibliography 275

Index 295

LIST OF ILLUSTRATIONS

BETWEEN PAGES 134–135

Portraits of N. M. Karamzin

BETWEEN PAGES 150–151

Illustrations from *Pis'ma russkogo puteshestvennika*

ACKNOWLEDGMENTS

THE BASIC RESEARCH for this book was begun in Cambridge in 1961, continued in the Soviet Union during a one-year post-graduate studentship to Moscow University and led in the first instance to a doctoral thesis, accepted at the University of Cambridge at the beginning of 1966.

Some of the findings of this initial and subsequent research have been published since 1964 in a number of scholarly journals; an article on Karamzin's versification which first appeared in the *Slavic Review* has been incorporated into chapter 6 of the present study and chapter 7 is substantially the same as an article which was published in the *Forum for Modern Language Studies*. I am indebted to the editors of both these journals for permission to reproduce these materials.

The writing of this book was completed at the Center for Advanced Study at the University of Illinois during the autumn and winter of 1968–69. I am profoundly grateful to the Steering Committee of the Center for the award of a post-doctoral fellowship and to my sponsor, Professor Ralph Fisher, Jr.

The early chapters of the book were read by Professor John Garrard of Dartmouth College, to whom I am indebted for his comments and criticism.

The task of preparing the typescript of my book was performed with immense patience and skill by Mrs. Susan Palmer.

Finally, I wish to record my respect for Professor Iu. M. Lotman of Tartu University, with whom I have corresponded but never met, but whose writings on Karamzin and his period since 1957 have been a constant stimulus to me in my own work.

A. G. Cross

Norwich, England
July 1969

INTRODUCTION

THE REIGN of Catherine the Great witnessed unprecedented ferment and development in Russian literature. Catherine herself fostered this activity in the belief that it would add luster to her reign and, a modest trend-setter in her own literary work, she successfully cultivated, particularly abroad, a reputation as an enlightened authoress. She was a capricious and arbitrary woman, anxious to keep control of what she had set in motion to a degree which brought eventually the destruction of some of the finest talents produced by her time. In cultural terms her reign was nonetheless a golden age, impressive by its own achievements and a necessary prelude to the age of Pushkin: there was an accelerated advance and enrichment in music, painting, architecture, literature, and there emerged Russians capable not only of slavish imitation of the West but of creative emulation. This sense of Russia's cultural emergence is caught in a typical, if mediocre engraving, published in 1801 with its accompanying lines of explanation: "The sun illuminates a wintery scene on one side but on the other draws from the earth grass and flowers by the speedy action of its rays: the symbol of enlightenment in our country."[1]

One of the few events from the brief reign of the unfortunate Peter III had been the decree of February 1762 which freed the nobility from obligatory state service; although many continued to serve, others took advantage of their new, official leisure to do nothing or to turn their energies to other pursuits. It was a decree which, it has been argued,[2] led to the alienation of the nobility from the state and the creation of an intelligentsia. Catherine naturally was concerned to channel the nobility's energies into enterprises which would ensure the well-being of Russia, as she conceived it. The first part of her reign is marked by the creation of institutions and societies of all kinds, the development of which was not always in line with what she had envisaged. The typical Catherine pattern of initiation, vacillation and ultimate repression may be illustrated in the field of literature by two examples, which are both connected with the name of N. I. Novikov (1743–1818).

In 1769 the publication of the Catherine-inspired *Pot-Pourri* [*Vsiakaia vsiachina*] was the signal for an intense but short-lived period of satirical journalism. Two years earlier she had promulgated her famous *Nakaz* and summoned deputies from all over Russia to participate in a legislative commission, and she envisaged the satirical journals as a platform for wider discussion of social and bureaucratic evils and malpractices and the creation of responsible public opinion. She succeeded admirably but her progeny was more responsible, independent, and critical than she had intended. The incisiveness of the criticism, the pointedness of the satire, particularly from the pen of Novikov, who had been a secretary to the commission, provoked Catherine to stifle what she had initially encouraged. The Pugachev Rebellion became a convenient excuse to curtail the activities of both the commission and the satirical journals by 1774. Nevertheless, from a literary point of view the satirical journals provided Russia with almost its first examples of good prose; Novikov at his best wrote lucidly, succinctly, and epigrammatically.

A decade later, Novikov was again the major figure in exploiting another of Catherine's important innovations. In 1783 she issued an *ukaz* permitting the setting-up of independent presses (vol'nye tipografii); the number of presses in Moscow and St. Petersburg quickly increased and presses were started in many provincial towns. Novikov, who in 1779 had moved from St. Petersburg to Moscow to take up a ten-year lease on the University press, had already initiated many of the revolutionary enterprises which led the historian Kliuchevskii to term the period up to 1789 "the Novikov decade."[3] He produced books which in quantity, quality, and variety set new standards in Russia and of 2685 books published between 1781 and 1790, 749 or 28 percent came from the Novikov presses.[4] Taking advantage of Catherine's *ukaz*, he, in collaboration with fellow freemasons, set up additional presses, including a "secret" masonic one and another connected with the Typographical Company (Tipograficheskaia kompaniia), which was formed in 1784. Catherine soon became alarmed by the extent of his activities and suspicious of the political loyalties of the Moscow freemasons. Although 1789 was the golden year of book publication in Russia (439 titles) it coincided with the French Revolution and Catherine's moves to curb free expression and enterprise within Russia. Novikov's empire was crushed and in 1792 he was imprisoned in the Schlüsselburg fortress. About twenty thousand books, impounded at Novikov's presses and bookshops, were burnt in Moscow in 1793–94, by which date two further repressive actions against prominent literary figures had been perpetrated: Aleksandr Radishchev's publication of his *Journey from Petersburg to Moscow* [*Puteshestvie iz Peterburga v Moskvu*] (1790) at a private press in St. Petersburg led to his exile in Siberia, and the publishing firm of the future fabulist Ivan Krylov had been raided and closed in 1793. The last decade of the eighteenth century witnessed a complete withdrawal from the very principle of free publishing Catherine had introduced and in 1796 the wheel turned full circle with the suppression of the independent presses. By this last year of Catherine's reign the number of books published was about half what it had been in 1789 and the figure dropped throughout the reign of Paul.

The vagaries of Catherine's rule need no further emphasis; it is the cultural benefits which her policy on publishing willy-nilly produced which are of immediate concern. There were about eleven thousand books published in Russia in the eighteenth century and of these about sixty-five hundred were published in the last twenty-five years. This indicates an obvious increase in numbers and also inevitably in variety. Although educated Russians had long read and continued to read works in French, and sometimes in German, Italian, and English, the Russian literary scene under Catherine presents unprecedented activity both in the translation of foreign works and the production of original work in all fields. In 1768 Catherine instituted one of her most enlightened projects, the Society for the Translation of Foreign books (Sobranie staraiushcheesia o perevode inostrannykh knig). In its fifteen years of existence the Society published 112 works, or 173 volumes of translation in all. The works translated covered the sciences, history, geography, and literature and the modern authors chosen included Montesquieu, Voltaire, Mably, Corneille, Diderot, D'Alembert, Blackstone, Swift, Fielding, Gellert, Tasso, and Goldoni.[5] There were soon cadres of translators in St. Petersburg and Moscow, some closely linked with literary journals, others formed by Novikov among the masons or at the university. The works of many European writers who had been no more than names to the Russian public became accessible in translations which varied widely in quality and fidelity; authors, representing different centuries, different cultures, different schools, were translated side by side. It is not surprising that original Russian literature in the period from the 1760's up to the late 1780's reveals curious and contradictory allegiances, a concertinaed history of European literature.

The reign of Elizabeth had seen the apogée of Russian classicism, a far from homogeneous movement or style as is obvious from the most superficial acquaintance with the work of the three authors most commonly associated with it—V. K. Trediakovskii (1703–69), M. V. Lomonosov (1711–65) and A. P. Sumarokov (1718–77). Trediakovskii and Lomonosov shared a similar social and educational background and were dissimilar not so much in what they strove for as theorists as in what they achieved as practicing poets. It was the fate of Trediakovskii to be ridiculed and parodied and of Lomonosov to be hailed as the "Russian Pindar." Sumarokov's allegiances moved from Trediakovskii to Lomonosov before he emerged as in many ways the most important and influential of Russia's classical triumvirate. More precisely described as "the Russian Boileau" than "the Northern Racine," he became by the 1750's the main theoretician and practitioner of pseudoclassicism, for which the source of inspiration was French literature of the seventeenth and eighteenth centuries. Although Trediakovskii and Lomonosov, particularly as exponents of the ode, may properly be discussed with reference to baroque poetic traditions, Sumarokov, despite his own particular characteristics and emphases, conforms more obviously to the image of the European classicist.

In 1748 Sumarokov published two epistles, the first "on the Russian language," the second "on poetry," in which he adopted and adapted material from Boileau's *Art poétique*. Acknowledging the richness of the Russian language, he emphasized the need for logic and clarity, intelligence and study, and in the second epistle he elucidated his conception of the genres in drama and poetry, outlining their salient characteristics and demanding harmony of style and subject matter. Recognized as the father of the Russian theatre, Sumarokov produced from 1747 a series of tragedies in the pseudoclassical mold and a number of freer and racier comedies. He practiced most genres of poetry, cultivating particularly the song (which he had defined at length in his second epistle). He was a constant and bold innovator, who was of paramount importance in the development of Russian literature throughout the remainder of the eighteenth century, although by the beginning of the nineteenth century his reputation was that of a mere hack writer. By the early 1760's there had emerged a distinctive Sumarokov school of talented but minor poets who accepted and developed what he had initiated. Originally a firm supporter of Catherine, he soon fell into disfavor and in 1769 moved to Moscow, where he died, a bitter and impoverished man, in 1777. The importance of Sumarokov lies not only in the field of literary theory and practice, but equally in his ideology. Proud of his membership in the nobility, he accepted a class hierarchy no less distinct than his genre division, but he insisted on the responsible and active role of his class, the true "sons of the fatherland." He subscribed to the concept of "enlightened absolutism" and his disagreement with Catherine led him to revise in 1768 his earlier tragedies and strengthen their contemporary political application, which is clearly in evidence in his later tragedies, written in Moscow, particularly his *False Demetrius* [*Dimitrii Samozvanets*] (1771). By the time he moved to Moscow, he represented an independent, even oppositional position, that of the alienated noble intelligentsia. His very removal to Moscow was a symbolic art, for it was there, in Russia's other and older capital, which Catherine so distrusted, that intellectual life, free from the restraints and direct surveillance of the court, flourished.

It is with Moscow that the work of two of the outstanding figures in Catherine's reign, M. M. Kheraskov (1733–1807) and Novikov, is profoundly linked, although both spent varying periods of time in St. Petersburg; both, like Sumarokov, were masons; both were to a greater or lesser degree at cross-purposes with Catherine; both adhered to the basic ideology propounded by Sumarokov. The elder of the two, Kheraskov, graduated in 1751 from the St. Petersburg Cadet Corps, with which Sumarokov had been closely connected since its opening in 1732. Kheraskov contributed poems to the first Russian literary journal, *Monthly Compositions for Profit*

and Entertainment [*Ezhemesiachnye sochineniia, k pol'ze i uveseleniiu sluzhashchie*] (1755), in which Sumarokov and other poets
from his circle, including A. A. Nartov and A. A. Rzhevskii, participated. Kheraskov soon moved to Moscow to begin his long association with Moscow University, also founded in 1755, and formed his
own influential literary circle; retaining his affection and respect
for Sumarokov, he pursued his own distinctive career.[6] During
Sumarokov's last years in Moscow Kheraskov was back in St. Petersburg, where he was instrumental in persuading Novikov to enter
the masonic order. Kheraskov returned to Moscow as Curator of
the University only in 1779, two years after the death of Sumarokov, and arranged the lease on the University press for Novikov.
One of Novikov's early and significant publications, in which he
was probably encouraged by Kheraskov, was the complete works of
Sumarokov (1781). In 1787 a second edition of this huge ten-
volume collection was brought out and in the preceding year all
Sumarokov's tragedies and comedies appeared in separate editions.
It is significant that the verses to Sumarokov's portrait prefacing
the complete works came from the pen of Kheraskov, who characterized Sumarokov as "this soaring, passionate, tender poet," rival-
ing Racine and La Fontaine[7]—an accolade which Novikov had
bestowed on him nearly ten years earlier.[8]

In 1779 Kheraskov completed his vast epic poem, *The Rossiad*
[*Rossiada*], and provided Russian classicism with its own example
in an important high-style genre, but Kheraskov had long since
cultivated other genres, both inside and outside the classical canon,
which prepared the way for sentimentalism, the predominant literary vogue in Russia at the turn of the century. It is in accord with
the neat but patently facile division to which the major European
literatures have long been subject that modern Russian literature is
said to reveal a progression from (pseudo) classicism to sentimentalism or preromanticism, from romanticism to realism. Sentimentalism is a term which has gained particular currency in Russian
literary history, although increasingly critics seek to trace its origins
to the 1760's and even late 1750's.[9] Their findings demonstrate
above all the constant flux and change in aesthetic principles and
ideas, the limitations of labels and their precise location in time.
To the extent that the term Russian classicism unites the work of
very disparate authors and plays down their contradictory, individ-

ual features, so Russian sentimentalism is a movement of widely differing talents, ideologies, and aims. Attempts have been made to emphasize the differences by polarizing "progressive" and "reactionary," "active" and "passive" tendencies, exemplified in the work of Radishchev and Karamzin respectively. It is a contrast which, crudely exaggerated and exploited, has led to a minimizing of Karamzin's importance and achievement. Nevertheless, consideration of Karamzin as a representative of "gentry sentimentalism" (dvorianskii sentimentalizm) does shed a revealing light on his literary and ideological position and the nature of his art. A comparison between classicism and sentimentalism on the basis of the work of Lomonosov and Karamzin provides a much starker contrast than a more meaningful one based on the work of Sumarokov and Karamzin.

The relationship between Sumarokov and Kheraskov and Novikov has already been alluded to; although Karamzin's best-known comments on Sumarokov are criticisms of his tragedies, it should be noted that these date from the beginning of the nineteenth century and that as a young mason, a protégé of Novikov and a sincere admirer of Kheraskov, Karamzin shared their enthusiasm for Sumarokov's work. As a political thinker Karamzin continues the Sumarokov tradition, emphasizing the prime role and responsibilities of the gentry, accepting the concept of an enlightened autocrat and a distinct hierarchy of classes, shunning revolution and believing passionately in the panacea of enlightenment. The obvious differences in their aesthetic views should not obscure their many points of contact, not least the similarity in their linguistic and stylistic demands. The transference of allegiances from the reason to the heart was not an anarchic release for the passions and feelings that classicism depicted and strove to control; Karamzin's sentimentalism was strongly moral and didactic, although its code was not as austere and lofty as Sumarokov's. For all his advocacy of the beauties of the feeling heart Karamzin eschewed extremes and sought a harmony of heart and mind. Sentimentalism is in many respects the meeting point between the two more self-conscious movements of romanticism and classicism. It is a transitional movement, avoiding abrupt change and blurring boundaries; it is analogous to its own favored state of melancholy, fusing elements of what was past and what was imminent.

It was the middle-style genres of classicism that Karamzin cultivated: love lyrics, elegies, songs idylls, pastorals, free from rhetoric and pomp, the products of the "quiet lyre," which the Kheraskov circle developed and which turned the attention from the abstract and general to the individual and the specific. It was an orientation which was sustained and nourished by other emerging, dominant genres in the 1770's and 1780's which were anathema to classicism and opposed vigorously by Sumarokov: the "mixed forms" of the *comédie larmoyante* and *drame sérieux* and the "English novel." It is not the intention here to trace in detail the transition from classicism to sentimentalism; the main lines of development have been noted in Soviet studies[10] and a recent English-language work provides a general survey of major trends, exemplified in original Russian works and translations.[11] Karamzin's emergence as the most significant representative of sentimentalism in Russian literature was obviously prepared by literary developments over preceding decades; he was a child of his age who quickly reached maturity and exercised great authority.

There is another method of periodization, peculiar to Russian literature, which is by reference to the achievement of certain individual writers, colossi in fact and in myth, whose activity, spreading to all aspects of literature, provided the stimulus and example for their contemporaries and posterity. It is a periodization which marks the development of a literature from infancy to maturity. Lomonosov, Karamzin, Pushkin, and Gogol' are the four names which serve as milestones along this path. They represent to some extent the four literary movements already named; they also by virtue of their particular strengths mark the alteration in the ascendancy of verse and prose throughout a century stretching from the 1740's to the 1840's. It is, nonetheless, a periodization which focuses attention on one author but does not inevitably categorize him; it admits of development and change in his work and ideas but acknowledges his intellectual leadership, his ability to influence, form, and create. Its limitations are obvious but not overwhelming: it seems to ignore or relegate the work of others, to minimize the complexity of the literary scene, to leave chronological gaps, but, given an awareness of these pitfalls, it is a scheme which, in the case of Karamzin at least, can be meaningfully exploited.

Lomonosov died in 1765, the year before Karamzin was born;

Karamzin began literary work in 1783 but achieved prominence only in 1791, and his literary career was effectively finished by 1804, when Pushkin was only four years old. Yet in the way Lomonosov's authority continued long after his death, Karamzin's work remained influential throughout the period he was engaged in writing his history. Although, as we shall see, Karamzin was instrumental in fostering the concept of a period in Russian literature to be identified with his name, as part of a general scheme of Russian literary development, the willingness with which his contemporaries and subsequent generations subscribed to the suggestion is an indication of their recognition of his great contribution to Russian letters. The present study seeks to examine the extent and nature of this contribution. Although there is a detailed analysis of his early years, particularly his literary activity in the period 1785–89, or what might be termed the prehistory of the Karamzin period, the main emphasis is on the work he produced between 1791 and 1803. The arrangement is basically chronological, moving from Karamzin's first journal (1791–92) to his second and last (1802–3), by way of his other publishing ventures, literary almanacs, and "pantheons." Separate chapters are devoted to his travel letters, his fiction, and his poetry which are isolated for a greater awareness of his achievement in the specific media of prose and verse. It is hoped that the study as a whole will contribute to a better appreciation of Karamzin's work "in its development, changes and fluctuations."[12]

N. M. KARAMZIN

A Study of His Literary Career

1783-1803

The transliteration system used is that recommended
by the *Slavic Review*.

All dates are given according to the Julian Calendar.

ONE

THE FORMATIVE YEARS

1766-1790

Nikolai Mikhailovich Karamzin was born on December 1, 1766, the second son of Mikhail Egorovich Karamzin, a retired army captain. The first ten years of his life were spent mainly at Znamenskoe, also called Karamzinka, a small family estate not far from the provincial capital, Simbirsk. Although his childhood was conventional and uneventful, Karamzin, influenced in his recollections of these early years by the fashions of western sentimental literature, was to stress the sensitive, melancholic sides of his character, his preference for lonely pursuits and the richness of his imagination; similarly, although his mother died before he was three years old, it is literary example which dictates the importance the images of the orphaned hero and his mother were to assume in his work.

At Znamenskoe Karamzin received his first unsystematic education: he began to learn German from a local German doctor and, somewhat later, French from the wife of a neighboring landowner. He read Aesop's *Fables* and seems to have developed a precocious taste for his late mother's collection of adventure novels, if we are to believe his novel, "A Knight of Our Time" ["Rytsar' nashego vremeni"] (1802-3), confessedly based on his reminiscences of childhood.[1] He then graduated to Charles Rollin's *Histoire de Rome* in the Russian version by Trediakovskii, a work of considerable ideological importance in the eighteenth century but for the young Karamzin primarily a rich pageant of heroic warriors.[2]

In 1776 he was sent to Simbirsk to attend a school run by a Monsieur Fauvel, but the following year he entered the Moscow boarding school directed by Johann Matthias Schaden (1731-97), a professor of moral philosophy at the university.[3] Karamzin recalls

1

the four happy years (1777–81) he spent there, his admiration for
Schaden and his love of languages, particularly German.[4] Elsewhere he writes of his introduction to German literature, specifically F. C. Gellert's fables and *Moralische Vorlesungen*, which
Schaden used to instill moral precepts in his young charges.[5] Karamzin also associates with Schaden's school the beginning of his
admiration for England, "the country most attractive to my heart,"
and remembers the feasts he would organize to celebrate the victories of the English admirals during the American War of Independence.[6] It is possibly at this period that he began to learn English.[7]
Karamzin tends to emphasize the childish nature of his interests,
but he also attended lectures at the university, possibly including
those delivered by Schaden himself. Many of Schaden's views on
religion, enlightenment, and government found an obvious response in Karamzin, and close parallels have been drawn between
passages in Schaden's lectures (seven extant from the period 1767–
93) and later articles and pronouncements by Karamzin.[8] Yet Schaden's views are not significantly different from the mainstream
Germano-masonic pedagogy, with its pronounced moral and religious basis, which dominated Moscow University and its *pensions*
in the 1780's and 1790's.

Although Karamzin indicates that he wished to continue his
studies at Leipzig University,[9] he left Schaden's in 1781 to join the
Preobrazhenskii Guard Regiment in St. Petersburg, into which he
had been enrolled as a child by his father in accordance with accepted gentry practice. Although he retired officially from the
Guards only in January 1784, Karamzin was in Petersburg less than
a year. Surviving military records show that he was on leave from
September 1781 until September 1782, and from February 6, 1783,
until retirement.[10] This period marks the beginning of Karamzin's
lifelong friendship with I. I. Dmitriev (1760–1837), a poet who
was to be credited by his contemporaries for achieving in poetry
what Karamzin was to achieve in prose. Dmitriev was an habitué of
the literary salons and theatres in the capital and had already contributed a number of translations and poems to literary journals.
Perhaps for the only time during the forty-five years of their friendship Dmitriev acted as Karamzin's mentor and guide in literary
matters; he encouraged him to attempt his first translations. Dmitriev recalls that Karamzin's first translation was "A Conversation

in the Elysian Fields between Maria Theresa and the Empress Elizabeth" (original unknown), for which he received from a bookseller a translation of Fielding's *Tom Jones*.[11] The piece, evidently a typical "conversation among the dead," was never published, but in 1783 there appeared Karamzin's version of Salomon Gessner's "Das hölzerne Bein," again in prose and from German, his strongest language. This German orientation was a natural outcome of his earlier education, but Dmitriev's friendship was fruitful in acquainting him with the work of both Russian and French writers. One of the few events from this period that Karamzin himself recalls in later years is the premiere of Denis Fonvizin's *The Minor* [*Nedorosl'*], performed on September 24, 1783.[12]

Karamzin's official reason for retiring from the Guards was the death of his father, although he wrote to Lavater that military service interfered with his studies. He goes on: "and so I was already in retirement in my eighteenth year and dreaming of devoting myself to books. At the same time I allowed myself to enjoy the pleasures of society, thinking, however, that they would not make a strong impression on me or turn me away from my books."[13] Nevertheless, Dmitriev portrays Karamzin at this time (1784–85) as an inveterate cardplayer, salon orator, and assured man-of-the-world, although reading widely, if "indiscriminately."[14] This is manifest in the ease with which Karamzin combines an enthusiasm for Voltaire's "Le Taureau blanc," which he proposed to translate, with the assiduous reading of Edward Young's *The Complaint, or Night Thoughts*.[15] By the beginning of 1785 Karamzin's great passion was for Shakespeare; he outlined his grandiose plans to the young Moscow freemason, Aleksandr Petrov (d. 1793), who comments with amusement that Moscow authors would be unable to get their work published when the presses were "engaged on the printing of the *Russian Shakespeare*."[16] The product of Karamzin's enthusiasm was to be a translation of *Julius Caesar*, published in 1787.

The letters Petrov wrote to Karamzin in May and June 1785, are the unique contemporary source of information on Karamzin's literary ambitions at this period—Dmitriev's memoirs were not written until 1823–24. The third letter, dated June 11, 1785, provides a particularly vivid characterization of the eighteen-year-old Karamzin's lofty plans and immature attainments.[17] "What is there missing on the subject of literature? Everything is there! You write about translations, about your own works, about Shakespeare, about tragic characters, about Voltaire's unjust criticism, as well as about coffee and tobacco." He comments ironically on "a most elegant treatise" on Solomon, written by Karamzin in German, in which "you rise above trivialities to such an extent that in three lines you made five mistakes in your German" and advises him to write in Russian for "there is nothing worse than to begin to demonstrate knowledge of some language or other by mistakes in that language."

In July 1785, Karamzin finally left Simbirsk for Moscow to join Novikov's Friendly Learned Society (Druzheskoe uchenoe obshchestvo, founded in 1781); instrumental in this move was I. P. Turgenev (1752–1807), a leading mason and founder of the Simbirsk lodge, The Golden Crown (Zlatoi venets), of which Karamzin had become a member in 1784.[18] Through Turgenev's influence Karamzin was able to overcome the temptations of society life and devote himself to serious study in the company of Petrov and other young masons. Dmitriev, who had observed Karamzin in St. Petersburg and in Simbirsk, was very conscious of the change in him; Karamzin was now "a pious student of wisdom, with a burning eagerness for self-perfection." It was in Moscow that "Karamzin's education began, not only literary but moral."[19]

The aim of the Friendly Learned Society, according to I. V. Lopukhin (1756–1816), a prominent Moscow mason, was "to publish spiritual books and instructions in morality in accord with the truth of the Scriptures and translated from the most profound foreign authors, and to aid good education."[20] Nevertheless, the actual activity of the Society was much less circumscribed, and if one half of Karamzin's work falls within Lopukhin's definition, the other half is clearly more in line with Novikov's wider publishing interests. Together with such similar institutions as the Pedagogical and Translators Seminaries, founded by Professor J. G. Schwartz (d. 1784) in collaboration with Novikov, the Society was closely connected both with the masons and Moscow University. When Karamzin arrived in Moscow, Schwartz had been dead over a year, but his influence remained strong; in the room Karamzin shared with Petrov there stood a bust of Schwartz.[21]

With Schwartz's death the authority among the Moscow masons he had shared and disputed with Novikov passed to Novikov, who in the course of the next seven years was to see both the order of masons and his considerable printing and publishing enterprises undermined and destroyed by Catherine. One of Karamzin's biographers has alleged that Karamzin showed no deep understanding of Novikov,[22] but his references over a period of more than thirty years to this key figure in Russian freemasonry reveal an awareness of the complexity and contradictions in his character and work. With typical masonic and sentimentalist disregard for Novikov's satirical writings, Karamzin wrote to Lavater of his transition to "a surer way of being useful to his country."[23] These useful services were both his active philanthropy, which Karamzin praises in the stanza devoted to Nikandr-Novikov in the poem "To Mishen'ka" ["Mishen'ke"] (1790), and his pioneering activity as bookseller, publisher, and editor.[24] Novikov's absorption in the more mystical pursuits of freemasonry remained foreign to Karamzin's nature and interests.[25] In a petition to Alexander I on behalf of the bereaved Novikov family in 1818, Karamzin writes that Novikov "as a citizen, useful by his activity, deserved public esteem; Novikov as a theosophical dreamer at least did not merit imprisonment: he was the victim of excusable but unjust suspicion."[26] At the time of his arrest Karamzin published a courageous appeal to Catherine on his friend's behalf, the ode "To Mercy" ["K Milosti"] (1792).

Two masons who enjoyed particular esteem in the Friendly Learned Society were Karamzin's "worthy man," Turgenev, and A. M. Kutuzov, the "kind K*" of *Letters of a Russian Traveler*. Turgenev was the translator of seminal masonic works, especially John Mason's *On Self-Knowledge*. The importance of this book for Turgenev himself is apparent from his dedication of the third edition of 1800 to his sons: "I am sure that it can be of true value to you. I am greatly indebted to this book for my own moral conduct."[27] Although all his translations are of strictly religious works and his influence on Karamzin is essentially moral, his general supervision of the work of the young translators in the Society and his own idiosyncratic views on translation assume particular significance in the context of Karamzin's literary development. Turgenev deliberately and exaggeratedly avoided foreign words and expressions, preferring to find or invent "Russian" equivalents. Thus he writes instead of *egoizm iachestvo, samstvennost', sobstvennoliubie* and *sobstenno-*

chestie.[28] It is a practice advocated later by Admiral Shishkov in the Shishkovite-Karamzinist controversies at the beginning of the nineteenth century. Turgenev's views were disputed by Kutuzov; defending the use of his own expression *negativnaia dobrodetel'* (a negative virtue), he writes: "However, believe me, in my opinion neither extreme is praiseworthy, neither the inappropriate use of terms nor their stubborn rejection, which frequently make our writings so obscure that after a short period of time we ourselves do not understand them. Find me one true author who would not use such terms; to invent and compose new words when we already have acceptable ones is almost impermissible, but it is our duty to use them once they become common currency."[29]

Kutuzov (1749–97), to whom Radishchev dedicated his *Journey from Petersburg to Moscow,* was one of the most profound and widely educated of the masons; he had studied with Radishchev in Leipzig and had a command of French, German, and English. By nature "quiet, taciturn and inclined to melancholy," he sought his salvation in self-knowledge, "that divine science."[30] All his life he retained an unswerving devotion to his friends, but his dedication to his ideals led to misunderstandings, to easily misconstrued actions, such as his subsequent criticism of Karamzin. His earnestness and erudition, together with his major translations of Young's *Night Thoughts* (1785) and Klopstock's *Messias* (1785–87), could not fail to impress the young Karamzin.[31] From being the "forgotten Rosicrucian" of Tarasov's 1910 article,[32] Kutuzov has come to be recognized as one of the most important early exponents of sentimentalism both by his translations and his original essays.[33] In an essay entitled "On the Attractiveness of Sadness" ["O priiatnosti grusti"] (1781), translated from Gellert, he describes the attractions of that twilight zone of the emotions, which are evident in his personal letters and which Karamzin was to affirm in his own poem "Melancholy" ["Melankholiia"] (1800).[34] Nevertheless, although championing the primacy of the heart over reason and mistrustful of the effectiveness of reason alone, he sees reason as a gift from God, which subservient "to faith, love and hope," guides man to truth.[35]

To a much greater extent than Turgenev, Kutuzov of the older generation of masons exerted a strong and continuing influence on Karamzin. Lotman has indeed been tempted to describe subsequent fluctuations in Karamzin's world view in terms of an opposition between "masono-Kutuzov ideology" (the evil nature of man, the need for inner regeneration) and the "Enlightenment-Rousseauist tradition" (the social determinants in man's conduct, utopianism).[36] At all events, in the spring of 1787 Kutuzov was sent to Berlin to pursue his studies in alchemy. Despite Karamzin's attempts to see him during his journey, they never met again; and Kutuzov died in 1797, a lonely and forgotten man.

It is Petrov who was, however, the supreme influence on Karamzin during his four years (1785–89) with the masons. They probably met when Karamzin was still with Schaden; by the spring of 1785 they were certainly intimate friends. Karamzin's sense of indebtedness and gratitude toward Petrov is exceptional even in an age of "passionate friendships"; the year before his death in 1826 Karamzin spoke to K. S. Serbinovich about Petrov, "whom he recognized as his teacher in his knowledge of the Russian language."[37] He explained in 1800 to a young Kazan' poet, Gavrila Kamenev, that Petrov's "taste was fresher and purer than mine; he corrected my scribblings, showed me the beauties in authors and I began to feel the strength and attractiveness of expressions."[38] As Karamzin notes elsewhere, Petrov was unwilling to write original works, but his translations "show the excellence of his style";[39] he translated from English, German, and French, ranging from such mystical works as *Khrisomander* (1783) and *Concerning the Ancient Mysteries or Secrets* [O drevnikh misteriiakh ili tainstavkh] (1785) to works for children, including a German grammar. This competence in German made him Karamzin's teacher in that language as well as in Russian. Karamzin's greatest tribute to his friend is the sentimental obituary, "A Flower on the Grave of My Agathon" ["Tsvetok na grob moego Agatona"], written shortly after Petrov's death in 1793. Under the guidance of Petrov, Karamzin developed his "first metaphysical concepts" and his "aesthetic sense." He believed that "the time of our acquaintance will always be the most important period of my life."[40]

Petrov's influence is thus reflected on three aspects of Karamzin's development: linguistic, aesthetic, and philosophic. Although Petrov would seem to be aligned by certain of his translations with the more mystically inclined masons, this is not apparent in his correspondence with Karamzin, where the emphasis, apart from a more tortured preoccupation with self-knowledge than ever Karamzin was capable of,[41] is essentially on literary theory and practice. Whatever else Petrov inherited from Schwartz, variously described as "a tireless enthusiast of enlightenment" and "a militant obscurantist,"[42] he adopted his view of the necessity of rules in art. The announcement of Schwartz's lecture course on European literature for 1782/83, which Petrov almost certainly attended, included the following passage: "In suggesting rules for all this [activity in all fields of the creative arts], in addition to the Ancients, Aristotle, Dionysius of Halicarnassus, Demetrius Phalereus, Cicero, Horace, Quintilian, there will be discussed from among the Moderns Batteux, Ramler, Hume, Boileau, Baumgarten and others."[43] Petrov's understanding of the application of rules to art is revealed in an important letter to Karamzin, dated August 1, 1787. Rules, he believed, do not inhibit but guide natural gifts and originality. Learning and culture are necessary for creative artists and "simplicity consists neither in genuine nor feigned ignorance."[44] Thus the reproduction of peasant speech, the description of *all* the phenomena of real life may be as pedantic as any uninspired imitation of literary models. His reluctance to praise Shakespeare unreservedly stems from his suspicion of his "naturalism" and his concept of genius as essentially cultured and not "wild." His undoubted mentor in such views is the abbé Charles Batteux, whose *Les Beaux arts, réduits à un même principe* (1746) he had recommended to Karamzin with subsequent far-reaching effect. Petrov's advice was prompted by Karamzin's views on Shakespeare, expressed in his foreword to *Julius Caesar*, published earlier that year, and judged solely against that document, it might seem unfortunate and retrogressive. However, as the final paragraph in his letter indicates, his view of life was considerably wider and more mature than Karamzin's. Petrov expresses his disappointment that Karamzin's recent stay in the country had not removed his earlier prejudices against country life and asks: "How can anyone find taste in *belles lettres*, in the artificial imitation of beautiful nature, when he finds nothing attractive in the original itself, even when it is presented in its finest aspect?"[45] Although Karamzin overcame this antipathy to real nature, this artificial stimulus in his appreciation of it remains throughout his work in the 1790's. Petrov's views both on true simplicity and delight in nature are anticipated in two articles in *Chil-*

dren's Reading, which have not previously been attributed to him. In the sixth letter of "The Correspondence between a Father and His Son about Country Life" ["Perepiska ottsa s synom o derevenskoi zhizni"], the Father upbraids his son for not admiring "natural" nature: "My poor, unfortunate son! What will become of you when such views do not move you, when you find pleasure only in the works of men and not of God?";[46] in the later "Conversation about Simplicity" ["Razgovor o prostote"], after praise for Fénelon's *Télémaque*, singled out in Petrov's letter to Karamzin, there follows a eulogy of simplicity in all its manifestations, including the arts: "In the arts simplicity is also one of the best qualities. It is found when an object is represented or described in keeping with its nature and without extra embellishment. It is the most beautiful nature which reveals its beauties without the intention of appearing beautiful: a green meadow covered with small flowers in comparison with a highly coloured flower-bed in which showy flowers, grown with the aid of art, are set out in order."[47] Although the orientation is thus on nature itself, art reproduces only what is beautiful.

Under Petrov's guidance Karamzin came to distinguish "the mediocre from the elegant, the elegant from the excellent, the studied from the natural, false talent from true."[48] In the survey which follows of Karamzin's original work and translations the clear interaction and at times opposition between Karamzin's independent interests and those encouraged in him by Petrov and the masons in general will be clearly seen.

The Wooden Leg [Dereviannaia noga] (1783)

IF THIS translation were not also Karamzin's first published work, its significance in the history of Russian "Gessnerism" would be as the only version of "Das hölzerne Bein" in the eighteenth century. It is unique among Gessner's idylls by the use of an incident from Swiss history and as such did not attract the attention of translators interested in the more traditional or conventional idyll. Only when Ivan Timkovskii produced his translation of Gessner's complete work was it again made available to the Russian public.[49]

Karamzin reveals no precocious talent as a translator. Although generally accurate, his version lacks the simplicity and harmony of the original; it exhibits that "mixture of Slavonic expressions and turns of phrase, characteristic only of German," which Timkovskii detects in all early Russian translations from Gessner.[50] Karamzin's selection of a Gessner idyll, and of "Das hölzerne Bein" in particular, is fully consistent with sympathies encouraged in him by his reading and education under Schaden. Gessner, whom Karamzin read "from his earliest years,"[51] describes that Golden Age of mankind for which the sentimentalist yearned; at this same time his own life in Switzerland seemed to recreate that age in the modern world. In a footnote to his translation of Albrecht von Haller's *Vom Ursprung des Übels*, published in 1786, Karamzin writes: "By 'happy creatures' Haller is referring to Alpine shepherds. All that I have heard about their way of life from people who have traveled through Switzerland enthused me. The thought of these happy people has often caused me to exclaim: 'O mortals! why have you strayed from your original innocence! why do you pride yourself on your false enlightenment!' "[52] Switzerland and pastoral innocence, Switzerland and freedom: such associations led Karamzin in translating "Das hölzerne Bein" to qualify the second *Freyheit* in the line "Freyheit, Freyheit beglückt das ganze Land" with the word *drazhaishaia* (most dear).[53] This enthusiasm for Swiss freedom in no way conflicts with his support for the English against the Americans or his adherence to Russia's system; it is a divorce between the ideal and the real in the realm of politics which he consciously retains all his life.

Karamzin's enthusiasm for Gessner and his work, his idyllic conception of Switzerland, that "land of freedom and happiness" (which his later scepticism led him to change to "land of freedom and prosperity"),[54] his exploitation of the Golden Age myth have been analyzed in detail in a separate study.[55] His successful emulation of Gessner as a stylist is manifest in "Palemon and Daphnis" ["Palemo ni Dafnis"], which he published in 1791. Although generally regarded as an original work, it is in fact a skillful adaptation of Gessner's idyll, "Der Sturm." Karamzin makes no attempt to reproduce every detail in Gessner's idyll, although despite a change of the shepherds' names from Lacon and Battus to Palemon and Daphnis, he retains essentially the same setting, development, and moral. He is now a true rival of Gessner in the simplicity and musicality of his prose and his mastery of syntax allows him to impart clarity and logic even to the longest sentences. Karamzin's originality lies in the way he has changed certain features in the original to conform with his underlying ideological purpose. Both idylls describe a storm at sea which brings death and destruction; although both begin in identical fashion, Karamzin dwells on the serenity and attractiveness of the scene in order to heighten the subsequent contrast with the storm and he rejects the final scene in Gessner's idyll as superfluous. He is intent on emphasizing the moral of "be content with your lot" and allows his shepherds to vie with each other in protestations of humility and contentment until the end.[56] He is warning against the specific storms of the French Revolution, persuading Russians to be content with their *status quo* and not imitate the French. Analogous use of this image of watching a storm from afar with direct application to France is found in his farewell letter from Paris in *Letters of a Russian Traveler* and in his essay, "Pleasing Prospects, Hopes and Desires of the Present Time" ["Priiatnye vidy, nadezhdy i zhelaniia nyneshnego vremeni"] (1803).[57]

On the Origin of Evil [O proiskhozhenii zla] (1786)

IN HIS first letter to Johann Kaspar Lavater (1741–1801), the Zurich philosopher and physiognomist, in August 1786, Karamzin acknowledges the influence of his "true friends and teachers" and it was probably at their request that he produced in that year his prose version of Haller's *Vom Ursprung des Übels* and participated in the translation of a work known as *Conversations with God* [*Besedy s Bogom*]. Nevertheless, Karamzin's personal affection for Haller's work is obvious both from the epithet "great" (velikii) he uses in the title to describe the author and from his own footnotes to the poem.

Polemicizing with Mandeville's fable, *The Bees*, Haller argues that despite the existence of evil "the best of worlds was called into being."[58] Written in 1734, at a time when Haller was deeply influenced by the work of Leibnitz and Shaftesbury, the poem expounds a comforting philosophy of religious optimism; at the same time, its social implications are in complete accord with the general conservative tendencies of the Moscow masons. Haller believes that "we are all equally endowed with the means to happiness; each has his share and no one is forgotten"; therefore, the peasant toiling for the noble, the mother with her family cares, and the scholar in his study should be content.[59] Identical tenets are basic to *Children's Reading for the Mind and Heart.*

Karamzin describes the appeal of Lavater's philosophy as "gentle sympathy for the misfortunes of others, consoling love, a tender appeal for resignation, which is the basis of our happiness on earth";[60] similar sentiments he finds in Haller, whose work is also linked with Pope's "Universal Prayer" and Thomson's "Hymn," which Karamzin translated two years later, by the recognition in deist terms of the infinite wisdom of the Creator and the wondrous harmony He created. These ideas are again underlined in *La Contemplation de la nature* by the Genevan philosopher, Charles Bonnet, which Karamzin was reading and translating at this time.[61] Such chapter headings as "The Goodness of the Universe" and "The General Connection or Harmony of the Universe" clearly indicate the message Bonnet was intent on propounding. Despite subsequent fulsome tributes to Bonnet, whom he considers superior in his wisdom to Plato,[62] Karamzin is sceptical about the ultimate value of "systematic" philosophers. He writes to Lavater: "Although this great philosopher of our time has revealed to me many new ideas, I am not, however, completely satisfied by all his hypotheses. Les germes, emboîtement des germes, les sièges de l'âme, la machine organique, les fibres sensibles—all this is very philosophical, profound, well-reasoned, and it could have been like this in fact, if at the creation of the world the Lord God had been guided by the esteemed Bonnet's philosophy; but I don't believe it was thus in fact, although I believe that God's wisdom far exceeds the wisdom of all our philosophers and is thus able to find more suitable ways for the creation and preservation of His works than those suggested by our Leibnitzes and Bonnets."[63] It is in this spirit that he is always ready to commend the poet who is able to suggest in a few words a "truth which we could not find in the numerous tomes of modern, fashionable theologians."[64] Haller, together with Thomson, provides him with a philosophy similar to Bonnet's, but poetically, suggestively, succinctly; in Haller he finds in addition idyllic set scenes in the manner of Gessner, sentimental tributes to friendship, "that sweet food of hearts," and the recognition that sensibility "although the source of tears is also the source of life."[65] The dedication of the translation to his brother, Vasilii, clearly indicated Karamzin's position.[66]

Conversations with God [Besedy s Bogom] (1787–1789)

ON NOVEMBER 18, 1786, a new periodical publication to begin in January of the following year was announced in the *Moscow News*.[67] It was to consist of three separate works: 1] *Conversations with God, or Reflections in the Morning, for Every Day of the Year* [*Besedy s Bogom, ili razmyshleniia v utrennie chasy, na kazhdyi den' goda*]; 2] *Reflections on the Works of God in Nature and Providence, for Every Day of the Year* [*Razmyshleniia o delakh bozhiikh v tsarstve prirody i provideniia, na kazhdyi den' goda*]; 3] *Reflections in the Evening, for Every Day of the Year* [*Razmyshleniia v vechernie chasy, na kazhdyi den' goda*]. Each work was to consist of four parts, each part of three monthly books; they were to be issued concurrently, but at different times in the month. In fact, in 1787 there appeared only three parts of each work; the fourth part of the second work appeared in 1788, and the fourth parts of the other two works only in 1789. They correspond to three independent German originals:

1] Christoph Christian Sturm's *Unterhaltungen mit Gott in den Morgenstunden auf jeden Tag des Jahres* (2 vols., Halle, 1768);

2] Sturm's *Betrachtungen über die Werke Gottes im Reiche der Natur und der Vorsehung auf allen Tage des Jahres* (2 vols., Halle, 1772);

3] Johann Friedrich Tiede's *Unterhaltungen mit Gott in den Abendstunden auf jeden Tag des Jahres* (2 vols., Riga, 1772).

These works were immensely popular, particularly Sturm's *Betrachtungen*, which enjoyed in England almost as many separate translations as editions from 1788 to the 1850's. Sturm's reputation was such that the one English translation of Tiede's work in 1838 was published under his name.[68] The esteem in which Sturm's work was held by the Moscow masons is reflected in what was for the period the huge edition of over ten thousand copies;[69] furthermore, A. A. Prokopovich-Antonskii, one of the original editors of *Children's reading*, a member of Schwartz's Pedagogical Seminar and possibly a participant in the Sturm translation, consistently recommended the publication to his pupils when he became Director of the Moscow University Noble Pension.[70] Although Sturm's work has been seen as an influence on Vasilii Zhukovskii during his days at the Pension, scholars have ignored its relevance for Karamzin. Karamzin's participation in the translation has been established on the testimony of Novikov and of Dmitriev as well as by the discovery of proof sheets corrected in Karamzin's hand.[71] What is still unknown is the extent of his contribution, although Dmitriev suggests it was no more than "two or three volumes of Sturm's *Reflections*, under the title . . . *Conversations with God*."[72] It should be noted, however, that Novikov named Karamzin as solely responsible for the whole translation at the end of 1786.

The two works by Sturm are not alike in tone or content. His *Unterhaltungen mit Gott* is a continuous confession of the author's inadequacies, his search for virtue and self-perfection, conveyed in a strongly emotional and pathetic style; its appeal, together with Tiede's very similar work, for masons with the pietist bent of a Lopukhin is obvious.[73] Sturm's *Betrachtungen*, on the other hand, although continuing the emphasis on virtue, is more varied in content and tone. Tikhonravov has characterized the work as "a sort of popular encyclopedia of natural history, pervaded from beginning to end with religious ideas."[74] In his preface to the third edition of his work (1784) Sturm speaks of his twofold design—to present reliable, factual knowledge and "to show the reader how he may derive lessons of wisdom and virtue from the contemplation of natural things"; to achieve these ends, he has made "no scruple to borrow from Buffon, Derham, Pulche, Niewntyt, Sulzer, Bonnet, and other writers of this class."[75] The logical place which Sturm's *Betrachtungen*—as well as the other two works on a different plane—holds in Karamzin's reading at this period is clear from this list of authors, especially Bonnet; what has been previously overlooked is that Sturm's work was used for a number of translations in *Children's Reading* and, together with J. H. Campe's *Kleine Kinderbibliothek*, was precisely one of "the German works" the editors in their program proposed to imitate, and plunder.[76] In part 5 for the first quarter of 1786 fourteen of the first twenty-five items are taken from Sturm. They have such titles as "Of comets," "The flux and reflux of the sea," "The utility of mountains," "Of subterraneous fires," and are almost all from the "Reflections" for the first two months. It is probable that these translations were by Petrov or Prokopovich-Antonskii and antedate by a year Karamzin's known participation in the journal.[77] One of the last pieces from Sturm to appear in the journal is "Contemplations on a Meadow" ["Lug"], a typical sentimental "botanizing" piece, which anticipates Karamzin's sketch "The Countryside" ["Derevnia"] (1792). In addition, Sturm's work contains numerous other pieces which echo Karamzin's philosophic and literary interests during his masonic period. Such are "Reflections on myself," "Reflections on oneself," "Spring is a picture of the frailty of human life, and an emblem of death" (cf. Karamzin's "Spring Song of a Melancholic" ["Vesenniaia pesn' melankholika"] (1788).

Julius Caesar [Iulii Tsezar'] (1787)

KARAMZIN's translation of Haller's poem was presented for scrutiny by the religious censor in August 1786; two months later it was followed by his version, also in prose, of Shakespeare's Julius Caesar.[78] Although the introduction is dated October 15, 1786, the translation itself was probably begun in Simbirsk in the previous year.[79] Its publication in 1787 coincides with the appearance in St. Petersburg of a translation from French of Richard III,[80] yet it is Karamzin's Julius Caesar, rather than the anonymous version of Richard III, which is the true landmark in the history of Russian appreciation of Shakespeare by virtue of its introduction and comparative fidelity to the English original.

Nearly forty years before these translations appeared, Sumarokov published his tragedy, Hamlet [Gamlet] (1748). He had become acquainted with Shakespeare's play in Pierre Antoine de La Place's prose version (1746) and saw merely the outline of a plot which could be adapted for a conventional pseudo-classical tragedy; he himself said that his play "except for the monologue at the end of the third act and Claudius's prayer hardly resembles Shakespeare's tragedy."[81] Sumarokov's use of Hamlet curiously anticipates a similar undertaking by J. F. Ducis, whose ignorance of English

led him to La Place's translation in his attempt to use Shakespearean subject matter within the Voltairean dramatic system; his
Hamlet was published in 1769. The gap in comprehension and accomplishment that separates La Place-Ducis from Pierre Le Tourneur and his *Shakespeare, traduit de l'Anglois, dédié au Roi* (20
vols. 1776–83) is similar to that between Sumarokov and Karamzin, for although Karamzin used the English text, he also used Le
Tourneur's translation and his introduction repeats to a marked degree the Frenchman's critical position.

The publication of the first two volumes of Le Tourneur's
translation, comprising *Othello, The Tempest,* and *Julius Caesar,*
as well as some one hundred and fifty pages of prefatory materials,
was the signal for furious polemics, in which Voltaire, the erstwhile
moderate champion of Shakespeare, took the leading oppositional
role. He slandered Le Tourneur for his lack of taste and patriotism;
feeling his own position in jeopardy, Voltaire wrote to le Comte
d'Argental: "c'est moi, qui le premier, montrai aux Français quelques perles que j'avais trouvées dans son énorme fumier. Je ne
m'attendais pas que je servirais à fouler aux pieds les couronnes de
Racine et de Corneille, pour en orner le front d'un histrion bar-
bare."[82]

Voltaire was fighting a losing battle against the "English tragedy" in the same way that a few years earlier Sumarokov had railed
unavailingly, despite Voltaire's support, against the "lachrymose
drama."[83] Karamzin had written to Petrov about "Voltaire's unjust
criticism" and in his introduction to *Julius Caesar* speaks slight-
ingly of "the noted sophist, Voltaire," who "was indebted to Shakespeare for the best passages in his own tragedies."[84] In Moscow he
received particular encouragement in his views from a man who had
himself been closely associated with the growing European acclaim
for Shakespeare, the Sturm und Drang poet, Jakob Lenz. Jakob
Michael Reinhold Lenz spent the last ten years of his life in Moscow, closely linked with the masons and for a time living in the
same house as Karamzin.[85] Lenz's support for Shakespeare in his
Ammerkungen übers Theater (1774) was possibly one of the factors influencing Karamzin in his choice of play. Of all Shakespeare's
works *Julius Caesar* was the center of particular discussion,
arising from Voltaire's own Shakespearean adaptations, *Brutus* and
La Mort de César. It is precisely the superiority of Shakespeare's

tragedy over Voltaire's that L. S. Mercier seeks to demonstrate in his *Du Théâtre, ou Nouvel essai sur l'art dramatique* (1773). Mercier's views, derided in France, enjoyed great popularity with the Sturm und Drang poets; Lenz's *Ammerkungen* supports Mercier's stand. After the appearance of Le Tourneur's translation, Mercier again praised the excellence of *Julius Caesar* in letters to the *Journal françois, anglois et italien* in 1777 and Le Tourneur in the preface to volume 7 quotes the German critic and editor of Shakespeare, J. J. Eschenburg's dismissal of Voltaire's criticism of *Julius Caesar* as "cold and jealous." Karamzin is thus clearly inspired to continue the refutation of Voltaire by translating the very play "the sophist" attacked. It was a move which had particular meaning in a Russian context, for both of Voltaire's tragedies had been translated by V. Ievlev in 1777 and 1783 and indeed the version of *La Mort de César* was republished in the same year as Karamzin's translation.

Following Le Tourneur, Karamzin singles out for particular praise Shakespeare's portrayal of Brutus; it had impressed not only Lenz and Mercier, but also Goethe and Herder. He is enthusiastic about Shakespeare's ability to reveal "the most secret springs within a man, his innermost impulses, the differences of each passion, each temperament, each form of life"; in a footnote to Caesar's characterization of Cassius in act 1 he remarks that "the following description of Cassius is a most excellent and lively description of a choleric temperament."[86] It is an interest in character which marks Karamzin throughout his career, dictated by the masonic wish "to know oneself" and the more general sentimental orientation on the contradictions of the human heart. Although Karamzin's praise for Shakespeare's psychological insight persisted, his accompanying admiration for the realistic use of language—"every degree of people, every age, every passion, every character speaks in its own language" —was soon significantly modified.

An important aspect of Karamzin's introduction is his attack on the artificial rules and conventions of pseudoclassicism by the glorification of genius and imagination; Shakespeare's "genius, like the genius of Nature, enhances with its glance both the sun and the atoms . . . His dramas, like the immeasurable theatre of Nature, are full of variety; however, together they form a complete whole, needing no correction from modern *theatrical* writers." An essential corollary of his respect for Shakespeare's work is fidelity in translation. He writes: "As regards my translation I have tried to translate as faithfully as possible, while at the same time trying to avoid expressions foreign to our language. However, let those judge *who are capable of judging fairly*. Nowhere have I changed the thoughts of my author, considering this impermissible for a translator." Against a background of eighteenth-century disfigurement and emasculation of English texts, Karamzin's intentions are commendable and historically important, although they correspond closely to the promises of Le Tourneur, who but a few years before had attempted to "tirer de l'Young anglais un Young français qui pût plaire à ma nation, et qu'on pût lire avec intérêt sans songer s'il est original ou copie."[87]

Karamzin achieves a fair rendering of what Shakespeare says, never of how he says it. He took great pains to ensure the accuracy of his translation, collating the French and English texts and using such additional sources as Farmer's *Essay on the Learning of Shakespeare* (1767); as a result, he often manages a version nearer to the sense of the English than does Le Tourneur, but his prose shows a curious mixture of styles, only part of which is a conscious, intended duplication of Shakespeare's stylistic shifts. He uses the same clumsy circumlocution as he did in *The Wooden Leg* in rendering Cassius's "And let us swear our resolution" by "I budem kliat'sia v nepremennom proizvedenii v deistvo nashego predpriiatiia"; his literalness is absurdly pedantic in ". . . Chtob predat'sia vrednoi mokrote noshchi i podvergnut' sebia nechistomu, dozhdevykh kapel' ispolnennomu vozdukhu, daby eshche uvelichit' bolezn' svoiu" for "To dare the vile contagion of the night, / And tempt the rheumy and unpurged air / To add unto his sickness" (act II, scene 1). Occasionally he is more successful, as when he retains some of the pace and epigrammatic quality of Caesar's "Let me have men about me that are fat . . ." in "Menia dolzhny okruzhat' liudi tuchnye, liudi krugloshchekie i takie kotorye noch'iu spiat. Kassii sukh; on mnogo dumaet: takie liudi opasny."[88]

Karamzin's translation and its enthusiastic foreword remained unique in eighteenth-century Russia, the one by its fidelity to Shakespeare's text, the other by its appreciation of Shakespeare's genius; they were before their time in Russia and were to be discovered for a more appreciative age by Belinskii, who wrote in 1836 that they showed that "even at that time there were bright and independent minds who did not regard as phantoms their intelligence and feelings, given to them by God, who trusted their intelligence and feelings more than all earthly authorities, liked to think in their own way and go against accepted opinions and beliefs, against all the Voltaires, Boileaus, Batteuxs and La Harpes, those threatening and powerful gods of their time."[89] Yet Belinskii's "unknown" translator, Karamzin, was soon to be wooed from what Petrov considered was Shakespeare's unnecessary contempt for rules and pedantic naturalism in language; he recommended to Karamzin the theoretical writings of the abbé Batteux in the hope of persuading him to a more orthodox viewpoint.[90] His success is evident from Karamzin's characterization of Batteux in *Letters of a Russian Traveler* as "the councillor of authors, who two years ago I used to read with dear Agathon, penetrating into the truth of his rules and analysing the beauties of his examples"[91] and from his subsequent refusal to imitate much that he had originally found admirable in Shakespeare's work. His pronouncements on Shakespeare remain largely eulogistic, although he comes to criticize the comic and vulgar elements in his tragedies.[92] His ensuing conscious orientation on the "middle style" precluded language realism, particularly in the portrayal of characters from the lower classes. Taste became almost as great a tyrant as the rules of pseudoclassicism he attacked; thus he advises Dmitriev in 1793 to use only those common words which have pleasant associations, *pichuzhechka* (a dear little bird), but not *paren'* (lad).[93] It was again advice assimilated from his mentor, Petrov, who agreed that "drunken peasants and the excrement of various animals are encountered in *nature*, but I would not wish to read a vivid description of them, either in verse or prose. They say that Shakespeare was a very great *génie*, but I'm not sure; for some reason his tragedies please me less than *Emilia Galotti*."[94]

Emilia Galotti (1788)

KARAMZIN reacted immediately to Petrov's stated preference for Lessing's play and produced a translation. He originally wrote a version specifically for the noted Moscow actor, Pomerantsev, who performed the role of Odoardo, but revised it carefully before publication in order to retain "the many beauties of this tragedy."[95] The published text is notably free from the stylistic unevenness, which mars his earlier translations, and is in keeping with his generally increased linguistic competence in evidence in *Children's Reading*.

In a brief prefatory note Karamzin dedicates his translation to readers of taste and discrimination, "to you, who are able to appreciate dramatic works and never compare Spanish farces with the dramas of Lessing—to you, who see in the former merely witty jokes, but in the latter, works of a philosopher, penetrating with his glance the depths of the human heart."[96] Three years later Karamzin reviewed the play in the drama section of the *Moscow Journal*. He considers it "a harmonious whole" and proceeds to praise Gotthold Ephraim Lessing, as he had Shakespeare, for being an observer of genius: "Everything, everything shows that the author has observed mankind not just for two days and has observed in a manner few are able to observe; Nature has given him a living sense of truth, which makes both author and man great."[97] He is particularly impressed by Lessing's depiction of Odoardo; this admiration had led him earlier, in his translation of Thomson's "Winter," to make an interesting change in the English original. Thomson briefly refers to Hamlet, Othello, and other characters from English tragedies and comedies;[98] these Karamzin rejects and substitutes his own pantheon, consisting of Sumarokov's Il'mena, Sinav and Oskol'd and Lessing's Odoardo.[99] No Brutus; instead, the pallid heroes of the Russian Voltaire.

Emilia Galotti apparently provided for Petrov and subsequently for Karamzin the best of Shakespeare without the shocks to refined taste, occasioned by comic and farcical interludes in tragedy. Lessing as a critic of Shakespeare has features in common with the more restrained Karamzin; both were attracted above all by the psychological richness of Shakespeare's characters; both were intent less on imitating his work than on using it to attack the French pseudoclassical theatre.[100]

Like his *Julius Caesar*, Karamzin's *Emilia Galotti* was a notable attempt to provide the Russian public with a faithful translation of a major work of European literature. Translations of Lessing's plays, including *Emilia Galotti* (1784), had been published previously, but like V. A. Levshin's version of *Miss Sara*

Sampson (performed but not published), with its additions "completely foreign to Lessing's spirit,"[101] they were not distinguished by their exactness. Karamzin's selection of both *Julius Caesar* and *Emilia Galotti* was dictated by purely literary considerations, although recent commentators have seen in the fact that both tragedies portray tyrants evidence of Karamzin's youthful free-thinking. The fact that *Julius Caesar* was among the "harmful" books burnt in 1794 on the orders of the Moscow Governor-General, A. A. Prozorovskii, is more a comment on Catherine's hysteria than the translator's oppositional tendencies. His genuine, if abstract, love of Roman virtue was nourished from his earliest years and existed in harmony with his support for the established order. A. V. Predtechenskii has suggested that there is no direct evidence of Karamzin's "loyalty" in these early years,[102] although there is reason to suspect that he was the author of an interesting insertion in the translation from Tiede on which he was working in 1786. In the "reflection" for January 24 is the passage: "How blessed is that country in which the monarch shows paternal concern for the welfare of his subjects! How quickly it moves towards perfection! Take for example Russia; let us turn our gaze upon that fortunate state and we will be convinced of this trust."[103] It was precisely the proof sheets for Tiede's *Reflections* for the months of January and February, corrected by Karamzin, which came into the possession of Pogodin.[104]

Children's Reading for the Heart and Mind
[Detskoe chtenie dlia serdtsa i razuma] (1785–89)

Emilia Galotti was Karamzin's last translation to be published separately during his association with the Friendly Learned Society. His other translations over the period 1787–89 were published in *Children's Reading*. His actual editorship began with part 9 in 1787, according to Dmitriev's reliable testimony, although it is conceivable that he contributed items in late 1785 and 1786, since Petrov was actively involved in the journal from its inception.

Children's Reading, issued as a free supplement to the *Moscow News* until the beginning of 1789, is an outstanding example of Novikov's efforts to provide suitable reading matter for Russian children. The opening editorial declares the intention to provide articles with general moral teaching (moral'nye ili nravouchitel'nye piesy) as well as popular scientific information; in common with many eighteenth-century journals, it aims to combine usefulness (pol'za) with attractiveness (priiatnost').[105] Although Gukovskii has dismissed the journal as "full of mysticism and unusually cloying moralizing,"[106] recent researchers rightly consider it the best children's work of the age; its educative effect on the young reader at the end of the eighteenth century is undoubted, and it was completely republished for a third time as late as 1819.[107] Its original editors included, in addition to Novikov, Petrov and Prokopovich-Antonskii, and among its contributors were V. S. Podshivalov, the future editor of Reading for Taste, Mind and Feelings [Chtenie dlia vkusa, razuma i chuvstvovanii] (1791–93) and an important, if unsung, figure in Russian sentimentalism, and N. N. Sandunov, later Professor of Law and Jurisprudence at Moscow University and a notable dramatist.[108]

The first eight parts of the journal generally conform with the promises in the editorial: the young reader is instructed, informed, and amused. The editors were quick to realize the particular appeal of the scientific articles and from 1786 greatly increased the proportion of such works, translating items principally from Sturm and Buffon. There is an obvious desire to provide diversity of form as well as of subject matter: fables, puzzles, Eastern and Oriental tales and allegories, plays, idylls, conversation pieces, occasional book reviews. The basic moral philosophy of the journal is embodied in the recurrent figure of Dobroserd (Goodheart), introduced by the editors as their personal friend and a shining example for children. In a series of tales and conversations with children, Dobroserd, or sometimes Father, expatiates on the virtues of obedience to parents, belief in God and the workings of Providence, the need for industry and application, the joys of altruism and, particularly, on the ideal of moderation.[109] In the elaboration of a positive moral code, the question of social inequality is inevitably discussed. The solution offered reveals clearly the ambivalence of the masons' position over serfdom; at the same time the number of articles and discussions devoted to the subject eloquently testify to the importance it holds for Novikov and his friends.

In the spirit of humanism and enlightenment the masons de-

mand respect for the peasant as a human being and as a most necessary member of society, who supplies food and income for the other
classes. The moral of the story, "The Peasantry" ["Krest'ianskoe
sostoianie"]—"He who despises a peasant is unworthy to feed on
bread"—is thus both humanitarian and economic:[110] a landowner's
care for his peasants not only satisfies conscience and justice but
ensures financial prosperity. The peasant is also seen sentimentally,
uncomplicated and naturally virtuous, free from the corruption of
the town; in short, he is the last link with a Rousseauist Golden
Age and thus an object of admiration for the feeling heart.

The masons were conscious of abuses of privilege by the land-
owners;[111] they appealed primarily to a sense of justice and kindness, but in one instance the *necessity* for such kindness is revealed
unobtrusively in the story of a general whose life was saved during
the Pugachev revolt by peasants to whom he had previously been
considerate and just.[112] Aware of peasant unrest, the masons at the
same time were anxious to preserve the existing social order; they
emphasize the validity of a class system, allegedly sanctioned by
God: "We are all creatures of the one God, who in his wisdom
and mercy divided us into different estates for the general good."[113]
Improvement can come only within the boundaries of one's class
for "it would be bad if we all shared a common lot. Then no one
would till the fields, no one would do for others what they
needed."[114] The same casuistry is used to justify inequality in posses-
sions, for without the existence of poverty, the rich would not have
such "beautiful virtues" as mercy and compassion for the needy.[115]
Social climbing is actively discouraged and contentment with one's
lot, however small, is the recommended panacea.[116] In this way an
uneasy compromise is reached between the sincere attempts of the
masons to raise the dignity of all men and to preach self-knowledge,
moderation, and contentment as the path to true happiness. They
fuse the potentially disruptive values of the Enlightenment with a
basically conservative philosophy.

Certain of these moral, pedagogical, and social views, particularly the ambiguous attitude toward the peasantry, were embraced
by Karamzin; and are reflected in both his later creative and publicist writings. They are also continued in *Children's Reading* under Karamzin's editorship, although the earlier editorial awareness
of its public is lost and the journal becomes absorbing primarily as

a record of Karamzin's personal literary and philosophical interests, of his competence as a translator and of his first attempts at
creative writing.

As sole editor during Petrov's absence from Moscow, Karamzin
decided on two full-scale translations to fill the journal: in parts
9–12 he published a partial prose translation of James Thomson's
The Seasons simultaneously with translations from the work of
Mme. de Genlis, which continued into part 15. Karamzin's enthusiasm for Genlis's work, which he retained all his life, echoes
the general European acclaim for the French authoress as an outstanding educationalist.[117] He translated the eleven stories which
comprised the original two volumes of *Les Veillées du château*
(1784) and from a third volume known as *Suite des Veillées du
château,* containing three "contes moraux à l'usage des jeunes
personnes," he selected the second story, "Daphnis et Pandrose,
ou les Oréades."

In his translations of *Les Veillées du château* Karamzin attempts a hesitant russification of the setting and characters. Thus
Paris becomes Moscow, the Marquis and Marquise de Clémire are
transformed into the Dobroliubovy and their daughters, Caroline
and Pulchérie, into Elizaveta and Katerina. The "Histoire de M. de
la Palinière" is even renamed the "Istoriia Gospodina Chudina."
Despite these changes, the majority of the stories retain their
European settings and other characters remain Olympie, Théophile, and Alphonse. Yet with or without the changes, the stories
are virtually devoid of specific local color; the action is largely independent of setting and consciously universalized. When within
a year Karamzin attempts to emulate Mme. de Genlis, he reveals
no wish to intensify the "Russianness" of his "true Russian story,"
"Eugene and Julia" ["Evgenii i Iuliia"].

In her preface to *Les Veillées du château,* Genlis outlines her
moral and pedagogic aims and prides herself on being the first author to be concerned with the "éducation du peuple" rather than
exclusively with that of the nobility.[118] Although Karamzin does
not translate this preface in the journal, his sympathy with her intentions is clear from an interesting footnote which he provides to
one of her tales. In "L'Héroisme de l'attachement" Genlis refers to
a work entitled *"l'avis au peuple,* ouvrage également intéressant et
estimable par son utilité et les principes d'humanité qui l'ont dicté"

and in a footnote identifies it as "de M. Tissot."[119] Karamzin intensifies the passage in the text to read: "Tissot's Appeal to the People, a most useful work, which enflames the heart of the sensitive reader with the purest fire of compassion" and adds: "Perhaps some learned and compassionate man would wish to compose such a book in our language, which would have as its subject the moral and physical welfare of our peasants; we could almost vouch for the great pleasure with which all patriots would greet such a work . . ."[120] This appeal to his compatriots for literary endeavors was to become characteristic of his future work as a journalist.

Genlis's stories abound in information on scientific discoveries and natural phenomena and recommend country life and sentimental respect for the peasantry. They thus echo earlier aspects of *Children's Reading*, but, although Genlis claims to be writing for well-educated twelve- and thirteen-year-old children, she describes in several stories tender and passionate, lawful and unlawful love in terms which would appeal to a young man of Karamzin's age, as Sipovskii notes.[121] In addition, Karamzin would have responded to the literary dress she gives to her moralizing; attacking dry moral treatises, she asks: "Pourquoi donc proscrire des ouvrages de morale le sentiment et l'imagination? Ce ne sont point de froids raissonnemens qui rendront les hommes meilleurs; ce sont des exemples frappans, des tableaux faits pour toucher et s'imprimer fortement dans l'imagination: c'est enfin *la morale mise en action*."[122] These precepts he was to follow in his own *conte moral*, "Julia" (1796). Two years earlier in Simbirsk Karamzin told Dmitriev that "from the choice of translation are judged the characteristics of the translator himself"[123] and in selecting Genlis's stories Karamzin was persuaded not only by their educational and moral aspects but equally by a personal identification with the heroes and heroines who undertook journeys through Europe to complete the education of their minds and hearts.

In this connection the story entitled "The Recluse" ["Pustynnik"] is particularly interesting.[124] Beginning with A. D. Galakhov,[125] scholars have credited Karamzin with the translation of fifteen stories by Genlis. The first twelve are from *Les Veillées du château*, but the remaining three were attributed to her on the basis of Karamzin's note after the fifteenth tale: "The end of Mme. Dobroliubova's stories."[126] Galakhov said that the last four tales came from other works of Genlis including her *Nouveaux contes moraux et nouvelles historiques;* Privalova writes categorically that the last three tales, excluding "Daphnis et Pandrose," were from that collection.[127] In fact, "Daphnis et Pandrose," although originally part of the supplementary third volume of *Les Veillées du château,* also appeared in the later collection of *Nouveaux contes,* which was published only in 1802 and comprised stories written mainly in the late 1790's. Galakhov evidently had not looked beyond the *Nouveaux contes,* but his remarks have been accepted without question. The thirteenth story, "L'Histoire de la Duchesse de C. . . , écrite par elle-meme" ["Istoriia gertsogini Ch."] is by Genlis and appeared in her *Adèle et Théodore, ou Lettres sur l'éducation* (1782), but the remaining two pieces are not to be found in her work. The only reason for mystification would seem to be Karamzin's wish to pass off his first original fiction as the work of Mme. Genlis, who, however, is never named in the journal, and to distract attention from the strongly autobiographical tale, "The Recluse."[128]

"The Recluse" shows the strong influence of Genlis's work in its general tone and certain particulars—the educational journey, the reverence for Gessner, the admiration for England, the negative attitude toward Voltaire—but these and other features are no less characteristic of Karamzin's basic interests and reading. The story would seem to provide interesting early evidence of Karamzin's tendency to romanticize events from his childhood and to devise sad dénouements for his fictional love affairs. Karamzin was also preoccupied with thoughts of foreign travel and his story anticipates not only the journey he was to begin less than a year later but also how he was to approach famous men and observe peoples and places. Travel had become "a necessity of my soul" (potrebnost' dushi moei).[129] The rationale was provided in the words of Professor L* to the Recluse, who was at that time a student at Leipzig University, the very university at which Karamzin had hoped to study: "You have made sufficient progress in the sciences, you have heard lectures on moral philosophy, which explains for us man's nature, but all theoretical knowledge is in a certain sense dead knowledge—it must be given life by practice, that is to say, by intercourse with men, by the careful observation of the workings of the human heart in society. Your present way of life does not allow you to learn much through experience or to observe men. And so, dear friend, leave the university; we shall travel through Europe for an intelligent and attentive traveler has the opportunity to acquire that living knowledge of the human heart which has a very great influence on our happiness."[130]

Parts 15–17 (end of 1788–beginning of 1789) seem a partial return to the character of the journal prior to 1787. There are several factual and informative pieces, along with small tales and fables, taken principally from the work of A. Berquin, the author of *L'Ami de l'adolescence*, a work recommended by Mme. de Genlis in the course of one of her own tales. Although it is impossible with any certainty to credit Karamzin with the translation of most of these pieces, one story in particular, "L'Inconstant" ["Nepostoianstvo"] is closely linked with Genlis's stories by its description of European travel.[131] Berquin's Zephyren is an antihero, who squanders his opportunities, but is finally brought to reason; in his last journal, *The Messenger of Europe* [*Vestnik Evropy*] (1802–3), when he is again deeply concerned with the problems of education and upbringing, Karamzin allows his negative hero to relate his story and leaves the moral implicit.[132]

There is a tendency to look beyond works designed specifically for children to materials from prominent European journals and for the first time the sources are cited: the *Spectator*, the *Rambler*, the *Town and Country Magazine*, the *New London Magazine*, Wieland's *Teutsche Merkur*. One piece, particularly "adult" in its tone and content is "An Extract from a Speech on the Eagerness to Imitate Foreigners" ["Otryvok rechi o stremlenii podrazhat' inostrantsam"] from the German of Joseph Reitzer.[133] Reitzer's attack on the foolish aping of foreigners recalls similar criticism in Novikov's satirical journals, but he is intent on achieving a balance between enlightened imitation, admiration for all writers and philosophers, independent of country, and true patriotic endeavor. As such it is consonant with Karamzin's own views throughout his life and expressed eloquently in his essay "On Love for One's Country and National Pride" ["O liubvi k otechestvu i narodnoi gordosti"] (1802).[134]

In parts 18–19 Karamzin again includes two major translations which reflect his own literary and philosophical interests. Firstly come his extracts from Bonnet's *La Contemplation de la nature*,

which have been discussed in connection with his translation from
Haller. They have, in addition, considerable interest for Karamzin's
attempts to render Bonnet's involved philosophical and technical
vocabulary into Russian. Thus he gives side by side *mchatel'noe
dvizhenie* for *mouvement projectile, borodavochki* for *papilles,
prelomimost'* for *refrangibilité,* etc.[135] Between the two halves of
his translation from Bonnet Karamzin published his version of a
drama by Christian Weisse (1726–1804), "The Arcadian Monument" ["Arkadskii pamiatnik"].[136] Although Weisse's work would
seem to be akin to Gessner's idylls, its moral implications align it
closely with masonic philosophy. Weisse in theory supports the
ideals and inspiration behind the myth of Arcadia, yet recognizes
that true happiness is to be found only within oneself: "Young
hearts / Do not torment yourselves with the desire / To find Arcadia beneath the sun! / You can find / Arcadia in a tranquil
soul. / Seek it there!"[137] Karamzin's own fascination with the
Golden Age and Arcadia lasts throughout his career. Recognizing
the Golden Age as an illusion, he is nevertheless enchanted by it;
emphasizing personal responsibility for happiness, he continually
seeks a general solution for all mankind.

Karamzin's apprenticeship as a translator led, in the year he
set out on his journey, to his first unquestioned original works, in
prose and verse. Inevitably the works he read and translated influenced strongly his first attempts. "Eugene and Julia," his first characteristic sentimental tale, takes its inspiration from Mme. de
Genlis, whereas his sketch, "A *Walk*" ["Progulka"], is pervaded
with motifs from the work of several writers, mainly poets.[138] Preeminent among these is James Thomson, whose *Seasons* Karamzin
had translated (with substantial cuts and interesting additions)
into prose and its concluding "Hymn" into verse. The epigraph to
"A Walk" is the second and third lines of the "Hymn," and Karamzin describes how "having taken up my Thomson, I went out of
town for a walk." The piece ends with Karamzin paying homage
to God, inspired by a reading of the "Hymn." Within this frame
Karamzin contrives a permutation of sentimental attitudes toward
nature and religion and both the settings and his emotional responses are guided by his reading. Thus the world of nature by day
—Thomson's world—gives way to night and the moon, inviting
inevitably a paean to Young;[139] musing on the effects of dreams
and sleep, he pays tribute to Homer and Ossian and the peace of

a starlit sky reminds him of Wieland. He contemplates the stars, thinking on the harmony of the universe and the plurality of worlds, in what is a digest of Bonnet's views.

Essentially a potpourri of self-conscious literary reminiscences, this "literary ramble" reveals Karamzin's assimilation of typical sentimental mannerisms and attitudes. Basic to the sketch is the author's absorption in his own emotions: "Everything has disappeared for me, everything except myself." He has a sense of uniqueness: "I feel keenly that I am alive and am something removed from all else: I am something whole." Karamzin has also acquired certain stylistic formulas, characteristic of his sentimental prose of the early 1790's. He is ever ready to fall on his knees—to express his religious emotion and to praise the singing of "Philomel"—or to enjoy "balsamic sleep." Anticipating his famed—and parodied—advertisement for the *Letters of a Russian Traveler,* he writes: "then I can better see, hear, feel and think." He uses such syntactical parallels as *uzhe... uzhe...* and *kogda... kogda... kogda...* as well as numerous exclamation marks and dashes to emphasize drama or intensity of emotion.

"A Walk" and "Eugene and Julia" are the beginning, however pale and unsure, of popular genres of sentimental prose cultivated by Karamzin; they point both to the continuity in his work and the maturity he was to achieve through his travels.

Early Verse

THE translation of Weisse's pastoral drama gave Karamzin an opportunity to practice various verse forms which coincide with the publication in the same journal of Karamzin's own first poems. Apart from a few lines from Thomson in the text of a translated story and Karamzin's twelve-line tribute to Gessner in part 16 there is no poetry in the journal before the six poems published in part 18. Five are by Karamzin, or attributed to him, the sixth is possibly by Podshivalov.[140] In addition, Karamzin produced three important verse translations from Thomson—the "Hymn" and "Lavinia," an inset tale from *The Seasons*—and Pope's "Universal Prayer."[141] He also began to include poems in his letters to Dmitriev, the majority of which were not published in his lifetime.

The dominant mood in his original verse fully accords with

Karamzin's characterization of himself as "a very strange melancholic."[142] His letters to Dmitriev and Petrov show him inclined to pessimism and fits of melancholy, induced by his sensitive nature, doubts in his own abilities and the more fatalistic aspects of masonic philosophy. In poems like "Often in this dark vale" ["Chasto zdes' v iudoli mrachnoi"] and "Happiness is truly found" ["Schast'e istinno khranitsia"] Karamzin is obsessed by the impossibility of prolonged earthly happiness and counsels moderation to avoid excessive sadness as well as excessive joy. The mood is elegiac, despite the promise of an afterlife ("To Mr. D** on His Illness" ["Gospodinu D** na bolezn' ego"]). In his "Anacreontic Verses for A* A* P*" ["Anakreonticheskie stikhi A* A* P*"] Karamzin laments his failure to be another Newton, another Thomson, or a great philosopher: "I grieve and weep bitterly / Sensing how little / Talent I have."[143] Nevertheless, poetry—and literature in general— is a major source of strength and consolation for Karamzin; he passes on to Dmitriev advice, essentially assimilated from Petrov: "Sing, brother, sing! To sing is not a bad occupation. He who practices poetry, who has developed its appreciation, will be bored in life less often than the next man; for boredom is an evil worm, which eats away the flower of our life."[144] The disillusionment he experiences comes from his inability to move from admiration of great writers to immediate and successful emulation. The shadow of his literary mentors still constricts his own originality; only after his journey did he become emancipated psychologically, although throughout his life his acknowledgment of foreign influences remained sincere and generous. This quality is shown in his early poetic manifesto, the long poem, "Poetry" ["Poeziia"], published only in 1792 but largely written, according to the author's own admission, in 1787.[145]

This poem, two hundred and eleven lines long, divides essentially into two parts which are followed by a coda of nineteen lines. The opening section of fifty lines outlines Karamzin's view of the divine nature of poetry, emphasized in the epigraph from Klopstock. Poetry is holy (sviataia) and "the eternal comforter of innocent, pure souls." Man sees the beneficence of God in nature and is guided by his emotions to sing songs of praise and gratitude. Karamzin moves to a survey of poets through the ages, whose work exemplifies his views. He speaks first of Moses and David and in a key passage emphasizes the didactic role of poets, "the chosen people" (izbrannyi rod): "In all, in all countries holy Poetry / Was the instructor of people, their happiness; / Everywhere it warmed hearts with love. / The sage by knowing Nature, knew its Creator, / And hearing His voice in the thunder and in the breezes, / In the forests and in the rivers, imitated on his harp / The heavenly chords, and the voice of this Poet / Was always the voice of God!" There follow short characterizations of Orpheus, Homer, Sophocles, Euripides, Bion, Theocritus, Moschus, Virgil, and Ovid. Karamzin notes in 1792 that he "is speaking only of those poets who most of all touched and occupied his soul at the time the poem was written." The location of this note after the listing of the Ancients would seem to suggest that his reverence for the Moderns persisted; the number of pastoral poets among the Ancients clearly points to his predilection for idyllic nature poetry. He then turns to British poets: Ossian, Shakespeare, Milton, Young, and Thomson. These poets are united, at least for Karamzin, by their ability to depict Nature—in its divine, human or natural aspects—and their inspired singing of melancholy. Karamzin sees nothing incongruous in his selection; in his introduction to *Julius Caesar* he had stressed Shakespeare's direct influence specifically upon Milton, Young, and Thomson. His survey finishes with tributes to Gessner and Klopstock, poets venerated by Karamzin and his friends. The poem concludes with a few optimistic lines on the future of Russian poetry and a personal dedication to poetry's joys and consolations, where he characteristically parades his own emotions before the reader.

Karamzin included "Poetry" in the first edition of his collected works in 1803 but omitted it from subsequent editions, seemingly embarrassed by his youthful fulsome tributes to foreign masters and preferring his poetic credo to be judged from later program-poems of the 1790's. In so doing, he tends to conceal the kinship with the Romantic movement of his early work—"Poetry," with its image of the "elected" poet, prophet, and interpreter of God's mysteries, the introduction to *Julius Caesar*, "rediscovered" by Belinskii, the ballads and criticism in the *Moscow Journal*. "Poetry" reflects, apart from a general reading of the "moral philosophers," Shaftesbury and his European popularizers, the specific influence of J. G. Herder's *Älteste Urkunde des Menschengeschlechts*.[146] Nevertheless, Karamzin, with his pronounced belletristic sympathies, assimilated many of his ideas from such "poet-philosophers," as Pope and Thomson. Thomson's influence on "Poetry" is evident in the form and content of the historico-literary section of the poem. Thomson's *The Seasons* abounds in rapid four or five line characterizations of philosophers, poets, and statesmen, predominantly British or Greek and Roman. In "Summer" he gives pen-portraits of Bacon, Shaftesbury, Boyle, and Locke, before turning to Shakespeare and Milton. Karamzin also turns directly from Shakespeare to Milton; for Thomson Shakespeare is "Nature's boast," for Karamzin, "Nature's friend," and both poets dwell on his knowledge of the heart. In "Winter" Thomson writes of "the Mantuan swain" and compares him with Sirius. After two lines on Homer, Thomson introduces "equal by his side / The British Muse," whereas Karamzin praises Ovid before a similar transition — "Britannia is the mother of the greatest poets," and the very use of "Britannia" points to Thomson's influence. Thomson's poem contains no references to French poets and their omission in Karamzin's poem reflects the strong Anglo-German orientation of his reading. Karamzin's poem has been compared with Lenz's "Über die deutsche Dichtkunst" (1775), with its marked English sympathies, characteristic of the Sturm und Drang poets in general.[147] Unlike Lenz's pessimistic view of the future of German poetry, Karamzin's attitude toward Russian poetry reflects an optimism shared by all eighteenth-century Russian poets, independent of their literary affiliations.[148]

Karamzin's early work is the product of an able student, not a precocious master. It is not absurd, however, to speak already of his contribution to Russian literature. This contribution lies not in his few original works, although his experiments with unrhymed verse are interesting, but in his translations. In the space of four years he produced translations of works by Haller, Sturm-Tiede, Shakespeare, Lessing, Genlis, Thomson, Weisse, Pope, and Bonnet. If the majority of these are but part of the spate of translations published in Moscow during the "Novikov decade," his translation of *Julius Caesar* and its enthusiastic preface occupy a special niche in Russian literary history.

In May 1789, Karamzin left Moscow to begin his European tour and left behind a society of freemasons, torn by internal dis-

putes and continually harassed by Catherine. In later years Karamzin described the masons as "none other than Christian mystics:
they interpreted Nature and man, sought a secret meaning in the
Old and New Testaments, praised ancient traditions, opposed academic wisdom, etc., but they demanded from their pupils true
Christian virtues, did not interfere in politics and were devoted
to the Tsar."[149]

In general, during the reign of Alexander Karamzin was intent
on minimizing his own connections with the masons. This is reflected in his substitution of the word "friend" (drug) for the
masonic "brother" (brat) in preparing extracts of Petrov's letters
for publication[150] and in his emphasizing an ideological break with
the masons by the time of his departure for Europe. He allegedly
told N. I. Grech: "I was drawn by circumstances into this society
in my youth and could not but respect the people in it who were
sincerely and selflessly seeking truth and devoted to useful public
activity. But I was completely unable to share their conviction that
some sort of secrecy was necessary for this and I disliked their ceremonies which always seemed to me foolish. Before my journey
abroad I told them frankly that without ceasing to respect the
honorable members of the society and to be grateful for their constant good will toward me I could no longer allow myself to participate in their meetings and was obliged to leave them."[151] Prozorovskii in his investigations into the affairs of the masons in 1792
could not help seeing a connection between Karamzin's journey
and the foreign missions of Kutuzov and of Nevzorov and Kolokol'-
nikov, students supported financially by the masons; Prince Nikolai
Trubetskoi, whom he was interrogating on this subject, replied,
however, that "as far as Karamzin is concerned, he was not sent
by us, but traveled as a tourist at his own expense."[152] The tradition, nevertheless, persisted that Karamzin was sent abroad by the
masons with instructions prepared by S. I. Gamaleia, and the recent discovery of a note by F. N. Glinka which records Karamzin
as saying that "the society which sent me abroad gave me traveling
expenses calculated for breakfast, lunch and supper" is positive,
if inconclusive, evidence of Karamzin's continuing dependence
on at least certain of the masons.[153] One can only speculate that
Karamzin was asked to contact German masons and Kutuzov, possibly with a view to procuring letters and information which could

not be sent through open channels. On his return from his travels Karamzin certainly continued to associate with many of the masons, although there is no doubt that their relationship was on a new and different footing.

The Friendly Learned Society (dissolved in name at the beginning of 1787, although its spirit and members remained) had been Karamzin's university, where he had spent four years acquiring that education of the mind and heart which inevitably left a deep imprint on his subsequent career as an author. Unattracted by the masonic quest for mysteries, he had shared the common enthusiasm for self-knowledge and self-perfection. Reconciled to "the unpleasant experience that everywhere there is evil,"[154] he did not extend this to an acceptance of the notion of the basically evil nature of man. He possessed an Enlightener's conviction that answers could be found for problems, which the masons were content to leave to faith. He alternated between a pessimistic view of life as a vale of tears and an optimism which stemmed from his love of great literature and belief in human progress.

Under the influence of Petrov and Kutuzov his feeling for language and distinctive literary tastes had developed, strengthening his desire to seek worldly fame as an author. It was a desire in direct opposition to the cautious anonymity, the modest contentment with translation or composition "for the few" encouraged by such as Petrov, Kutuzov, and M. N. Murav'ev. Karamzin's reading had made him familiar with many of the leading writers of the eighteenth century; he was fluent in French and German, translated proficiently from English, knew a little Italian and Greek. In general, he received the literary education of a cosmopolitan in the approving eighteenth-century sense of a man equipped to take his place in a brotherhood of enlightened minds, rising above nationalist squabbles and imbued with a love of humanity and true enlightenment, such as Wieland describes in *Die Abderiten*. It is hardly surprising that Karamzin desired nothing so strongly as the opportunity to travel, to meet and talk with famous authors.

« TWO »

The *Moscow* Journal

1791~1792

According to an entry in the record of arrivals and departures which the St. Petersburg chief of police kept for Catherine, Karamzin arrived in the capital on July 15, 1790, some fourteen months after his departure for Germany.[1] Before the recent discovery of this document the only evidence to contradict Karamzin's own assertion in *Letters of a Russian Traveler* that he arrived in Russia in September had been a letter from A. A. Pleshcheev to Kutuzov, which gave his arrival in August.[2] It is possible that Pleshcheev is referring to Karamzin's arrival in Moscow after spending some three weeks in St. Petersburg and that the confusing indication "from Moscow" in the police record arose from a misreading of his passport. Karamzin may well have finished his journey by land, mindful of the difficulties he had encountered originally in attempting to leave St. Petersburg by boat.[3] Shtorm in his commentary on the police document attempts mistakenly to relate Karamzin's movements on his return to the undoubtedly false dating of the English letters in *Letters of a Russian Traveler*. Karamzin could hardly conceal his whereabouts from the authorities and his presence in St. Petersburg was dictated by his wish to gain the collaboration of Dmitriev and, through him, of Derzhavin and other writers in his projected journal. With regard to *Letters* itself, there could be no intention to mislead Catherine's officials, since part 5, in which the English letters appeared, was published for the first time in 1801; it was obviously immediate and distant posterity that Karamzin wished to deceive, successfully if unnecessarily.

"At last I returned—(the very same person who had set out, only with some new experiences, some new knowledge, a greater

35

ability to feel the beauties of the physical and moral world)":[4] in his obituary for Petrov Karamzin was answering the accusations of his masonic friends that "those accused foreign countries have made a different person of you."[5] On his return to Moscow Karamzin stayed with the Pleshcheevs, Aleksei Aleksandrovich and Anastasia Ivanovna, whose friendship brought from Karamzin subsequent fulsome tributes in verse and prose. Pleshcheeva certainly found him "completely different and what is worse, he himself thinks that he is better now than he was previously";[6] she shared with Kutuzov doubts about Karamzin's continued attachment to them, about his cosmopolitanism and his intention to publish an account of his travels. In July 1790, before Karamzin's return, she had written to Kutuzov that "if he writes anything I will not read it, and my first demand will be that he should not publish any of his descriptions";[7] nevertheless, in the *Moscow News* for November 6, 1790, there appeared the announcement of Karamzin's forthcoming *Moscow Journal*, in which *Letters* figured prominently.[8] Karamzin had made no secret of his wish to publish an account of his travels[9] and it is certain that he did not expect the hostility that the announcement and the first numbers of his journal provoked among his so-called friends, who, according to Pleshcheeva, "wish him every possible misfortune and at the same time profess that they love him dearly."[10] A flurry of letters, written between December 1790, and June 1791, by M. I. Bagrianskii, I. V. Lopukhin, and N. N. Trubetskoi to Kutuzov and by Kutuzov to his various correspondents, deride Karamzin's aims, his ability, vanity, immaturity, and lack of patriotism.[11] Kutuzov even wrote a parody of Karamzin, which he sent to Trubetskoi for possible inclusion in a rival journal.[12] In marked contrast, nowhere in Karamzin's published work or correspondence is there a malicious personal reference to any of the masons.

Announcing his journal, Karamzin projected its contents under five headings: 1] original Russian works in verse and prose; 2] foreign works, selected principally from German, English, and French journals, together with notices of recently published foreign books; 3] critical reviews of Russian books, mainly original, but also deserving translations; 4] notices of plays performed in Moscow; 5] descriptions of noteworthy events and anecdotes about famous modern authors. Karamzin welcomed contributions in accord with his plan, which excluded "only works which are theological, mystical, too academic, pedantic or dry." Polemically emphasizing his own position, he requested anything, "which in a well-ordered country may be printed with official permission." Kutuzov, not without justification, saw further evidence of Karamzin's ideological break with the masons: "I have just received a letter from Plescheev, enclosing a copy of Karamzin's 'Announcement,' from which I see that his former relationship with us has changed."[13] Karamzin's stand is curiously near to that taken by I. I. Melissino, the curator of Moscow University and a bitter opponent of Schwartz and Novikov, who had announced in the *Moscow News* in May 1789, the establishment of a Society of Friends of Russian Scholarship (Obshchestvo liubitelei rossiiskoi uchenosti). The statutes, discussed at the first preliminary meeting of the Society on May 25, 1789, a week after Karamzin left Moscow for St. Petersburg, stressed the need to avoid "any sort of futile and useless mystical or mysterious philosophising."[14] Despite his insistence that his Society was formed in opposition to the defunct Friendly Learned Society, Melissino failed to obtain Catherine's approval because of suspected links with what she called "that crowd" (skopishche).[15]

Karamzin's announcement does not signal a renunciation of his past; it merely clarifies an attitude toward literature and philosophy, which masons like Kutuzov interpreted now as a betrayal. He remained consistent in his love of artistic literature, moral in content, attractive in presentation and style, exemplified in the work of Thomson and Haller. A similar literary orientation undoubtedly induced masonic poets such as I. A. Dmitrevskii, F. P. Kliucharev, and Kheraskov to contribute to Karamzin's journal.[16]

In his foreword to the first number of his journal Karamzin wrote: "Many foreign journals lie before me; I will take none of them as an exact model, but will make use of them all."[17] His judgment of the type of journal the Russian reading public would welcome was excellent; avoiding the parochial appeal of the masonic journals and antipathetic to the means of the satirical journals which had enjoyed such a vogue in the early years of Catherine's reign, Karamzin made the *Moscow Journal* the broadsheet of Russian sentimentalism. To retain the attention (and subscriptions) of his reading public, primarily the gentry, which was enjoying a greater degree of leisure than ever before, Karamzin had not only to produce a journal with lively and varied, essentially contemporary, content but perfect a style which would attract even those who affected to despise their native language and literature. By general European standards the *Moscow Journal* is an accomplished example of the eighteenth-century literary journal, mixing the "useful" and the "pleasant" in its appeal to readers with taste and a feeling heart.

The first number provides a good example of the general organization and variety of the journal. A poetry section of six poems by Kheraskov, Derzhavin, Dmitriev, Karamzin, and Petrov, is followed by the first *Letters of a Russian Traveler*. Then comes "A Suicide" ["Samoubiitsa"], an anecdote included in *Letters* in a later edition but singled out for the particular contemporary interest in the psychology of the suicide. The second half comprises a review of a recent performance of Lessing's *Emilia Galotti* and two book reviews, the first of Kheraskov's *Cadmus and Harmonia* [*Kadm i Garmoniia*] and the second of François Le Vaillant's *Voyage dans l'intérieur de l'Afrique*, translated from an original review by S. R. N. Chamfort in the *Mercure de France*. Such was the basic formula during the first year, with an occasional change in emphasis by the introduction of more translated material, both fictional works and book and Paris theatre reviews. In the second year of publication (1792) there was a considerable increase in translated works and a succession of Karamzin's own original tales. The earlier extensive Russian book and dramatic reviews were by contrast greatly reduced, but the staple of the journal remained throughout Karamzin's *Letters*, which ended with the description of his arrival in Paris.

Karamzin's skill in organizing the poetry section of his journal undoubtedly assured his initial success. Derzhavin and Kheraskov, the acknowledged leading poets of St. Petersburg and Moscow respectively, gave authority to the journal by readily contributing their latest poems and were clearly among the few established writers who were willing to acknowledge Karamzin's enterprise and talent. By a deliberately ambiguous stratagem in the closing lines of his poem "Poetry," Karamzin seems to acknowledge his gratitude to both poets. The poem, which, according to a note, was composed in 1787, was published for the first time in September 1792, in the *Moscow Journal* and contains the following lines in its closing section: "O Russians! the time will come / When poetry will shine among you, like the sun at midday. / The darkness of night has disappeared—already Aurora's light / Shines in **** . . ." Once considered by commentators who believed the omitted word to be "Moscow" as an indication of Karamzin's excessive opinion of himself as a poet, the number of asterisks and metre suggest a four-syllable word with a second-syllable stress. If the poem reflects Karamzin's sympathies in 1787, the poet is undoubtedly Kheraskov;[18] in the context of the *Moscow Journal* it may be seen as one of a series of mutual compliments between Karamzin and Derzhavin.[19] Karamzin received contributions from other poets in Derzhavin's circle, such as N. A. L'vov and V. V. Kapnist, and from poets close to Kheraskov in Moscow, Kliucharev, Dmitrevskii, S. S. Bobrov, and Podshivalov (members of the Friendly Learned Society and the last two also contributors to *Children's Reading*) and Iu. A. Neledinskii-Meletskii. Few poems were in fact signed, most were designated simply by initials, but the three poets who dominate the journal by the number of their poems as well as by their characteristic and conflicting styles are Derzhavin, Dmitriev and Karamzin himself. There are eighteen poems by Derzhavin, nineteen by Karamzin and approximately forty-three by Dmitriev. Derzhavin is the poet near to Court life, writing of Catherine's *vel'mozhi* and official functions but defending his independence and high calling as a poet; Dmitriev, encouraged by Karamzin's advice and suggestions, is the salon poet, alternating Voltairian satire and epigrams with sentimental love songs and achieving fame for his wit and polished and precise language; Karamzin is the private poet, singing of melancholy, nature, true friendship, the mysteries of art and poetry, and experimenting with new and expressive poetic forms and metres.

It is nevertheless the prose of the *Moscow Journal*, Karamzin's prose, which gives the journal its significance in eighteenth-century Russian literature. Karamzin had earlier in a letter to Lavater pointed out the lack of good prose writers in Russia[20] and he strove to fill precisely this gap. Stressing the importance of foreign writers in the evolution of his prose style, he explained how "intending to appear on the stage [of Russian literature], I was unable to find one Russian writer worthy of imitation and although I paid tribute to the eloquence of Lomonosov, I did not fail to note his *wild* and *barbarous* style, completely alien to our time, and I tried to write in a purer and livelier fashion. I had in mind a few foreign authors; at first I imitated them but later wrote in my own style, which was not borrowed from anyone."[21] In the *Moscow Journal*, there was published approximately half of *Letters of a Russian Traveler*, together with a series of tales, of which the most famous and influential are "Poor Liza" ["Bednaia Liza"] and "Natalia, the Boyar's Daughter" ["Natal'ia, boiarskaia doch' "]. They will be discussed in subsequent chapters, but it is interesting to consider at this point the relative novelty of the publication of his stories in a literary journal and the stimulus they gave to original Russian prose fiction. Over the years 1730–90 only *seven* original novels or stories were published in Russian journals, although some 426 foreign works were published and republished. In the following decade the popularity of the novel and short story (written in Russian) grew considerably: the total of 403 translated works nearly equals the total for the preceding sixty years and the fifty-eight original Russian works represent a figure eight times greater than the earlier one. Karamzin's role in this sudden creative activity on the part of Russian authors would seem to be of paramount importance. According to Sipovskii's table, from which these figures are extracted, the one Russian story appearing between 1785 and 1790 was his "Eugene and Julia" (anonymously and unnoticed) and of the nine original works appearing during the two years of the *Moscow Journal* five were his.[22]

The controversial features in the journal were not the stories or the poetry but the book and drama reviews; they were an attempt to resolve a particularly touchy and persistent problem in eighteenth-century Russian literature. Previously, occasional book reviews had appeared in such journals as G. F. Miller's *Monthly Compositions for Profit and Entertainment* [*Ezhemesiachnye sochineniia, k pol'ze i uveseleniiu sluzhashchie*] (1755) and particularly Novikov's *St. Petersburg Scholarly News for 1777* [*Sankt-Peterburgskie uchenye vedomosti na 1777 god*]. Karamzin developed the well-intentioned criticism which Novikov had initiated, made it a regular feature of his journal and founded it on clearly defined critical principles.

Karamzin had spoken in his announcement of his wish to note "the good and the bad impartially," but his strongest defense of criticism is found not in one of his own reviews or program-statements but in his intervention in a controversy between Podshivalov and F. O. Tumanskii, a notorious pedant who plagued Karamzin with unacceptable contributions and became his bitter enemy.[23] Podshivalov had reviewed Tumanskii's *On the Improbable Myths by the Greek Writer, Palaephatus [Palefata grecheskogo pisatelia O neveroiatnykh skazaniiakh]* (1791) negatively but with restraint in view of the numerous absurdities in Tumanskii's explanations of the myths and of the curious mixture of Russian and Slavonic in his style.[24] Printing Tumanskii's reply the following month, Karamzin accompanied it with a series of footnotes, defending criticism as necessary for the development of a national literature. He counters Tumanskii's argument of "do not judge and you will not be judged": "You therefore wish there to be no criticism at all? What was German literature thirty years ago, and what is it now? And is it not partly due to strict criticism that the Germans have begun to write so well?"[25] He refutes the view that criticism is for small minds and frustrated authors by referring to Lessing and Moses Mendelsohn and insisting that "taste and knowledge" are requisites of the critic.[26]

Tumanskii typifies the Russian author, vain and resentful of criticism, for whom literature was a mere pastime and whose efforts, however inept, were to be complimented, never censured. Karamzin's position is very near to that of Novikov in his *Windbag [Pustomelia]* (1770): "Some people affirm that it is easier to criticize than write . . . but I am not convinced and believe that to criticize with judgment and taste is as difficult as to write well."[27] For Novikov specific and effective literary criticism was an integral part of his arguments for satire "against the person" (na litso) rather than the general and weak satire "against the vice" (na porok), advocated by Catherine; Karamzin at this period of his career was able to endorse "strict criticism" without extending this to an acceptance of satire. His program is nonetheless again anticipated by Novikov in the *St. Petersburg Scholarly News*, when he writes: "But since the critical reviewing of published books and other material is one of the main aims in publishing this kind of journal and in fact may be considered the soul of its body, we request our enlightened public to allow us the freedom for responsible criticism. We are inspired to this not by the desire to censure the

acts of others but by the public good; thus we do not wish by this
step to offend conscientious writers, editors, and translators; indeed
our criticism will observe extreme moderation and with great care
be kept within the bounds of decorum and good behavior."[28] Karamzin possessed not only the good intentions but equally the
ability to write good reviews. Novikov and his friends were not always so fortunate; M. A. Dmitriev recalls a gathering of litterateurs
at Novikov's house in Petersburg and the unsuccessful attempt to
write a review of Kheraskov's epic *The Rossiad* (1779): "At that
time it was still impossible to grasp such a large work of poetry—
there was nothing but unaccountable astonishment and enthusiastic praise."[29] Karamzin's first review in the *Moscow Journal* was of a
work by Kheraskov, an action which prompted the mason N.
Trubetskoi to write to Kutuzov: ". . . he has even dared to write a
review of *Cadmus*"[30] and brought ridicule from Ivan Krylov and
A. I. Klushin in their *Spectator* [*Zritel'*].[31]

Under one of two rubrics, "About Russian Books" and "About
Foreign Books" some forty works were reviewed or listed by Karamzin. Despite Karamzin's initial wish to review "particularly original"
Russian works, foreign works predominate, a fact which mirrors
faithfully the state of the Russian book market. Of the forty books
reviewed, twenty-seven come under the foreign books section and
of the remaining thirteen only four are original Russian works. All
the reviews of works published in Russia were written by Karamzin
himself and he also provided short evaluations of some of the foreign language books. The major reviews in this section were translated and carefully edited by Karamzin from leading foreign journals. In common with all his translations they reflect his own
interests and tastes. It is also interesting to note the emphasis given
to book criticism in the first year and the sporadic nature this
feature acquired in the following year. Of the eight original major
reviews written by Karamzin seven appeared in 1791, together with
the four principal translated reviews. In 1792 Karamzin's criticism
of N. P. Osipov's *Virgil's Aeneid In Reverse* [*Virgilieva Eneida,
vyvorochennaia na iznanku*] (1791) was the only extensive review
in either book section, although his brief notes on other books are
not without significance.

Karamzin's first book review in the *Moscow Journal* of Kheraskov's *Cadmus*, was challenging in several respects: firstly, the se-

lected work had been published in 1789 and was already well-known to the reading public; secondly, its author was a venerated literary figure, particularly in Moscow, where the journal had most subscribers; thirdly, despite its generally respectful tone, the review is no mere homage but critical and polemical. Although several of the translated reviews are longer, it is the most detailed of those written by Karamzin himself and is the only review of an original Russian *prose* work in the journal. It sets the characteristic form of general assessment, followed by a résumé of the contents with extracts which invite specific literary or ideological comment, which leads finally to linguistic and stylistic criticism.[32]

His opening remarks immediately reiterate the opposition to the academic and the pedantic indicated in his "Announcement": "The philosopher who is not a poet writes sometimes extremely dry moral dissertations; the poet accompanies his moral with captivating images, brings it to life in his characters and produces a greater effect." This in turn is closely connected with the following review of Vaillant's travels, where the author is praised for his ability "to write, to enliven and diversify his scenes and he holds now our mind, now our feelings, now our imagination. I have heard it said of his book that it is not sufficiently scholarly. This reproach may not be without foundation, for his book in fact is not boring; and in many genres a work has to be boring in order to gain a reputation for profundity and scholarship."[33] Kheraskov is a true "poet-philosopher," whose aim was "to write a second Télémaque." The mention of Fénelon's work gives Karamzin his first opportunity to polemicize with Kheraskov and certain aspects of pseudoclassical poetics. He argues: "In his foreword the esteemed author says that his *Cadmus* is not a *poem* [poema] but a simple story, but when a story is not history but fiction, then it is, I think, a poem, epic or not, but still a poem, written in prose or verse but still a poem, which according to the generally accepted meaning in other languages signifies any work of imaginative power. Thus a comedy or novel is a poem." European precedents for such a definition were numerous; nearly two hundred years previously Cervantes had spoken of the epic in similar terms and Karamzin was equally familiar with the preface of the novel Fielding wrote "in imitation of Cervantes," *Joseph Andrews*. Nevertheless, in Russia, where pseudoclassical poetics were still persuasive, Karamzin was among the first to attack genre hierarchy and agitate for the importance of prose. A year later he began his note on Florian's *Gonzalve de Cordoue, ou Grenade reconquise* with the words "this heroic novel or prosaic poem," adopting the description from an original review in the *Mercure de France*.[34] In a similar spirit he describes Ludovico Ariosto as "a novelist" (romanist), whose exuberant imagination "invents hero after hero, adventure after adventure and wonder after wonder" in his "heroic poem" *Orlando Furioso*.[35] The persistence of the opposition to Karamzin's views may be seen in an article by I. I. Martynov published in 1804, in which he praises Karamzin's reviews as "exemplary" (primery v retsenzii) but refers to the authority of Batteux and La Harpe to affirm that "a work written in prose is never called a poem."[36] The fact that many eighteenth-century Russian translations of verse originals were in prose blurred genre divisions, although it is interesting that Kheraskov in his preface, which Karamzin avoids quoting directly, specifically moves the emphasis from verse versus prose to a question of content and manner in defining the epic. On such grounds he refuses to accept Fénelon's *Télémaque* as an epic, even when Trediakovskii recast it in hexameters in his *Tilemakhida* (1766).[37] Trediakovskii had prefaced his poem with a translation of A. M. Ramsay's *Discours sur la poésie épique, et sur l'excellence du poème de Télémaque* (1719), which, as is obvious from the title, defined Fénelon's work as an epic poem. Karamzin was known among the masons as "brother Ramsay" or "Lord Ramsay," a name suggested, it has been argued, by the similarity of the last two syllables of his name with that of the Scottish mason,[38] but it is possible that in addition he may have been the translator of Ramsay's *Discours*, which was published by Novikov in 1787.[39] In August 1788, Kutuzov mentioned in a letter to Turgenev "the new poet Lord Ramsay, or simply Karamzin"[40] and there seems no earlier usage of the name; in addition, Ramsay's work contains many ideas, albeit unoriginal, on the nature of poetry which Karamzin himself propounds.

Karamzin proceeds to a short résumé of the contents of Kheraskov's work and then to extensive extracts designed to exhibit its various "beauties." It is a technique which he uses for a specific purpose. Not only is he intent on pointing out the strengths and weaknesses in the work under review from a literary angle but on isolating passages which have an independent ideological interest out of context. He uses the ideas of others, which to change the tense of his "Announcement" "in a well-ordered country *have been* printed with official permission." Thus he quotes Cadmus's speech on government to the Thessalians, in which Kheraskov argues that A] an aristocratic ruling clique would be self-defeating, B] rule by the people would lead to chaos, C] laws are not sufficient in themselves, and D] one ruler in one state is the solution encouraged by Nature itself—one head to one body, and Karamzin adds the comment: "Who can fail to feel the persuasiveness of these deliberations?"[41] Then follows the speech of a bard who refuses to prostitute his art and demands the right to sing his own songs; it is the position of Derzhavin's murza in the first poem in the journal and Karamzin comments with approval: "This is the language of a poet who feels his worth!" A third quotation on the meeting of Cadmus and Harmonia with their son, whom they do not recognize, has the commentary: "The description of the youth is beautiful, as is the description of the vague feelings of parental love. As yet they do not know that he is their son, but already they love him. I do not know who will not be moved by this, who will not feel the beauty of this passage, but I know that he has feeling neither for the beauties of Nature nor for the beauties of Poetry." It is not so much Karamzin's injection of pathos into a scene which hardly deserves it as his categoric division into "the feeling" and "the unfeeling" which is characteristic. Examples of these tactics can be found in the quotation on Truth in the review of Voltaire's *Henriade*, the increasing irony toward Lavater in the passage from Coxe's *Sketches of the natural, civil, and political state of Swisserland*, quoted allegedly to show the excellence of the translation, the lucid exposition of the main ideas in Thomas More's *Utopia*, "this political novel, which is very obscure in the Russian translation."[42]

Recommending *Cadmus* as "a work, worthy of the reader's complete attention," Karamzin proceeds to further criticism, since "they say that there is no work perfect in everything." On reading certain passages, he finds "that smacks too much of modernity; it is against the spirit of those times from which the fable has been taken." His understanding of the literary conventions of the modern epic is clear from his comparison between Homer's and Fénelon's Telemachus: "Take any shepherd—Swiss or Russian, it makes no difference—dress him in Greek clothes and call him the son of the King of Ithaca: he will be nearer to Homer's Telemachus than any child of Fénelon's imagination, who is nothing more than the ideal image of the French dauphin, guided not by the Greek Minerva but by French philosophy." Karamzin criticized Ariosto, who "despised verisimilitude in his fictions, despised unity of action";[43] he was essentially a representative of modern poetry, which Karamzin defined in another review as concerned "with pleasure and amusement."[44] Kheraskov and Fénelon are excused for their willful anachronisms, however, because of their underlying moral purpose; they thereby perpetuate the seriousness of the Ancients while writing in an attractive style. In keeping with such views Karamzin chose as the epigraph to part 7 of his journal Shaftesbury's "poets in early days were looked upon as authentick Sages, for dictating rules of life, and teaching manners and good sense: how they may have lost their pretension, I can't say."

Finally, Karamzin turns his attention to Kheraskov's language, pointing out words "to which our ears are unaccustomed" and objecting to the use of certain words in the plural rather than the singular—an interesting criticism of what was a distinctive stylistic feature of English sentimentalism.[45] His verdict that "*Cadmus* will live with *The Rossiad* and *Vladimir*" proved all too correct—by the next generation the three works were completely forgotten; nevertheless, to a greater degree than his reviews of works enjoying a kinder fate Karamzin's review of *Cadmus* demonstrates his critical techniques.

Epic poems were the subject of several substantial original reviews, but Karamzin is more concerned with the manner and the quality of the verse than the content in Voltaire's *Henriade* and Ariosto's *Orlando Furioso*. Confronted with Osipov's mock-epic Karamzin states that "it is required only that the jokes should be in fact amusing; otherwise they will be intolerable for readers possessing taste."[46] He finds that although there is some effective parody, "unfortunately there is much that is weak, drawn-out, too coarse; also many lines which are impure or offensive to the ear."[47] Karamzin's constant preoccupation with the demands of refined taste effectively inhibits his appreciation of comedy. His criticism of Osipov's work is in line with his rejection of such works as Voltaire's *Candide* and Gay's *The Beggars' Opera*, both considered witty but tasteless,[48] and his dislike of English comedy.

Much more compatible with sentimental aesthetics are the novels of Samuel Richardson, containing "the best philosophy of life, propounded in the most attractive way." Richardson is "a skilled painter of man's moral nature," able to maintain a reader's interest through eight volumes, whilst "describing nothing but the most usual scenes in life."[49] The ability to depict character inevitably links Richardson with Shakespeare: in yet another addition to Thomson's "Winter," Karamzin followed the paean to Shakespeare with "O Richardson! your works will always be Britain's pride and monuments of the art of painting man's heart."[50] He praises Richardson's portrayal of Lovelace "in whom we see such a remarkable but natural mixture of good and evil qualities—Lovelace, sometimes noble and kind, sometimes a monster." This interplay of contradictory impulses and passions fascinated Karamzin; he describes Lessing's Prince in *Emilia Galotti* in similar terms[51] and attempted schematically to create their Russian counterpart in the figure of Erast in his story "Poor Liza."

Karamzin believed that Richardson and Fielding taught the French and Germans how to write novels that were "a history of life,"[52] but they belonged to a past generation of outstanding English poets and novelists. "Modern English literature does not deserve the slightest attention: they are writing here now only the most mediocre novels and there is not one good poet," he wrote in a letter from England,[53] but the *Moscow Journal* reveals his eagerness to herald a possible revival. In 1792 he devoted two reviews to recent English works; in F. Sayers's *Dramatik Sketches of the Ancient Northern Mithology* he detected "a rich imagination, natural simplicity, Ossianic painting and the flowers of Greece"[54] and the appearance of Thomas Holcroft's *Anna St. Ives* allowed him to pronounce: "Thus English literature rises again. Sayers and Holcroft have appeared on the scene and the public crowns them with laurels."[55] Holcroft "writes as though inspired, like a poet"; he relates completely credible adventures and characters worthy of Shakespeare and surpasses even Richardson. It was an enthusiasm which Karamzin came to regret. The review which had opened with the words: "A rare novel!" (roman, kakikh malo!) was replaced in the second edition of the journal by the brusque dismissal: "A run-of-the-mill novel!" (roman, kakikh mnogo!).[56]

Karamzin was on much surer ground with the translated review of Ulrich Bräker's *Lebengeschichte und natürliche Abenteuer eines armen Mannes von Tockenburg.* In its realistic evocation of peasant life it was equaled in eighteenth-century German literature only by Jung-Stilling's *Jugend,* which Karamzin held in particular esteem.[57] "There are observations and insights into the human heart of which a Montaigne would not be ashamed, or any scholar or observer of the heart—and what is more, the hero of this history is a simple peasant."[58] The German reviewer, after an inevitable comparison between Bräker and Rousseau, finishes with the sentimental appeal, characteristic of Karamzin's own reviews: "Now let the reader judge the Genevan with the man from Tockenburg, and whoever says not only with his tongue but feels in his heart that Homo sum, humani nihil, etc., let him take the book and read it from cover to cover!"[59] It is a work in all respects central to the *Moscow Journal's* artistic aims and propaganda for the classlessness of the feeling heart.

Karamzin's dramatic criticisms are quantitatively and qualitatively as significant as his book reviews.[60] They appear as two separate features, "Moscow Theatre" and "Paris Theatres"; the second of these was translated and adapted from N. E. Framéry's "Les Spectacles" section in the *Mercure de France* and consists of short notices of the latest operas, vaudevilles, and plays in revolutionary Paris. Karamzin's major dramatic reviews appeared again during 1791 and the interest in 1792 is minimal. Of the eleven plays reviewed as "Moscow Theatre" only N. P. Nikolev's *Spoilt Darling* [*Baloven'*] was an original Russian work and the remaining ten were translated or adapted from foreign originals. Seven of these were German and three were French. European domination of the book market is thus paralleled by a similar phenomenon in the theatre.

Karamzin's forewords to *Julius Caesar* and *Emilia Galotti* indicate truth to (human) nature as his primary demand of the dramatist. His contrast between French classical drama and the works of a Shakespeare or a Lessing is based on a division between dramatists who are guided by dead rules and conventions and those who have an intuitive understanding of the workings of the human heart. The former may produce works which exhibit taste and purity of style but lack imaginative insight and the power to move an audience. The performance of the Russian *Le Cid,* an adaptation of Corneille's original by Ia. B. Kniazhnin, gives Karamzin the opportunity to continue his campaign against French tragedy.[61] *Le Cid*, the least regular of Corneille's plays and the only one to find sympathy among the Romantics, contained, in Karamzin's opinion, a few "good scenes and touching feelings" and "many beautiful lines," a concession already made by D'Alembert in his attack on French tragedy and particularly on Corneille's *Cinna*, which Karamzin quotes at length in his review. D'Alembert speaks of "cette froideur" which is "le grand défaut, selon moi, de presque toutes nos pièces de théâtre." Karamzin endorses his view of "terreur et . . . pitié" as the basis of tragedy and embarks on a contrast between French tragedy and Shakespeare in terms of the relative charms of a regular French garden and wild nature—one of the most overworked figures of the age, but one used earlier by Voltaire specifically to demonstrate French superiority. Karamzin's major criticism of *Le Cid* is the mixed response which the dénouement evokes in the audience. "The dénouement of a drama must invariably be sad or happy for the spectator and leave him with pure, unmixed feelings." This ineptitude in the dramatist is distinct from the psychologically motivated switches from sadness to joy in a character's response to a situation, such as he appreciates in *Emilia Galotti* or Racine's *Iphigénie*.

Lessing's play in fact satisfies all Karamzin demands of true theatre. A particular feature of his review is his constant stressing of the "naturalness" of the character's reactions (estestvenno; natural'no), but it is of an essentially "theatrical" kind: he relates it to strong, emphatic acting, to the marriage of words and exaggerated gesture and play of the eyes. This is clear both from a footnote on a performance of *Le Cid*, which he saw in Paris,[62] and from the lines he addressed to the actor Pomerantsev in the role of Odoardo: "He who the emotions of an unhappy father / By art was able to convey to the hearts of all spectators / Who by strong acting and weighty words, / When on the stage, possessed the spectators' souls."[63] Here pity is stressed; in Karamzin's insertion in Thomson's "Winter" it is the terror inspired by Odoardo's murder of his daughter: "Terror possesses the spectators; then their hearts soften and tender tears pour from their eyes."[64] In a later piece Karamzin describes the cathartic effect of Sophocles's *Oedipus:* "Oedipus dies. Horror on all faces—in the soul a sweet pleasure. O wonder of

art! Who will explain your mysteries?—O Sophocles!"[65] But Karamzin is inclined to blur the line between true tragedy and the facile
emotions aroused by melodrama. In his review of F. J. Bertuch's
Elfriede he finds that the author "does not know that great art of
striking our hearts which so many of his countrymen have, as it
were, appropriated. He is no Goethe, Schiller, Klinger or Kotzebue."[66] This linking of Kotzebue with the Sturm und Drang dramatists is revealing. Karamzin held Kotzebue in particular esteem at
this period of his career; he speaks of him as "a genius"[67] and "one
of Germany's true poets";[68] to a marked degree he was one of the
instigators of the Kotzebue vogue in Russia, toward which he was
later ironical.[69] He judges the success of Kotzebue's *Menschenhass
und Reue* in Moscow by its tear-jerking effects: "In the boxes and
stalls I saw tears falling: the most flattering praise, which only a
dramatic author can enjoy."[70] In an earlier extract from *Letters of
a Russian Traveler* he describes how "at the entrance I wiped away
the last sweet tear" after witnessing a performance in Berlin,[71] although in a later edition, he was to modify his praise.[72]

Karamzin's only attempt to write a play is an unfortunate
mixture of Kotzebue and Shakespeare. The first scenes of "Sofiia", a
one-act play in eleven scenes, were published in the same number
of his journal as his notice on Kotzebue's drama.[73] Possible evidence
of his reading of Shakespeare are the short scenes, the constant
change of setting as well as Sofiia's final monologue, reminiscent
of a favorite passage from *King Lear*. The plot revolving around the
infidelity of a young wife who abandons her husband for her lover
and repents too late is clearly taken from Kotzebue's play, as a
comparison with the résumé in *Letters of a Russian Traveler* shows.
Karamzin seeks to provide a series of scenes designed to move and
harrow the reader in the best melodramatic tradition. In the opening scene, in which Sofiia attempts to tell her husband that she is
leaving him, Karamzin introduces pathetic exclamations as a means
to heighten the tension. Sofiia and Dobrov vie with each other in
their use of "My God!" (Bozhe moi), which Karamzin believed
particularly poignant.[74] Apollon Grigor'ev records that the play
"was read avidly,"[75] but the general falsity of the dialogue under-
lines Karamzin's wisdom in abandoning further dramatic works
and concentrating on prose.

A more interesting feature of the play is the attempt to create a
recognizable Russian background. He transferred the European

bourgeois drama to a suitable Russian environment—the country estate of the middle gentry; he introduced peasant servants to comment on the action and stylized their speech by the use of occasional proverbs and characteristic speech patterns. His use of names such as Sofiia, Ivan, Anna, Parasha, Le Tiens and, less plausibly, Dobrov are in keeping with views expressed in a review of Collin d'Harleville's *L'Optimiste*. In his attempt to russify the play the translator renamed the characters Zlanet, Buremysl, Izveda and Premila; Karamzin objects that such a procedure never allows the spectator to forget he is in the theatre: "The drama must be a faithful representation of society; it is essential that the characters in it not only act but are named the same as they are in society," i.e., by name and patronymic.[76] He insists that if a play is to be adapted to Russian conditions, the action should be realistically motivated; therefore, he argues: "Zlanet, who has lost all his money, wants to live more moderately and gives his servants their freedom. There is something here which is also un-Russian. If a member of the gentry became impoverished then he would either sell his servants or release them with passports, i.e., for a certain period, not for ever."

Karamzin's conception of the theatre as "a faithful representation of society" (vernoe predstavlenie obshchezhitiia), consonant with the concern of Lessing and Diderot for realistic middle-class tragedy, is part of a generally impressive program for the drama. He demands psychological truth and motivated action, strong emotions and moving scenes, naturalness in dialogue and speech, russification, when necessary, in complete accord with existing Russian customs. He is always conscious of the difference between what is to be read and what is to be spoken; he emphasizes that "the drama cannot tolerate any long orations; it consists of *acts*—the very word is expressive. If an author wishes to deliberate, let him write a dissertation, or a conversation piece or what he will—only not a drama for the theatre."[77] He is consequently equally attentive to the quality of performance and almost all his reviews end with detailed and informed comment on the actors. He stresses the need for an actor to understand and live completely his part, so that the illusion of real life is created and the falsity of the theatre transcended. On the debit side is the invitation for emotion for emotion's sake and over-acting.

The detailed discussion of plays and theatres which is found in

Letters of a Russian Traveler is a necessary complement to the dramatic reviews as such. The interdependence of *Letters* and the content of the journal is apparent in many contexts and with regard to the drama Karamzin refers the reader in the course of his review of Kotzebue's play to *Letters* for a detailed résumé of the action. Although *Letters*, as published in the *Moscow Journal*, represents only half the complete account of Karamzin's travels, his remarks on the French and English theatre, which appeared in 1801, may be conveniently included at this juncture. The example of Shakespeare remains the constant touchstone in his criticism of French drama; he finds that Marie Chénier tends to substitute words for action in *Charles IX*[78] and in his letters from Paris declares: "I still have not changed my opinion about the French Melpomene. She is noble, majestic, beautiful; she never moves, never astounds my heart in the way the Muse of Shakespeare and some (in truth not many) Germans do. French poets have a refined, gentle taste and are models in *the art of writing*. Only in terms of invention, enthusiasm and a deep *feeling for Nature*—forgive me, hallowed shades of Corneille, Racine and Voltaire—they must cede pride of place to the English and Germans."[79] He nevertheless finds much to commend in the theatres of Paris, particularly the acting and dancing, the artistry of the presentation, the attractive buildings. He is delighted by the "so-called Italian Theatre, where they perform only French melodramas"; he admits it is his favorite spectacle, which he visits more than any other.[80] It is equally characteristic that he should be attracted to the French comedy, which he considers infinitely superior to its English and German counterparts. "English comedies are in general either boring or coarse, indecent and offensive to delicate taste; and the German, apart from a few of mediocre quality, are completely undeserving of attention."[81] In his review of K. D. Dittersdorf's *Apotheker und Doktor* he objects to "the jokes which make only 'the gods' laugh."[82] The contemporary English theatre failed to impress him; he was repelled by a careless and inartistic performance of *Hamlet* and especially by the audience's enthusiasm for the gravediggers' scene.[83] He criticizes the post-Shakespearean theatre for "Shakespeare's bombast without Shakespeare's genius" in its tragedies and confusing intrigue and caricature in its comedies.[84]

This reference to Shakespeare's bombast is particularly interesting in view of Karamzin's general restraint in attempting to comment in detail on the Englishman's style and language. However, his obvious distaste for such stylistic features emerges in his comments on Schiller's *Don Carlos*: "the author writes in the spirit of Shakespeare. Only there are some excessively flowery expressions (as there are in Shakespeare), which although they show the author's wit are nonetheless out of place in the drama."[85] Karamzin believes that "the simpler the language of a play the better."[86] In his review of a translation of J. C. Brandes's *Der Graf von Olsbach* he objects to *sie* and *onoe* as never used in normal conversation and unattractive to the ear.[87] The translator of *L'Optimiste* is commanded for a version which is "pure and smooth" (chist i gladok), but criticized for the use of both unnecessary gallicisms and ugly slavisms. Karamzin quotes the line: *ono nichego proizvest' ne mozhet, razve uchinit' navsegda menia neshchastnoio* and finds that "here together are both a gallicism and a slavism. Dear Premila who says this translated from the French 'il ne fera que'; and *razve* —in the sense in which it is used here—and *uchinit'* instead of *sdelat'* cannot be used in conversation, particularly by a young girl."[88] His heavily ironical review of Nikolev's *Spoilt Darling* ends with an attack on "*astonishing* jokes at the expense of poor old grammar; verbs, cases, pronouns, in short, nothing escaped."[89]

This concern with style and language is equally evident in his book reviews. His attitude toward the use of slavisms is implicit in a review of *Romantische Gemälde der Vorwelt*, translated from *Allgemeine deutsche Bibliothek*, where the author is criticized for "several unacceptable words, with which he seems in love, like our best authors in this genre who from time to time turn over the compost of our language and drag out in triumph various obsolete words, long since replaced by others much better and equally expressive—although there are very good old words which should be re-introduced."[90] His reviews of *Clarissa* and *Orlando Furioso* condemn the use of words like *daby* and *koliko*, again particularly when put into the mouth of young girls.[91] He is indignant at loose and careless syntax and stupid translation: he returns the Russian *Clarissa* to the publisher, because "such mistakes are unpardonable, and whoever translates in such a fashion spoils and mutilates a book and deserves no mercy from the critic."[92] His complaints about the virtual illiteracy (bezgramotnost') of many Russian writ-

ers run through his letters to Dmitriev at this period[93] and are given
literary expression in his satirical fable "The Nightingale and the
Crows" ["Solovei i vorony"].[94]

He believes that with such works as *Clarissa* "the language
usually constitutes one of its main merits,"[95] whereas it is often the
unique distinction of a work in verse. His requirements of the
translator of Voltaire's *Henriade* and Ariosto's *Orlando Furioso*
are consequently higher. "It is necessary not only to express the
poet's thoughts, but express them with the same accuracy, the same
purity and attractiveness as in the original; otherwise a poet loses
almost all his value."[96] He finds a few successful lines in the Russian
version of the *Henriade*, but a translator should "translate everything well, or at least almost everything." Karamzin was preoccupied with the specific difficulties of translating poetry; in September
1791, he wrote to Dmitriev: "It is difficult, my friend, to translate
poets; but if I publish my journal in the coming year (which seems
unlikely however), I shall try to translate some small passages from
ancient and modern poets."[97] He believed that "it is easier (in my
opinion) to write an epic poem in twenty cantos in Russian than
to make a good translation of the ten cantos of the *Henriade*."[98]

Karamzin's careful attention to the quality of translations is
consistent with both his general stylistic and linguistic concerns and
his belief in the importance of translations for the enlightenment
of Russia. He praises the translation of Buffon's *Histoire naturelle*
as a civic act: "Every Russian who loves the enlightenment of his
homeland should rejoice that this useful work, unique of its kind, is
being translated into Russian and by learned men who know the
subject and are equally proficient in both languages."[99] He demands
honesty and accuracy from the translator; he insists that the public
be informed from which language a translation is made: "Some of
our scribes, or writers, or translators—or call them what you will—
act moreover in a most unforgivable fashion. Presenting the public
with various works, they do not say that these works are translated
from foreign languages. The trusting reader accepts them as Russian works and frequently is amazed that the author who is able to
think so well expresses himself so badly and incorrectly. Civic
honesty at least obliges us not to appropriate something belonging
to another person either by deeds, words, or *silence*."[100] Karamzin
himself delights in pointing out the *true* original, usually French in

the case of English works. He cites impermissible gallicisms, although in his review of a translation of Thomas More's *Utopia* his examples do not so much clinch his case as indicate inadequacies in his English.[101]

If Karamzin's reviews expound his theory of translation, his numerous translations reveal his practice. The gulf which separates Karamzin's translations in the *Moscow Journal* from all that he published before his journey, in style and accuracy if not in content, is remarkable; Karamzin himself was well aware of this when he refused to allow the publisher S. I. Selivanovskii to include anything from *Children's Reading* in the enlarged second edition of *The Pantheon of Foreign Literature* [*Panteon inostrannoi slovesnosti*] in 1818.[102] He explained to Fedor Glinka how he had perfected his style "by means of the fireplace. And in such a way: I would translate one and the same thing once, twice, three times, and when I had read it through and deliberated, I would throw it into the fire, until at last I achieved something worth publishing."[103] Kamenev records similarly how Karamzin "confessed that before publishing the *Moscow Journal* he used up a lot of paper and that only by first writing badly and indifferently can one write well."[104]

The translations fall more or less into two groups, the first of which consists of fictional works—short stories, extracts from novels and plays, sentimental rhapsodies, poems—and the second includes works of a general literary and philosophical nature—biographies of leading German authors, excerpts from travel accounts, meditations, precepts. The majority of these latter features appeared in the second year of the journal, in keeping with a promise in the editorial letter at the end of 1791.[105] There is a close interdependence between the literature which Karamzin chose to translate and his reviews and particularly his *Letters of a Russian Traveler*. Almost all the foreign authors are mentioned in *Letters*; many of them Karamzin had met and talked with. There are translations from Barthélemy, Engel, Florian, Garve, Goethe, Herder, Kotzebue, Marmontel, Meister, Mercier, Moritz, Ossian, Schiller, Sterne, Vernes, and Wieland—names which occur many times in the journal and are evidence of Karamzin's constant popularization of recent European literature. Certainly in a literary respect the *Moscow Journal* could well receive the name of Karamzin's later journal, the *Messenger of Europe*.

Karamzin's translating activity in *Children's Reading* is primarily connected with the stories of Mme. de Genlis; in the *Moscow Journal* she cedes pride of place to J. F. Marmontel. Translations of nine of his tales, which appeared originally in the *Mercure de France* from 1790 onwards, give to Karamzin's journal a continuity which parallels that provided by *Letters of a Russian Traveler*. Marmontel's stories were generally considered accomplished examples of the storyteller's art, unique, Karamzin believed, in style and taste.[106] Marmontel likewise replaced Genlis as a direct influence on Karamzin's own original fiction. The other tales Karamzin selected are all imbued with typical sentimental and preromantic elements. In the hierarchy of French storytellers Karamzin placed Mercier after Marmontel and Florian,[107] but gave translations from all three. Florian's "Valérie," Mercier's "Anecdote historique, tirée d'une ancienne chronique d'Allemagne," together with Wieland's "Cordelia" exhibit a love of the supernatural and the trappings of the Gothic novel.[108] Kotzebue's "Maria Salmon" is a much more conventional tale of innocence triumphant and rewarded and in its emotional appeal is linked with the important translations from Sterne.[109] The witty, idiosyncratic, iconoclastic Sterne was imitated to a limited extent by Karamzin at a later stage of his career, but it is the Sterne of the obliging tear and the most sensitive of sensibilities who is represented exclusively in the four translations from his work which appeared in the *Moscow Journal*. Karamzin was the translator of the passages from *Tristram Shandy* and *A Sentimental Journey* about Maria, "the victim of sensibility and love" as he described her in the footnote where the author is extolled as "the original, inimitable, sensitive, good, witty, kind Sterne";[110] the other two translations, entitled "The Poor Man and his Dog" and "The Story of Le Fevre" were not, however, by Karamzin, but to them he appended a rapturous tribute to Sterne: "Incomparable Sterne! In what learned university were you taught to feel so tenderly? What rhetoric revealed to you the secret of touching with two words the most delicate fibers of our hearts? What musician commands the sounds of his strings as skillfully as you command our feelings? The times I have read Le Fevre and the times my tears have poured onto the pages of this story!"[111] The "divine" melancholy Karamzin also found in Sterne was an even greater attraction in the Ossian poems of Macpherson, accepted unquestioningly as genuine relics of an old and fascinating culture. Karamzin published versions of "Carthon" and "The Songs of Selma," negatively reviewed by Tumanskii in his *Russian Storehouse* [*Rossiiskii magazin*] (1792–94), where he waged an active but self-defeating linguistic polemic against Karamzin.[112]

Karamzin's interest in other "lost" cultures led him to translate scenes from *Sakuntala*, a Sanskrit drama by Kalidasa; it was an interest given wide European respectability by the writings of Herder but in the *Moscow Journal* is justified by a translated review of G. E. Groddeck's *Uber die Vergleichung der alten besonders griechischen mit der deutschen und neuern Litteratur*. "Are not beauty and perfection something very relative or rather something which in all their purity you will find in no one nation and no one work of art?"[113] Since taste, the guide to beauty and perfection, is also subject to change, dogmatic support for Greek (or French) culture would obscure the relative historical merits of works in other national literatures, the beauties of which a critic must attempt to discern. In his own short foreword to *Sakuntala* Karamzin proclaims: "The creative spirit resides not in Europe alone; it is *a citizen of the universe.* Man everywhere is man; everywhere he has a feeling heart and in the mirror of his imagination holds both the heavens and the earth. Everywhere Nature is his teacher and the main source of his pleasures."[114] Kalidasa is thus elevated to a position alongside Homer. "Above all it [*Sakuntala*] may be called a beautiful picture of ancient India, in the same way that Homer's epics are pictures of ancient Greece—pictures in which we can see the character, customs, and habits of its people. Kalidasa is for me as great as Homer. They both received their brush from the hands of Nature and both portrayed—Nature."

"Mankind and nature are the two great subjects. He, only he can be a poet who penetrates with his gaze into mankind and nature deeper than other men, who finds there beauties hidden from the gaze of other men."[115] In this footnote to a translation of F. Bouterwek's "Apollo, Erklärung einer alten Allegorie" Karamzin is applying specifically to the poet Professor E. Platner's remarks on the character of genius during the lecture on aesthetics, "the science of taste," which Karamzin heard in Leipzig[116] as well as stressing yet again the seriousness of "the Russian traveler," who "devoted his attention to nature and man above all else."[117] Throughout his journal Karamzin is concerned with the poets, novelists, and dramatists who reveal genius in their imaginative work but at the same time he is eager to commend factual and descriptive works which provide raw materials. This is evident on the one hand in his reviews of Vaillant's and Coxe's works and his noting the publication of James Bruce's *Travels to Discover the Source of the Nile* (1790) and on the other in the sympathetic review of Bräker's autobiography and of the memoirs of Benjamin Franklin and Goldoni as well as his interest in and translations from J. P. Moritz's *Magazin zur Erfahrungsseelenkunde* (1783–93). Of this journal he wrote: "It includes descriptions of various events in a man's life, worthy of note or arousing astonishment and all that relates to the interesting knowledge of man and is able better to explain to us ourselves, our soul, our heart."[118] Karamzin could well have added to his earlier epigraph from Pope: "Pleasures are ever in our hands or eyes"—the equally applicable "the proper study of mankind is man."

In view of such interests and enthusiasms it is not surprising that Karamzin's basic optimism and idealism, which during his masonic period compete with transient moods of pessimism and despondency, assert themselves strongly in the *Moscow Journal*. He is intent on fashioning a working philosophy of life which accommodates the coexistence of good and evil, the search for truth and enlightenment, and the acceptance of limits to man's capacity for understanding. He writes with obvious sympathy of Platner, "an eclectic philosopher, who seeks truth in all systems without attaching himself to any of them in particular, who for example agrees with Kant on one point and with Leibnitz on another, or contradicts both of them."[119] Karamzin turns to such self-recommending sources as J. J. Engel's *Der Philosoph für die Welt;*[120] he translates a piece by Christian Garve, which praises "the appealing sisters" Nature and Science and the way of life dedicated to their study;[121] he includes two pieces by the Lutheran, J. V. Andreae (1586–1654), the first of which contained a series of aphorisms on philosophy, politics, religion, and death, for which Karamzin has obvious sympathy.[122] Discussing the philosophy of Collin d'Harleville's optimist, Karamzin agrees with its basic tenets but adds that "it is not possible to agree with it so easily when he says that illness is not an evil because there are doctors, that impotent old age is not an evil because an old man is like a patriarch, that there are only one or two deceivers and thieves in the world."[123] He thus retains his view of the great evils existing in the world which are at odds with the basic goodness of man. In this context the review of Vaillant's travels is important for the sympathy for the Hottentots, "a meek and good-natured people," and the reflection that "perhaps it is also necessary to revise those observations on which some philosophers base their ideas of human nature and present it as evil and forever incapable of change."[124] Karamzin's position is expressed most clearly in two articles, one original, the other translated. An apochryphal exchange of letters between Bayle and Shaftesbury[125] argues that doubt is inevitable and essential for the truth seeker, who refuses the easy solution, examines contradictions, and attacks systems and dogma. Life is a voyage which is ended by death before man achieves the peace and knowledge he pursues.[126] In "Various Fragments (From the Notes of a Young Russian)" ["Raznyye otryvki (Iz zapisok odnogo molodogo rossiianina)"] Karamzin states his strongly Rousseauistic views on a number of obsessive themes, including happiness, death, evil, immortality, genius, human nature, and concluding with a rapturous vision of universal brotherhood.[127] It elicited an immediate reproach of "servility toward man" (chelovekougodnichestvo) from his friend Petrov, who sensed how far Karamzin now stood from the basic masonic teaching.[128]

The hostility which some of the masons showed from the beginning could not but be increased by subsequent material in the journal. The excesses of masonry are exposed in the story of the charlatan Schröpfer included in *Letters of a Russian Traveler;*[129] Karamzin there calls Cagliostro "a second Schröpfer" and in a later number of his journal includes extracts from *The Life and Deeds of Giuseppe Balsamo, the so-called Count Cagliostro,* in which his system of "Egyptian Masonry" is exposed.[130] Karamzin attacks such charlatans in the name of Enlightenment, "one spark from which will light up the abyss of fallacies."[131] Karamzin also published an epigram by Dmitriev on John Mason's *On Self-Knowledge,* the masonic "bible" translated by Turgenev,[132] and he himself alludes to his own relations with the masons in his "imitation of Lichtwer," the poem "The Strange People" ["Strannye liudi"].[133]

Karamzin's journal aroused suspicions of much deeper significance than betrayal of masonry. A. T. Bolotov (1738-1833), a noted agronomist, editor of Novikov's *Economic Magazine* [*Ekonomicheskii magazin*] (1780–85), and the author of famous and extensive memoirs, wrote in a revealing passage: "It must be said that this young and appealing writer, despite all the perfections of his style, possessed the vice of transgressing to an excessive degree the bounds of strict decency and particularly in scenes of passion; it is therefore desirable that he should refrain somewhat from this and also from an excessive attachment to the present harmful freedom which is distracting the whole world and many characteristics of which he displayed already in the *Moscow Journal*." Referring specifically to Karamzin's subsequent almanac *Aglaia*, but obviously again mindful of the earlier journal, Bolotov adds: "There still remained a great doubt about his ideas on religion and the law."[134] When Bolotov speaks of Karamzin's sexual license, he is undoubtedly referring to the seduction of Liza, the meeting of the lovers in the prose poem "Night" ["Noch' "], the description of the Turkish girl's naked charms in "Liodor," and Sofiia's indiscretions. Karamzin's play seems to have been particularly suspect; M. N. Zagoskin devotes a long passage in his novel *The Seducer* [*Iskusitel'*] to a discussion of its morality.[135] Karamzin himself was aware that he was inviting criticism; he said of Kotzebue's *Menschenhass und Reue*: "The author has dared to bring onto the stage an unfaithful wife, who, forgetting her husband and children, runs away with her lover."[136]

The political aspects of Bolotov's criticisms were developed in the masonic correspondence, which the masons themselves knew was subject to official scrutiny (perliustratsiia) and therefore potentially compromising for Karamzin. The masons paraded their own patriotism and the innocent nature of their activities but did not hesitate to criticize Karamzin for contempt for Russia and idolatry of the West. At the end of January 1791, Bagrianskii wrote to Kutuzov: "Tout ce qui regarde la patrie, est dit avec mépris et une injustice vraiment criante. Tout ce qui regarde les pays étrangers y est dit avec extase. Entre autre la pauvre Livonie est maltraitée au dernier degré. Il faut la passer, dit-il, les yeux fermés. La chère Courlande n'est rien que la terre promise, et il est étonnant comme les Juifs se sont trompés."[137] Government suspicions were inevitably aroused, although in his interrogation of the masons in 1792 Prozorovskii limited himself to questions about the connection between

Karamzin's journey and masonic activities. Undoubtedly Karamzin's work was closely watched; it should not pass unnoticed that Prozorovskii, hardly inspired by a love of literature, was among the first to subscribe to Karamzin's journal.[138]

Karamzin was moderate, eclectic, basically apolitical; his major concerns were literature and cultural enlightenment; his beliefs humanist and liberal. He was not as outspoken and critical as Radishchev, but did not stand as far from "the first Russian radical" as some would seem intent on asserting; he represents a liberating and liberal force in a particularly reactionary period of Russian history. The evidence of Karamzin's independence in the *Moscow Journal* is not insubstantial. In a letter from Leipzig he alludes to Radishchev and Kutuzov under the initials R* and K* and offers no correction to Platner's view that "many of your fellow-countrymen sought enlightenment at Leipzig University and, I hope, not in vain."[139] More important is Karamzin's courageous appeal to Catherine on Novikov's behalf in his ode "To Mercy." The ode, in which Catherine and Mercy are identified, contains the clearest expression of Karamzin's political and social philosophy at this time. He demands intellectual freedom, the natural development of (peaceful) human desires and faculties and personal security. In return a grateful nation will give loyalty to the throne, for "A throne will never be shaken / Where it is retained by love."[140] Karamzin nevertheless considered the original wording of certain lines too bold; Petrov asked him to "send him" the poem "To Mercy" as it was originally written; "I will not show it to anyone, if you think it necessary."[141] Karamzin restored the lines after Alexander came to the throne and they appeared in all subsequent editions of his work; the lines on the natural rights of man—"As long as you shall not forget the rights, / With which man is born"—are echoed in the two odes Karamzin addressed to Alexander at that time. A further, if more devious, example of Karamzin's willingness to speak out against injustice and arbitrary action is again connected with Novikov. In the May 1792, number in which "To Mercy" was published there appeared Karamzin's review of Osipov's *Aeneid*, containing the remark: "About the tribute or dedication in verse . . . I shall say not a word."[142] Osipov's long, flattering dedication was addressed to I. S. Sheshkovskii, the son of Stepan Ivanovich Sheshkovskii, Catherine's chief inquisitor and Novikov's interrogator.

In political terms Karamzin was always what Petr Viazemskii was to term Pushkin—a liberal-conservative.[143] Pogodin relates how immediately after his return from abroad Karamzin at dinner with the Derzhavins "expressed certain opinions not altogether in accord with the accepted way of thinking in Russia"[144] and Kutuzov even speaks of "a French Revolution" occurring in Karamzin's ideas,[145] but the basic orthodoxy of his views on the Russian political structure would seem to be borne out by his comment on Kheraskov's reasoning in *Cadmus and Harmonia* and by the philosophy of "leave well alone" in his idyll *Palemon and Daphnis*. Despite his nonacceptance of revolution in theory and in French practice, he never lost a sense of proportion; like his shepherds he continued to look calmly on troubled waters. There is no truly negative judgment on the French Revolution in the journal; at one stage in his summary of *La Liberté conquise* he writes that "popular unrest, the storming of the Bastille, etc., are presented, which can be of interest only for a Parisian audience,"[146] but it is important that he does continue to review the latest French theatrical and literary events. An English visitor in Paris at this time says of the theatre: "One powerful engine that has been brought to bear against the clergy, as well as against the monarchy, is that old enemy of the former, the stage. I lately saw *les Victimes cloîtrées* at the Théâtre de la Nation, a piece evidently written to inspire horror and indignation against the priesthood, and to place the monks in particular in the most atrocious point of view."[147] J. M. Boutet de Monvel's play, together with J. Fiévée's *Les Rigueurs du cloître*, are among the plays listed by Karamzin, a confirmed opponent of religious asceticism.[148] He also translates such sentiments as "the theatre must be as truthful as history, condemning tyrants and great evil-doers and praising good rulers, famous and virtuous men."[149] At the beginning of 1792 Karamzin listed Volney's *Les Ruines, ou Méditations sur les Révolutions des Empires* and Mercier's *De J. J. Rousseau etc.* with the comment that "these two books may be termed the most important works of French literature in the past year."[150] Karamzin was familiar with the contents of these works from the extensive reviews which had appeared in the *Mercure de France* and the *etc.* in the Mercier title is, as Lotman has pointed out, the willful suppression of the remaining words *considéré comme l'un des premiers auteurs de la révolution*.[151] However, the earlier information that "all which recalls this great writer is pleasing to the French and thus this play [*J. J. Rousseau à ses derniers moments*] was greeted with loud applause"[152] would seem to indicate Karamzin's increasing intention to avoid censorship difficulties. In 1791 Karamzin had enjoyed particularly good relations with the journal's censor, A. A. Barsov, Professor of Rhetoric at Moscow University since 1761; he related how he would take a number of blank pages to Barsov for the official imprimatur, and when he had later written his copy, he would send it directly to the publisher.[153] Barsov died on December 21, 1791, and Karamzin's privileges were obviously not extended.[154]

Deeply interested in what was happening in the West, Karamzin was nonetheless truly patriotic; it was a patriotism which was in harmony with his famous declaration in *Letters of a Russian Traveler*: "Everything *national* is nothing before the human. The main business is to be men and not Slavs. What is good for men cannot be bad for Russians and what the English and Germans have invented for the use and advantage of man is *mine*, because I am a man."[155] In the *Moscow Journal* Karamzin wrote predominantly about things European—places and people he had seen during his travels, reviews and translations of foreign works, portraits of foreign authors. Contemporaries like Zhukovskii saw one of the journal's outstanding achievements in the awakening of "l'intérêt pour la littérature étrangère."[156] Heinrich Storch in his *Gemälde von St. Petersburg* (1793–94), discussing the lack of "philosophical publications" in St. Petersburg, mentioned Karamzin's journal as introducing Kant's philosophy into Russia.[157] Yet Karamzin's journal was the organ of Russian literature, manifest above all in his own original stories, set in Russia, and in travel notes about Europe, but a Europe seen through the eyes of a Russian traveler, conversing with eminent foreigners, listening and recording, but also informing about Russia, and describing later what he felt and saw in an attractive "new style." It was these works—stories like "Poor Liza" and "Natalia, the Boyar's Daughter" and *Letters of a Russian Traveler*—which were translated and published in a number of European languages and made him the first Russian writer to achieve a truly European reputation.

Karamzin sought to inspire Russians to produce a worthy Russian literature; his idealism and enthusiasm were inevitably considered presumptuous and conceited, but his motives were commendable and his own achievement considerable. At the end of 1791, which he termed "a black year," he addressed a typical "dream" to his public: "If only there would be formed here a society of young, active people, endowed with *genuine* talent; if only these people— with a sense of their worth but without the arrogance characteristic of base minds—would dedicate themselves completely to literature, join their talents and before the altar of the beneficent Muses vowed zealously to propagate all that is noble, not for their own fame but from a worthy and selfless love of good; if only my most cherished dream would once become real, then with joy, sincere joy, I would efface myself into complete anonymity and leave this respected society to publish a magazine, worthy of the good will of the Russian public."[158] The dream was not realized; Karamzin went on to dominate Russian literature for a whole decade, continuing to produce the work which gave rise to the concept of "the Karamzin period" in Russian literature. Twenty-five years after Karamzin composed his appeal, Viazemskii looked back with respect on his achievement: "Karamzin in the *Moscow Journal* destroyed the Gothic towers of a decaying literature and on its ruins laid the foundations of a new European publication, which awaited for its ultimate completion skilled, industrious hands."[159]

The journal enjoyed an undoubted success with the Russian public, although Karamzin regretted that he did not have enough subscribers to allow him to improve the quality of the publication. According to the lists published in the journal, he achieved some 258 subscribers in the first year and 274 in 1792. Apart from Novikov's *The Drone* [*Truten'*] and *The Painter* [*Zhivopisets*] no other eighteenth-century Russian journal commanded such an audience. Of journals contemporary with Karamzin's, Krylov's *Spirits' Postbag* [*Pochta dukhov*] (1789) had some 80 subscribers and his *Spectator* [*Zritel'*] (1792) had 169. Although the majority of Karamzin's subscribers were from Moscow and many others from St. Petersburg, there were a considerable number from Simbirsk (his hometown), Tula, Orel, and Kaluga; even more interesting is the spread throughout provincial Russia which Karamzin's journal achieved: in all, fifty-two towns are indicated, ranging from the capitals (Karamzin characteristically always calls Moscow the capital in his work) to the large provincial centers, from smaller towns to the fortress outposts. Several of the subscriptions are designated

to offices, institutions, and clubs, but behind every provincial sub-
scription stands a legion of potential readers among families and
friends. The continuing popularity of the journal as a whole, as opposed to individual works by Karamzin which were republished in
other format, may be gauged from a second edition in 1802–3.

THREE

Letters of a Russian Traveler

1791~1801

Letters of a Russian Traveler was an important integral part of Karamzin's "plan" for the *Moscow Journal*, at the same time reflecting faithfully its variety of subject matter and form. It is Karamzin's outstanding literary achievement in the eighteenth century and the work, which, together with "Poor Liza," ensured his contemporary success and popularity. Conceived after the manner of western models, *Letters* was in its turn widely imitated in Russia.[1] Its appeal was essentially a dual one. On the one hand, it was seen as the bible of Russian sentimentalism to which enthusiasts turned to imitate the "correct" aesthetic and moral response to sentimental set-pieces and situations, the cadences and phraseology of sentimental style; on the other hand, it provided a mass of information about life in the major European countries, mirroring the basically educational motives behind Karamzin's journey. It is from the standpoints of sentimentalism and enlightenment that the work will be examined, but it is important first to consider its complex genesis and publishing history.[2]

Although inevitably and justly associated with the *Moscow Journal* and Karamzin's early reputation, the letters which were published by the end of 1792 represent half of the complete work: they cover Karamzin's journey from Moscow through Germany and Switzerland and end with his arrival in Paris. Karamzin resumed their publication in the two volumes of his almanac *Aglaia* (1794–95), but abandoned the strict chronological sequence of his journey. Thus the excerpt in 1794 is entitled "Journey to London" and begins just before his arrival at Calais and ends with his arrival in London; the excerpt in the following year switches back to

Karamzin's stay in Paris and gives three letters in an order which was changed in the second edition. What has become known as the first edition was spread over a period of five years and lacks one hundred and sixty-five pages in the order of pages of the final version.[3] The second or, as Karamzin called it, "new" edition of *Letters* appeared in 1797, or at least the first four volumes did. Volume 4 closed with words which by that time had acquired somewhat ominous ambiguity: "The people still love the blood royal" (2, 460) – from a letter already included in *Aglaia* (1795). In Paul's reign only seven pages on the history of Paris and a few brief impressions and street scenes were thus added to what had already appeared in print. It was only with the accession of Alexander in 1801 that the two remaining volumes were published and the complete *Letters* became available to the public.[4]

The responsibility for this complex and drawn-out publishing history rests primarily with the censorship: Karamzin wished to speak on subjects which were actively discouraged in the last years of Catherine's reign and throughout Paul's. It is significant that volume 5 begins: "Should I speak about the French Revolution?" (2, 460) and is followed by the cautious words: "You read the newspapers; therefore, the events are known to you." The completion of the second edition does not, however, indicate merely the eventual overcoming of censorship difficulties, for in the interim Karamzin's own attitude to events in France and Europe had been modified. Karamzin became his own censor, guided by the most conservative and cautious views of his maturity. Volumes 5 and 6, as published in 1801, are in many ways more a valuable complement to his work in the *Messenger of Europe* than a faithful reflection of the *Moscow Journal*. This is not to suggest that the final three hundred pages of *Letters* are an entirely new composition dating from the close of Paul's reign; it is clear from the passage on England which was published in 1794 that much, possibly all, of the work had been written by that date and that Karamzin was as yet selecting inoffensive excerpts. Retaining the basic material, Karamzin would seem to have omitted certain passages and added new thoughts and reflections.

If the publishing history is important for ideological and linquistic reasons, the genesis of the work affords considerable literary interest. Karamzin successfully encouraged the idea that *Letters* had originally been written by the author from abroad to his friends, specified for the first time in the dedication to the 1797 edition as the Pleshcheev family. In his introduction at that time he declares that "he described his impressions not at leisure, not in the quiet of his study, but where and how they arose, on the road, in pencil on scraps of paper."[5] These impressions, noted on scraps of paper or in a travel diary, formed the basis of *Letters of a Russian Traveler*, which was a work completely independent of the few real letters he managed to send to the Pleshcheevs, Petrov and Dmitriev. Recording what "he saw, heard, felt, thought,"[6] Karamzin added later "in the quiet of his study" information culled from accounts of earlier travelers and from all manner of guide books and manuals. His method is near to that of Bishop Coxe, whose introduction to the second edition of his work on Switzerland he quotes with obvious sympathy in the *Moscow Journal*.[7] Sipovskii by a careful collation of texts has demonstrated the extent of Karamzin's considerable indebtedness to foreign sources, but Karamzin who had fulminated against the deceit of translators in his journal saw nothing contradictory in his own procedure. As he notes in *Letters*, he tests the descriptions left by others against his own observations (2, 442) and he is well-informed about the literary and historical associations of the places he visits. In the course of his work he refers to authors who belong to the various species of "Idle Travelers, Inquisitive Travelers . . . ," catalogued by Laurence Sterne at the beginning of *A Sentimental Journey*, and *Letters* itself belongs to the hybrid travel accounts, part informative, part sentimental, of which Moritz's *Reisen eines Deutschen in England* and C. M. Dupaty's *Lettres sur l'Italie en 1785* are notable contemporary examples.

Karamzin reveals considerable skill in sustaining the illusion of a real correspondence. He refers to facts and incidents to be understood only by a small circle of intimates, designates many people simply by initials and on one occasion omits a section of a letter as too personal for publication (2, 312). The epistolary form allows him to change swiftly from one subject to another, to describe, philosophize, rhapsodize, to insert touching sentimental scenes and anecdotes, to alternate nature descriptions with conversations en route, to be melancholic, reflective, flippant, ironic. He succeeds in capturing the feeling of immediacy and freshness he seeks. He is concerned with the minutiae of travel—food, accommodation, costs, discomforts—to a degree that brought a verdict of "futile" and "superficial" from Belinskii;[8] against similar criticism from his contemporaries Karamzin argues that "a man in traveling clothes, with a stick in his hand and a bundle on his shoulder is not obliged to speak with the cautious discrimination of some courtier surrounded by courtiers or of a professor in a Spanish wig, sitting in a large academic chair, and whoever seeks in a travel account mere statistical and geographical information is advised to read Busching's *Geography* instead of *Letters*."[9] It is interesting that he defends the content of his work not by analogy to existing works of travel but to the novels of Richardson and Fielding, his chroniclers of "life as it is": "but if we read without boredom in Richardson's and Fielding's novels that, for instance, Grandison drinks tea twice a day with dear Miss Byron, that Tom Jones slept exactly seven hours in some village inn, then why not forgive the Traveler some trifling details?"[10]

Karamzin was in little doubt as to the originality and success of his work. In an essay of 1797 for the French émigré journal *Le Spectateur du Nord* he wrote: "Cet ouvrage doit en partie son succès à la nouveauté du sujet pour les lecteurs russes. Depuis assez longtems nos compatriotes voyagent dans les pays étrangers; mais aucun d'eux, jusqu'à présent, ne s'est avisé de la faire sa plume à la main. L'auteur de ces lettres a eu le premier cette idée, et il a parfaitement réussi a intéresser le public."[11] Karamzin's fellow-countrymen traveled to Europe in increasing numbers throughout the eighteenth century, as diplomats, students, and tourists, and some of them, if not traveling pen in hand, recorded what they saw and did. Sometimes their impressions are included in actual correspondence with friends or even in official dispatches, sometimes they are the subject of memoirs or specific accounts, which were almost invariably published long after their author's death. Two widely differing accounts published before Karamzin's *Moscow Journal* were Radishchev's *Life of Fedor Ushakov* [*Zhitie Fedora Vasil'evicha Ushakova*] (1789) and N. A. Demidov's *Journal of a Journey... through Foreign Countries* [*Zhurnal puteshestviia... po inostrannym gosudarstvam*] (1786), which had negligible effect on the reading public. Demidov's brief notes, published in a small private edition, are of some interest for his comments on cultural life, art galleries and museums in France, Switzerland, Italy, and England. Karamzin's impressions of England are antedated by two accounts in journals: Princess Dashkova's "The Journey of a Russian Noblewoman through Some English Provinces" ["Puteshestvie odnoi rossiiskoi znatnoi gospozhi, po nekotorym anglinskim provintsiiam"] (1775)[12] and the anonymous "Russian in England" ["Rossiianin v Anglii'] (1794),[13] which are significant for their comments on parts of England Karamzin never visited.[14] On the evidence of certain passages in *Letters* it seems probable that Karamzin was acquainted with the manuscript of Count F. V. Rostopchin's *Prussian Journey* [*Puteshestvie po Prussii*] published only in 1849,[15] but it is unlikely that he had access to Fonvizin's highly critical impressions of European life contained in letters to relatives and Count I. Panin in the years 1762–87, although his insistent enquiries to Dmitriev in 1788 about Fonvizin's proposed journal, "Starodum, or the Friend of Honest People" ["Starodum, ili drug chestnykh liudei"] indicates his interest in their promised publication.[16] Fonvizin's commentary on French life and personalities provides a revealing contrast to Karamzin's indulgent, good-natured descriptions of similar scenes and people;[17] they provide a Russian parallel to the travel accounts of Sterne and Smollett, although Smollett's *Travels through France and Italy* was written after and against Sterne's.

If Karamzin was not the first Russian to record and publish his impressions of Europe, he was certainly the first to capture the imagination of the Russian reading public with such a work and inspire contemporary writers to emulate him; as a successful and original work of Russian literature, *Letters* was unique. Foreign works in the original and translation prepared the way for Karamzin's work and although its differences from Sterne's A *Sentimental Journey* are obvious, its success was first and foremost the triumph of a new literary fashion. It was the sentimental traveler, the Russian Sterne, whom Karamzin's contemporaries sought and found in *Letters* and it was *Letters* as the example of the sentimental manner and mannerism that his opponents parodied. Karamzin's own estimate is found in his announcement, in his preface to the second edition, in the text of *Letters* and with the pretense of objectivity in the *Spectateur du Nord* essay. There he writes: "C'est un jeune homme, avide de voir la nature là où elle se présente sous des aspects plus riants, plus majestueux que dans notre pays, et surtout avide de voir les grands écrivains, dont les ouvrages ont développé les premiers facultés de son âme: il s'arrache des bras de ses amis et part seul avec son coeur sensible. Tout l'intéresse: les curiosités des villes, les nuances qui distinguent leurs habitans dans la manière de vivre, les monumens qui lui rapellent quelque fait de l'histoire, quelque événement célèbre; les traces des grands hommes qui ne sont pas plus, les sites agréables, la vue des champs fertiles et celle de la mer immense."[18] The journey was thus a further stage in Karamzin's education. *Letters* is both the account of what he saw and felt and what he believed he should see and feel; it is often at one and the same time a reflection of Karamzin's true character and aspirations and of a general European tradition of sentimental literature. In the letter from Cronstadt which brings the work to a close, Karamzin emphasizes the personal value of *Letters*: "Here is the mirror of my soul in the course of eighteen months! After twenty years (if I live that long!) it will still be attractive for me— if only for me! I shall look and see what I was, how I thought and dreamt; and between us, what is more absorbing for a man than himself?" (2, 790). But *Letters* remained for his fellow Russians a mine of attractive and entertaining information on European life, conveyed by a sympathetic traveler seeking "the wise link of sociability" which disarms prejudice and superstition: "In a word, my friends, a journey is food for our spirit and heart. Let a hypochondriac travel in order to be cured of his hypochondria! Let a misanthrope travel in order to love mankind! Let whoever is able travel!" (2, 148).

　　Letters is essentially a work in four parts, which correspond to the principal countries Karamzin visited. Linking these parts and giving unity to the whole is the figure of the traveler himself. Each of the four countries has a particular center of interest for Karamzin: Germany—writers and scholars; Switzerland—Arcadian simplicity; France—epitomized in Paris, the home of culture and the social graces; England—national enlightenment, public and political institutions. This interest in turn dictates a diversity of manner and style. Karamzin is much more serious and scholarly when writing about England than about France; his long-held view of the French as a fickle and effervescent nation leads him to minimize, not merely out of censorship considerations, the importance of the French Revolution. In Switzerland Karamzin remembers his reading of Gessner and Haller and the idyllic manner predominates, whereas in Germany he is concerned primarily with individual writers and philosophers, anxious to provide precise pen-pictures of each "Great Man" he meets.

Germany was the home of most of the living writers he admired; his beloved English authors—Pope, Thomson, Young, Sterne —were long since dead, and there were no contemporary writers he attempted to meet in London. Similarly Haller, Gessner, Rousseau, and Voltaire were only to be conjured up in the imagination by visits to places connected with their life and writings. In Lyons he met the German poet Friedrich Matthisson, and Marmontel and Barthélemy in Paris, and he gives detailed descriptions of Bonnet and Lavater in Switzerland, but Germany had a host of writers whom he hastened to see and describe. Kant, Nicolai, Ramler, Moritz, Platner, Weisse, Herder, and Wieland are all "interviewed" and their conversations recorded; only Goethe eludes him. This is the series of letters which was published in the *Moscow Journal* and led to a wider knowledge of German literature and writers among the Russian reading public.

In his descriptive techniques Karamzin was self-confessedly influenced by the physiognomical theories of Lavater, according to which a person's character could be discerned from the shape of his head and features. He is ill-disposed toward a Frenchwoman because "her physiognomy and habits do not please me" (2, 16), but responds to the German poet J. A. Kramer, who had his "good nature written on his face" (2, 6). Nicolai's "high forehead indicates a highly calculating man" (2, 69), but when Karamzin begins to describe Herder by the same method, he laughs at his own obsession: "I am afraid, my friends, that you might consider me a physiognomical wizard" (2, 147). Nevertheless, he later essays an appraisal of the English nation in physiognomical terms: "I also looked at Englishmen, whose faces may be divided into three types: the morose, the good-natured, and the bestial. I swear to you that nowhere have I chanced to see so many of the last as here" (2, 674). Karamzin shared his physiognomical enthusiasm and an ironic awareness of its absurdity with a number of European writers: Harley, the hero of Henry Mackenzie's *Man of Feeling*, a celebrated work of sentimental fiction already known in Russia, is, for example, often deceived by his foible and duly reprimanded that "as for faces—you may look into them to know whether a man's nose be a long or a short one."[19]

Karamzin's meeting with Kant in Koenigsberg, the first of the series, illustrates his typical approach to "the Great Man": "I am a Russian gentleman, I love great men and wish to express my respect to Kant" (2, 29–30).[20] The subsequent interview clearly conveys the mixture of reverence for the man and incomprehension before the subtleties of his philosophy which marks all Karamzin's further references to Kant. He opposes Kant of the European reputation, the "famous, profound, subtle" philosopher to Kant, observed in his physical environment, "the small, skinny old man, extremely white and delicate." His final verdict continues the contrast: "Everything is simple, except . . . his metaphysics" (2, 32). Karamzin's contradictory assessment of Kant was in complete accord with an already widespread European attitude but for a Russian audience it was novel and informative. At the same time such meetings are an obvious device for communicating Karamzin's own views on literature and philosophy. His meeting with Nicolai, for example, is devoted almost entirely to a discussion of the Berlin Jesuits, ending with typical idealist rhetoric: "Where does one find tolerance, if even philosophers and enlighteners—for this is what they call themselves—show so much hatred of those who think differently from themselves? For me the true philosopher is the man who can live in peace with everyone, who loves even those who disagree with his way of thinking. The errors of the human mind should be demonstrated with noble fire and without malice" (2, 68).

Throughout his journey Karamzin exhibits his humanism and tolerance, not only in religious matters but in all fields of intellectual and emotional activity. He writes with sympathy of the plight of the Jews in Frankfurt, attends services in the churches of different orders and sects and praises Voltaire primarily as an active philanthropist and an opponent of obscurantism. Concerned not with the views that divide men among themselves but with the qualities that unite them, Karamzin manages to write warmly of almost all the people he visited in Germany—and Switzerland. He looks for kindness, sentiment, humanity rather than wit, originality, individualism; he is particularly delighted to find his writers in situations which enhance their qualities and justify his belief that the great writer is necessarily a good man in his everyday life. Weisse in Germany and Lavater and Bonnet in Switzerland, depicted in the circle of family and friends, reassure him that "one glance at a good man is happiness for him in whom the sense of good has not coarsened" (2, 131). Only once is Karamzin near to being disillusioned by such encounters; he recalls it in his *Spectateur du Nord* essay: "Kant, Nicolai, Ramler, Herder, l'accueillent avec une aménité et une cordialité qui l'enchantent; et alors il se croit transporté dans ces tems anciens, où les philosophes alloient voir leur semblables dans les pays les plus éloignés et trouvoient partout des hôtes hospitaliers et des amis sincères. Mais quand l'immortel auteur d'Agathon, dans un accès de mauvais humeur lui dit: 'Monsieur, je ne vous connois pas!' il est étonné, pétrifié, déjà il veut s'éloigner et renoncer à sa manie pour cette sorte de visites."[21] Yet as a result of this unexpectedly cold reception, Karamzin's description of his first meeting with Wieland evinces a humor and irony lacking in the more predictable meetings. Between his two visits to Wieland he describes a second meeting with Herder, where by contrast the cordiality of his reception provokes the accolade: "Dear friends, it is pleasant to see at last that man who was already so well known and dear to us from his works and whom we imagined or tried to imagine to ourselves. Now, it seems to me, I shall read the works of Herder's genius with ever greater pleasure, when I remember the author's appearance and voice" (2, 148). A second visit to Wieland, comfortingly for Karamzin, reverts to type.

Meetings such as these with Herder and Wieland are the act of homage from a student to his teachers and represent Karamzin in the guise of "the young Scythian" Anacharsis, who traveled "to adorn his reason with knowledge" (2, 509), but to reduce the first part of *Letters* to a succession of interviews is to ignore its variety and readability. The early letters describe other incidents and conversations in coach and inn which contrast in their vivid detail and liveliness of language with the more formal meetings. The transition between the letters from Germany and those from Switzerland is in one respect not strongly marked: the meetings with Lavater in Zurich and Bonnet in Geneva are a continuation of the earlier series and recorded in greater detail, for Karamzin met his long-admired philosophers on several occasions. Lavater is seen in his many roles as philosopher, preacher, active philanthropist and family man and the resulting picture is in accord with Kant's earlier evaluation of Lavater as a man with a good heart, led astray by his dreams. If Lavater and Bonnet are the living representatives of the great men Karamzin associates with Switzerland, their influence on his view of the country is secondary to that of earlier writers. It is the writings of Gessner, Haller, and, above all, Rousseau which hold the key to the beauties of the landscape, the attractions of the republican system, and the character of the people.

Imitating Rousseau, who had written in *Les Confessions*: "En entrant sur la territoire de Berne, je fis arrêter; je descendis, je me prosternai, j'embrassai, je baisai la terre et m'écrirai dans mon transport: Ciel! protecteur de la vertu, je te loue, je touche une terre de liberté!"[22] Karamzin describes how "having traveled two versts from Basel, I leapt out of the carriage, fell on the flowering banks of the green Rhine and was prepared in my delight to kiss the ground" (2, 203). Karamzin's enthusiasm for the lakes at Lausanne and Zurich, the majesty of the Alps, and the Rhine waterfall derives to a marked degree from Rousseau's example, as does the expression of his religious emotion in strongly pantheistic terms. Like Rousseau, Karamzin prays on a mountain top, sensing the nearness of the Creator (2, 270-71), and experiences a union with nature which elicits the thought that "the fear of death is a consequence of our deviation from the ways of nature" (2, 204). He imagines himself in the Golden Age, and his descriptions of the Swiss shepherds and peasants are in the spirit of the idyll. A peasant's care in washing a cup and bringing him water causes him to wonder "why were we not born in those times when all men were shepherds and brothers? With joy I would reject many of life's comforts (for which we are indebted to modern enlightenment) in order to return to the original state of man. All *true* pleasures— those in which the heart participates and which make us genuinely happy—were enjoyed by people then and to a greater degree than now . . ." (2, 278-79). He continues in this Rousseauist vein until he leaves his shepherd who, Karamzin insists, already enjoys all the fruits of true happiness. Idealist and optimist, Karamzin interprets all by the formula: the simple, natural life equals virtue and contentment. Accordingly, he looks down into a valley, where "cottages are smoking, the dwellings of poverty, ignorance and— perhaps of peace. Eternal Wisdom! what variety there is in your physical and moral worlds!" (2, 265). Sharing some young peasants' food, "I told them that their simple and carefree life pleased me greatly and that I wished to remain with them and milk cows" (2, 272). A peasant wedding is the excuse for praising the tender feelings of Alpine shepherds and their understanding of "the language of the heart!" (2, 283). All Karamzin's chance encounters in Switzerland, together with the stories he narrates, harmonize with the overall impression of a life in Arcadia. Visits to Gessner's monument, meditations on his life and work, extensive quotations from Haller's poem "Die Alpen," Rousseau's pervasive influence, and, specifically, the links of *La Nouvelle Héloise* with the lake at Lausanne provide the literary references which sustain the illusion of the promised land.

The image of the Swiss shepherd, projected against a backcloth of mountain peaks and green valleys, preoccupied Karamzin but not to the extent of minimizing his keen interest in the urban life of Switzerland and questions of its economic and political stability. He notes that "although in Basel the people has no legislative power and cannot elect its representatives, the government of this canton may, however, be called partially democratic, since the path to the highest distinctions in the republic are open to everyone and people of the lowest class are members of the big and small councils which make laws, conclude peace, set taxes, and elect their own members" (2, 199). Annoyed by the persistent begging of children, Karamzin forecasts the possible downfall of the Swiss republic in terms which anticipate his political commentaries in the *Messenger of Europe*: "Young scamps may in time become big ones and spread through their country a dangerous moral illness from which sooner or later freedom dies in republics. Then, dear Swiss, the balmy air of your mountains and valleys will not help you, the beauty of your tender goddess will die and your tears will not revive the old corpse!" (2, 254). The delicate balance is still maintained, because "perhaps in no other town in Europe will you find, my friends, such unspoilt morals and such piety as in Zurich," where "wise legislators" knew that "luxury is the grave of freedom and good morals and tried to prevent its entering their republic" (2, 240–41). Such views are in keeping with Karamzin's political thinking elsewhere in the *Moscow Journal* and reiterated later more forcefully. He is able to discuss the condition of the

Bernese peasants in economic, nonidyllic terms: "The, so to speak, flourishing state of the Swiss peasants comes mainly from the fact that they pay almost no taxes and live in complete freedom and independence, giving the government only one tenth of what they harvest. Although some of them have up to fifty thousand rubles in capital, they nevertheless dress simply . . ." (2, 257). A parallel with the lot of the Russian serf is implicit; it was a problem Karamzin approached with some caution in his sketch "A Country Festival and Wedding" ["Sel'skii prazdnik i svad'ba"].[23]

All the passages on Swiss life and government are retained in the final version of *Letters*; apart from some criticism of the character of the inhabitants of Basel and Lausanne Karamzin's picture of Switzerland is overwhelmingly approving. In preparing the second and third editions, however, he introduced small, but significant changes, illustrating on the one hand a more biased attitude toward the French Revolution and on the other deflating what he considered had been excessively naïve reactions in himself. In the first edition, for instance, Karamzin had followed Rousseau's example by actually kissing the Swiss earth; retaining this version in the second edition, he felt the need to add: "At that time I was only twenty-four years old." Similarly, his effusion on the Golden Age was subsequently given the footnote: "A dream of the imagination" and in the final edition: "When was that?" Although in 1791, apparently unaware of any falsity or attitudinizing in himself, he was sharply critical of other sentimental travelers he met, such as the Danish poet H. Baggesen and his companion Count A. Moltke: "Both of them love sighing and exclaiming. The Count beats his brow and stamps his feet, and the poet Bag* folds his arms and gazes at heaven when Lavater is speaking enthusiastically about something" (2, 250–51).[24]

Karamzin's account of Switzerland offers little modification to what his literary mentors had conditioned him to feel and see; in contrast, it might have been expected that his letters from a France involved in revolution would be an immediate eye-witness account, independent of long-standing authorities. The fact that Karamzin has left a leisurely, tourist's account of life in Paris is to be explained, censorship apart, by the aims he pursued on his journey and a lack of concern about the Revolution at this stage of events: he is interested in the Revolution only insofar as it affects his understanding of the French character or interferes with his wish to see historic places and meet prominent people. Nevertheless, the few allusions to the Revolution in the first edition (up to his arrival in Paris) are given more negative coloring in the second edition. Thus "the street noise" (ulichnyi shum) becomes "the noise of drunken rebels" (shum p'ianykh buntovshchikov) and a victim of the mob was no longer "dragged" (vlachimyi) along the street, but "torn to pieces" (terzaemyi). On the evidence of such changes one can only speculate that Karamzin modified passages in volumes 5 and 6 prior to their eventual publication in 1801. In the *Spectateur du Nord* Karamzin quoted a passage on the Revolution which did not appear in the published *Letters* but prefacing these lines in which he declared that his ideas on the events "ne sont pas assez mûres" are the significant words: "Enfin l'auteur va parler de la revolution... On s'attendroit à une longue lettre, mais elle ne contient que quelques lignes."[25] Karamzin at no stage of his life countenanced violence and upheaval, and his belief that "every civil society upheld over centuries is sacred for good citizens and in the most imperfect one cannot but be amazed by the wondrous harmony, organization, and order" (2, 462), although published in 1801, is fundamental and unchanging. It is closely linked with the opening section of his farewell letter from Paris:

I have left you, dear Paris, with regret and gratitude! In the midst of your noisy events I lived peacefully and happily as a carefree citizen of the universe; I looked at your troubles with a quiet soul, as a peaceful shepherd looks from a hill at the stormy sea. Neither the Jacobins nor the aristocrats did me any evil. I listened to arguments, but did not argue; I entered your wonderful temples so that my eyes and ears should be enchanted where the gleaming god of the arts shines in the rays of the intellect and talent, where the genius of glory majestically reclines on its laurels! (2, 648)

The commentary on this passage comes in the *Messenger of Europe*, where Karamzin insists that "an evil Royalist is no better than an evil Jacobin. There is only one good party in the world: the friends of mankind and goodness. They form in politics what the eclectics do in philosophy."[26] His faith in "good men" and their ability to prevail, which was temporarily shattered by the events of the French Terror, reasserts itself.

Karamzin's picture of Paris in the spring of 1790, despite the paucity of political comment, is nonetheless absorbing. Not primarily concerned with the new personalities produced by the Revolution—although he has left an amusing account of visits to the National Assembly, where he heard Mirabeau and the abbé Maury "continually in single combat like Achilles and Hector" (2, 644) — he was interested in the life of the upper classes, in the depiction of which he is frequently ironic. He has left a portrait gallery of the hosts and habitués of the salons—Mme. Glo*, who contradicted all his literary judgements; Mme. N*, with her dreams of a simple life in Switzerland, and her jealous suitor, Baron D*; the abbé D*, with his stern pronouncements on Racine; the abbé N*, sighing for the former brilliant social life. Karamzin seems intent on showing how little things had changed with the Revolution or how quickly and easily the French adapted themselves to new conditions. He emphasizes their fickle, volatile nature; in 1786 he described them as "madcaps," and his view in 1790 is not revised:

Fire, air—and the character of the French is described. I know of no nation more intelligent, fiery and fickle than yours. . . . Sensitive to an extreme, he [the Frenchman] falls in love with trouble, fame, great undertakings—but lovers are inconstant! The moments of his enthusiasm, frenzy, hate may have terrible consequences: an example of this is the Revolution. It would be a pity if this awful political change should also change the character of a people that is gay, witty and attractive! (2, 646–47)

Karamzin's letters are essentially a sentimental homage to "France—this most beautiful country in the world, most beautiful for its climate, its works, its people, its arts" (2, 433). Descriptions of places in and around Paris which have strong historical, literary, and sentimental associations abound. Karamzin visited Chantilly, Marly, Versailles, Fontainebleau, Ermenonville, he meditates on the mont Valérien and in the Bois de Boulogne, but it is Paris, with its famous buildings and streets, its contrasts of opulence and poverty, its "wondrous variety," which dominates Karamzin's letters:

Here it is, I thought, here is the city which for centuries was the model for all Europe, the source of taste and fashion the name of which is pronounced with awe by scholars and non-scholars, philosophers and fops, artists and ignoramuses in Europe and Asia, America and Africa.

The name which became known to me almost as soon as my own, about which I have read so much in novels, heard so much from travelers and dreamt and thought so much! (2, 438)

Karamzin's comments on the French character and the contrasts of Paris are near to Rousseau's in *Les Confessions,* but Karamzin refrains from similar critical conclusions. He is completely enchanted: "Paris is a unique city. Perhaps nowhere else can you find so much material for philosophical observations, nowhere are there so many curious objects for a man able to appreciate the arts, nowhere so many distractions and amusements" (2, 494).

Karamzin's visit to Paris dispels his old prejudices; his visit to England had the opposite effect. He arrives with enthusiasm: "I am in England—in that country which I loved in my childhood with such enthusiasm and which by the character of its inhabitants and degree of national enlightenment is certainly one of the first states in Europe" (2, 659), but at the end of his visit, he writes: "I would come to England again with pleasure, but I leave it without regret" (2, 782). His final letter from England is a résumé of his thoughts on the country and its people: "Now I have seen Englishmen at close quarters, I do justice to them, I praise them— but my praise is as cold as they are themselves" (2, 773). He pays tribute to the beauty of Englishwomen, the general enlightenment, the sense of honor which, he believes, stems from British trading traditions, English philanthropy, more in evidence abroad than at home, where poverty is considered almost a crime. He considers the English reserved, silent and cold—and there is no more damning epithet in the sentimentalist's vocabulary; their humor is coarse and heavy and their reputation as profound philosophers merely a consequence of the sluggishness with which blood flows through their veins. He re-endorses a widely held view of England as a land of eccentrics, melancholics, splenetics, and suicides. The favorable impressions of France are continually used as a contrast to English deficiencies. Disputing Fielding's apologia of English humor, Karamzin writes: "Leave any playfulness of wit to your enemies, the French. Be rational if you wish but allow me to believe that you have no subtlety, no attractiveness of mind nor that lively fusion of thoughts which produces social graces" (2, 775). He reacts against English xenophobia, which makes foreigners seem "some sort of imperfect, pitiful people. 'Don't touch him,' they say in the street, 'he's a foreigner—which means 'he's a poor man or an infant' " (2, 780). It is a verdict prompted by his earlier reflection that "I wish to live and die in my dear homeland; but after Russia there is no country more attractive to me than France, where a foreigner frequently forgets that he is not among his own people" (2, 780).

Karamzin's interest in Paris and London, which he calls the two highlights of his journey, leads to an obvious difference between the various parts of *Letters*. In Germany and Switzerland Karamzin had been a sentimental *traveler*, journeying from place to place in search of entertainment for the heart and mind; in Paris and London he becomes a temporary resident with time to describe at leisure and in great detail historical buildings, places, and streets. He makes excursions to surrounding places of interest, but his narrative is more sedate and predictable. His letters on England are the least sentimental in the work; they are a cautious and considered investigation into manners and institutions with an emphasis on the imperfections in the parliamentary system and electoral procedure. Obviously mindful of would-be constitutionalists and reformers in Russia, he warns that "all civil institutions must be in accord with the character of the people; what is good in England would be bad in another country" (2, 779) and seeks to commend those aspects of English life which he considered worthy of imitation by virtue of their nonpolitical nature. He praises the Greenwich Hospital, the Vauxhall Gardens, trial by jury, educational facilities, and widespread literacy which, together with the respect for family life, contributes to a life of peaceful harmony and prosperity, attainable, Karamzin believes, within any system "the soul of which is justice" (2, 779). The visit to England was an important stage in Karamzin's education; believing originally that "to be English is to be brave, magnanimous, and sensitive, and also to be a true man" (2, 773), Karamzin soon lost his illusions. He learnt instead how potent and selfish a force patriotism was.

Only England, or Englishmen, failed to meet Karamzin's expectations. In Germany his faith in great men had been largely justified; in Switzerland he had been impressed not only by the natural beauty and the simple, good life of the shepherds but also by the system of government; France had exceeded his hopes and,

the Revolution notwithstanding, he found the French a delightful
and civilized people. From this time dates his assiduous reading of
French literature; it is French salon-culture which influences his
subsequent literary undertakings and language reforms.

Firm in his belief that "what is good for humanity cannot be
bad for Russians," Karamzin is at pains to distinguish its cultural
implications from the political. Informing himself during his journey of French and English political history from such works as
Gabriel de Mably's *Observations sur l'histoire de France* and J. L.
Delolme's *Constitution d'Angleterre, ou état du gouvernement
anglais,* he retains a negative attitude toward politics and political
reform. An illustration of his idealistic faith in great men rather
than political institutions to guarantee the welfare of nations is
the contrast he makes between the French statesmen, Richelieu
and Colbert. Richelieu he portrays as "a cunning minister but a
fierce man, an implacable enemy, a boastful patron of the arts but
the envious persecutor of great talents" (2, 571), he embodied not
the Christian religion but "the monster called Politics," described
in Voltaire's *Henriade*. Colbert was a state's ideal servant: "a great
minister, the glory of France and Louis XIV! He served the King,
attempting to increase his revenues and power; he served the people, attempting to enrich it by means of various helpful institutions
and trade; he served mankind, aiding the speedy progress of the
sciences, useful arts and literature, not only in France but also in
other lands" (2, 575). Karamzin praises all men who, he believes,
had contributed to the spread of enlightenment through the ages.
Monarchs, philosophers, scientists, statesmen, writers: Colbert, Copernicus, Descartes, Franklin, Henri IV, Linnaeus, Montesquieu,
Newton, Peter the Great, Rousseau, Voltaire. His tributes are generous and his enthusiasm for science typical of an age unaware of
any divorce into "two cultures." He is confident that mankind was
progressing inevitably toward perfection: "Where Homers and Platos lived there now live ignoramuses and barbarians; but in Northern Europe there lives the singer of the *Messias*, to whom Homer
himself would have conceded his laurel crown, and at the foot of
the Jura Mountains we see Bonnet and in Koenigsberg Kant, before
whom Plato is a child in matters of philosophy" (2, 433).

Karamzin is an accomplished practitioner of the typical
eighteenth-century game of "name-dropping"; in contrast to the

pseudo-classicist's gallery of mythological figures and Greek and Roman heroes, Karamzin has a pantheon peopled with figures dear to the Enlightenment and symbolic of man's attainments and progress. He has a corresponding, not always interchangeable, set of writers and poets, venerated by the sentimentalist. At its best it is a form of literary shorthand, at its worst, a meaningless and naïve following of fashion. Although Karamzin at times seems guilty of a mere parade of famous names and the passing on of secondhand information, there is a basic consistency and purpose in his field of reference. He was a perceptive and indefatigable reader and his work is rich in informed comment on a variety of subjects, particularly on the arts.

The exaggerated emotional response is characteristic of Karamzin's preferences in his self-acknowledged fields of competence, literature and the drama; it is predominant in his comments on music, painting, and sculpture, fields in which he emphasized he was not "an expert" (znatok). Styling himself "an amateur of music" (2, 80), he relies of necessity on his feelings to distinguish the cold professional from the true artist: it is a distinction reminiscent of the epigraph from Rousseau to part 4 of the *Moscow Journal*: "J'ai toujours senti que l'état d'auteur n'était, ne pouvait être illustre et respectable, qu'autant qu'il n'était pas un métier." He criticizes the Italian singers, Todi and Marchesi, because they do not "move his heart" and "lack soul," qualities which he finds in the French singers Chenard, Lais, and Rousseau (2, 79–80, 471). Discussing the merits of certain composers, Karamzin characteristically finds much to commend in both Gluck and Piccini; conscious that they represented opposing sides in an earlier musical controversy in France, he supports his views by recalling that Rousseau had preferred Piccini but was moved by Gluck's *Orphée*: "Thus do great men acknowledge the injustice of their opinions!" (2, 542). For Handel and Haydn Karamzin reserved his unqualified admiration. In London he enthused: "I have heard the music of Pergolesi, Jommelli, Haydn, but I have never been as moved as I was by Handel's *Messiah*. It is both sad and cheerful, wonderful and full of feeling" (2, 676). Haydn's work represented man's highest achievements in music and provided one of life's greatest joys; it was *The Creation* which he was to translate in 1801. The emotions aroused in him by Haydn's *Stabat Mater* and Jommelli's

Miserere are his assurance of his soul's immortality: "Who will prove to me that my soul, open to such holy, pure, and ethereal joys, does not have within it something godlike and imperishable?" (2, 676).

Karamzin's rivals in painting to Haydn and Handel in music are Michaelangelo and Raphael, but it is Correggio who occupies a place of particular esteem and affection. Karamzin believed that "his brush is an example of tenderness and agreeableness" (2, 99) and it is to these specific qualities that Karamzin refers in his later poems, "Il'ia of Murom" and "A Picture" ["Kartina"]. If Correggio appealed to the sentimentalist by the soft and voluptuous nature of his canvases, Salvator Rosa represented the increasing vogue for wild nature and mysterious characters. In his extensive commentaries on the artists represented in the Drezden gallery, extracted in good measure from A. I. D'Argenville's *Abrégé de la vie des plus fameux peintres* (1745), Karamzin alludes to Rosa's talent for landscape painting and later as he surveys the scenery around Frankfurt, he exclaims: "So many landscapes worthy of the brush of Salvator Rosa or Poussin" (2, 168). It is a pairing of artists in strict accord with Thomson's "Or savage Rosa dash'd or learned Poussin drew"; equally in line with the tastes of his age is his praise for the paintings in Boydell's Shakespeare Gallery in London. He considered the work of Gavin Hamilton, Benjamin West, and Angelica Kauffman "very good and expressive," but it was Henry Fuseli's fantastic treatment of Shakespearean themes which moved him with "their astonishing power, their astonishing imaginative richness." He suggests that "if the dreamer-poet were to be resurrected, he would embrace the dreamer-painter" (2, 701). Elsewhere in *Letters* Karamzin pays tribute to paintings by Holbein, which he saw in Basel, and to the work of Rubens, "the Dutch Raphael" (2, 501), but it is on "the French Raphael," Charles Lebrun, that he exhausts his superlatives. In Paris he made a special visit to the Carmelite Monastery to see Lebrun's *Magdalene* and record his response:

I never thought nor imagined that a painting could be so eloquent and moving. The more I look at it the deeper I penetrate with my feelings into its beauties. All is charming in the Magdalene: face, figure, hands, disheveled hair which serves as a cover for her lily-white breasts; most charming of all are her eyes, reddened by tears . . . I have seen many famous paintings, have praised and been astonished by their art, but this painting *I would wish to possess; I could be happier with it*; in a word, *I love it!* It would stand in my lonely study, always before my eyes! (2, 561)

But it is not the magic of the picture which moves Karamzin; it is his knowledge of its sentimental history, of the fact that Louis XIV's mistress, Louise de la Vallière, was the Magdalene, which holds "its secret charm for my heart." Karamzin's designation of various "national Raphaels," if understood to denote more than the supreme accolade of achievement, is another indication of his eclecticism. He shows no hesitation in acclaiming both Poussin and Rubens, who had given their name to rival factions in a bitter artistic dispute of an earlier age, when the description of Rubens as "the Dutch Raphael" would have seemed heretical.[27]

Karamzin's views on sculpture were markedly influenced by the "new criticism" of the period. When he paid tribute to the famous dead, Karamzin commented, whenever the occasion presented itself, on the monuments and statues erected to their memory. He shared with many contemporary artists "le plaisir des tombeaux," but his appreciation of tomb sculpture was at the same time based on his attitude to death as something to be welcomed rather than feared. The grave was a place of peace and joy and not of horror; it is an opposition which his poem "The Cemetery" ["Kladbishche"], originally published as "The Grave" ["Mogila"] in 1792, exploits. Death is the sister of Sleep, suggested explicitly by Karamzin in his design for a monument to Gessner (2, 200–201), and death is a merging with nature. He therefore takes particular delight in tombs and monuments which were set in poetic natural surroundings, such as Rousseau's tomb at Ermenonville. In his dislike of monstrous tombs and unnatural burial practices he is at one with Herder and Lessing, who had both written works with the title *Wie die Alten den Tod gebildet*, and with Mercier's remarks in *Le Tableau de Paris*.[28] His views are clearly expressed in his criticism of two pieces of sculpture by Jean Baptiste Pigalle —the tomb of the Maréchal de Saxe in S. Thomas, Strasbourg, and the tomb of the Comte d'Harcourt in Notre Dame. Of the first he writes:

The artist wanted people to be amazed by his art: in the opinion of experts he achieved his aim. Not being an expert, I looked at the figures,

at the first, the second, the third, and was as cold in my heart as the
marble from which they were made. Death in the form of a skeleton,
dressed in a cloak, revolted me. The Ancients did not represent it in this
way and woe betide modern artists who frighten us with such interpreta-
tions! I would prefer to see a different expression on the hero's face. I
would ask him to pay more attention to grieving France than to that
hideous skeleton. In short, Pigalle, I feel, is a skillful artist but a poor
poet. (2, 188)

Commenting earlier on Phidias's famous Laocoön, Karamzin had
been impressed by the expression of physical pain and paternal anguish—and his praise for the artist was precisely: "Phidias was a
poet" (2, 183). His appreciation of Pigalle's second work derives,
as does his love of Lebrun's *Magdalene*, from its sentimental associations. "They say that the tender Countess, endlessly mourning
the death of her loved one, saw exactly such a dream: the artist represented it according to her description—and never has Pigalle's
chisel so strongly acted upon my feelings as in this touching, melancholic creation. I am sure that his heart participated in the work"
(2, 570).
    An interesting aspect of Karamzin's sentimental judgments is
his understanding and use of the word "Gothic." The first Russian
to introduce elements of "literary Gothic" into his work, Karamzin
in his role as a sentimental enlightener was completely opposed to
the Gothic in its historical connotations: it was for him a synonym
of medieval obscurity and barbarism. He saw the time of the Cru-
sades as a period when war was all important and the fourteenth
century presented endless barbarities. His intellectual and artistic
kinship with Thomson is reaffirmed when he quotes the passage
on Peter the Great from *The Seasons* in which "Gothic darkness"
is attacked. The Middle Ages implied intellectual stagnation and he
could find little to commend in the work of Chaucer, Erasmus, or
Rabelais. Unable to appreciate "the strange taste of those past centuries" (2, 111), he granted Gothic architecture nothing more than
a certain "boldness" (smelost') and dismissed Notre Dame as "a
Gothic building, huge and respected for its antiquity" (2, 569).
The view of his contemporary Chateaubriand that "you could not
enter a Gothic church without feeling a kind of awe and a vague
sentiment of the Divinity"[29] would obviously have been meaningless for Karamzin.

Karamzin emphasized the personal factor in his aesthetic judgments, but behind them stood the authority of an age. His subjective responses reflect the Zeitgeist of the late eighteenth century and his "I" is not to be divorced from the "we," the European men of feeling. Karamzin's originality lies precisely in the skill and panache with which he purveyed European tastes and fashions to a Russian audience. Undoubtedly it was the overtly sentimental tone of Letters which guaranteed its success and it is interesting to examine in some detail Karamzin as a representative sentimental man, the product of both natural inclination and pronounced literary influence, a person in whom it is sometimes difficult to separate genuine response from expected response, true feeling from sentimental fiction. In a work avowedly the mirror of Karamzin's soul, the Rousseau and the Shalikov, the alpha and omega of the literature of feeling, are found side by side. Letters, nevertheless, set the norm for Russian sentimentalists in all matters of content and style.

At the center of the sentimental mystique was the cult of the feeling heart (chuvstvitel'noe serdtse) or sensibility (chuvstvitel'nost'). It is in his propaganda for the naturally virtuous heart, which confers both infinite bliss and infinite sorrow on its possessor, that Karamzin is linked with Sterne, Rousseau, and Goethe as the most eloquent apologists of the age of feeling. Goethe's Werther extolls "this heart of mine, of which I am so proud, for it is the source of all things—all strength, all bliss, all misery."[30] Sterne sings of "dear sensibility! source inexhausted of all that's precious in our joys, or costly in our sorrows!"[31] Karamzin, no less than they, praises sensibility and its riches. The heart assures men of the existence of an afterlife, when reason is powerless to help; sensibility is the key to all deeds of philanthropy, compassion and magnanimity, which in their turn enraptured the man of feeling. On reading an inscription dedicated to Gellert, Karamzin exclaims: "It is pleasant, delightful for every feeling heart to see such inscriptions and to know that truth, not flattery, engraved them" (2, 121). He is ever ready to respond to canonized sentimental set-pieces: on one occasion he watches in ecstatic silence the reunion of an elderly French emigré couple with their children: "You have flown by, moment of silence and peace! but you have left deep marks on my heart which will always remind me of man's sensibility—for it turned us to stone as we saw father and mother, son and daughter embrace each other with ardor and delight!" (2, 197). Like Goethe, Karamzin delights in the innocence of children as they play with their mother; like Sterne and Mackenzie's Harley, he responds with compassion to illness and madness; mindful perhaps of Thomson's pity for the worm, wriggling on the angler's hook, he believes that a snake, although "a malicious creature," was created in God's infinite wisdom and, therefore, deserving of mercy; after the example of Goethe, Sterne, Young, and a legion of their epigones, he meditates among ruins on the rise and fall of civilizations, repeating *sic transit gloria mundi.*

Sensibility was a *sine qua non* of all artists and all who would appreciate true art. It was confidence in the infallibility of his feelings which allowed him to appreciate a Gluck opera, a Phidias sculpture, a Lebrun painting, to attack the supposedly cold art of Racine and Corneille and to mistake maudlin sentimentality for rich emotional *aperçus.* He left a performance of Kotzebue's melodrama in a state of emotional exhaustion: "Will you believe, my friends, that I count this evening among the happiest in my life? Let them show me now that the arts do not influence our happiness! Yes, I will always bless their effect, whilst my heart beats in my breast—whilst it is sensitive!" (2, 73). Inseparable companions of sensibility are melancholy and tears. Although Karamzin's friend, Lenz, was the victim of "deep melancholy" (2, 10), melancholy and tears are far from indications of life's tragic side; they were in themselves a source of pleasure. With the advent of autumn Karamzin experiences grief mixed "in my heart with some sweet pleasure" (2, 332). Melancholy is for Karamzin a goddess (2, 391) and elsewhere apostrophized as "Holy, heavenly Melancholy, mother of all the immortal works of the human mind" (3, 396). "The tender tear of melancholy," which Karamzin shed at Rousseau's grave (2, 624), was but one of the tears for all occasions with which Karamzin emulated Sterne or the lachrymose Harley. Karamzin draws attention to Sterne's amusing precision in describing tears, but his own observations are no less detailed. He weeps tears of gratitude for unexpected hospitality, wipes away "the last sweet tear" after Kotzebue's play, weeps from the beauty of Haydn's music and is ready to weep as homage to Lebrun. To weep is an anticipated pleasure: Karamzin takes up his Gellert, determined "to read, to feel and—perhaps to weep" (2, 121). It happens, however, that an excess of emotion leaves him incapable of tears.

Karamzin's emotional arsenal held more than the subtleties of tears and melancholy: exhaustion and swooning are further indications of intensity of feeling. He faints twice before the imposing beauty of waterfalls, but in general his joy in nature is expressed in silent reverence. In keeping with Rousseau's teaching of silent homage to the Divinity, Karamzin describes how "I bent my knees, directed my gaze at heaven and brought the sacrifice of heartfelt prayer" (2, 270). Although Karamzin was in principle intent on rendering nuances in feelings and nature, he follows Rousseau in acknowledging his inability to describe intense emotional states; faced with the beauty of a Swiss valley or waterfall, he regrets that the pen cannot rival the paintbrush and is ready "to throw down his pen" (2, 280–81). Some situations induced emotional exhaustion, others demanded physical stamina: Karamzin sat looking at the sea for an hour, gazed at the panorama of Danzig for two hours and was prepared to spend a whole day in contemplation of the Rhine. He subscribed to the belief that "distance lends enchantment to the view" and seeks out vantage points from which to look down on cities and valleys. A final characteristic he shared with many contemporaries is his enthusiasm for literary rambles. In the way the appeal of a painting or sculpture was increased for Karamzin by knowledge of its genesis, the beauty of a region was inevitably enhanced when there existed some literary description of it or real and fictional associations. Goethe and Klopstock are connected for him with the lake at Zurich; Twickenham and Windsor appeal for their links with Pope. He seeks traces of Rousseau on the Ile de St. Pierre, visits Ermenonville, where memories of Rousseau's life crowd in on him, and goes to Vevey "with Rousseau's *Héloise* in my hands" (2, 302).

A literature devoted to nuances of feeling and meaning and lyrical description could not have been successful without a fine instrument—"the new style," invariably associated with the name of Karamzin. Almost all the compliments Karamzin's contemporaries bestowed on his early work made reference to the attractiveness of his style. Bolotov praised "the sweetness and especially the attractiveness, predominant in all his works and language";[32] F. N. Glinka recalled young officer-cadets in St. Petersburg reading and learning by heart "his musical prose and verse, which were so easily retained in the memory";[33] S. N. Glinka mentioned, improbably in view of the date of the dramatist's death, Kniazhnin's enthusiasm for Karamzin's "new, lively, spirited style."[34] Not all were so impressed: N. Ia. Ozeretskovskii, who succeeded Kniazhnin as instructor in the Cadet School in 1791, was, according to S. N. Glinka, "of a completely different opinion from Kniazhnin. Seeing the enthusiasm with which we were reading *Letters of a Russian Traveler*, he once made me read aloud the letters on the Alps. I began to read. Ozeretskovskii, as was his wont, paced up and down the room and when I had finished reading like an inspired Pythia, he said sullenly and curtly: Well, what's that? A pompous, pretentious style, a soap bubble, filled with wind. Prick it with a pin, the wind will fly out and nothing will be left."[35]

The sentimental lexicon which Karamzin canonized in his work was already partially familiar to readers of the eclogues, elegies, and love poems of such poets as Sumarokov and Kheraskov, of the translations from writers such as Gessner, Rousseau, and Young; and of certain existing Russian novels and plays. Karamzin popularized certain already existing words and expressions, introduced calques and neologisms, not haphazardly but *systematically*. His new style was first and foremost a syntactical revolution; he strove for clarity, simplicity, logic, based on a philosophy of language, on a clear understanding of what to say and how best to say it. In a review of a Russian grammar written by a Frenchman, Jean-Baptiste Maudru, he objects to the view that in Russian words may be placed anywhere: "It seems to me that there is a law governing word position in Russian; each position gives a phrase a particular sense, and where it is necessary to say: *solntse plodotvorit zemliu* [the sun enriches the earth], it would be a mistake to say: *zemliu plodotvorit solntse* or *plodotvorit zemliu solntse*. There is always only one best, i.e., true, order in the positioning of words; Russian grammar does not define it, but so much the worse for bad writers! and the right to make a mistake is no asset" (3, 600).

The immediate stylistic impact which Karamzin's prose had on his contemporaries may be appreciated from the first of the *Letters of a Russian Traveler*, dated Tver', May 18, 1789, which was also the first piece of prose in the *Moscow Journal*. Karamzin describes his emotions when he set out on his journey and left behind his beloved friends; an apostrophe to the mysterious workings of the heart is the excuse for the analysis of the contradiction between his long-standing desire to travel and his melancholy at the time of parting. Within this frame he contrives a mosaic of references to his past life and experiences, to the character of his friend, Petrov, and to reflections on the transience of happiness. Karamzin employs a strongly emotive vocabulary in keeping with the exclusively sentimental content of the letter: *serdtse* (seven times), *chuvstvo* (five times), *vostorg, radost', udovol'stvie, pripadki, melankholiia, sleza* (twice), *uzhas, grust', utesheniia; milyi* (five times), *nezhneishie, priiatneishaia, zhelaemyi, liubezneishie, liubeznyi* (three times), *nravstvennyi, dragotsennyi, bezdushnyi, blagopoluchnyi, priiatnyi, shchastliveishii, radostnyi, trogatel'nyi, grustnyi, gorestnyi; podgoriunivshis'; razmiagchen, rastrogan; khotet', grustit', plakat', chuvstvovat', zameret', vyplakat'.* Many other words acquire in context distinct emotional coloring: *mechta, voobrazhenie; izlivat'sia, osirotet', proshchat'sia, rasstat'sia, onemet', ostavit', priviazat',* and *prosit'.* Of sentimental key words, such as *serdtse, chuvstvo, sleza, trogatel'nyi,* only *chuvstvitel'nyi* is missing, reserved for the opening of the following letter. Karamzin's liking for the superlative form of an adjective is clearly in evidence and is a characteristic technique in the sentimentalist's attempt to stress the intensity and exclusiveness of his experience and feelings.

The emotional appeal and effectiveness of the letter is, however, achieved by syntactical and orthographic devices. Karamzin extends his principle of the "harmonious whole" (garmonicheskoe tseloe) to the smallest syntactical unit: each phrase is carefully structured and contributes to the overall unity of the letter. The two basic devices Karamzin employs are repetition—usually of words within a single sentence—and parallelism—a series of sentences or subordinate clauses similarly constructed. The short opening paragraph shows the kind of effect repetition produces. In the opening sentence: *Rasstalsia ia s vami, milye, rasstalsia!*—he places the emphasis on the act of parting by inverting the personal pronoun and the verb and repeating the verb again at the end, balancing the sentence and at the same time turning it back upon itself. In contrast to this hermetic effect, the final phrase of the second sentence shows a different position of the verb and its repetition in a different tense, which opens it out in accordance with the idea of prolonged separation: *a ia besprestanno ot vas udaliaius' i budu udaliat'sia!* A third example shows Karamzin repeating the verb to avoid the use of a conjunction and isolate the aspects of his loneliness, physical and spiritual: *Drug vash osirotel v mire, osirotel v dushe svoei*! To intensify the emotional effect Karamzin also repeats adverbs (*No polno, polno!*) and nouns (*O serdtse, serdtse!*) and occasionally introduces synonyms instead of simple repetition: *byl razmiagchen, rastrogan*. Examples of syntactical parallelism are the three negative rhetorical questions in the second paragraph and the three nouns with subordinate clauses dependent on *na* later in the same paragraph. In his striving for logic and harmony Karamzin consciously restricted the use of the conjunctions *i* and *a*: in a letter of 459 words, divided into twenty-nine sentences, which vary in length from one word to seventy-three, *a* appears three times and *i* thirteen (including five occasions when it is used for noun doublets, i.e., *mysli i chuvstva*). Within a complex sentence he relates the parts to the whole on the basis of parallel clauses dependent on prepositions and such words as *gde* and *tam*, as well as by the liberal use of dashes. The letter in general abounds in question and exclamation marks, rows of dots and—dashes. Grech wrote of his tutor who "had read "Poor Liza" with rapture and loved to place dashes everywhere, in imitation of the fashionable Karamzin",[36] it was a technique constantly employed by Wieland among authors Karamzin particularly admired and it was a feature which Shishkov attacked.[37]

The letter is an excellent example of Karamzin's mastery of his chosen method, of his ability to marry content and style. Yet the abuses to which his style lay open, its mannerisms and artificiality are evident. In the sense that Karamzin called Sterne "original, inimitable" he too was unique in Russian literature; few of his contemporaries had his feeling for language and harmony or the technical accomplishments to go beyond facile imitation of sentimental words and attitudes. It is to Zhukovskii and even more, to K. N. Batiushkov that one should look for the true inheritors of Karamzin's prose reforms, authors who followed the spirit of his work, not its outward trappings.

The contribution *Letters of a Russian Traveler* made to Russian literature was varied and considerable. Although its contemporary appeal is attributable first and foremost to the transitory vogue of sentimentalism—it was both the first and best example of a Russian sentimental journey—it possesses more durable qualities. The first Russian prose work of extended length to be consistently readable and entertaining, *Letters* provided its readers with abundant information on European culture. It is a work marked by an often naïve enthusiasm, but this is found alongside passages based on acute and critical observation. Historically, *Letters* represents the first detailed published account of a Russian's journey through western Europe and analysis of European life and culture; in its turn it became the first Russian prose work widely known in the West.

The man who more than any other was responsible for establishing Karamzin's reputation in Europe was a minor German litterateur, J. G. Richter (1763–1808), whose translations of Karamzin's stories, *Letters of a Russian Traveler* and articles from the *Messenger of Europe* became the "originals" for translations into other European languages. His version of *Letters, Briefe eines reisenden Russen*, which was published in six volumes in Leipzig in the years 1799–1802, has become a venerated German classic and was reprinted in 1922 and again in 1959. Richter, close to the latest literary developments in Moscow, where he was employed as a tutor until 1804, submitted his translation for Karamzin's approval; Karamzin deciphered for him names denoted in the Russian text only by initials. The first appearance of Karamzin's name in English periodicals is closely connected with Richter's first, almost unknown work, *Moskwa. Eine Skizze* (Leipzig, 1799), which contains comments on Russian literary works and personalities.[38] In the survey article "Foreign Literature of the Year 1799," published in the *Annual Register* (1800) there appear the following lines on Karamzin: "At Moscow, M. Karamsin has published "Travels into several Countries of Europe," in six volumes. These travels originally made their appearance in the Moscow Journal, in the form of letters to the author's friends. In that form they met with such general approbation, including that of the late empress, who was an excellent judge of literary productions, that the author was encouraged to collect them in one body, with additions and improvements. In the foreign critical journals they are highly praised for the information and entertainment which they afford, and the justness, delicacy, and benevolence of sentiment which pervade them."[39] The same information in a somewhat different and expanded form, but still from Richter, was published later that year in the *Monthly Magazine* as "Russian Literature!—Extract from a Letter from Moscow, 2d of March, 1800."[40]

The first review of Karamzin's *Letters* appeared revealingly in the *German Museum,* which published the first English translations of "Frol Silin," "Poor Liza," and "Julia"—all from Richter's German.[41] Prefacing a summary of Karamzin's journey from Moscow to Germany is a short assessment of the work, in which it is suggested that the travels "do not excite so lively an interest as some other works of this class, since in respect to sentimental observations, they are inferior to the modern travels of Baggesen the learned Dane, called *The Labyrinth,* . . . but they abound in observations equally just and striking, and contain some information relative to Russian literature, and many entertaining anecdotes."[42] Two years later a further review was published in the *Anti-Jacobin* and extensive extracts were given from Karamzin's stay in Zurich.[43] The sympathetic reviewer places Karamzin's importance in the context of Europe's growing awareness of Russian progress in all fields: "In Mr. Karamsin, the display of their talents still farther improves upon us: and we see in him an instance of a Russian whose writings are studied on the Continent; not merely as exhibiting new features in the Russian character, but as giving pictures of European life and manners, which have been marked by the eye, and pourtrayed [sic] with the pencil, of elegant and impressive genius—as being rich in judgments concerning men and things, of which the sagacity and liberality might do honour to any mind, however polished, and however wise."

In September, 1803, an English translation of Karamzin's *Letters* was published by Andreas Andersen Feldborg (1782–1838), a Dane who lived in England almost continuously between 1802 and 1816 and the translator of numerous works into English during that period.[44] His translation was "from the German" and attracted wide critical attention the following year. In January 1804, the *Edinburgh Review* published a heavily ironic attack from the pen of Henry Brougham.[45] The review opens: "A book of travels by a native of Moscow, excites the same sort of interest with any uncommon natural phenomenon—a horse in Venice, for instance— or a tree in Scotland" and Brougham suggests that it is only "the rarity of a Russian work, and the amusing badness of the author's head" which prompt any attention. He ridicules Karamzin as a representative of those "sentient beings" who "refer everything to themselves, and [to] consider their own concerns as the objects upon which all eyes are turned"; Karamzin is trivial in his interests, boorish in his approaches to writers and scholars, inaccurate, and misled by "ignorance and imagination." The tone of this review and the belief that Karamzin had written in German provided the excuse for a political broadside from the *Anti-Jacobin*: "That translation has, indeed, been represented as the original, in the Edinburgh Review, a work of which the presumptuous ignorance, the petulant tastelessness, the incredible blunders, the lumpish dullness would not, even for the sake of its virulent slander, be endured in any other country in Europe but Great Britain."[46] The *Anti-Jacobin*'s own review was in keeping with its earlier comments on the German translation;[47] the reviewer is indulgent and avuncular, prepared to excuse "a mawkish strain of *sentimentality*, and *universal philanthropy*" on account of the author's youth and the accepted circumstances of the work's composition: "written on the spur of the moment, without previous reflection or study, the sentiments flowing warm from the heart, and intended only for the ear and the bosom of friendship." The review ran to no less than fifteen closely printed pages; the prolixity of other reviews was excused for similar reasons of the uncommonness of a Russian work. Reviewers in the *Monthly Review*, the *Annual Review*, and the *Annual Register* all found much to commend and quote;[48] their major criticisms, naturally enough, were provoked by Karamzin's comments on England, which were termed "erroneous" and attributable to his association only with members of the Russian embassy.

Karamzin's work—his tales (translated also by Feldborg from the German and published in 1803) and his *Letters*—attracted considerable attention; his name had become known, although his reputation was essentially that of a literary curiosity. It was only with the publication and fame of his history that his name was voiced with respect rather than condescension and he took his place in *The Pantheon of the Age*.[49]

FOUR

SENTIMENTAL FICTION

1789~1803

R EVIEWING IN 1803 a French translation of four of his early stories, Karamzin expressed his amusement and surprise that Henri Coiffier, the translator, should criticize "Frol Silin" as a *conte* rather than consider it a simple "description of good deeds."[1] Yet the very nature of sentimental fiction as practiced by Karamzin encouraged this confusion: despite our knowledge that Frol had been a real person, a Simbirsk peasant, Karamzin's objections seem strangely misplaced, from the point of view of both form and content.

Reacting strongly against the principal prose form of pseudo-classicism—the interminable adventure novel with its involved and fantastic plot, incredible coincidences and puppet-like characters, Karamzin sought simplicity and naturalness, a world peopled by recognizable men and women, experiencing the joys and sadnesses of life, such as might, theoretically at least, befall anyone at any time in any estate. Literature was not to be divorced from life; it was part of life. In Russia Karamzin's stories were the first to establish this link and "Poor Liza" is the outstanding tribute to his success.

Earlier than Karamzin, writers like Fedor Emin with his *Letters of Ernest and Doravra* [*Pis'ma Ernesta i Doravry*] (1766) and Pavel L'vov, the author of *The Russian Pamela* [*Rossiiskaia Pamela*] (1789), had attempted to assimilate the manner, form, and subject-matter of Rousseau's *La Nouvelle Héloise* (1761, first translated into Russian in 1769) and Richardson's *Pamela* (1740, translated in 1787). Although they anticipated scenes, attitudes, even turns of phrase which Karamzin was to incorporate into his own work, they lacked the command of language and form, which

96

were the basic and essential components of his undoubted revolution in Russian prose. In linking Karamzin's name with Rousseau and Richardson, it must be emphasized that he followed them not in form but in theme. The age of the novel was not to come in Russia for another half-century. Karamzin worked in the minor genre of the short story, which demanded a high degree of formal organization and linguistic exactness. The importance of this orientation is to be traced through Pushkin to Lermontov and Turgenev.

Although Russian Julies and Pamelas began to proliferate, Karamzin's Liza was the first character in Russian literature to step out of literature into life. Karamzin's contemporaries saw him as the talented reporter of the tragic fate of a girl who had lived near Moscow and died in a pond near the Simonov Monastery; the scene of her death became the object of sentimental pilgrimage. Karamzin recalled in 1817 how "twenty-five years ago I composed there "Poor Liza": a simple tale, but so favorable for the young author that thousands of curious people went there to seek traces of Liza."[2] Aspiring young authors like Gavrila Kamenev and I. A. Ivanov went to pay homage at the *Lizin prud* and were struck by Karamzin's exact description of the setting.[3] An amusing account of Karamzin's popular fame is in a letter from A. F. Merzliakov to Andrei Turgenev, dated August 3, 1799, which gives the conversation between a peasant and a craftsman about Liza.[4] Liza and Frol Silin were thus to an equal degree real people and imaginary heroes: to separate them would be to destroy the sentimental illusion Karamzin had been preeminent in creating.

An analysis of the terms Karamzin employs to define the nature of his stories upholds such a view. Karamzin uses the word *povest'* (tale) on three occasions in subtitles to works; his first story, "Eugene and Julia," is "a true Russian tale"; "Poor Liza," originally without a subtitle, was later called "a Russian tale" (rossiiskaia povest') and "Martha the Mayoress" ["Marfa-posadnitsa"] he termed "an historical tale" (istoricheskaia povest'). On the other hand, "The Beautiful Princess and the Fortunate Dwarf" ["Prekrasnaia tsarevna i shchastlivyi karla"] was described as "an old fairy tale or a new caricature" (starinnaia skazka ili novaia karrikatura) and "The Deep Forest" ["Dremuchii les"] as "a fairy tale for children" (skazka dlia detei). Yet the difference in genre, suggested here in the use of *povest'* and *skazka*, is not consistently observed. When Karamzin published the first collected edition of his works in 1803, volume 6 was entitled *Povesti* and included the stories mentioned above (with the exception of "Eugene and Julia"), together with "Natalia, the Boyar's Daughter," "Julia," "The Island of Bornholm" ["Ostrov Born'golm"], and "Sierra Morena," which had originally been introduced as "an elegiac fragment from the papers of N."[5] *Povesti* was obviously a suitable collective word for stories of different types and in 1794 Karamzin had published a separate edition of his Marmontel translations under the title *Novye Marmontelevy povesti*. Nevertheless, Karamzin elsewhere refers to Marmontel's stories as *skazki*, calls "Poor Liza" a *skazka* and describes himself as a *skazochnik*. Evidently, he saw no basic difference between the two words.

In addition to *povest'* and *skazka* Karamzin uses other words which illustrate the identification he was seeking between the sentimental story and real life. They are "true story" (byl'), "history" (istoriia), "fable" (nebylitsa), "romance" (roman), and "fiction" (vydumka). Having originally called "The Beautiful Princess" a *skazka*, he then refers to it as a *povest'*, whereas the events of "The Deep Forest" are described as a *starinnaia byl'*. Karamzin called "Natalia" *odna byl', ili istoriia*, which he had heard from his grandfather's grandmother, who had a reputation for *skazki*; within a line he is speaking of the *povest'*. The opening of "The Island of Bornholm" juxtaposes three types of story: *budem rasskazyvat' drug drugu skazki i povesti i sviakie byli* ("We shall tell each other tales and stories and all kinds of true events") and this is followed by the assertion that "I am narrating, narrating the truth and not fiction." This in turn echoes "Poor Liza" (already called a *povest'* and *skazka*), when the author regretted he was writing "not a romance, but a sad true story." In "A Knight of Our Time" Karamzin, characterizing his own story as a *romanicheskaia istoriia*, attacked the fashionable *istoricheskie nebylitsy*. He insists that "I am not a liar and have not invented a single one of his [the hero, Leon's] words or actions," for once more, "you are reading not a romance but a true story."

Karamzin thus was clearly advancing an antithesis between fact and fiction, truth and untruth: on the one side were grouped *istina, byl', povest', istoriia,* and *skazka* and on the other, *vydumka, nebylitsa,* and *roman*. Karamzin recognized a genre distinction be-

tween the short story and the novel, and on publishing a second in-
stallment of "A Knight of Our Time" in 1803, described it as a
roman.[6] Nevertheless, in the context of the truth-untruth polemics
roman always implies an extravagant and formless romance, *neskla-
ditsa*, and as such had been criticized by a long line of writers from
Cervantes to Fielding.

The number of Karamzin's works which fall within the category of *povest'* has fluctuated at the whim of critics and editors. In
the present study sixteen stories are analyzed:[7] "Eugene and Julia"
(1789), "Frol Silin" (1791), "Liodor" (1792), "Poor Liza"
(1792), "Natalia, the Boyar's Daughter" (1792), "The Beautiful
Princess and the Fortunate Dwarf" (1792), "The Island of Bornholm" (1794), "Sierra Morena" (1795), "Athenian Life" ["Afinskaia zhizn'"] (1795), "Tender Friendship in a Lowly Estate"
["Nezhnost' druzhby v nizkom sostoianii"] (1795), "The Deep
Forest" (1795), "Julia" (1796), "Anecdote" ["Anekdot"] (1802),
"My Confession" ["Moia ispoved'"] (1802), "A Knight of Our
Time" (1802–3), "The Sensitive and the Cold" ["Chuvstvitel'nyi
i kholodnyi"] (1803), and "Martha the Mayoress" (1803).[8] Also
included in this chapter is a discussion of hitherto neglected minor
prose pieces, published principally in the *Moscow Journal*, which
are essentially prototypes of the poem in prose.

"Eugene and Julia"

"EUGENE AND JULIA" was Karamzin's attempt to emulate Mme. de
Genlis; its interest lies precisely in the ease with which he adopted
her narrative manner and in his assimilation of characteristic elements from her stories. The very title, linking the names of two
young lovers, is reminiscent of similar pairings in Genlis's work:
"Eugénie et Léonce," "Alphonse et Dalinde," "Daphnis et Pandrose," "Olympie et Théophile." The Russian characteristics of
Karamzin's story are, despite the subtitle, as superficial as his russification of her stories: the mere mention of Moscow and the setting
of a Russian estate. All the other elements in the story are consciously Europeanized, from the portrayal of Eugene and Julia as
noble and virtuous sentimental soul mates to the cultural background—the epigraph in French, the reference to Klopstock's

"*Willkommen silberner Mond*," set to music by Gluck, as well as the required reading of "the works of the true philosophers, who wrote for the good of mankind."

Karamzin's story is nearest of all to Genlis's "Eugénie et Léonce," but differs by its tragic dénouement (Eugene catches a fatal chill on the eve of his marriage to Julia). Genlis's pronounced didacticism inclined her to happy endings; Karamzin, who at this period regarded himself as a "very strange melancholic" and wrote verses on the impossibility of human happiness, saw tragedy as the inevitable fate of all sensitive souls. Nevertheless, in other ways he remains faithful to Genlis. The idealization of the main characters —exemplary virtue, religious devotion, philanthropy, receptiveness to the beauties of nature, poetry, and music, and pure, nascent love, instructed by the birds and bees but directed toward lawful union, and above all, emotional richness, that *chuvstvitel'nost'* without which a character was deprived of the sympathies of author and reader: all this Karamzin found in Genlis, together with the linguistic clichés for every sentimental attitude and situation.

The links between "Eugene and Julia" and Karamzin's later stories are obvious, but Karamzin was to achieve a comparative subtlety of characterization and mastery of construction which are completely absent from his first pale effort.

"Poor Liza"

"POOR LIZA" is likewise a tragic tale, but Karamzin is no longer concerned with a love sanctioned by parents and society (although in nineteenth-century fiction, the ward, exploited and abused by her "protectors" was to become a familiar figure). His subject is unhappy love, caused not only by a flaw in the character of Erast, Liza's lover, but by social factors. Death, which brought unhappiness in "Eugene and Julia," is the release from despair and unhappiness in "Poor Liza." It was Karamzin's introduction of the suicide motif, popularized in *Werther*, into a typical sentimental homage to the fine and sensitive souls to be found among the lower classes of society which assured the success of "Poor Liza."

As Karamzin himself noted, "Poor Liza" was "a simple story" and its theme was anticipated in works he had translated or read. In "Il le fallait" (translated by Karamzin as "Tak dolzhno byt' ")

Marmontel relates the story of a nobleman's marriage to a humble servant, whom he had unjustly slandered but not seduced. Marmontel's ending is happy, but there is a moment when tragedy is imminent: "elle m'a dit, en m'embrassant, qu'elle allait se noyer."[9] This became the tragic dénouement of Karamzin's tale—a dénouement intimated even more clearly in Werther's story of a simple girl who, betrayed in love, commits suicide. The suicide scene was possibly also influenced by Ophelia's death in *Hamlet*, which he had seen in London and commented: "Only Ophelia interested me: a beautiful actress, beautifully attired and so touching in the madness scene."[10] The pastoral setting for his story, the relations between Liza and her mother and their quiet, secluded life—all these were present in another foreign source, Thomson's "autumnal tale" "Lavinia," which Karamzin had twice translated, in prose and verse. Once more, the endings differ, but there is a marked similarity in the characterization of the heroines.

Liza, in fact, conforms to the European stereotype of the peasant heroine—innocence, purity, simplicity, and an infinite power to love. Yet despite the conventions, Karamzin manages to impart some psychological depth to Liza's portrayal, precisely when her ideal qualities are undermined by the demands of "unlawful love." It was only when their virtue and innocence were assailed that Pamela and Clarissa became absorbing characters for the eighteenth-century reader. Karamzin was clearly aware of this; furthermore, he recognized the attraction of their seducers, even though as a moralist, he might naïvely wonder at a London servant girl's preference for Lovelace over Grandison and her lack of regard for Clarissa.[11] Erast, Karamzin's would-be Lovelace, is no less of a stereotype than Liza, but more interesting precisely because he is the instrument of discord and tragedy. He is not evil, merely inconstant and irresponsible: "quite a rich gentleman, with reasonable intelligence and a good heart, good by nature, but weak and fickle." Erast's basic goodness of heart is stressed at the end, when he is tormented by conscience: for the sentimentalist, only the absence of conscience is the indication of the truly evil. Karamzin's criticism of Erast after his rejection of Liza is of a strictly moral order: "My heart bleeds at this minute. I forgot the human being in Erast—I am prepared to curse him—but my tongue does not move—I look at the sky, and a tear rolls down my face." The social issues are concealed and he leaves his readers with the thought that Liza and

Erast are reconciled in heaven, a characteristic sentimental solution
which is suggested again in Karamzin's narrative poem, "Alina."[12]
If Karamzin skirts ultimately the social implications of his tale, they
are earlier clearly delineated, particularly through Liza, and are
closely linked with his use of pastoral motifs and the myth of the
Golden Age.

"Poor Liza" has been called "Karamzin's reminiscences from
the world of Gessner's idylls";[13] the pastoral elements, however, are
not merely used as a backcloth to the action but woven into the
plot and motivate the tragic dénouement.

Liza's beauty made an impression on his heart at their first meeting.
He used to read novels, idylls; he had a lively imagination and often
took himself mentally to those times (which might or might not have
existed), when, if we are to believe the poets, all people wandered carefree through the meadows, bathed in clear springs, kissed like turtle
doves, rested beneath roses and myrtles and in happy idleness spent their
days. It seemed to him that he had found in Liza what his heart had
been seeking. "Nature calls me to its embrace and its pure delights," he
thought and decided to leave society life—at least for a time.

Not only is Karamzin's scepticism about the existence of a Golden
Age apparent but also the likely temporary nature of Erast's enthusiasm. Erast is conscious of playing a part. Not so Liza: she, too,
weaves her own pastoral, but for very different reasons. Seeing a
young shepherd by the river, she sighs "If only he who now occupies
my thoughts had been born a simple peasant, a shepherd" but is
clearly conscious that it is a daydream (Mechta!). It is this realization that a happy love with Erast is impossible which makes Liza
think in terms of shepherds and shepherdesses; for her, they are not
bookish, unreal characters, but a part of her reality, her *possible*
happiness. Subsequently the two concepts merge, although Erast's
fictional world is dominant. Erast arrives and Karamzin remarks
"Her dream was partially fulfilled," but "partially" refers to Erast's
arrival and the affection he shows her, not to a change in his station
in life. Their love affair progresses completely in the spirit of an
idyll; they always meet by the pond and afterwards Liza returns to
her mother and Erast to Moscow—and real life. Erast refuses to let
Liza tell her mother of their love; this would break the illusion
which becomes so complete that Erast himself is near to believing
in it: "I shall live with Liza like a brother with his sister, he

thought, I shall not abuse her love and shall always be happy!" The author immediately chides Erast for not understanding his heart and its changes, and thereby prepares the reader for the imminent crisis in their relationship. Liza's mother, despite her liking Erast, sees her daughter's happiness in marriage to a rich peasant suitor. Erast's reassurances to Liza are once more part of his sentimental fiction, but Liza argues realistically that he will not marry her because she is a peasant. This intrusion of social differences is paralleled by a disillusionment in the realm of feeling. Liza gives herself to Erast, but the very height of their love foreshadows its end. Erast emerges from the world of the idyll into a world of all too familiar sensations: "Liza was no longer for Erast that angel of purity who had earlier inflamed his imagination and entranced his soul. Platonic love was replaced by feelings of which he could not be proud." Inevitably, Erast leaves Liza; despite his moments of sincerity and his final repentance, his conduct was selfish and fraudulent. In his dénouement Karamzin shows himself psychologically and socially more realistic than the high-minded L'vov, who had urged "it is better to marry a peasant girl who is good-natured than a noble and rich countess or princess who is evil-natured and extravagant."[14] Karamzin's true originality in the development of an essentially unoriginal theme lies precisely in his skillful exploitation of the rift between books and reality, ideals and human nature. He has embodied in a work of fiction his own ambivalent attitude to the Golden Age and at the same time expanded the techniques and subject matter of the idyll. In an anonymous essay, published in 1795, "On the Nature of the Idyll" ["O svoistve idillii"], there is an analysis of the themes and characters of the idyll which ends with the view that "innocent pastoral love must be free from all the vices which are caused by the corruption in the city."[15] It is this clash of two cultures which Karamzin exploited, effecting the transition of the traditional idyll into the sentimental short story.

"Tender Friendship in a Lowly Estate"

PERHAPS the most famous line ever written by Karamzin—"for even peasant women know how to love" (ibo i krest'ianki liubit' umeiut) —characterizing incidentally not Liza but her mother, is in itself nothing more than a felicitously phrased version of a sentiment already hackneyed in European and Russian literature. In translating Mme. de Genlis's *Les Veillées du château*, Karamzin encountered such statements as "il [Ambrose, a servant] possédait des vertus sublimes; et sous un extérieur si grossier, il cachait l'âme la plus sensible et la plus elévée" and "la princesse . . . apprit avec autant de plaisir que d'attendrissement, qu'il n'y a point d'états, point de classes où l'on ne puisse trouver les sentimens nobles et généreux."[16] Marmontel frequently wrote, and Karamzin translated, such sentiments as "Ah! la fierté, l'élévation d'âme sont des vertus de la nature" and "Je sais que la fortune est l'idole du monde; mais, parmi les âmes communes, il se retrouve encore des coeurs nobles et généreux."[17] In Russia L'vov had anticipated Karamzin in his preface to *The Russian Pamela* with "we also have tender hearts, great souls in a lowly estate and noble sensibility," a belief he reiterated in *Roza and Liubim*.[18] Nevertheless, Karamzin was directly responsible for inspiring such sentiments in subsequent Russian writers, as is evident from the phrasing of V. Izmailov's "every peasant woman also knows how to feel" (chuvstvovat' umeet i vsiakaia krest'ianka).[19]

Closely linked with this humanitarian aspect of "Poor Liza" are Karamzin's "Frol Silin" and "Tender Friendship in a Lowly Estate." In the second of these, published in the second volume of *Aglaia*, Karamzin is pursuing a dual purpose. On the one hand he is continuing his sentimental propaganda for the "classlessness" of the feeling heart: the typical coda of "Reader! this is no fiction," followed by the pathetic cry of "such souls, such friendships, and in such an estate! – Misanthrope! . . ."; on the other he is insisting on the happiness to be gained within each class. Mme. M*, the noblewoman who "interviews" the two loving sisters, Masha and Aniuta, asks them "Thus you are completely content with your condition, my friends" and is at once reassured "Certainly, madame!" Karamzin was continuing the sermon he had preached in "Palemon and Daphnis," insisting on the compatibility of spiritual contentment and material insufficiency. What is more, Mme. M* who "always goes to see them and never parts from them without emotion" is seeking emotional satisfaction and not attempting to ease their lot. The blame for their straitened circumstances is laid on Masha's late husband and on "those people who led him astray and taught him evil things."[20]

This story is connected with "Poor Liza" and with every passage Karamzin wrote in which his peasant characters speak by the contrast between his willingness to attribute fine qualities to his characters and his reluctance to reproduce their true manner of speech. Liza speaks like a well-bred young lady; Masha and Aniuta are sentimental heroines par excellence in word and deed. The theoretical justification for such an approach was provided by Marmontel in the third of the stories Karamzin translated for the *Moscow Journal*. Dervis objects to the language Juliette puts into the mouth of her nurse, whose story she is relating: "Voilà, reprit Dervis d'un air un peu malin, voilà, pour une paysanne, un langage bien élégant! Monsieur, répliqua Juliette, je ne répète pas son langage à la lettre; je le traduis fidèlement."[21] The peasantry, freed from any impurities in speech and habits which would adulterate its spiritual qualities, is thus offered up for the admiration of the privileged classes.[22]

"Frol Silin"

FROL SILIN is the only male character in Karamzin's gallery of admirable peasants, who, incidentally, are never serfs. L'vov had been particularly anxious to show that Russia had its Pamelas and Basiles (a Marmontel peasant hero) and Karamzin's creation of Frol Silin gave new impetus and direction to an already existing genre.[23] It is the form which Karamzin gave to his description of Frol Silin's good deeds and generosity to his less fortunate neighbors during a famine which is of particular interest. "Frol Silin" is a sentimental version of the classical ode, with prose replacing verse and a peasant extolled instead of a prince: "Let Virgils extol Augustus! Let eloquent flatterers praise the magnanimity of the mighty! I wish to praise Frol Silin, a simple countryman, and my praise will consist in a description of his deeds which are known to me." It is a curious and probably unknowing response to the following lines in the satirical journal *Miscellany* [*Smes'*], published in 1769: "Does [the peasant] possess virtues? Even that I don't know. Although poets praise virtues in a lyrical voice, I have never read a panegyrical ode to a peasant or to the nag on which he ploughs."[24]

"The Beautiful Princess and the Fortunate Dwarf"

A LESS controversial use of a traditional formula is evident in "The Beautiful Princess and the Fortunate Dwarf," which begins "Once upon a time in a certain kingdom in a certain state there lived a good king." The subtitle indicates that Karamzin's intent was far from straightforward: in one sense, his story is a traditional fairy tale but in another it is a modern parody, in which he laughs gently at contemporary customs as well as at old literary conventions. As Sipovskii has noted, the theme of the love of a beautiful princess for a hunchbacked dwarf is near to Perrault's "Riquet à la houpe,"[25] but Karamzin's tale is best seen against the tradition of the parodying fairy tale, exploited by Mikhail Chulkov in his *The Mocker* [*Peresmeshnik, ili Slavenskie skazki*] (1766–68).

Published in the *Moscow Journal* in August 1792, "The Beautiful Princess and the Fortunate Dwarf" is linked with "Natalia, the Boyar's Daughter," which appeared in the October–November issue, by the theme of physical and spiritual beauty. In "Natalia" Karamzin writes: "Socrates said that physical beauty is always an indication of spiritual beauty . . . And my own experience does not contradict that opinion and I am loath to believe the anecdote of the Leipzig student and the ugly Jew, which Anton Wall relates in his *Bagetellen*."[26] Natalia is consequently beautiful in body and soul; so is the heroine of Karamzin's fairy tale, but not the hero, who true to the later Romantic formula, conceals rare spiritual beauty and intellectual accomplishments beneath an ugly exterior. Sturm's *Betrachtungen* contains an article contrasting the song of the nightingale with its commonplace appearance, which gives rise to "a number of useful and edifying thoughts. For instance, we may learn from her this truth, that homeliness of body is sometimes united with amiable qualities, and does not preclude mental beauty. How unjustly do those act, who, attaching themselves only to the features of the face, and qualities merely external, neither praise nor blame anything but what strikes their senses; and who despise, or treat with asperity, those of their fellow-creatures who have bodily defects: let us learn to judge with more equity. Yes, a man deprived of the advantages of figure and fortune, may manifest in his conduct a wise and holy mind, and thus render himself worthy of our esteem."[27] Sturm hereby pays homage to God's wisdom; characteristically, Karamzin uses the contrast to illustrate the transforming power of secular love: "I love him, said the Princess—and after these words, the dwarf appeared almost handsome to the populace."

"The Deep Forest"

IN "The Deep Forest" Karamzin again exposed the conventions of the genre of the fairy tale. He indicates that his tale had been "composed in one day on the following set words: Balcony, forest, ball, horse, hut, meadow, raspberry canes, oak, Ossian, stream, grave, music," and that these words were to be used in the given order. Karamzin sought to encourage his public, child and adult, to play literary games in verse and prose. He had been impressed by Lavater's daughter's attempts at such games,[28] and he himself left several examples in verse. Karamzin deliberately uses stock devices from the fairy tale—wondrous and mysterious happenings, white rabbits guiding him through a wood, balls of fire—and at the end gives a "scientific" explanation of events, in line with his general scepticism toward the supernatural and allegedly inexplicable. Despite the generally light and playful tone of the narrative, Karamzin's preoccupation with the Reign of Terror again obtrudes: the old hermit in the forest forsees "the times of horror," when "the rivers will flow with blood and the groans of the unfortunate will drown the noises of the storm."

"Natalia, the Boyar's Daughter"

IN HIS introduction to "Poor Liza" Karamzin comments on the engravings on the doors of the Danilov Monastery: "All this refreshes in my mind the history of our country—the sad history of those times, when the fierce Tartars and Lithuanians ravaged with fire and sword the regions surrounding the Russian capital, and when unhappy Moscow, like a defenseless widow, awaited help from God alone in her cruel misfortunes." It is to the time of Muscovy's struggle against the Lithuanians that Karamzin turns for the setting of "Natalia, the Boyar's Daughter." Natalia is Karamzin's first historical tale and in this sense the direct predecessor of "Martha the Mayoress," but it is no less a truly sentimental story, closely linked with all Karamzin's stories in the *Moscow Journal*.

The sentimentalizing of a nation's past was a characteristic Karamzin shared with a number of European writers, although in his translations from Marmontel he even intensifies the French author's praise of old French virtues.[29] "Natalia" opens with a long paean to "those times, when Russians were Russians, when they dressed in their own clothes, walked in their own way, lived according to their own customs and spoke with their tongue in harmony with their heart, that is to say, they spoke what they thought." Criticizing contemporary aping of the West, he attempts to instill a sense of pride and purpose in the Russian gentry. Liodor, in the story of the same name, "affirmed than then [in times gone by] there was more *spirit* in our gentry, more characteristic *firmness* than nowadays, when in the chase for the brilliant *exterior* of other nations we have abandoned all by which God and Nature wished to distinguish us from other nations—abandoned all, forgotten *ourselves* and become students in all things and masters in none."[30] It is a theme which is developed at length in "A Knight of Our Time" in the description of the provincial gentry of the middle of the eighteenth century.

"Natalia" is Karamzin's attempt to make old *Rus'* the homespun counterpart of Arcadia; although as an enlightener, he could not recommend a return to the past, he was willing to develop its possibilities in fiction. In his eagerness to use the *starina* for moral criticism of contemporary society he confuses what is worthy of praise with what is not. Oblivious to the irony, he comments on the peasants whom Natalia is watching: "peasants who even in our time have in no way changed, who dress the same, live and work as previously they had lived and worked, and among all the changes and disguises still present us the true Russian physiognomy."

This moral preoccupation as well as the humorous style in which the story is told link "Natalia" with "The Beautiful Princess." Karamzin frequently breaks his narrative to reveal the artificiality of a given literary device or the alleged change in moral attitudes. Sterne would seem to be his mentor in this type of jocular, self-conscious literary technique; indeed at one point in "Natalia" Karamzin writes: "Dear reader, forgive me this digression! Not only Sterne was a slave of his pen." The two stories are equally close in their "historical" aspect. "The Beautiful Princess" is obviously first and foremost a fairy tale, with a timeless setting and action, whereas "Natalia" is set in a specified historical period and loosely based on certain historical events and facts. Nevertheless, the treatment in both stories is stylized and conventional. This extends equally to the use of language. In "The Beautiful Princess" he uses in italics such expressions as "a patterned cloth" (skatert' branaia) and "an undecipherable deed" (tarabarskaia gramota) to give a period flavor to his story and elsewhere "translates" into a modern idiom supposedly period documents—this he was also to do in "Martha the Mayoress." In "Natalia" he draws attention to his technique in a footnote to a conversation between Natalia and her lover Aleksei: "The reader will guess that lovers in olden days did not speak exactly the same as they speak here, but we would be unable now to understand their language. It was necessary only *in some way* to imitate the old coloring."

A comparison equally instructive for illustrating the sentimental character of "Natalia" and for illuminating the lineage of Natalia herself and the nature of the central conflict is with "Poor Liza." Despite the fact that Liza is a peasant's daughter living at the end of the eighteenth century and Natalia is the daughter of a mighty seventeenth-century boyar, they are essentially one and the same sentimental heroine. Both are young, innocent, naïve; both are unable to read or write; both are ignorant of love until nature conveniently awoke them to its mysteries; both become involved in clandestine love affairs resulting in a subsequent change of allegiance from parents to lovers. What differentiates them is their ultimate fate. For Liza there is disillusionment and death, for Natalia marriage and happiness, eventual recognition for Aleksei from the Tsar and Natalia's father. Liza yielded to Erast and "it seemed that Nature was *lamenting* Liza's lost innocence"; the thunder rolled and Liza, anticipating Ostrovskii's Katerina, was afraid "lest the thunder should kill me like a sinner." Natalia, however, only yielded to Aleksei when they were married, for earlier "the goddess of purity presided unseen in Natalia's room." The use of the word *neporochnost'* is an echo of the scene in "Poor Liza."

It is arguable that Karamzin was motivated by social prejudices in distinguishing between the fates of his heroines, since Aleksei, although an outlaw, is Natalia's social equal and the restoration of his former titles is merely a final stage to complete their happiness; yet the difference would seem to result equally from the different literary conventions Karamzin was following. Despite the nearness of the heroines and the sentimental coloring, "Poor Liza" was pre-eminently a new phenomenon, a product of the interest in the peasant and the simple, often tragic events of everyday life, in essence an anecdote; "Natalia," on the contrary, was in the earlier tradition of the adventure novel, reworked in a modern idiom. Indicative of this tradition is the character of Aleksei Liuboslavskii, the son of a banished aristocrat, attempting to prove his father's innocence; courageous, handsome, noble, he is the male counterpart of Natalia—a pair of ideal lovers, physically and spiritually beautiful, rewarded after a series of vicissitudes by happy marriage and parental blessing. Likewise the action itself—Aleksei's band of friends living in the forest, his success as a warrior, Natalia's transvestite exploits in battle—was in keeping with the type of novel Karamzin, through his hero Leon in "A Knight of Our Time," recalls reading in his youth, where amidst "a multitude of various people on the stage, a multitude of wondrous actions, adventures and the workings of Fate" the heroes and heroines remain faithful and virtuous.

Karamzin was reverting to an old tradition, but with ironic detachment, manipulating and parodying its devices, "psychologizing" its characters, compressing it into a new form. At the same time "Natalia" is a sentimentalist's polemic with the motives and actions of the characters in the seventeenth-century "Story of Frol Skobeev" ["Povest' o Frole Skobeeve"], reasserting the power of love and the attractiveness of personal and civic virtues.[31] In its turn, "Natalia" carried its influence into the nineteenth-century, and a number of scholars have explored the possible parallels with Pushkin's *Eugene Onegin*.[32] "Natalia" provides just one example of Pushkin's wide use (particularly in *The Tales of Belkin*) of themes and characters from Karamzin's work for the purposes of imitation and parody.

"Liodor"

"LIODOR," begun in February 1792, was never completed. Despite Petrov's prompting and an intimation to Dmitriev that he was preparing to continue the story,[33] Karamzin in fact showed little inclination to do so. Instead, he went on to write "Natalia" and "The Beautiful Princess." Although "Liodor" was never included in any edition of Karamzin's work during his lifetime, it is as "finished" as certain other pieces that were. "Liodor" apart, "The Island of Bornholm," "A Knight of Our Time," as well as the poem "Il'ia of Murom" all promised sequels when first published, and in each case the promise was unfulfilled. It would seem that Karamzin had simply lost interest, or, more probably, they were already finished in the sense that Karamzin had achieved his initial artistic intention. He was continually experimenting, indicating new genres, new subject matter, pointing the way for others; but the fragment, the incomplete manuscript, the mysteriously inconclusive scene or anecdote were recognized and fashionable genres of sentimentalism and preromanticism. "Sierra Morena," for example, was originally subtitled "An elegiac fragment . . ." and the sketch "The Village" ["Derevnia"] was also called "A Fragment."[34] P. N. Sakulin believed that "Il'ia of Murom" was deliberately left unfinished because Karamzin's interest was in the love scene and the initial delineation of Il'ia's character rather than in the description of his epic deeds.[35] "The Island of Bornholm" is more obviously a complete work, since its effect is directly dependent on its atmosphere of vagueness and mystery. Bolotov, Karamzin's contemporary, waited impatiently and naïvely for the sequel and the elucidation of the mystery.[36] The story intrigued even the Dowager Empress Maria Fedorovna who years later, in 1815, enquired about the ultimate fate of the unfortunate lovers.[37]

"Liodor" ends at a highly intriguing juncture, which is curiously and exactly paralleled in "A Knight of Our Time." Liodor, who is relating his life story to the narrator and his friends, describes how he saw a beautiful Turkish girl undressing in the moonlight by a pool. He fainted from intense emotion at the sight and was roused by the yapping of her little dog, which chased him from the garden. In "A Knight of Our Time," the young Leon lies in the grass and watches the Countess Mirova bathing, until he is put to flight by her three English hounds. The tone of the narrative is quite different, but the incident described identical. In both cases Karamzin had judged the moment appropriate for ending his stories; the reader is left to exercise his own imagination. The "unsaid" was as important as the "inexpressible" in sentimentalism's aesthetics.

"Liodor" has been described as another attempt to introduce motifs from *Werther* into a "Russian" story.[38] If "Poor Liza" is a development of a secondary theme in Goethe's novel, then "Liodor" shows an orientation on the character and life story of Werther himself, combined with a strong Ossianic influence that was probably in itself suggested by *Werther* rather than an indication of Karamzin's own blending of two sympathetic authors.[39] Equally important is Karamzin's fusion of these literary influences with details from his own autobiography, which produced a new variation on the characteristic image of the storyteller in Karamzin's work.

The narrator, the inevitable "I" of earlier stories, who acts as intermediary between the readers and the events of the story and invites their participation, gives to the narrative both a sense of authenticity and a feeling of intimacy. In the early tales the narrator is always the same person, the sympathetic man of feeling, who dictates the mood: elegiac sadness in "Poor Liza": "Ah! I love those subjects which touch my heart and make me shed tears of tender sorrow," bantering humor in "Natalia": "I hear your *sweetthundering* words: 'Continue, my dear great-grandson!' So I will continue, I will, and arming myself with a pen, I courageously begin the history of 'Natalia, the Boyar's Daughter'" and in "Liodor" autumnal melancholy: "The cold winds had already blown paleness and darkness into sad nature, when Agathon, Izidor and I left for the country—to enjoy melancholic autumn." Using the introductions to modulate the tone of the subsequent narrative, the narrator emphasizes the reality of his heroes and heroines in the codas to the stories; on three occasions (in "Eugene and Julia," "Poor Liza," and "Natalia") he describes a sentimental visit to their graves.

In "Liodor" the narrator plays a more important role in the action of the story: his life in the country with his friends and his meeting and conversations with Liodor form the frame to Liodor's account of his life. Furthermore, the identification of the narrator with the author of *Letters of a Russian Traveler* is easily appreciated by the reader of the *Moscow Journal:* the narrator refers to his favorite walking stick, mentioned in the early letters, and to Aglaia, already apostrophized in "The Bird of Paradise," "Innocence," and "The New Year," as well as in the *Letters.* Occasionally, the allusion is to be understood only by Aglaia herself, as when she is asked to imagine Izidor after his serious illness, or when the narrator apologizes to her for reviving the sad memories linked with the deaths of both Izidor and Agathon. It is at such times that the reader feels, and is required to feel, that he is eavesdropping on a private conversation. In addition, "Liodor" is related to the content of *Letters* by other details and references: such are the narrator's comments on the complexities of Kant's metaphysics, the "truth" of physiognomy, the mention of "my friend Lavater," and the view of the French as the most attractive nation in Europe.

"The Island of Bornholm"

IN THE last pages of "Liodor" the hero describes his travels and his impressions of peoples and places—Leipzig, France (Paris and Marseilles), and Spain. In his almanac *Aglaia* Karamzin develops this tendency to place a Russian hero in a foreign, exotic setting, instead of writing stories set in Russia, as he had done in the *Moscow Journal.* "The Island of Bornholm," "Sierra Morena," and "Athenian Life" form a triptych of stories which represent a further stage of development beyond the earlier sentimental story of the "Poor Liza" type toward romanticism proper.

"The Island of Bornholm" was a new event in Russian literature, a successful Russian version of a Gothic tale which intrigued and fascinated Karamzin's contemporaries. Karamzin would seem to be familiar with the work of the leading British exponents of the genre, Horace Walpole, Clara Reeve, and Anna Radcliffe, although the only oblique reference at this period was Karamzin's pilgrimage to Strawberry Hill.[40] Mrs. Radcliffe's *The Mysteries of Udolpho* coincided with the publication of the first volume of *Aglaia* (1794), in which "The Island of Bornholm" appeared, but she had already published such works as *The Sicilian Romance* (1790) and *The Romance of the Forest* (1791) with the recurring figure of the persecuted maiden, shut away in a castle dungeon, which Karamzin introduced into his own work. Karamzin's only reference to Mrs. Radcliffe is in his essay "Historical Reminiscences and Notes on the Way to the Monastery of the Holy Trinity" ["Istoricheskie vospominaniia i zamechaniia na puti k Troitse"], written in 1803 when her European fame was at its height. He has a clear understanding of the "scenic props" required by the genre: "Mrs. Radcliffe might have used this palace [built by the Empress Elizabeth at Taininskoe] and composed a horror novel about it; there is here everything necessary for her art: empty halls, corridors, high staircases, remains of rich ornaments, and (what is most important of all) the wind blows in the chimneys, whistles through the broken windows and bangs doors, bringing down showers of gilt. I myself walked up its rotting staircases when it was thundering terribly and the lightning was flashing; it could indeed work strongly on the imagination."[41] In the *Moscow Journal* Karamzin had also translated Wieland's "Cordelia" and Florian's "Valérie" with their elements of the mysterious and the supernatural; in "Poor Liza" he describes "the gloomy, Gothic towers of the Simonov Monastery" and the howling of the wind through the empty rooms and over the grass-covered graves.

Soon after landing on the island of Bornholm the narrator comes across "a large Gothic building, surrounded by a deep moat and a high wall." Thereafter every detail is designed to sustain the feeling of suspense and the aura of mystery. Led into the castle by a strange, silent man in black, the narrator describes how "in the first hall, surrounded by a Gothic colonnade, there hung a lamp directing a pale, weak light onto rows of gilded columns, which had begun to fall apart from age." He meets the owner of the house, burdened with years and a great and deep sorrow. During the night his sleep is disturbed by nightmares of vengeful knights in armor and winged monsters, whereupon he ventures into the garden and finds in a dungeon "a young, pale woman in a black dress." "You perhaps know my story, but if not, don't ask me, for God's sake, don't ask," but a series of hints and allusions makes the reason for her imprisonment and her relations both with the old man and the original young stranger on the Gravesend beach all too obvious.

The narrator learns the true story, "a most terrible story—a story which you will not hear now, my friends; it will be left for another time. Now I shall only say that I learned the secret of the stranger of Gravesend—a horrible secret!"

Obviously there would be no sequel and structurally the work is complete, in a way the other "unfinished" works are not. Bolotov himself, in demanding a sequel, shows that he wanted stated in black and white what he already understood. Karamzin had brought to his Gothic tale not only its exterior decor and its qualities of mystery and suspense but also its typical characters, particularly the star-crossed lovers, and the *frisson* of the age—incest. The song of the young stranger, which introduced the theme, became extremely popular with the Russian public and was ultimately parodied by Gogol' through Khlestakov in *The Government Inspector*.

A further aspect of the story which contributed toward its effect and appeal is its relation to *Letters of a Russian Traveler*. In "Liodor" the details to be appreciated by the reader of *Letters* lend authenticity to the tale; "The Island of Bornholm," on the other hand, is related as an incident which happened to him during the journey to a similar audience of intimate friends. Avoiding discrepancies between his "fact" and his "fiction," Karamzin notes in both works his seasickness and his drenching from the high waves. Although *Letters* contains no mention of Bornholm, the setting for his story would seem to have been inspired by his reading and translating Ossian on board ship: "What a holiday for my imagination, filled with Ossian! I wanted to see the wild shores of Norway on the portside, but my gaze was lost in the darkness."[42]

"Sierra Morena"

KARAMZIN's imagination again enjoyed a "holiday" with the composition of "Sierra Morena." Liodor indeed had called Spain "that fatherland of novels, which was always represented in my imagination in an attractive light." Spain, as the conventional setting for stories of strong passions, is found in stories by Florian and Marmontel and Karamzin's Spanish local color is little more than details recollected from a story by Mme. de Genlis which he had translated for *Children's Reading*.[43] The names of places and characters are selected primarily for their melodic qualities in an impressive prelude to the tale.[44] In a recent study a suggestive parallel was made between Karamzin's story and the ballad of "Brave Alonso and Beautiful Imogine," which appeared in chapter 9 of Lewis's *The Monk*.[45] This, on the one hand, reflects Karamzin's continued interest in the English Gothic novel and his immediate creative response, and, on the other, would date "Sierra Morena" at the beginning of 1795.

Nevertheless, Elvira and Alonso are pale figures and secondary to the narrator, who is concerned with an account and analysis of his own feelings, which range from initial happiness to ultimate misanthropic disillusionment. The narrator for the major part of the tale is the expected Karamzin sentimental hero, but precisely from the moment he is rejected by a remorseful Elvira he shows signs of a rebellious and bitter nature, a man at war with the world. Like Werther he is rejected by the woman he loves and the world becomes "cold and dark"; he travels, seeking fashionable philosophical solace amidst the ruins of Palmyra, consumed by melancholy and "keenly feeling the futility of all sublunary things." In Europe he becomes "the plaything of the malice of people once loved by me" and he inveighs against the "cold world. I have left you! Mad beings called men, I have left you! Rage in your wild frenzies, tear and murder each other! My heart is dead for you and your fate does not move it." Karamzin's hero is not a Romantic rebel, but at such moments there is an undoubted anticipation of his characteristic attitudes.

This condemnation of the world is traceable to Karamzin's strained relations with his friends on his return from Europe but more particularly to his disillusionment in the course of the French Revolution: it is a disillusionment which runs as a leitmotif through his private letters, his publicist and philosophical writings, and his fiction. His anguish was deep and sincere, but it was also a source of creative strength, manifest above all in "Athenian Life."

"Athenian Life"

THE STORY is built on the contrast between the real world of horrors which the author cannot face and the ideal world to which his imagination takes him. Karamzin's thesis is that "we are more learned than the Greeks, but the Greeks were more intelligent than us," for they were concerned above all with the "important art of happiness."[46] To escape the modern world Karamzin would willingly exchange his frockcoat for a Greek tunic and "in moments of pleasant thought, I do exchange it—I wrap myself in a purple cloak (in my imagination, of course), cover my head with a large, floppy hat and step out in Alcibiades's shoes with measured pace and philosophical solemnity—into the square in ancient Athens." The account of such an imaginary visit is Karamzin's attempt to show people of very different interests and views living together in harmony. Karamzin sees happy toilers in the fields, hears Plato discoursing on Socrates; he visits the theatre and attends a feast where the subjects of conversation are love, poetry, philosophy, and wine, and the guests "all swear to live and die as friends of the gods and men." But the dream is shattered, the beguiling illusion ended: "O my friends! everything passes, everything disappears! Where is Athens? Where is Hippius' house? Where is the temple of pleasure? Where is my Greek cloak?—Dreams! dreams! I sit alone in my study in the country, in a poor dressing gown and see nothing before me, except a guttering candle, a used sheet of paper and the Hamburg newspapers, which tomorrow morning (not before, because I wish to sleep peacefully tonight) will inform me of the terrible madness of our enlightened contemporaries."

Although clearly rooted in the circumstances of Karamzin's personal crisis, "Athenian Life" is a notable manifestation of the Hellenist dream. In his essay "Melodor to Philalet" ["Melodor k Filaletu"], which was published in the same volume of *Aglaia*, Karamzin described Greece's appeal as "there everything entices the eye, the soul, the heart; there reside in splendor Lycurguses and Solons, Codruses and Leonidases, Socrateses and Platos, Homers and Sophocleses, Phidiases and Zeuxises—in a word, there we should marvel at the refined workings of the mind and morality."[47] Such an image of Greece Schiller idealized in his *Uber naive und sentimentalische Dichtung*, which was published soon after Karamzin's work.

A possible influence on Karamzin's attempt to convey the spirit of Athenian life was Wieland's *Geschichte des Agathon* (1766–67), for which he expressed particular admiration,[48] but the direct source of ideas and themes was the abbé Jean-Jacques Barthélemy's *Voyage du jeune Anacharsis* (1788), a work he consistently championed throughout his career. "Athenian Life" follows in broad outline and often in exact detail Barthélemy's account in the second volume of Anacharsis's life in Athens.[49]

The formal independence of Karamzin's work is obvious; above all "Athenian Life" is remarkable for its pronounced lyrical qualities, underscored by typical Karamzinian syntactical devices in the prose and by the introduction of eight poems and songs, which evoke a variety of moods and display Karamzin's metrical virtuosity. The introduction of songs into the text of his stories began with "Liodor," where he quotes the Italian song sung by the Turkish girl; in "The Island of Bornholm," the stranger's song, given as a translation from Danish, has an important structural function. Karamzin consciously used the songs in these three stories to heighten their foreign and exotic background; apart from a few lines from his own poem "Virtue" ["Dobrodetel' "], quoted in "A Knight of Our Time" but without any specific lyrical or structural intent, Karamzin avoids their use in his pronouncedly "Russian" tales.

The Poems in Prose

THE LYRICAL qualities of "Athenian Life," evident in almost all of the stories published in the *Moscow Journal* and *Aglaia*, link it with other minor prose forms which Karamzin cultivated precisely in this first period of his work. Karamzin's experiments with the prose idyll led him from initial translations of Gessner to an original reworking of "Der Sturm" and ultimately to the transformation of the genre into the sentimental short story in "Poor Liza." In "Frol Silin" Karamzin attempted a prose counterpart to the lofty panegyrical ode, an experiment consistent with his belief that the epic also could be written in prose. He also created a group of works which may justifiably be termed poems in prose, even if the theory and practice of such a genre belong essentially to the nineteenth century.

Two such poems in prose were included by Professor Iu. M. Lotman in his edition of Karamzin's complete verse in 1966.[50] The first is a version of a song Karamzin heard in Zurich during his travels and the other is the dedication to the second volume of

Aglaia; both are short in length and with an apparent stanzaic arrangement and are thus more easily accommodated in a collection of Karamzin's verse. Nevertheless, the prose poem, particularly as it was practiced by Baudelaire in French and Turgenev in Russian, has a much more supple and varied form than Lotman would seem to grant it. It embraces not merely the prose equivalent of a lyric poem but also of descriptive and narrative poems; its length varies from a few lines to several pages; it may or may not have the formal organization of a poem, and, although a hybrid, it has its own rhythm, which is that of prose. "A certain harmony, which is not inferior to the harmony of verse" Karamzin found in Gessner's prose and brought to his own.[51]

In addition to the two works designated by Lotman, six further works may be included in the category of poems in prose:[52] "Innocence ["Nevinnost"], "The Dedication of the Grove" ["Posviashchenie kushchi"], "The Bird of Paradise" ["Raiskaia ptichka"], all dating from 1791; "The New Year" ["Novyi god"], "Night" ["Noch"] , "The Countryside" ["Derevnia"], all from 1792. "Innocence," "The New Year," and "The Bird of Paradise" are connected with the dedication to *Aglaia* as elaborate compliments to Aglaia-Pleshcheeva, but are distinct from it in their allegorical character, highly artificial in sentiment and diction, abounding in sentimental periphrases but syntactically highly organized. "The Dedication of the Grove" is close to them in form and language but it is an invocation to Fantasy, which combines motifs from Thomson and Goethe's "Meine Göttin."[53] Thomson's influence is clearly discernible in "The Countryside," which is essentially a work in two parts: a carefully wrought lyrical prelude followed by a description of "My day" in the country. "The Bird of Paradise," when first published, had a footnote explaining that "the idea of this piece was taken from a Russian folk tale and shows that in Russia we have long understood the wondrous effect of music on the human heart. I find in this fiction something poetic."[54] This thematic link with a Russian folk tale has led one Soviet scholar to term "The Bird of Paradise" a short story,[55] but Karamzin himself had adopted the neutral term of *piesa.* A stronger story line is evident in "Night," although the eventual meeting of the lovers is a mere finale to the highly charged description of the lover's emotions as he awaits his Chloe.

"Night" provides a good example of the degree of formal

organization Karamzin achieved in his prose poems. It is written in
twelve paragraphs, ranging from five to twenty-two lines in the
large type of the *Moscow Journal* or between four and sixteen lines
in the 1848 edition. The opening four small paragraphs form a
lyrical introduction to the piece. In the first three paragraphs Karamzin makes insistent use of the imperative form of the verb (four
times in paragraphs one and three and three times in paragraph
two), addressing the moon, the stream, the trees and flowers. These
paragraph-stanzas represent a sequence of appeals to the senses—to
the sight, the hearing, the smell. The fourth paragraph reverts to
the hearing, in a climax of sound and melody in the nightingale's
song. Paragraphs five to eight form a counterpoint of examples of
love and lovelessness against a background of nature, until the re-
currence of Chloe's name (mentioned in the opening paragraph) in
paragraph eight anticipates the dénouement, which is prepared in
paragraph nine by the uniting of the motifs of the opening four
paragraphs: "High has climbed the clear moon; brightly shines the
murmuring stream; the trees, flowers, grass pour forth their am-
brosia; loudly sings the nightingale from the branches of the rosemary." The accelerated movement of the final paragraphs is emphasized by the typical Karamzinian device of the meaningful dash.
The lovers embrace and faint from their emotion and the piece
finishes with a rapturous apostrophe to "Love, Love, the reason and
aim of our life." There is not a trace of realistic description or
psychology; Karamzin's aim is to recreate a typical set piece of
rococo sensualism, an artefact of well-worn verbal formulas,
moulded by alliteration, clausal parallelism, and poetic cadences.

The literary precedent and inspiration for Karamzin's prose
poems would seem to come from Herder's *Paramythien*, a new
genre of the *Nachdichtung*, which has been described as "an extremely free translation or paraphrase of materials from foreign
literatures, especially the classical, with far-reaching modifications
to make them acceptable to contemporary readers."[56] Karamzin
called them "the tender products of a fertile fantasy, which breathe
a Greek spirit and are as beautiful as a morning rose."[57] This appreciation appeared in the *Moscow Journal* three months after the
publication of two of Herder's *Paramythien*, "Die Lilie und die
Rose" and "Nacht und Tag," allegedly not translated by Karamzin
himself.[58] These were followed in the next issue by Karamzin's

"Innocence," which has distinct similarities with "Die Lilie und die Rose." "Innocence," "The New Year," "Night," and particularly "The Dedication of the Grove" contain numerous references to Greek mythology and Karamzin resorts to footnotes to explain their application to his readers; "The Bird of Paradise," on the other hand, shows his use of a Russian source for similar aims.

"Julia"

IF KRESTOVA's dating of "Sierra Morena" is accurate, it would have been written shortly after "Julia," which was seemingly completed at the end of 1794 for inclusion in a never published third volume of *Aglaia* and eventually appeared separately at the beginning of 1796. "Julia" represents a new departure in Karamzin's fiction and emphasizes the essential Protean nature of Karamzin's undertakings, such as suggested in his poem "Proteus" (1798). Karamzin required of contemporary drama a faithful representation of society, one aspect of which was the use of first names and patronymics rather than conventional or "meaningful" names; it was a requirement, however, which he ignores in his prose fiction. All his heroes and heroines bear conventional, "international" first names: Julia and Eugene, Liza and Erast, Elvira and Alonso, Liodor, Agathon, Izidor. A necessary exception is his historical tale "Natalia." "Julia" (1796) continues the tradition with Julia herself, Aris, and a Prince N*. In addition, for the first time he introduces "meaningful" names, which characterize the person and are directly linked with the traditions of the eighteenth-century Russian comedy and satirical journals. Legkoum (Featherbrain), Pustoslov (Windbag) and Khrabron (Braggart) are three of Julia's typical admirers, amusingly and economically portrayed. In "A Knight of Our Time" Karamzin resorts to the same device to indicate the positive virtues of his "provincial matadors."

It is not so much this satirical note, already evident in a more general way in "Natalia" and "The Beautiful Princess," as the depiction of fashionable society which sets "Julia" apart from Karamzin's earlier work. An early prototype of the Russian *svetskaia povest'*, "Julia" is particularly interesting for the introduction of a faceless, gossipy, ill-informed, Griboedovian "public opinion." It gives an illusion of depth to the main characters, who stand out precisely because they have a definite personality, a "face." The negative portrayal of society is an essential aspect of the story's main theme.

The superiority of country life over that in the city was an *idée reçue* of sentimentalism and Karamzin had set his previous "Russian" stories in the country. The opposition is largely implicit and little attempt is made to depict city life; only in "Poor Liza" is there a hint of its corrupting influence. By contrast, "Julia" makes the opposition explicit: not only does the action alternate between Moscow and Aris's country home, but the characters themselves embody different aspects of the theme. Aris, quiet and unspectacular, is the symbol of natural conduct. He is governed by his heart and the dictates of conscience and decency; he represents the joys of family life, constant, if unexciting, love. Prince N* is a society lion and habitué of the salon, the cynical advocate of a "love without chains" philosophy. Between them stands Julia, a typical sentimental heroine of the complex variety, a society beauty, calculating and egotistical, but not immoral or corrupt. She is a version of Marmontel's Hortense de Livernon who "était née avec une âme honnête, un coeur sensible, et un esprit léger,"[59] or the female counterpart of Erast in "Poor Liza." Aris's explanation of her character is that she is fundamentally virtuous but easily led astray by "the immodest wish to please, the fruit of imprudent upbringing and bad example." She wavers between Aris and the prince, only temporarily happy, soon seeking change and distraction. Her final conversion comes when she achieves the required balance of heart and mind and realizes that true happiness is to be found in her role as a mother, living not for herself but for another, away from society and its futility.

References to works by Rousseau provide a commentary on the basic theme of the story: when Julia begins to tire of country life she shows her change of heart by criticizing a passage Aris was reading from *La Nouvelle Héloïse* on the "bliss of mutual love," but it is to *Émile* that she turns in order to "prepare herself for the calling of a mother." Yet "Julia" is not a Rousseau-inspired work; it merely reflects the diluted Rousseauism which was part of the general equipment of the sentimentalist writer. It is essentially a Marmontelesque narrative, as its French translator de Bouilliers[60] and the anonymous Russian reviewer in the *Patriot* noted.[61] Recent commentators, particularly P. Brang, have demonstrated the influence of Anton Wall's work,[62] although Sipovskii earlier pointed to the close similarities in plot with Marmontel's "L'heureux divorce."[63] "Julia" is truly a *conte moral*, preaching a code of homely morality, possibly inspired by Karamzin's reflections on his own intensified social life.

Despite the continuing tension between his love of florid periphrasis and his structurally well-organized stories, Karamzin achieves considerable psychological depth and subtlety. Not only does Julia herself exhibit a greater complexity than Liza or Natalia or even Erast, but she is surrounded by other carefully delineated characters in Aris and Prince N*. If the theme of the tale is the opposition of natural and unnatural values, exemplified by these three characters, the plot relies on a manipulation of the stock device of the "eternal triangle." The story develops according to the formula: Julia—Aris—Prince N*, exit Aris. After the prince abandons Julia, the formula is repeated, but with the significant change that Julia is by now Aris's wife. The parallel between these first two stages of the story is emphasized by the letters that Prince N* in the first instance and Aris in the second write to Julia. The prince's letter of rejection allows the repeat of the triangle; Aris's letter—an amusing anticipation of Lopukhov's "I am leaving the stage" note in Chernyshevskii's novel *What Is To Be Done [Chto delat']*—occasions the dénouement. The happy and moral ending results from the formation of a new triangle: Julia—her son, Erast—Aris. This is made possible initially by Julia's repentance and rejection of the prince, although, as his footnotes indicate, Karamzin was very conscious of the contrived nature of this change of heart and equally of Aris's *deus ex machina* appearance.

"A Knight of Our Time"

SOME six years passed between the publication of "Julia" and Karamzin's first fiction in the *Messenger of Europe*. Although the interim period is marked primarily by Karamzin's work as a poet and translator, he was contemplating new works in prose. In 1799 he wrote to Wilhelm von Wolzogen, Schiller's brother-in-law:

"depuis quelque temps je ne fois que des vers et des plans pour des ouvrages en prose."[64] The previous year he had written to Dmitriev of his projected novel "A Picture of Life" ["Kartina zhizni"];[65] although no work with this title was ever published, the reference is almost certainly to the first drafts of what became "A Knight of Our Time." At the end of chapter 5 appears the date 1799.

Karamzin produced a new and rich synthesis of literary influences which are evident in his earlier fiction, but at the same time has freed himself of other and stronger influences. There is no trace of Marmontel's manner or typical subject matter; instead, as V. K. Kiukhel'beker noted, Karamzin "is imitating Sterne—and not without talent."[66] In "Natalia, the Boyar's Daughter" Karamzin had drawn attention to his Sternian manner *en passant*, but only in "A Knight of Our Time" is it displayed with any degree of invention and panache. The characters in the novel owe little to Sterne, although Karamzin was conscious of possible analogies when dissociating his hero's father from Uncle Toby. Karamzin delights in what Viktor Shklovskii has called Sterne's "exposing of the narrative device" (obnazhenie priema).[67] Thus the work is divided into chapters, although chapter 2 is a paragraph of twelve lines and chapter 4 "was written only for the fifth." In chapter 3 he declares that there is little to write about childhood, but adds that he has no wish "to conceal the sandy infertility of my imagination and quickly put a full stop," for he could find "sufficient flowers to adorn the chapter"; he enumerates the variety of styles and subjects he could offer and proceeds to give examples with a commentary on their distinctive features. After one false lead to suggest the end of the chapter, he adds a further page, before abruptly announcing: "I am saving paper and the attention of the reader and so—end of chapter!" It is noticeable that Karamzin's imitation of Sterne is confined to the early chapters written in 1799; although the humorous tone is necessarily continued in the succeeding chapters, there is less attempt to draw attention to the mechanics of the narrative.

"A Knight of Our Time" is Karamzin's attempt to write a *Bildungsroman*, to portray the youthful development of his hero Leon. It is an attempt in accord with his admiration for Moritz's *Anton Reiser*, which he praised as "a most curious psychological book in which he describes his own adventures, thoughts, feelings,

and the development of his spiritual qualities" and he adds revealingly: "I prefer the *Confessions* de J. J. Rousseau, Stillings *Jugend-
geschichte,* and *Anton Reiser* to all the systematic psychologies in
the world."[68] Karamzin fictionalized events from his own childhood, as he explained in a footnote when the work was published,[69]
and Dmitriev and K. S. Serbinovich have both testified to the basic
truth of the narrative. This in turn has led to an abuse of the story
for biographical purposes, although Karamzin is clearly influenced
more by existing literary example than by actual reminiscences. His
aim was specifically to write a novel, not an autobiography.

The title clearly indicates the type of person he wished to create. Leon is the portrait of an idealist, a latter-day Don Quixote,
guided by high ideals and warm impulses, a foe of materialism and
atheism. The analogy with Don Quixote is invited not only in the
title but within the work, when Karamzin refers to Leon's quixotic
imagination, nurtured by the reading of adventure novels. The image is a persistent one in Karamzin's fiction and publicist writing; at
the probable time of the novel's conception, Melodor in *The Dialogue on Happiness* was professing: "I am already bored with being
a Don Quixote, chasing after an imaginary Dulcinea, an empty
dream, and making old people laugh with my piteous sighs," to
which Philalet rejoins: "That is the lot of all the knights of our
time."[70]

Karamzin traces his hero's development from his birth to the
age of eleven. His attention to the formative influences on a child,
his belief that the early years are critical for a child's character and
subsequent development make "A Knight of Our Time" an important milestone in Russian literature. He carefully describes Leon's
mother, her own qualities of love and virtue, her propensity to
melancholy, which she fostered in her son, the effect of her early
death. Leon's father is drawn with equal care and his sterling qualities are emphasized in the description of the society of provincial
noblemen who pledge their lives to the service of their ideals and
each other. Particular attention is paid to Leon's education, the
books he read; Karamzin describes the novels with their fantastic
adventures as "a hothouse for a young soul, which ripens prematurely from such reading."

Not all the episodes Karamzin selects as important in Leon's
development are psychologically and artistically convincing. De-

spite the author's usual assurances that the event was no mere invention, the story of Leon's miraculous escape from a bear is extravagantly melodramatic, although the underlying idea of the mysterious workings of Providence in the lives of men is characteristic of Karamzin's work at this period. In the elaboration of the relationship between Leon and Countess Mirova Karamzin still pays tribute to the unfortunate tradition of rococo sensualism with his suggestive innuendo and ultimate Acteon-Diana set piece.

Rousseau's account in *Les Confessions* of his life with Mme. de Warens has been seen as a likely influence on Karamzin's story,[71] although Karamzin added embellishments of his own devising. Countess Mirova is, nonetheless, well-observed and drawn. Although her biography does not explain the "strangeness" of her passion for Leon, as Karamzin hoped, it does provide a convincing picture of her relationship with her husband. Not only is there a great difference in age between them, but also in temperament. Despite persistent suitors, she remains virtuous and faithful "by system and reason," although as she admits in a letter to a friend: "one could say that we lived with our souls as one from the moment I ceased to look for a soul in him." She needs a child to give meaning to her life: Leon fills this need and drives away her boredom in the country. Karamzin's analysis of her dilemma, of her search for fulfillment in life and the compromise that accepted morality and marriage have imposed upon her, contains the elements of true tragedy. Psychologically it is much subtler than Karamzin's overtly moralizing treatment of the subject in "Julia," and it has certain interesting parallels with his subsequent sketch "The Sensitive and the Cold."

"The Sensitive and the Cold"

"The Sensitive and the Cold" develops a series of character contrasts adumbrated in "A Knight of Our Time"; there are analogies between Leonid, the cold hero, and Count Mirov, between Erast, the sensitive hero, and a combination of the young Leon and N*, the tender, languorous suitor, described in the countess's letter as knowing "so well how to speak to a woman's heart," and between Calliste, Leonid's wife, who is prompted, unlike the countess, by her husband's coldness to respond to her suitor, and the Countess Mirova. In "A Knight of Our Time" the countess refers to the Saint-Preux–Julie–Wolmar relationship in Rousseau's *La Nouvelle Héloise,* but of all Karamzin's work it is "The Sensitive and the Cold" which shows the clearest indebtedness to Rousseau's novel.[72] Erast and Leonid are Karamzin's version of Saint-Preux and Wolmar, and indeed Erast is called "the new Saint-Preux."

Karamzin's basic thesis, advanced in his introduction, is that "indifferent people are prudent in everything, live more peacefully in this world, cause less trouble, and more rarely disrupt the harmony of society; but only people of feeling make great sacrifices to virtue, astound the world with great deeds, for which, in Montaigne's words, *un peu de folie* is always necessary; they shine with imaginative and creative talents. . . ." The passage, as R. V. Ivanov-Razumnik pointed out,[73] is an almost literal translation from Kant's *Anthropologie,* but it is equally a long-held belief of Karamzin's as well as a general contention of European sentimentalists. Some months before his story appeared in the *Messenger of Europe,* Karamzin published a translation from the *Universal Chronicle* of a piece entitled "The Prudent Man" ["Blagorazumnyi chelovek"], a variation on the same theme: "Prudence acts on life in the same way rules do on a work of art; it makes a man cautious, but cannot uplift the spirit; it averts injury but cannot bring any real advantage; it avoids mistakes but cannot lead to fame since it destroys daring which is sometimes fatal but without which wonder and loud acclaim cannot be earned."[74] Yet the original formulation would seem to be Rousseau's "il n'y a que des âmes de feu qui sachent combattre et vaincre; tous les grands efforts, toutes les actions sublimes sont leur ouvrage: la froide raison n'a jamais rien fait d'illustre, et l'on ne triomphe des passions qu'en les opposant l'une à l'autre."[75] Not surprisingly, a similar opposition is found in *Werther,* which, Karamzin opined, could never have been written without *La Nouvelle Héloise;*[76] Goethe, with his greater talent for narrative, allows Werther to propound the idea in an argument with Albert.[77]

Closely linked with this fundamental opposition between reason and feeling is Karamzin's understanding of character. In his introduction Karamzin polemicizes with the view that environment is totally responsible for a person's character and believes that "Nature alone creates and bestows: upbringing only forms." Reason and will are unable to change inborn qualities. His arguments are directed not only against his constant foes, the "systematic" theorists and philosophers, but against his own views in "A Knight of Our Time," where he refers to Locke in describing "the blank sheet of his [Leon's] sensitivity." Later he attributes to Leon's mother's tender care the basis of his character: "Initial upbringing almost always decides both the fate and the main qualities of a person. Leon's soul was formed by love and for love"; elsewhere he sees Leon's early reading as responsible for the "moral character" of his life. In *Letters of a Russian Traveler* Karamzin attempted to make a distinction between "temperament" and "character": "Temperament is the basis of our moral being and character its chance form. We are born with temperament but without character, which forms gradually as a result of exterior impressions."[78] By the time of writing "The Sensitive and the Cold" Karamzin's understanding of character corresponded to the earlier idea of temperament.

Although inevitably Karamzin's contrast between his "two characters," as the story is subtitled, is somewhat schematic, Leonid and Erast are convincing to an extent his earlier, facilely "complex" characters are not. This is primarily attributable to Karamzin's maturity in handling autobiographical material and the comparatively objective and detached role of the narrator. Karamzin is no longer intent on promoting the narrator of his earlier stories, the "man of feeling"; the transition to a more epic narrative position is perceptible between the two parts of "A Knight of Our Time" and in the wish to allow characters and their actions to speak for themselves.[79]

Despite the equations of lack of feeling and egoism[80] and sensitivity and altruism and Karamzin's inevitable sympathies for the latter, Leonid and Erast are not simply black and white characters, villain and hero. Leonid embodies distinct features of Karamzin's late lamented friend, Petrov: the description of his early life, his moments of rare sensitivity, his relationship with Erast, founded on the attraction of opposites.[81] Erast has much in common with Karamzin himself, or, in fictional terms, represents an extension of Leon in "A Knight of Our Time." The careers of Erast and Leonid are depicted and contrasted from school bench to army and on to government service. Their paths diverge until after their respective marriages, when Erast becomes involved with Leonid's wife and

Leonid subsequently resists Erast's, for "what prudent man would sacrifice an old friend to their momentary whim?" Erast is in constant pursuit of happiness, forever seeking change, inspiring love and hate, wasting his money, health and emotions, for "the sensitive man is a natural spendthrift"; he dies, virtually forgotten. Leonid goes from strength to strength, indifferent to the deaths of his wives, children, and friends, gathering fame, respect but not love —to which he is indifferent anyway: "*Non-suffering* seemed to him enjoyment and indifference the talisman of wisdom."

The implications of the story are obvious: despite his excesses, it is the man of feeling who lives life whereas the prudent man merely exists. Artistically, it is Leonid rather than Erast, who is the interesting figure. Commentators have seen in him a prototype of Tolstoi's Karenin and even the first portrait of the bourgeois in Russian literature,[82] although Karamzin with his own considerable Leonidian prudence was propounding a middle road of moderation, such as advocated by Philalet in *The Dialogue on Happiness.*[83]

"My Confession"

"My Confession" forms with "The Sensitive and the Cold" and "A Knight of Our Time" a group of character sketches unrivaled in Karamzin's earlier work, but at the same time it is unique from a narrative point of view. Written in the form of a "letter to the editor," it is a remarkable self-portrait of an irreverent, immoral young aristocrat, who records his rake's progress through life. In the general context of the *Messenger of Europe* it is a satire of fashionable gentry education with its abuse of opportunities and refusal to acknowledge that "a noble name is an obligation to be a useful man in a state and a virtuous citizen in one's homeland."[84] Yet it is much more than a routine piece of moralizing; the count is more real than any other character in Karamzin's work, despite the fact that he is a caricature, whose only natural ability is precisely for the drawing of caricatures. Karamzin stands outside the narrative, relying for his effect on the unconscious irony which pervades the count's confession.

The count inevitably invites comparison with Leonid, the "cold" hero, although there are notable differences. Leonid is not a disruptive influence in society; his indifference does not prevent the able fulfillment of his obligations. The characteristic he shares with the count is not his prudence, although the count was advised "to be moderate and prudent in life," but his egoism. Both live their lives without attacks of conscience and are totally indifferent to the fate of others; both would wish to repeat their lives without change. The count, however, feels himself an exceptional being: "Nature produced me as a completely special person and . . . Fate impressed all the events in my life with some seal of excellence"; he has a clearly defined philosophy of moral anarchy and scepticism: "All the world seemed to me a disordered game of Chinese shadows, all rules a rein on weak minds, all obligations an unbearable constraint." Life possesses no meaning; it is a dreamworld, in which all play out their part fatalistically, indifferently.

Karamzin's creative and publicist writings in the *Messenger of Europe* reveal a tendency, reaching its peak in "My Confession," to question the accepted authorities of his youth as well as specific features of his earlier works. The count's story contains a deliberate and creative critique of both philosophic and stylistic aspects of Karamzin's *Letters of a Russian Traveler*, which had been finally published in the previous year. The count's "favorite words," "Chinese shadows" echo the last line of *Letters*, and his story is an ironic comment on Karamzin's "and (between ourselves) what is more interesting for a man than himself?" when that man is not a "man of feeling" but an egoist; even his praise for the "respected spendthrift" is a shaft against the extravagant emotionalism of the "sensitive" Erast. Karamzin's linguistic practice at the time of the *Moscow Journal*—word calques, the translation of French phrases—is also mocked in the count's use of *iazyk poves, liubovnoe dezhurstvo*, his defense of the word *vliublennost'*. The title of the work clearly suggests a parallel with Rousseau's *Les Confessions*, and the count refers to the general vogue of confessional literature which gives his own work a justification independent of any wider interest for the reader; once more it is an ironic echo of the closing paragraph of *Letters*. His further remarks on the proliferation of works with such titles as "my efforts" or "the secret journal of my heart" suggest inevitably Karamzin's own *My Trifles* and the imitations they inspired. Finally the count prides himself that his work will be distinguished by its *lack* of moral intent and its brevity. In this respect it is clear that Karamzin in these literary polemics goes beyond self-criticism to criticism of other current works, such as A. E. Izmailov's *Eugene; Or, The Fatal Consequences of Bad Upbringing and Company* [*Evgenii, ili pagubnye sledstviia durnogo vospitaniia i soobshchestva*] (1799–1801).[85]

In the *Messenger of Europe* Karamzin discontinued his practice in his earlier journal of reviewing specific Russian literary works; a facet of his new position, however, was the increasing use of the forms and techniques of satirical journalism, particularly in his socio-political writings. *My Confession*, written in a succinct and aphoristic style, is the sole example of Karamzin's undoubted talent for realistic satire in fictional form.

"Anecdote"

THE autobiographical form of "My Confession" with its negative hero precludes the direct moralizing intervention of its real author, Karamzin. In "Anecdote," however, Karamzin once more resorts to overt moralizing. It is the fictional representation of his "Thoughts on Solitude" ["Mysli ob uedinenii"], also written in 1802, where he writes: "Man is not created for eternal solitude and cannot remake himself. People offend him, people must console him. There is poison in the world, but also its antidote."[86] Using favored conventional names, Karamzin relates the story of Liodor, whose happiness is blighted within the space of three days by the deaths of his fiancée, Emiliia, and his best friend, Milon. The distraught Liodor decides to enter a monastery, where his grief slowly lessens with the passage of time until "he was banished from the monastery for indecent actions which I refuse to describe!" This "phenomenon of the human heart" leads Karamzin to reflect: "we shall be unhappy when Providence wishes to deprive us of our joys, but we shall remain in the theatre until the last act—we shall remain until that moment when a mysterious bell shall call us to another place."

The piece is pervaded by a poignancy which is rare in Karamzin's work; it originates in circumstances of Karamzin's own life and is conveyed by the narrative position he adopts. Karamzin's own despair at the sudden loss of his first wife (also addressed as Emiliia in the poem of that name) underlies the story, which is told as an anecdote, originally related by a Mr. P*. Karamzin's position is thus at two removes from the actual events; he is the worldly-wise philosopher, the experienced observer of the human heart, who uses the particular incident for generalizations on death, grief, religion, immortality. The narrative is restrained and free from pose, giving a meaningful renewal to such clichés as "there are sorrows which should not be described. Each according to his sensitivity can imagine them."

"Martha the Mayoress"

KARAMZIN'S irony against certain types of sentimental literature in "My Confession" was directed in the preface to "A Knight of Our Time" against historical novelists, whose "historical fables" were "a pretty puppet play." He declared that "I have never been a follower of fashions in dress; nor do I wish to follow fashions in authorship; I do not wish to awaken the slumbering giants of mankind." Yet at the beginning of 1803 he published "Martha the Mayoress," perhaps his most famous and influential story after "Poor Liza"; instead of the "Numuses, Aureliuses, Alfreds, and Charlemagnes" he had ridiculed, he chose to portray Martha and "one of the most important events in Russian history," the subjection of Novgorod, which is the alternative title of his story. Martha, unlike those characters, was "passionate" (italicized in the text), the quality, without which a "person is a puppet."

"Martha the Mayoress" marks an intermediate stage between "Natalia, the Boyar's Daughter" and the *History of the Russian State*; it is the first and only story Karamzin subtitled "an historical tale" and by comparison with "Natalia, the Boyar's Daughter" reveals different demands on historical material and distinct differences in tone and style. Despite its close relation to historical fact, "Martha the Mayoress" is, nevertheless, not history but fiction; in Karamzin's words, it is designed "for the lovers of history and—of tales."[87] The conscious liberties Karamzin took with certain historical characters, events and facts are clear from a comparison with the relevant passages in his *History of the Russian State* and have been discussed at length by Soviet commentators;[88] these discrepancies are significant to the degree they affect the conception of Martha and the implications of the story.

The link between "Natalia, the Boyar's Daughter" and "Martha the Mayoress" lies in their common fictional, rather than historical, aspects. Kseniia, Martha's daughter, is a typical sentimental heroine, particularly close to Natalia by her upbringing, her life in the *terem*, her sweetness and innocence, described by similar analogies to spring and turtle doves. Nevertheless, she is a much paler figure than either Natalia or Liza; her role in the story is purely secondary and her youth and naïvete are a foil to her mother's power and passion. Miroslav, Kseniia's husband, is the counterpart of Aleksei Liuboslavskii; a youth "of wondrous beauty," he is a great warrior, and "his birth is shrouded in mystery; but the blessing of the Almighty has clearly marked out this youth." This element of mystery is developed in subsequent events—Miroslav's refusal to kill Tsar Ivan in battle, Ivan's visit to Miroslav's grave—which clearly suggest that Ivan was Miroslav's father. A third character who is anticipated in Karamzin's earlier work is the hermit, Theodosius, whose ability to read forebodings of tragedy in the heavens and whose life in "the deep forest" recall the hermit in the tale of that name.

The parallel between "Natalia, the Boyar's Daughter" and "Martha the Mayoress" is sustained in the descriptions of battles, although there is greater evidence of Karamzin's acquaintance with, and use of, the techniques of the Russian epic tradition and chronicles. Between the publication of the two stories had come Karamzin's "immersion" in Nikon and the discovery and publication of *The Igor' Tale*, the importance of which he was among the first to champion.[89] Although Karamzin now works with a deeper understanding of period style and language, the effect he achieves is not totally dissimilar. In his earlier story, written under the stylistic influence of Sterne and similar authors, the narrative tone is light, sentimental, frequently humorous; linguistically, Karamzin essayed only a token imitation of the "ancient coloring." The historical pretense is more sustained in "Martha the Mayoress"; instead of retelling a story, Karamzin is "editing" an old manuscript, allegedly written by a Novgorodian boyar, in which "he has corrected only its obscure and unintelligible language." These "corrections" inevitably involve the introduction of the phraseological and syntactical patterns of his canonized sentimental style. The tone, differing markedly from that of "Natalia, the Boyar's Daughter," is lofty and serious, an example of what might be termed Karamzin's patriotic civic sentimentalism, which pervades his publicist writings in the *Messenger of Europe.* It marks that synthesis of sentimental and classical elements, which Mordovchenko has controversially termed "neo-classicism," opposing it thereby to the pseudoclassical tradition (continued at the beginning of the nineteenth century in the work of Admiral Shishkov and his followers) and to the earlier lachrymose sentimentalism.[90]

This civic pathos is the new element in Karamzin's fiction; he has chosen a subject which is politically instructive and artistically effective. "Martha the Mayoress" exploits the implications of one of his favorite paradoxes: ". . . emotionally I shall remain a republican, but still a faithful subject of the tsar of Russia."[91] In his role as editor, he attempts in his preface to indicate the moral and political complexities of the ensuing historical events: "Wise Ivan was obliged to join the province of Novgorod to his kingdom for the glory and strength of his country: praise be to him! However, the opposition of the Novgorodians is not the revolt of some Jacobins; they were fighting for their ancient charter and rights, granted to them in part by the Great Princes themselves, by Iaroslav, for instance, who ensured their freedom." He goes on to censure the Novgorodians for their lack of *prudence*, that *blagorazumie*, which he obviously condones in nations and the excess of which he condemns in individuals.

A tribute to his comparatively objective narrative position is the vehement denunciation of Karamzin for his "atheism and anarchy" by P. I. Golenishchev-Kutuzov, admittedly one of the most reactionary of Shishkovites: "What a rebellious spirit and what an empty fiction, the sole aim of which is to inflame with its republican spirit! He has put into the mouth of a drunken and stupid old woman an orator's speeches in defence of Novgorodian liberty and made her speak like Demosthenes. And is it permitted to distort with fictions an historical event which happened as long ago as two hundred years—and to what end—Jacobinism?"[92] Karamzin is at pains to dissociate the Novgorodian resistance specifically from the events of the French Revolution; he sees their cause as just, but ill-advised. Yet the lessons learnt from France and from the fate of the Swiss Republic which are elaborated in the political commentaries of the *Messenger of Europe* are basic to his story. Karamzin believes that a republic can exist only where an almost impossibly high

Engraving by Lips, 1801

Lithograph from portrait by Damon, 1805

Portrait by Tropinin, 1814

Portrait by Varnek, 1819

standard of civic virtue is maintained; he suggests that its absence was one of the reasons for Novgorod's fall.

The political debate in the tale is carried out between Martha, the spokesman for Novgorod's heritage, and Prince Kholmskii, Ivan's emissary and the advocate of autocracy and a united *Rus'*. Kholmskii and Martha both have their own interpretation of Novgorod's history: Kholmskii refers to Riurik and a common Russian tradition whereas Martha evokes Vadim and Novgorodian independence. Speeches by Martha punctuate the succeeding events until finally Kholmskii returns to address the people of Novgorod. He voices what may be considered the quintessence of Karamzin's own political philosophy at this period: "not freedom, often fatal, but organization, *good organization, justice and security* are the three pillars of civic happiness." In his first speech Kholmskii equates the position of peoples under an autocracy and in a republic, "for a people must always be obedient"; Karamzin removes from the people the right to revolt, for he sees the overthrow of tyrannical monarchs as an act of God alone. Nevertheless, Karamzin shows both the power and the inconstancy of the people: easily swayed by strong personalities, it quickly forsakes Martha for Ivan, but it retains a sense of its own republican dignity, manifest in its original reception of Kholmskii and, more particularly, in its refusal to acknowledge Ivan whilst the gallows is still standing. In the phrase "the people still was silent" (narod eshche bezmolvstvoval) there is a direct anticipation of the closing scene of Pushkin's *Boris Godunov*, although there the continued silence is a polemic with the eventual acclamation of Ivan by the Novgorodians.[93]

"Martha the Mayoress" presents an essentially unhappy mixture of historical, oratorical, and sentimental elements. Its strength lies not in its static political speechifying or sentimental interludes, but in the portrayal of the character of Martha. She *embodies* an ideology; the other characters are wooden and lifeless. Ivan, her counterpart, possesses no distinct personality; he is the ideal Little Father of the Russians: "Ivan in Iaroslav's house entertained lavishly the most noble Novgorod boyars and with his imperial hand scattered gold among the poorest citizens, who sincerely and warmly praised his philanthropy. Not a menacing foreign conqueror but a great Russian tsar had conquered Russians: the love of a father-monarch was shining in his eyes." It is precisely from the wish to destroy the ideal in Martha that she emerges as a living and credible figure. The preface contains the key to Karamzin's approach to her character. She is described as "this wonderful woman who knew how to command the people and wished (very inappropriately) to become the Cato of her Republic." Commenting on the alleged original document, Karamzin finds that "the secret motive, which he has given to Martha's fanaticism, proves that he saw in her only a *passionate*, fervent, and intelligent woman, not a great or a virtuous one." Golenishchev-Kutuzov attributes the wish to inflame to Karamzin but it is in Martha herself that he depicts this ability; he describes how "in order to inflame their minds even more, she shows the chain, rattles it in her hand and throws it to the ground: the people in a frenzy of anger trample the chain underfoot." Martha is Karamzin's version of the revolutionary orator, a Mirabeau manipulating the populace, encouraging it to resist Ivan, reviving it when it despairs. Karamzin would seem intent in sustaining the analogy even in her fate; contrary to historical fact, she is beheaded before the populace. Martha's patriotism is not disinterested, her devotion to Novgorod is accompanied by suspicion of the people in whose name she speaks. The "secret motive" behind her actions is her love for her husband and the oath she swore before he died "to be the eternal foe of all the enemies of Novgorod's freedom: . . . to die as the defender of its rights." This makes her drive the people relentlessly, "unreasonably," until her final acceptance of defeat, the ambiguous *sovershilos'* ("it is finished" / "it has come to pass"). She is a tragic heroine, who despite all the portents of disaster, challenges fate until the end: "the fate of people and of nations is the secret of Providence, but our actions depend solely on ourselves, and that is enough." She consciously prepares herself for martyrdom. She rejoices when her sons are killed in battle, which allows her to identify herself with the bereaved mothers of Novgorod and at the end she invites execution and dies proud and unafraid:

"Subjects of Ivan! I die as a citizen of Novgorod!"

It is the psychological depth Karamzin gives to his portrayal of Martha which lifts the story above the level of the politico-didactic novels of authors such as Kheraskov. His analysis of the motivation behind Martha's actions is the climax to his interest in the workings of the human heart and the story as a whole is an interesting attempt to give life to history, however uneven and anti-historical the result.

"Martha the Mayoress" was Karamzin's final essay in narrative fiction. Essentially a collection of short stories, totaling little more than four hundred pages and composed over a period of fifteen years, his fiction as a whole has an interest and importance which are essentially not mirrored in the considerable influence exerted by only one or two of his tales. "Poor Liza" and "Martha the Mayoress" enjoyed enormous and immediate popularity and "Poor Liza" in particular prompted numerous imitations and adaptations;[94] both were made the subject of long, drawn-out plays.[95] Other stories, such as "The Island of Bornholm," certainly caught the imagination of contemporary readers, without inspiring specific imitation, whilst "Natalia, the Boyar's Daughter" retained its popularity far enough into the nineteenth century for Pushkin meaningfully to parody its characters and plot. On the other hand, stories which in recent times have increasingly attracted the attention of scholars and have led to a more sympathetic appraisal of Karamzin's achievement were comparatively neglected in their time. From different periods of Karamzin's career one might name in this category "Liodor," "Athenian Life," "My Confession," and "A Knight of Our Time." Kiukhel'beker for instance was full of praise for "A Knight of Our Time," which he read in exile in 1832, but was initially unaware of Karamzin's authorship. An explanation for this neglect lies in the selection and disposition of Karamzin's writings in his collected works. The stories which were popular from the time of their publication into the nineteenth century were all re-published outside the journals and almanacs in which, with the exception of "Julia," they originally appeared; they appear in the volume of tales in the collected editions of 1803, 1814, and 1820. The neglected works are to be found in the miscellany sections ("Athenian Life," "My Confession," "The Sensitive and the Cold") or were excluded ("Liodor," initially "A Knight of Our Time").

Belinskii saw Karamzin "not merely as a reformer, but as an initiator, a creator";[96] his words are particularly applicable to Karamzin's fiction, which has a diversity and richness largely obscured

by the fame and/or notoriety of "Poor Liza." Establishing prose as
a worthy medium of artistic expression, Karamzin left distinctive
Russian examples of stories popular in contemporary western literature. His range embraces the sentimental peasant story, the Gothic
tale, the *conte moral*, the historical tale, the psychological character-
sketch, a would-be *Bildungsroman*. There is a development from
the story with few characters and virtually devoid of plot toward
the major form of the novel. In this development, as well as in other
respects, "Julia" is the pivotal work. The unfinished "A Knight of
Our Time" represents the limit of this trend in fictional terms, although his monumental *History of the Russian State* might be seen
as its logical culmination. No longer obliged to assert the "truth" of
his work, he assumes the *persona* of the responsible historian, but
brings to his task his artistic talents for a lively depiction of events,
a sentimental-psychological interest in character, and an exacting attention to style. His work was read by the Russian public as though
it were an exciting historical novel—from an author, whose favorite
relaxation from his historical labors was the reading of the novels of
Walter Scott; it was praised not only as the first distinguished history of Russia but as a great event in Russian literature.

Although there are obvious contrasts between Karamzin's early
stories and his fiction in the *Messenger of Europe*, they result from
Karamzin's deepened appreciation of the artistic potentialities of
sentimentalism. All his work falls between its historical and aesthetic boundaries and to see such later stories as "My Confession,"
"The Sensitive and the Cold," and even "A Knight of Our Time"
as a mere "critique of sentimentalism"[97] is to assume that the rejection of certain stylistic mannerisms implies the renunciation of its
philosophical and aesthetic tenets. As Kanunova rightly stresses,[98]
Karamzin's work shows the evolution of sentimentalism, not its rejection. All his stories are united by his interest in the psychology of
characters, in the depiction of their emotions: "Poor Liza" and "A
Knight of Our Time" differ in the artistic means he employs to reveal character. Karamzin's stories show, at one end of the scale, his
close contacts with pseudoclassicism and at the other, his anticipation of further developments in nineteenth-century fiction through
romanticism to realism. His characters in the stories of the 1790's
are understood statically and simplicistically, even when professedly
"complex"; characters like Leon and Martha are seen in the round,
shaped by environment and circumstances.

An indication of Karamzin's development is the changing role of the narrator. In the stories published in the *Moscow Journal* the narrator is a key figure, the "man of feeling" who is responsible for directing the reader's responses, setting the mood; in the main *Aglaia* stories he becomes even more of a "character," indeed the hero-narrator who tells of his exploits against the exotic backcloths of Spain, Bornholm, and Ancient Greece, all equally real and equally imaginary. These stories show Karamzin at his most subjective and lyrical; they are tone poems, escapist dreams in which the continual confrontation in Karamzin's work of the ideal and the real is at its most acute. The stories in the *Messenger of Europe* provide far greater variety in the narrative "point of view"; on the one hand, the effusive "I" narrator is replaced by a more detached and objective "we" and on the other, when the first person narration is used—in "My Confession"—the hero is an anti-hero, a vehicle for the author's irony.

With Karamzin's increasing emphasis on the portrayal of man in society and a truer understanding of the complexity of personality there is a subsequent loss of other characteristic features of his earlier tales, principally their lyricism. This lyricism comes from the sentimental poeticization of the beauties of the emotions and of nature and the carefully devised syntactical structure which supports it. In the depiction of character lyricism tends to replace analysis; in nature descriptions the particular detail which would arrest or detract is rejected for the general which merges into the overall picture. It is remarkable, nevertheless, that Karamzin is credited with making contemporary readers responsive to the beauties of the Russian countryside. F. N. Glinka recalled that "he seemed to give the key to nature itself, revealing its comforting beauties even in our northern land"[99] and Gogol' was even more enthusiastic: "I am now living in a countryside exactly like that described by the unforgettable Karamzin. It seems to me that he copied the Little Russian countryside—to such a degree are his colors vivid and like the local countryside."[100] The most famous passage of this type occurs in the prelude to "Poor Liza," where a general description in the spirit of Thomson's *The Seasons* is combined with the noting of specific Moscow landmarks.

Although the Russian coloring in his stories is relatively superficial, there is little doubt that Karamzin emphasized the "Russianness" of his work from the beginning and not merely during his consciously patriotic phase at the beginning of the nineteenth century. He wished to provide the Russian public with stories about Russian life or alternatively in which a Russian played a prominent role. His was a "Russianness" which the reading public he addressed, and was partly responsible for creating, was prepared to accept, for his approach was by talented assimilation of European literary example—content, form, and style—and not by its rejection.

Karamzin's debt to European authors is great and obvious, notwithstanding his own justified pride in his originality and the attempts by Russian scholars, both before and since the Revolution, to emphasize his use of Russian literary traditions. Apart from general reminiscences of Thomson, Gessner, and Ossian, specific prose writers to influence his work at different periods and to different degrees include Mme. de Genlis, Goethe, Rousseau, Anton Wall and, principally, Sterne and Marmontel. The translator of Karamzin's tales into English inevitably drew the parallel with Sterne and with reference to *Letters of a Russian Traveler* stated that "he has certainly attempted, if not to imitate a Sentimental Traveller, at least to display an entire comprehension of whatever that admirable writer composed."[101] A later commentator, Sir John Bowring, was not so impressed; he saw Sterne as a bad influence on Karamzin's work, "since the pecularities which characterize him are only tolerable because they are original."[102] Bowring was referring to Karamzin's early prose work and was not acquainted with "A Knight of Our Time," where Karamzin exhibited a talented assimilation of Sterne's narrative manner. For the French critics, on the other hand, the automatic comparison was with Marmontel. De Bouilliers, who translated "Julia" in 1797, believed Karamzin was a writer able to "rivaliser avec les Marmontels et les Florians";[103] Coiffier saw even "Natalia, the Boyar's Daughter" as a "Marmontel narrative," a view Karamzin disputed with justice in the specific instance, although Marmontel's influence is pervasive in his early stories.[104] Karamzin's enthusiasm for Marmontel, whom he had met in Paris in 1790, is founded on a clear appreciation of his talents as a storyteller: "I saw the author of those attractive tales, who in what seems the easiest, commonest type of composition is able to be unique and inimitable."[105] Marmontel as "the author of unique tales" is placed alongside Voltaire, Rousseau, Thomas, and earlier writers for perfecting the French language in an essay of 1803.[106]

Marmontel enjoyed an unrivaled European reputation in Europe by the end of the century and translations of his stories in English magazines, for example, far exceeded those from any other contemporary European writer's work.[107] It was therefore high praise for Karamzin to be compared with the foremost exponent of the short story by foreigners and fellow-countrymen alike. This is clearly shown in an important article, "A View of Stories or Tales" ["Vzgliad na povesti ili skazki"], published anonymously in 1804 in the *Patriot*.[108]

The author attempts to define "this new type of composition," which Marmontel is credited with introducing, in terms which are strikingly applicable to Karamzin's own work: "To depict the contradictions in one's struggle with oneself, to reveal the secrets of the heart, covered nowadays by such a dark veil; to investigate the action of the passions, which are more inflamed in our time than ever before, to show, when opportune, the role of fate and the strength of prejudices, finally, with the aid of concealed moralizing to harmonize the reason and the passions, nature and society—this is the important task of the composer of tales, this is the sense in which even tales may be called a school of morals, and storytellers teachers of mankind." Karamzin is praised as the most talented foreign imitator of Marmontel and "Julia" is noted as the work which justly earned him comparison with the master in Russia and abroad. Karamzin's own specific qualities as a storyteller are summarized on the basis of "Julia": "Liveliness of narrative, beauty of expression, examples of painting in prose, faithful representation of society, finally all the flowers of the imagination and all the charms of language adorn it—a distinction all the more striking because the author had to struggle with a poorly developed language, softening it for tender expression and making it supple for light turns of phrase."

The beauties of the "new style" rightly impressed Karamzin's contemporaries and without his command of language Karamzin's simple tales would have lost much of their appeal and effectiveness. Yet the mature Karamzin, who was wont to dismiss the works of his youth as unimportant,[109] felt the need to revise his stories before their inclusion in his collected works. His concern was primarily stylistic, although inevitably from a man who willingly subscribed to Buffon's dictum that "le style, c'est l'homme même," the changes reflect shifts in his philosophical and aesthetic position at the beginning of the nineteenth century. It is remarkable that "Poor Liza" was in fact subject to few changes, whereas "Natalia, the Boyar's Daughter" received very careful revision. The reason is to be found in Karamzin's exclusively historical concerns in the last two decades of his life which led him to feel a greater genre division between the two stories than had originally existed. With the experience of "Martha the Mayoress" behind him he wished to increase the historical aspect of his earlier tale; thus he excluded most of the facetious contemporary allusions—to mesmerism, Montgolfier's balloon, Anton Wall's *Bagetellen*—as well as certain rococo similes and metaphors which had appeared in the first edition and which were at the same time absent from "Poor Liza." A logical consequence of Karamzin's criticism of meaningless tears, expressed in the preface to the second volume of *Aonides* (1797) and in translated items in the *Messenger of Europe*, is the exclusion of a whole song of praise to "tears, blessed tears." Equally his earlier endorsement of love as the great, ruling passion in life has given way to a more sober viewpoint, a refusal to identify with his characters. Thus the passage "Whoever blames Natalia, whoever accuses her for leaving her parents' home with a young man she has seen only three times and from whom she has heard but a few pretty words . . . does not know what love is, does not know its omnipotence" becomes "Together with our reader we sincerely blame Natalia, sincerely accuse her . . . but love is so terrible [uzhasnaia]."[110]

Karamzin's fiction, when judged in its entirety, faithfully mirrors his development and reveals him as an author of considerable talent and attainment. His work was a necessary and important prelude to the emergence of the great Russian novel of the nineteenth century and a direct springboard to the romantic fiction of Beztuzhev-Marlinskii and to the prose of Pushkin. Karamzin brought to Russian fiction a clear sense of form, an exact, supple style, a gallery of pale but well-delineated characters, including glimpses of the idealized Russian women of the later Russian novel, the beginnings of psychological analysis, and a feeling for nature. His fiction was another of the cornerstones on which the concept of the "Karamzin Period" is based.

From *Aglaia* to
The Pantheon of Russian Authors

1793-1801

I AM GROWING OLD along with you, my friend! Already the bounds of my brow are widening. What can be done? Tears will not help; sighs will rack the chest. We shall attempt to pass the time in the best way, or to shorten it in the most pleasant!"[1] With gentle irony the twenty-seven-year-old Karamzin greeted the New Year of 1793 in a letter to Dmitriev, but the remaining years of Catherine's reign brought a series of misfortunes and events, both personal and public, which had begun in 1791 and which were in marked contrast to his ever increasing fame and popularity as an author. In March 1793, his closest friend, Petrov, died in St. Petersburg, where he had been Derzhavin's secretary since the spring of 1792; the Pleshcheevs, with whom he was living, soon became involved in serious financial troubles and Karamzin decided to sell his remaining part of the family estates to help them; in 1794–95 rumors were rife in Moscow that he had been exiled to the country—a fate which had befallen the masons, I. P. Turgenev and N. N. Trubetskoi. He spent as much time as possible out of Moscow at the Pleshcheev estate of Znamenskoe, although he kept himself informed of current literary news, particularly the attacks against him by Krylov, Klushin, Tumanskii, and Nikolai Emin. He suffered periods of ill health and moods of despondency, which were deepened by news of events in France. His letters to Dmitriev, which faithfully mirror his state of mind during this period, omit all discussion of the French Revolution apart from an early ironic reference to the "free French" (vol'nye frantsuzy);[2] the *Moscow Journal* and *Let-*

ters of a Russian Traveler show Karamzin's wish to preserve a balanced and objective viewpoint. The chaos and bloodshed which 1793 brought to Europe and France, however, disillusioned him deeply: "Would you believe how much the terrible events in Europe trouble my soul? I run into the darkness of the woods but everywhere the thought of the destruction of cities and the death of people grips my heart. Call me a Don Quixote, but that knight could not love his Dulcinea as passionately as I love mankind!"[3] It was again literature which continued to play its role as his comforter and confidant: "Write when bored, write when sad: that is the greatest benefit of our trade, which is not called a trade."[4]

He notes in his letters the detention of the editors of the *Spectator* and the government action against the serf poet, Ivan Rozov, for alleged "blasphemy"[5] and writes to Derzhavin that "the present time is not favorable for literature."[6] Nevertheless, in the remaining years of Catherine's reign, he published—in 1794, *My Trifles* [*Moi bezdelki*] (2 parts), the first volume of *New Tales by Marmontel*, and the first part of *Aglaia*; in 1795, the second part of *Aglaia*, a translation of Mme. de Staël's *Méline*, and produced throughout the year a feature entitled "Miscellany" ["*Smes*,"] for the *Moscow News*; and in 1796, he published a second edition of *Aglaia* (2 parts), his short story, "Julia," and the first volume of a poetry almanac, *Aonides* [*Aonidy*].

The popularity of the *Moscow Journal* was such that Ridiger and Klaudius, the University printers, persuaded Karamzin to collect his original pieces for a separate edition, which appeared less than two years after the end of the journal as *My Trifles*. Bolotov, in a comment revealing for the reading habits of the time, wrote that "it was good to have it in such a small format so that it could serve as a book for the pocket and be used for pleasant reading during walks."[7] F. N. Glinka recalled the great impact the collection had on provincial society: "He awoke new life, aroused numerous unknown concepts, spoke in the language of feeling and in return received universal sympathy."[8] The first part of *My Trifles* consisted of twelve prose pieces, headed by the now famous "Poor Liza"; the second part opened with "Natalia, the Boyar's Daughter" and was followed by a selection of Karamzin's poems, not all of which had in fact appeared in the *Moscow Journal*. In the second edition of 1797 Karamzin brought all his prose into the first volume and devoted the second to an expanded selection of his poetry, under the epigraph from B. J. Saurin: "J'aime encore les vers, je le dis, et sans honte." Karamzin's title, reminiscent of Wall's *Bagetellen*, reflects the period's ironic, self-depreciating attitude toward literary work, the cult of minor forms, *vers fugitives*, in reaction to the odes and collected works under the title of *Tvoreniia* [*Creations*] of classicism; *My Trifles* was soon followed by Dmitriev's *And My Trifles* [*I moi bezdelki*] (1795) and P. A. Pel'skii's *My Odds and Ends* [*Moe koe-chto*] (1803). Inevitably, the vogue was parodied; N. M. Shatrov wrote: "Collecting his minor works, / A Russian Frenchman called them "My Trifles" / But a wit, who read them, said: / Nothing startling here, / The title alone is just."[9]

In the epilogue to the *Moscow Journal* Karamzin outlined his plans for a new almanac, which "must differ from it [the journal] by a most strict choice of works and generally by the purest, i.e., the most carefully polished style, for I will not be obliged to publish it by a fixed date."[10] In a postscript to the first volume of *Aglaia*, he again emphasizes the importance of style: "I would like to write in a different fashion from the majority of our writers; but strength and ability are not always equal to the intention."[11] The two books of *Aglaia* reveal Karamzin's attainment of a supple and graceful prose style unequaled in eighteenth-century Russian literature; they show his continued experiments with form, but above all they illustrate a period of deep crisis in his life and thought. In *Aglaia* "there are only Russian works; there are no translations."[12] Furthermore, apart from one poem by Dmitriev and two by Kheraskov, all the works are by Karamzin himself. Decorated in suitable sentimental fashion with engravings of entwining rambler roses and cupids, *Aglaia* offered the reader Karamzin in all his roles from the *Moscow Journal*: the sentimental poet, traveler, storyteller, philosopher, and enlightener. Derzhavin was highly impressed by the charms of what he called "Aglaia Nikolaevna"[13] and it is a description which indicates the reader's constant awareness of the author's personality, of the intimate autobiographical background against which all the works are projected, from a passionate rejection of Rousseau's attack on enlightenment to an artistic manifesto.

The sense of loss occasioned by the death of Petrov is a major theme of the first book. In the opening dedicatory poem, "An Offering to the Graces" ["Prinoshenie Gratsiiam"], his paean to the "Mild Goddesses, favorites of the heavens, / Friends of the gentle muses and all imperishable beauty" is interrupted by the thought of Petrov, but this is the excuse for extolling yet another virtue of the Graces—their ability to comfort the bereaved and dejected.[14] In a more than usually mawkish addressal "To the Nightingale" ["K solov'iu"] the death of Petrov leads to thoughts of his own end;[15] the transience of human life and terrestrial happiness underlies his "Epitaph of the Caliph Abdul Rahman" ["Epitafiia Kalifa Abdula-Ramana"], a poetic version of a small prose piece published in the *Moscow Journal*.[16] Karamzin's most impressive tribute to the memory of Petrov is the elegiac prose obituary, "A Flower on the Grave of My Agathon," a form possibly suggested by a work Lenz wrote after his arrival in Russia, *Etwas über Philotas Karakter* (*Ein Veilchen auf sen Grab*) (1780). It is characteristic of Karamzin's esteem for his friend that he should choose as an epigraph the lines on Brutus from *Julius Caesar* ending "This was a man!"; equally characteristic is the opening to the piece: "Agathon is no more! . . . My friend is no more!—Reader! you did not know him—he was neither rich nor well-born," where a man's stature and importance are judged not by public acclaim but by the author's personal relationship with him.[17] It is a polemical orientation which is felt more strongly in verse; three years later Karamzin wrote a poem "On the Death of Prince G. A. Khovanskii" ["Na smert' kniaziia G. A. Khovanskogo"] (1796), which began: "Friends! Khovanskii is no more!" and included the lines: "Khovanskii was in no way famous; / He was . . . simply a good man."[18] As a good man who "Loved Nature and men," Bonnet receives Karamzin's accolade in his "Inscription for the Grave of Bonnet" ["Nadgrobnaia nadpis' Bonnetu"];[19] in contrast the strongly pacificist Karamzin, on hearing of the fighting in Europe which began in the spring of 1793, rebukes Man who "Massacres his brothers and friends, / Born like him for happiness" ("Spring Feeling" ["Vesennee chuvstvo"]).[20]

Acutely aware of the strong reaction to the events in France which had swept through Europe and Russia, Karamzin at the beginning of 1793 wrote "On the Sciences, Arts and Enlightenment" ["Nechto o naukakh, isskustvakh i prosveshchenii"];[21] his "few notes, few thoughts on this important subject" are the first example of the publicist essay which became characteristic of the *Messenger of Europe.* Stylistically, the essay offers an interesting alternation of highly charged emotional and lyrical passages—the hortative introduction and the concluding personal dedication to the Muses —with lucid and well-reasoned argument. It is a refutation of the attack on enlightenment contained in Rousseau's prize-winning essay, *Discours sur la question, proposée par l'Académie de Dijon, si le rétablissement des sciences et des arts a contribué a épurer les moeurs?* (1749). Karamzin realized that the relevance of Rousseau's essay was perhaps even greater in the 1790's than it had been in the 1740's: "The author is no longer alive, but his work exists; fools read it—the very people who read nothing else—and under the aegis of the famous citizen of Geneva malign enlightenment." The immediate cause of his essay was the appearance of an anonymous German piece, "in which the poor sciences suffer in a frightful way," but it is typical of Karamzin's position that his anxiety to preserve "true" enlightenment from the forces of reaction was accompanied by no less a concern to dissociate it from the forces of upheaval and revolution: "All men have a soul and heart: consequently all may enjoy the fruits of Art and Science—and whoever enjoys them becomes a better person and a most peaceful citizen —most peaceful, I say, for he finds everywhere and in everything a thousand pleasures and delights and has no cause to curse fate and complain of his lot." Rousseau's posthumous fame as "the father of the French Revolution" is clear from the pages of the *Moscow Journal,* but Karamzin, advocating moderation and a balance of feeling and reason, was intent on preserving *his* Rousseau. In his long letter from Ermenonville in *Letters of a Russian Traveler,* he writes of the false pupils of Rousseau and adds: "I think that contemporary French orators also should not pursue him with their pompous praises: the sensitive, good-natured Jean-Jacques would have declared himself the first enemy of the Revolution."[22] In "On the Sciences" he declares: "I respect your great gifts, eloquent Rousseau! I respect the truths which you have revealed to your contemporaries and to posterity—truths which are henceforth inerasable from the boards of our knowledge—I love you for your kind heart, for your love of mankind." Therefore, he wishes to expose Rousseau's dangerous "dreams as dreams, (your) paradoxes as paradoxes" and to suggest that he was misled by "vanity, which is a weakness of even the greatest minds."

His critique of Rousseau's work was in a sense suggested by Rousseau himself. Karamzin describes the essay as "a logical chaos, in which only a deceptive order or the spectre of order is discernible; . . . It is a collection of contradictions and sophisms, offered —and one must be just to the author—with considerable art"; in *Les Confessions* Rousseau had written: "Cependant cet ouvrage, plein de chaleur et de force, manque absolument de logique et d'ordre; de tous ceux qui se sont sortis de ma plume, c'est la plus faible de raissonement et le plus pauvre de nombre et d'harmonie."[23] Karamzin attempts a systematic refutation of Rousseau's arguments, particularly his belief that enlightenment leads to a fall in morals; the burden of his essay is contained in a series of aphorisms—a form which he cultivated particularly in the 1790's: "Courtesy, affability, is the flower of society"; "Morality, one of the most important sciences, the alpha and omega of all the sciences and arts"; "Enlightenment is the Palladium of good behavior." To give authority to his arguments, he lists his Great Men, whose very existence and achievement, he feels, expose Rousseau's fallacious thesis. He refers to "the Newtons and Leibnitzes," "Bacon, Descartes, Haller, Thomson, Gessner" and awaits the appearance of future Bacons, Newtons, Lockes, Condillacs, and Bonnets; such men represent man's progress toward enlightenment, the realization of his inborn potentialities. He insists that education is necessary for all classes of society, including the peasantry; it brings respect for one's fellow men, allows good to be distinguished from evil, inculcates good morals. According to Karamzin's utopian vision, "the enlightened peasant" affirms the justice of the order of things and contentedly combines the tilling of his fields with the reading of Homer.

The sciences were the consequence of man's natural thirst for knowledge; the arts were born of his social and moral instincts. The essence of all art was "the imitation of Nature," which gave rise not only to "the utilitarian arts" (poleznye uskusstva), such as the ability to build houses, but also to "the fine arts" (iziashchnye iskusstva), which embellish life.[24] The arts and sciences refine society and contribute to good morals, which is based on Karamzin's assumption that the practitioners are themselves good men. To the elaboration of the necessary connection between great writing and good morals Karamzin had devoted his essay "What Is Necessary for an Author?" ["Chto nuzhno avtoru?"], which preceded "On the Sciences" in *Aglaia*.[25] For Karamzin "talent, knowledge, wit are not enough to make an author. He must have a good, tender heart, if he wishes to be the friend and beloved of my soul." The written word reveals the quality of its author, for "a writer always represents himself in what he creates, and frequently against his will." It is a conviction expressed throughout his career, beginning with his translations from Mme. de Genlis: his words on Gessner are an echo of the characterization in "Églantine, ou l'indolente corrigée."[26] In his second letter to Lavater in 1787 he writes: "Your image, created by my imagination, cannot be completely unfaithful; it cannot but resemble completely its original, for my imagination borrowed the coloring for it from the works of your spirit."[27] In *Aglaia* itself his position is anticipated in the epigraph from Bonnet—"les esprits bien faits qui ne peuvent lire mon coeur, liront au moins mon livre"—and in the epitaph for him. Karamzin concludes his essay: "in a word: I am sure that a bad man cannot be a good writer" and in the final lines of "On the Sciences" he puts himself among the writers whose work will be respected by posterity for its author's moral worth. It is a contrast between genius and evil which Pushkin was brilliantly to exploit in *Mozart and Salieri* [*Motsart i Sal'eri*].[28]

Of Karamzin's contemporaries Murav'ev stands nearest to him in the propaganda of such views on morality and art; in "The Concept of Rhetoric" ["Poniatie ritoriki"] there is a passage which anticipates Karamzin's essay: "Literature presupposes as its subject the perfection of *moral* or *intellectual* beauty (le beau idéal). All its efforts are put to its acquisition or imitation. There can be no beauty which is separate from truth and virtue. Only a noble soul, only an elevated mind is in a position to comprehend and represent its merit. All is bad in literature which is bad in morality and sound reasoning. Consequently before beginning to write, one must know how to deliberate and feel."[29] Karamzin in "What Is Necessary for an Author?" defined art in similar terms as something "which must be concerned only with what is noble, must represent beauty, harmony, and spread pleasant impressions *for the sentiments*" (v oblasti chuvstvitel'nogo). The word *iziashchnyi*, italicized in the original and translated here as "noble" rather than "elegant," has distinct moral connotations in Karamzin's usage.

Both Karamzin and Murav'ev use the word in translating belles lettres and *beaux arts* but the moral inference is more obvious in other contexts. Thus in his translation of *Julius Caesar* he renders Shakespeare's "worthiness," "most noble" and "gentle" by *iziashchnost'*, *iziashchneishii*, and *iziashchnyi* respectively;[30] the word is used no less than fifteen times in his version of Haller's *Vom Ursprung des Übels* for *gut* and *schöne*.[31]

Karamzin's idealist conception of the artist was conditioned by his whole course of reading from his schooldays; it was part of the harmonious optimistic philosophy popularized by authors whom Karamzin read and translated, such as Pope, Bonnet, Batteux, and Engel. "What Is Necessary for an Author?" would seem, however, to hark back to the founder of the school, Shaftesbury. As an epigraph to part 7 of the *Moscow Journal* Karamzin had adopted lines from Shaftesbury which occur in the third treatise of his *Characteristics*, entitled "Soliloquy or Advice to an Author" (1710);[32] although there is no formal similarity between Karamzin's typically succinct essay and Shaftesbury's rambling treatise, there are obvious analogies between the titles and basic ideas.

The first part of *Aglaia*, for which almost all the works had been completed by the middle of 1793, was published in the spring of 1794;[33] it was only in the second part, which appeared in 1795, that Karamzin's extreme disillusionment with events in France during the summer of 1793 became apparent.[34] It made known to the public at large the anguish he had expressed in private letters to Dmitriev, although a passage in "On the Sciences" showed his growing concern. "The poets' Golden Age will come, the age of good morals—and there, where now bloody scaffolds rise up, there virtue will sit on a shining throne."[35] Nevertheless, he had still viewed civilization's achievements and prospects with optimism and enthusiasm; it was precisely a loss of optimism, a sceptical attitude toward the triumph of good which were to characterize the verse and prose of the second volume. It is Karamzin's *Candide*, that "witty and repulsive novel," which he recalls in those letters from England which bear the mark of later reflection before their eventual publication in 1801. Quoting Voltaire's "il faut cultiver notre jardin," he writes that these words "often echo in my heart after exhausting deliberations on the secrets of fate and happiness."[36] It is an analogy suggested by the epigraph to *Aglaia* from

Illustration from Karamzin's *Pis'ma russkogo puteshestvennika*
Translated by J. G. Richter (Leipzig, 1799–1802)

Illustration from Karamzin's *Pis'ma russkogo puteshestvennika*
Translated by J. G. Richter (Leipzig, 1799–1802)

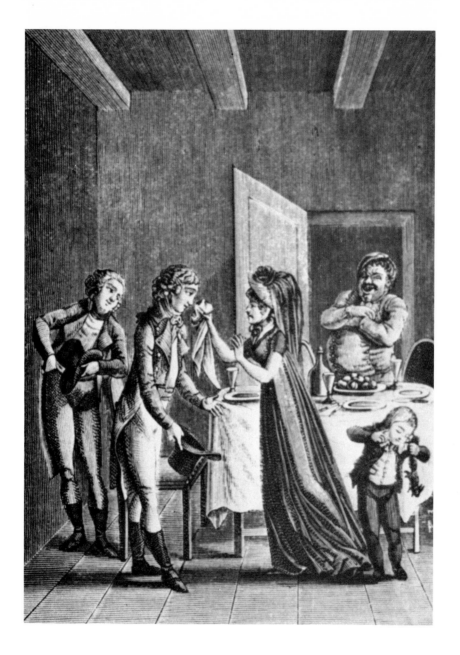

Illustration from Karamzin's *Pis'ma russkogo puteshestvennika*
Translated by J. G. Richter (Leipzig, 1799–1802)

Illustration from Karamzin's *Pis'ma russkogo puteshestvennika*
Translated by J. G. Richter (Leipzig, 1799–1802)

Montaigne: "Je veux que la mort me trouve plantant mes choux; mais nonchalant d'elle, et encore plus de mon jardin imparfait."

The theme of lost illusions is the refrain to the volume. In the dedication to Pleshcheeva he writes: "The phantoms of my youth have disappeared; the burning desires have been extinguished in my heart: my imagination is still. Nothing attracts me in the world. What is there to seek? What is there to strive for? . . . for new sorrows? They will find me by themselves—and without complaint I will shed fresh tears."[37] Although in his "Epistle to Dmitriev" ["Poslanie k Dmitrievu"] (1794) he stresses his love of humanity and wish to help enlightenment—that "passion for good" and "desire for the general welfare" which are required of the true author,[38] he confesses: "But time, experience destroy / Youth's castle in the air; / Bewitching beauties disappear . . . / Now I see a different world,— / And I clearly see that like Plato / We shall not establish republics,— / Like Pittacus, Phales, Zeno / We shall not soften cruel hearts."[39] He seeks his salvation in the love of true friends— of Pleshcheeva: "your tender, generous, sacred friendship provides all the value and happiness in my life,"[40] and of Dmitriev: "Love and friendship—with these / One finds comfort beneath the sun!"[41] He turns away from a world where virtue is abused and asks only for "a peaceful cottage," "To which evil and ignorant men / Would never find the way, / And where, without fear or hope, / We could live together in peace."[42] The virtuous find consolation in their lack of personal responsibility for the evil in the world and await their reward in the afterlife. Karamzin is left with a religious faith which is a resigned and fatalistic acceptance of the ways of Providence. In need of this religious support he addresses a "Song to God" ["Pesn' Bozhestvu"], "composed for that occasion when the madman Dumont said in the French Convention: 'There is no God!' "[43] It is an equation of the madman and the atheist which he inherits from Rousseau and is repeated in "Philalet to Melodor" ["Filalet k Melodoru"]: "I will look up at the sapphire sky and I will look at the flourishing land, I will place my hand on my heart and say to the atheist: 'You are a madman!' "[44]

The consolations of religion—and of literature. Literature now became an end in itself, an escape from reality: "For a moment we will forget ourselves / In the magic of beautiful fictions!"[45] It was an idea which he develops in a letter to Dmitriev in August 1796:

"A poet has two lives, two worlds; if the real world is boring and unpleasant for him, he leaves for the land of imagination and lives there according to his taste and his heart, like a devout Mahomedan in paradise with his seven houris. Vive et scribe!"[46] Not unexpectedly, in a period marked by his preoccupation with *Les Confessions*, Karamzin is here adapting for a different context Rousseau's description of the conception of Julie and his imagined "sérail de houris"; Rousseau attains "le pays de chimères" and "oubliant tout à fait la race humaine, je me fis des sociétés de créatures parfaites, aussi célestes par leur vertus que par leurs beautés, d'amis surs, tendres, fidèles, tels que je n'en trouvais jamais ici-bas."[47] But into the fantasies Karamzin creates—of Ancient Greece in "Athenian Life" or of the remoteness of the woods in "The Deep Forest—his anxieties about the real world intrude.

The exchange of letters between Melodor and Philalet ["Melodor k Filaletu" and "Filalet k Melodoru"] is Karamzin's explicit discussion of the crisis in his world view.[48] In a letter to Karamzin in 1816 Novikov suggested that Melodor was Karamzin and Philalet Petrov,[49] a view which is modified but not discredited by Galakhov's later conjecture that Melodor and Philalet represent two sides of Karamzin's own nature.[50] Petrov's moderating influence on Karamzin during their years in the Friendly Learned Society has been discussed earlier, as has Karamzin's portrayal of his friend in such works as "A Flower on the Grave of My Agathon" and "The Sensitive and the Cold." Petrov was Karamzin's alter ego, an essential part of his own character. The Melodor-Philalet debate is equally a continuation of the Bayle-Shaftesbury correspondence from the *Moscow Journal*, revived in a new historical context. Melodor embodies the despair Karamzin experiences when practice failed so miserably in his eyes to uphold the proud theories of the Enlightenment. "We considered the end of our century to be the end of mankind's main misfortunes and thought that an important general fusion of theory and practice, idea and action would follow, that people would be convinced through morality of the beauty of purely rational laws and would begin to enact them to the letter and in the shade of peace, under the roof of tranquillity and serenity they would enjoy the true benefits of life." Melodor asks: "Where now is the comforting system? . . . It is destroyed to its foundations." His despair leads him to an indictment of his age: "Age of Enlightenment! I do not recognize you —in blood and flame I do not recognize you!" Melodor is the Karamzin who supported active enlightenment and involvement in life, for whom *to be good* was less important *than to do good;*[51] he fears for the future and believes that the *Mizosofy,* the reactionary opponents of enlightenment, whom Karamzin had attacked in "On the Sciences," will triumph. Melodor views the world with unrelieved gloom and pessimism: "now everything existed for me without aim." Philalet is intent on persuading Melodor that the future is not as dark as it might appear; he systematically "corrects" Melodor's views and reaffirms a philosophy of reasoned optimism. He believes in mankind's gradual progress toward perfection and defends with passion enlightenment: "Enlightenment is always beneficial; enlightenment leads to virtue, showing us the close link between private and general good and revealing an inexhaustible source of bliss within our own hearts; enlightenment is the panacea for the uncorrupted heart and mind; enlightenment alone by its invigorating warmth can dry this mud of morality which annihilates with its poisonous vapors all that is noble and good in the world; and only in enlightenment shall we find a true antidote for all mankind's misfortunes!" Despair led Melodor to seek solace in the company of trusted friends; Philalet's optimism, however, does not counsel his former passionate involvement with the world's problems. Philalet's philosophy is tempered by experience and offers resignation and faith rather than the activity of a dedicated enlightener. Nevertheless, the defense of enlightenment is categoric and this provides the stimulus for Karamzin's continued activity as a writer and a search for an explanation of contemporary events in philosophy and history.

At the end of 1794 the editors of the *Moscow News* announced a new feature, to be written by "the respected and kind editor of the *Moscow Journal, Aglaia,* etc."[52] and in the course of 1795 some one hundred and sixty-nine small translated and original items appeared under the general title of "Miscellany." Bolotov found among the first items "some truly very curious ones and completely in the Karamzinian spirit," but was sceptical that the readers' interest and the initial variety could be maintained throughout a whole year.[53] The variety to which Bolotov referred and which Karamzin had promised in his short foreword included anecdotes,

articles on foreign literature, translations from ancient and modern
philosophers, natural history, travelers' notes, prose poems—in
short, the *Moscow Journal* in microcosm. Although Karamzin
emphasizes his interest in "recent English and German books" and
his use specifically of London newspapers, there is a striking predominance of translations from or anecdotes about French authors: Bayle, Bonnet, Buffon, Corneille, Dorat, Fénelon, Fontenelle, Helvétius, La Bruyère, La Rochefoucauld, Malesherbes,
Montesquieu, Racine, Rousseau, St. Evrémond, St. Pierre. Equally
significant is the number of moralists and philosophers in this list:
classical, materialist, sentimental; Karamzin was pursuing a typically eclectic course in rebuilding his philosophy of life. He translates a series of La Rochefoucauld's maxims and a passage from
St. Evrémond with a pronounced Horatian view of life. Karamzin
seems intent on continuing the Melodor-Philalet debate through
translations. He quotes La Bruyère on the essence of happiness:
"To be with those people whom we love is bliss for us, to think
and speak with them, say not a word to them, think about them,
think about the most trivial things, but always be near them, only
with them—it is all the same—we are delighted, we are happy."[54]
This idea of happiness found among one's friends and in a tranquil, moderate life is echoed in other passages, but friendship is
already caring and living for others rather than for oneself: "Base
souls! Be eternal idols for yourselves; never sacrifice anything for
friendship and never know the meaning of friendship!"[55] This is
one step from Fénelon's creed: "I love my family more than myself, I love my country more than my family, I love humanity more
than my country."[56] In this context one of the final numbers of
"Miscellany" is particularly important and is almost certainly an
original piece by Karamzin. Entitled "The Deliberations of a Philosopher, an Historian and a Citizen" ["Rassuzhdenie filosofa,
istorika i grazhdanina"],[57] the philosopher and the historian advance views near to, but not identical with, the arguments of Philalet and Melodor. The philosopher advocates the temperate life,
free from all obligations and concerned only with self: "Happiness
resides within my heart. The earth does not belong to me." His
reliance on the intellect is criticized by the historian, although his
belief that "a man is created not to be learned but rational" is an
extension of Karamzin's conception of the enlightened peasant in

"On the Sciences": "To be enlightened is to be rational, not a scholar, not a polyglot, nor a pedant."[58] The historian looks to history for an understanding of the world; reiterating Karamzin's long-held view that "the philosopher loses himself in systems," he sees history providing a powerful, corrective moral force: it is an anticipation of the burden of the *History of the Russian State*. Finally, the citizen states Karamzin's tenets for a viable and accessible code —patriotism, love of family, honest toil, belief in God.

Karamzin's aversion for systems on the one hand and politics on the other is basic to his description of a new German literary journal, Schiller's *Die Horen*, "the aim of which is to increase in people's hearts *the feeling of good and beauty*. Not a word about politics, not a word about academic metaphysics!"[59] Elsewhere he finds Francis Bacon's analogy of Nature with a pyramid, which has experience as its foundation and metaphysics as its apex, "brilliant and just, despite the systems of *fashionable critical philosophy*."[60] He continues to stress the cardinal importance of feeling: "all is accomplished by feeling in the heart of a tender man; everything in the world touches his soul; everything moves him"[61] and praises the possessors of "the good and feeling heart" in all estates and at all times. The feeling heart is moral; it is also thereby receptive to the aesthetically beautiful; "despite the darkness of our age" it "still finds new food" in Goethe's *Wilhelm Meisters Lehrjahre*[62] and Schiller's journal, "a rare phenomenon in literature" for being "comprehensible, edifying for the soul and adorned with the flowers of the Graces." It is significant that Karamzin's perennial concern for the status of "the fair sex" as arbiters of taste and social intercourse should take on a new urgency at this time, manifest above all in his famous epistle "To Women" ["K zhenshchinam"] (1795) but also in items in his "Miscellany."[63]

Karamzin declined the editors' invitation to continue his contributions in 1796. His prose publications in the last year of Catherine's reign were limited to "Julia," which he had originally projected for a third volume of *Aglaia*, and three translated stories for the Petersburg journal, the *Muse* [*Muza*]. All three were from familiar sources. Kotzebue's "Wer hatte das geglaubt?" (translated as "Kto by semu poveril?") is a tale of a couple who lead separate lives but, brought together by chance, find new delight in each other's company;[64] in its treatment of the tribulations which beset society marriages it parallels Karamzin's "Julia," which in its turn bears the mark of Karamzin's reading of Anton Wall. However, Karamzin's selections from Wall's *Bagetellen* for the *Muse* are quite different. The second of them is in close accord with Karamzin's propaganda for general religious tolerance and in its setting and theme parallels his dream of universal brotherhood in the last of his "Various Fragments" in the *Moscow Journal*.[65] It is also a warning against hasty enlightenment: "What I wish to do must be prepared: for the people are unenlightened and a sudden light blinds" and as such anticipates an insistent theme in the *Messenger of Europe*.

"Catherine II died on November 6 and Paul I is our Emperor. Let us see what changes there will be."[66] Karamzin's attitude toward Catherine during her lifetime was reserved and cool; it was rather "a conspiracy of silence," particularly effective against the background of general fulsome praise for Catherine from a writer whose basic patriotism and adherence to the Russian monarchic system is unquestionable. "To Mercy" was a noble and courageous document, prompted by her interference in the nation's cultural life and arbitrary use of power. Praise for Catherine in the *Moscow Journal* comes not from Karamzin but from other contributors. His few references to her in the period 1793–96 are limited to two brief and conventional allusions to her greatness in his poetry[67] and to a footnote in his essay "On the Sciences," which was omitted from subsequent post-Catherine editions. He lends authority to his own arguments in favor of enlightenment and education by noting "Such are the ideas of our great Monarch, who has opened the way to enlightenment for all her subjects by the creation of national schools."[68] His position is made explicit in his "Reply to My Friend, Who Wanted Me to Write an Ode to Catherine the Great" ["Otvet moemu priiateliu, kotoryi khotel, chtoby ia napisal pokhval'nuiu odu Velikoi Ekaterine"] (1793, published 1796);[69] he asks to be excused for loud singing is foreign to his "quiet Muse." In 1794 he attempted to dissuade Dmitriev from writing odes: "My friend, let our poetasters write such works. Do not humble the Muses and Apollo";[70] that such a position was more than a sentimentalist's opposition to the genre is obvious from his willingness to write odes to Catherine's successors, Paul and Alexander.

Karamzin greeted Paul's accession with an enthusiasm consonant with the long-held hopes of the Moscow masons—one of the major reasons behind Catherine's persecution of Novikov and his friends had been her suspicions of a conspiracy against her in favor of Paul.[71] Paul's generosity toward the disgraced masons heartened Karamzin; he hastened to inform his brother, Vasilii, of their return to favor[72] and in the eleventh stanza of his ode to Paul declared: "Freedom with mercy has appeared; / Paul is on the throne; you are forgiven."[73] Paul had shown the mercy Catherine had lacked and Karamzin pointedly omits any mention of her in his ode. Instead he links Paul with Peter the Great: "Peter I was the beginning of everything; / But with Paul I there shone / In Russia the happiness of people." Paul is indeed preferred to Peter, because "Peter was *great,* You *appeal to hearts*"; he is endowed with all the attributes of the sentimental man: friend of the poor and homeless, bringer of happiness, generous with tears and patron of the arts and enlightenment. His accession seems to have revived Karamzin's fond illusions of a possible Golden Age, which less than two months earlier he had acknowledged as a fiction: "You are presenting me prematurely with a patent of citizenship in the future *Utopia.* Sometimes I concern myself quite seriously with such plans and overworking my imagination, enjoy in advance this height of human bliss. Why should we not compose novels, when our life is nothing but a novel, in part like the novels of Mlle. de Scudéry."[74] This same letter to Prince A. I. Viazemskii reveals, however, that he had acquired a balanced, "historical" view of European events. "Military events have taken another turn in Germany. The French have lost a lot. Wondrous things are happening! The history of mankind becomes more interesting with each century. Some say there is nothing new here; others say everything is new and nothing repeats itself. Whatever the case and however the present war may end, we can say boldly that important and great changes are in store for the political system of Europe."[75] This passage, together with the detailed discussion of French affairs in a letter to his brother in November 1795,[76] anticipates Karamzin's remarks on the French Revolution which are contained in his essay for the *Spectateur du Nord:* "La révolution française est un de ces événemens, qui fixent les destinées des hommes pour une longue suite de siècles. Une nouvelle époque commence; je le vois, mais Rousseau l'a prévu. Lisez une note dans *Émile,* et le livre vous tombera des mains. J'entends des déclamations pour et contre, mais je suis loin d'imiter les crieurs. J'avoue que mes idées là-dessus ne sont pas assez mûres. Les événemens se suivent comme les vagues d'une mer agitée; et l'on veut déjà regarder la révolution comme finie! Non! non! On verra encor des choses étonnantes; l'extrême agitation des esprits en est le présage. Je tire le rideau."[77]

This new, absorbed interest in Europe was counterbalanced by the dashing of any hopes he might have cherished for new cultural and civil liberties in Russia. Paul was soon to introduce restrictions which made Catherine's reign seem by contrast benevolent and tolerant. Karamzin was above all dismayed by the caprices of the censorship which led to an almost complete curtailment of the import of foreign books into Russia and a suppression of politically innocuous works within the country. "The censorship stands like a black bear on the road; they carp at mere trifles."[78] His sense of frustration was such that by the end of 1798 he could write: "I may disappear alive, as an author. The Moscow censors have rejected my 'Epistle to Women' in the new edition of *Aonides*. A similar fate awaits *Aglaia, My Trifles, Letters of a Russian Traveler*, that is to say that probably the censors will want to scratch out and correct any new editions, and I would prefer to abandon everything rather than agree to such a loathsome operation; and thus in a year's time perhaps not one of my books will be on sale. Dying as an author, I exclaim: 'Long live Russian literature!' "[79] Finally, in 1800 Tumanskii, the enemy of Karamzin since the days of the *Moscow Journal*, took advantage of the prevailing mood to show his professional zeal as the Riga censor and to vent his personal spite by stopping the German translation of *Letters* as well as submitting a report on the allegedly seditious nature of Karamzin's work.[80]

Karamzin did not die as an author, although the amount of original work he published under Paul was not great. He wrote principally verse which reflected both the distraction he sought in the salons of Gagarina and Dolgorukaia and his moments of despondency and crisis, occasioned not only by public events but also by an unhappy and protracted love affair. One poem, in particular, described in a moving letter to Dmitriev as his epitaph, expresses tersely and poignantly his state of mind: "God gave me the light of reason: I looked for truth, / And everywhere saw lies—the lamp I extinguish. / God gave me a heart: I suffered— / And my heart I return to God."[81] He published no prose fiction, but began the novel which became "A Knight of Our Time." His only published work in prose was A *Dialogue on Happiness* [*Razgovor o shchastii*] (1797), which contributes a further chapter to the Philalet-Melodor debate.[82] Although the piece ends with the reiteration of Philalet's belief that "to be happy is to fulfill faithfully wise, natural laws and since they are based on the general good and opposed to evil, then *to be happy is . . . to be good,*" Melodor's scepticism is earlier apparent: "Your philosophy is quite comforting; only not many people will believe it." It is an echo of Bayle's description of Shaftesbury's optimism as "an attractive dream."[83] Galakhov has pointed to the close similarities between Karamzin-Philalet's arguments and Pope's in the "Essay on Man"[84] and it is significant that when once more (in 1803, after the death of his first wife) Karamzin wished to condemn his inclinations toward optimism, it is against Pope (and Leibnitz) that he turned, declaring "Optimism is not philosophy but an intellectual game: philosophy is concerned only with clear truths, however sad; it rejects lies, however attractive."[85] This belief forms a leitmotif in his letters to Dmitriev in 1797—the year he published his *Dialogue on Happiness*. In March he wrote: "One must believe in Providence; each of us will receive what is ordained for us and what we deserve; I want nothing else and agree to be patient if I deserve neither happiness nor peace"; in August: "It is necessary to submit as indifferently as possible to the dictates of Fate. Life is a game; et tres souvent ce jeu ne vaut pas la chandelle. Faisons toujours bonne mine!"; in October: "I have no farseeing plans. I do not crawl before happiness—No! Le dos contre le dos! When my heart begins in its old fashion to sigh and argue, I order it to be quiet. Hope is a coquette; it seeks only slaves, deceives them and laughs."[86] The stoicism which Philalet rejects is characteristic of his creator.[87]

A few pages survive from Karamzin's notebooks for the years 1797–98; they are essentially a collection of quotations from authors he was then reading and recorded for the sympathetic response they found in him and as such form a personal sequel of his "Miscellany."[88] Two quotations have an obvious application to his situation under Paul; in a period of restricted civil liberty he saw in man's freedom to *think* as he chose his sole inalienable right. J.-J.

Pompignan's lines "Soyons de notre esprit les seuls législateurs; / Vivons libres du moins dans le fond de nos coeurs; / C'est le trône de l'homme; il règne, quand il pense" are echoed in a later passage: 'Il se faut réserver une arrière-boutique, toute notre, toute franche, en la quelle nous établissons notre vraie liberté." It is again possibly as a result of his reassessment of Paul that he projected an article on Peter the Great, with whom he had hopefully linked Paul in his 1796 ode. "Ideas for a Panegyric to Peter I" ["Mysli dlia pokhval'-nogo slova Petru I"] reaffirms Karamzin's dedication to the concept of universal enlightenment;[89] it echoes his defense of Peter in *Letters of a Russian Traveler* by reference to the French historian P.-C. Levesque and his belief that "the progress of nature is always the same: one enlightenment and one way to perfection and happiness!" To further enlightenment Karamzin was even prepared to justify "certain cruelties": "Constant soft-heartedness is incompatible with greatness of spirit. Les grands hommes ne voyent que le tout." It is a view which holds the key to his seemingly paradoxical love for Robespierre, "the threatening tribune" with "his selflessness, dedication, and strength of character."[90] If such a view equally condones a particular form of despotism, the panegyric in general is an implicit rebuke to Paul for lacking the essential greatness of soul. In the same year that he outlined his panegyric Karamzin wrote the poem, "Tacitus" ["Tatsit"], from which P. A. Viazemskii, meditating on the Decembrist uprising shortly after the event, was to draw an argument in favor of popular opposition.[91] Karamzin had said of Tacitus's Rome: "We should not grieve about it: / It deserved its misfortune of dire troubles, / Bearing what cannot be borne without debasement."[92]

Both the panegyric and the poem point to Karamzin's growing historical interests and are linked with passages in the later parts of *Letters*. In his defense of Peter the Great he speaks of "Tacitus, Hume, Robertson, Gibbon" as the models to follow[93] and in the letters from England, after characterizing the English novelists, he continues: "Robertson, Hume, Gibbon gave to history all the attractiveness of an absorbing novel by their intelligent disposition of action, vividness of adventures and characters, ideas and style. After Thucydides and Tacitus, no one can compare with the Historical Triumvirate of Britain."[94] This in turn leads to the entry in his notebook for June 12, 1797: "If Providence spares me; if what is more frightening for me than death [blindness?] does not happen . . . I will concern myself with history. I will begin with Gillies; then I will read Ferguson, Gibbon, Robertson—read with attention and make notes; and then I will begin on the Ancients, particularly Plutarch."[95] David Hume, missing from this list as an historian long since studied and admired, taught Karamzin that bloodshed and violence in a nation's history were not inevitable obstacles to enlightenment and an age of reason; he considered it a mark of English enlightenment that Hume's history was read and discussed by ordinary London tradesmen.[96]

One further entry in Karamzin's notebook on love, "puissance souveraine qui peut tout et contre la quelle rien ne peut,"[97] is pertinent both to his personal life at this time and his essay entitled "Quelques idées sur l'amour," which he appended to a letter to Dmitriev in December 1797.[98] Dominated by his passion for Princess P. Iu. Gagarina and confessing that no one in love could describe his love, he nevertheless attempted to philosophize on the subject; it is reminiscent of a similar piece in *Letters* with an identical title, "Ideas on love" ("mysli o liubvi"), which was read to habitués of a Paris salon by the abbé D*, although it was the composition of his sister, Marquise L*.[99] Karamzin reversed the roles, signing his essay Md. de Lim**. The Rousseauist contrast between the "amans passionés," whom Karamzin celebrates as "toujours l'objet de mon culte," and the "hommes froids et pervers" anticipates his later sketch, "The Sensitive and the Cold." A feature of his essay is his assured command of French; it reflects his intense reading of French authors and his letters to Dmitriev abound in French words and phrases. Visiting Karamzin in 1800, Kamenev noted: "Karamzin uses a great number of French words; there is probably one French word for every ten Russian."[100] It is possible that the essay, which was never published, was intended for the *Spectateur du Nord*, the editors of which had requested contributions from him and where the first translation of his story, "Julia," had appeared in January 1797.[101]

Closely linked with the surviving pages of his notebooks for 1797 is Karamzin's one major undertaking in the reign of Paul, which reflects both his love of foreign literature and the considerable role translation played in his literary activity. The result of economic necessity and the desire to serve the Russian public—"reason tells me to bedeck necessity with flowers"—*The Pantheon of Foreign Literature* [*Panteon inostrannoi slovesnosti*] was designed as "a collection of *every* type of work, important and unimportant; therefore, it may include a tale, a fragment, an Arabian anecdote." It was to be "a sort of journal devoted to foreign literature," in which the articles were selected from Greek, Latin, English, French, and German originals, "some for the ideas, others for the language." Unfortunately, "the huge and new plan" of the work did not impress the censors: "I have translated several speeches by Demosthenes, which would have adorned *The Pantheon*; but the censors say that Demosthenes was a republican and that one should not translate such authors—and neither Cicero nor Sallust. Grand Dieu! What will become of my *Pantheon*?"[102] Three small volumes were eventually published in 1798 and included selections from Cicero and Sallust, together with Lucan, Tacitus, and Plutarch of Classical authors, but omitted Demosthenes.[103] Despite his awareness of the censorship's excessive suspiciousness, Karamzin refused to have his reading and translating prescribed for him. Although there is nothing which may be termed inflammatory or seditious in the works he translated, some of the contemporary authors he selected were known for their radical views. In his notebook Karamzin had written a number of quotations from Hérault de Séchelles, a man closely connected with the early events of the French Revolution and guillotined along with Danton in 1794; he translated these as "Ideas and Anecdotes" ["Mysli i anekdoty"], together with others which eulogized Franklin and stressed the moral implications of Tacitus's work.[104] Karamzin provided translations from both of these long-admired and "dangerous" authors. He also translated an extract from *Man As He Is,* an obviously self-commending title, but omitted the name of the author, Richard Bage, well known for his "thorough-going radical and French Revolutionary sympathies"; [105] this was followed by equally innocuous selections from William Godwin, "a new author, able to think and write" in Karamzin's view,[106] but regarded with suspicion by English conservative circles: "All creeping creature, venomous and low, / Paine, Williams, Godwin, Holcroft, praise Lepaux."[107] Although such considerations may serve to maintain the independence of Karamzin's position in a period of reaction and stern censorship, *The Pantheon*'s center of interest is elsewhere.

The Pantheon served Karamzin's own needs under Paul; until he was able and wished to speak again in his own voice, he resorted to the words of others. From the point of view of both style and content *The Pantheon* was his own creation: "Until I publish my own trifles, I wish to serve the public with a collection of other people's work, not contrary to good taste and written in a not altogether common style—that is, a not altogether contemptible style."[108] It is the stylistic declaration of *Aglaia,* in combination with the content of his "Miscellany." Although no consistent pattern is discernible in the arrangement of the three volumes, certain themes are persistent; the translations reflect his own sympathies in matters of religion, morality, and enlightenment. His justification would seem to be found in the following quotations from Godwin: "Is not our mind satisfied most of all by the search for enlightenment in the school of those people who better than any others have enlightened their own minds" and "whoever is able to profit from his reading mingles his own ideas with those of an author, analyzes, compares, weighs the writer's proofs, and accepting what is good, rejects what seems to him false."[109]

The extracts which open *The Pantheon* were taken principally from Cicero's *De Natura Deorum* and are arranged and translated in such a way that Cicero speaks as a typical eighteenth-century optimistic philosopher.[110] Cicero, with a faith based on "conviction of the heart" and alien to excessive intellectual probing, pays homage to "a superior Ruler," "a Divine Reason," who had organized the harmony of the universe. He considers true faith inimical both to social unrest—"civil laws without religion cannot always keep man from evil deeds"—and to fanaticism and superstition—"our faith must be reasonable, enlightened, not harmful, unfortunate superstition." Such ideas are echoed elsewhere in *The Pantheon,* principally in the form of Eastern allegories or touching "true stories." In Henry Mackenzie's "Story of La Roche" David Hume learns from the Swiss pastor, La Roche, the comforts of faith and finds that "happy, happy is he who has never doubted the truths of religion";[111] but true religion, which brings self-knowledge and spiritual peace, is also the stimulus to active good, and the bishop Las Casas, in another translation, is praised as one of "the active friends of mankind" for his work among the American Indians.[112] Man is created to live in society and the hermit Galeb is called upon to "return to the world; try to do as much good as possible; love what is noble in the physical and moral worlds."[113] It is the moral of the Persian poet Saadi's "Thoughts on Solitude" ["Mysli ob uedinenii"]: "I do not recommend complete solitude to anyone: man is always in need of man; but seek him only in order to be useful to him. Do good in society only from a love for good."[114] Held up for admiration for the examples they give to and in society are Socrates, epitomizing the virtuous, religious man, martyred by an unjust world, and Cato, praised for his humanity and sense of civil honor.[115]

True religion brings stability and peace to society; similarly, true enlightenment cannot but serve virtue and justice. The monarch-enlightener in "Enlightenment" ["Prosveshchenie"] asserts that "an enlightened people will submit to me more willingly . . . because it will judge better the justice of my laws."[116] The obligations of the monarch are developed at length in another piece by Saadi. A ruler's happiness is the happiness of his people and is maintained by justice: the hero, Kozroes Parvis tells his son: "If you wish to be loved, then deserve love. Do not be excessively fearsome, for hatred is never far from fear." The use of force does not bring stability to a kingdom, for "an army will subdue slaves for you; but slaves are not subjects."[117] The application of this "lesson to Tsars" to Paul is inescapable; Saadi's words are essentially a restatement of Karamzin's ode to Paul. It takes its place in a line of political pronouncements, beginning with "To Mercy" and ending with the two odes to Alexander in 1801 and the *Historical Panegyric to Catherine II* [*Istoricheskoe pokhval'noe slovo Ekaterine II*] of 1802.

Karamzin's concern for the conduct of monarchs is paralleled by his interest in a code for the individual in society. Perhaps as a result of his own thoughts on marriage, he translated extracts from Plutarch under the title "Rules for Married People" ["Pravila dlia suprugov"] and a more somber passage from Bage in which the egoism of a society-loving wife leads to her husband's madness.[118] He continues to stress the balm of friendship in a piece by Rivarol and quotes Montesquieu as saying "I am in love with . . . friendship."[119] His preoccupation with the meaning of happiness is continued in the first of the passages from Godwin, where the view of the need for individual independence and contentment with a little in life echoes *The Dialogue on Happiness*.[120] A requisite for happiness in Karamzin's case was literature and its comforts are duly stressed.

The literary theme in *The Pantheon* is sustained in a series of translations in which problems of style and method are discussed;[121] it is likewise manifest in a critical article on the Ossianic poems,[122] which is consonant with his view of poetry outlined in the introduction to the second volume of *Aonides* (1797), and in his own footnotes to a translation from Lucan.[123] Finally, he included such passages as Tasso's description of Armida's garden from *Gerusalemme liberata* for the appeal of their "language" rather than their "ideas."[124]

The attractions of style and language which Karamzin perceived in the originals was only to a limited degree communicated to his readers. His dilemma suggests itself in the epigraph from P. D. Écouchard-Lebrun, which he adopted for each volume of *The Pantheon*:

> *Gardez-vous bien du mot-à-mot:*
> *Horace et le Goût le renie.*
> *Tout pédant traduit comme un sot.*
> *C'est la graçe, c'est l'harmonie,*
> *Que doit rendre un libre Génie.*
> *Le plus fidèle traducteur*
> *Est celui qui semble moins l'être:*
> *Qui suit pas-à-pas son auteur,*
> *N'est qu'un valet qui suit son maître.*[125]

Such an attitude had led the French to their "tasteful" travesties of the "barbaric" English, and although Karamzin himself required accuracy of a translator, his demand for a graceful and harmonious style was paramount. Some attempt to convey stylistic differences is perceptible in his earlier translations,[126] but his increasing stress on purity of style led him to impose his cultured "middle style" on disparate authors. This tendency was noted in an anonymous review, published in the year following his death; the reviewer, although exaggerating Zhukovskii's technique, remarks: "I do not remember who (possibly Voeikov) noted very justly that in Karamzin's translations everyone spoke in the same way: Cicero and Rousseau, Franklin and Buffon; with Zhukovskii, on the contrary, you find complete diversity: he translates for you not only the author's thought, but also his expression, as he finds it in the original."[127] The list of authors indicates that it was precisely *The Pantheon of Foreign Literature* the writer had in mind.

Karamzin's foreign pantheon was to be matched three years later by a Russian pantheon of a somewhat different nature. The transition is marked in the "Lettre sur la littérature russe," which appeared in the *Spectateur du Nord* at the end of 1797.[128] In this essay Karamzin was able to include comments on the French Revolution, which were as yet unpublished in Russian, and to develop his ideas on the significance and direction of Russian culture. The major part is devoted to a eulogy and résumé of his own *Letters*, but in the opening pages he gives a brief survey of Russian literature. Committed to the belief that "le génie est de tous les climats," he describes Russian folk and epic poetry in terms of a general European background of naïve pastoral and chivalresque romance. He finds "une mélancholie, un doux penchant à la tristesse" characteristic of Russian folk songs and compares the recently discovered *Igor' Tale* inevitably with the "plus beaux morceaux d'Ossian." Turning to post-Petrine Russia, he concedes that "il [the Russian] modela sa langue sur celle des allemands, des français, et notre poésie, notre littérature devinrent l'écho et la copie des leurs." It was an admission he had made with greater regret in his story "Liodor." Russian literature's few attainments were attributable to insufficiently developed taste, artistic inadequacy, and lack of dedicated study, but above all to the absence of enlightened values in Russian society: "c'est que dans un pays où le rang fait tout, la renommée a peu de charmes." He recognized that "en général on fait chez nous plus de vers que de prose; parce qu'à la faveur de la rime l'on se permet plus de négligences, qu'on peut lire une jolie chanson en société à une jolie femme, et qu'un ouvrage en prose demande plus d'idées mûres." Karamzin fought to establish what Pushkin in the 1820's could still term "despised" and "lowly" prose, and thirty years before Pushkin he recognized the degree of intelligence and thought which prose demanded and that without a distinguished body of prose writing Russian literature could not claim maturity. His own view of prose writing an an exacting discipline is well expressed in a letter to Dmitriev in 1799: "If my health improves, I shall start this summer to write *prose* to prevent my mind from coarsening."[129]

Karamzin made no mention in his essay of any Russian authors, apart from himself and the "bard" Boian (or Baian, in Karamzin's spelling). A French public, almost totally unacquainted with Russian literature, might have expected at least a listing of leading contemporary authors; Dmitriev obviously did, and Karamzin argued that "it seemed to me that it was necessary to write about Russian literature in such a way for *foreigners*, lightly, without excessive detail, with a turn of phrase à la françoise . . . They requested from me *a few lines* on Russian literature in general and in addition, extracts from my letters. But what more can I say? We must write as things appear to us; let others judge as they appear to them."[130] Karamzin had, in fact, little regard for existing Russian literature; it was an attitude which inevitably ran counter to national prejudice, although it in no way impaired Karamzin's general patriotic sentiments. As Mordovchenko has rightly pointed out, Karamzin retained all his life "the ability to combine propaganda for European enlightenment with a message of patriotism."[131] Russian literature was still in its infancy by European standards, but possessed distinctive features and looked to a bright future — it was essentially the same message as contained in his "Poetry," written a decade earlier. Karamzin's sense of his own role in the emergence of Russian literature was not without a certain justifiable vainglory. His references in print to Russian authors and works, apart from the reviews in the *Moscow Journal*, were very few. His attitude is clearly revealed in comparison with that of three of his friends, who represent three different generations of writers— Murav'ev, Dmitriev, and Batiushkov. All possessed a good acquaintance with Classical and European literatures, but they do not hesitate to mention and quote earlier Rusian poets—whereas Karamzin quotes only himself. Murav'ev in his "Suburban Dweller" ["Obitatel' predmestiia"] supplied each chapter with an epigraph from Sumarokov, Bogdanovich, Fonvizin, Lomonosov, Kheraskov, and others;[132] Dmitriev acknowledges not only the influence of French writers but also of Sumarokov, Vasilii Maikov, and Murav'ev;[133] Batiushkov in his prose essays quotes among others Derzhavin, Dmitriev, and Murav'ev.[134] Karamzin recognized the influence on himself of no Russian writer. He spoke with respect of Derzhavin, Dmitriev, and Kheraskov; and in his early work there are one or two references to Sumarokov, which are out of keeping with the eulogy of Shakespeare but were probably dictated by the respect in which Sumarokov was held, particularly by Novikov. Kamenev noted Karamzin's objections to Dmitriev's praise of Fonvizin and Bogdanovich and his criticism of Lomonosov's prose style.[135] Karamzin nevertheless acknowledge Lomonosov's importance; he thought of writing a panegyric to him in 1798 and composed a verse tribute "To Lomonosov's Portrait" ["K portretu Lomonosova"], in which he echoed the general appraisal of him as the "Russian Pindar."[136] In 1818 he termed Lomonosov Russia's only "classic" (klassicheskii avtor).[137]

Toward the end of Paul's reign Karamzin's reading took him from European to Russian historians; in 1800 he wrote: "I am up to my ears in Russian history. I sleep and see Nikon and Nestor."[138] In that year he agreed to collaborate with P. N. Beketov on a work to be entitled *The Pantheon of Russian Authors* [*Panteon rossisskikh avtorov*] and published in the reign of Alexander (1801–2), which gave him the opportunity to write critical appraisals of earlier historians and of authors whom he had not considered worth enumerating "for foreigners." The work was published in four large folders, each of which contained five portraits with succinct biographical and criticial notes by Karamzin. The biographies were arranged chronologically and began with the already canonized father of Russian literature, Boian, and ended with Lomonosov. No further folders were issued, although Karamzin added biographies of Sumarokov, Fedor Emin, Maikov, N. N. Popovskii, and M. Popov when *The Pantheon* was included in his collected works. The period thus covered ended with the 1770's; no living authors such as Derzhavin and Dmitriev, no recently deceased writers such as Fonvizin or Kniazhnin were included.

Despite the limitations of these "brief notes" (notitsy),[139] Karamzin's work was a significant contribution to Russian literary history and invites comparison with the only existing work in Russian of a similar nature, Novikov's *Attempt at an Historical Dictionary of Russian Authors* [*Opyt istoricheskogo slovaria o rossiiskikh pisateliakh*] (1772), to which Karamzin alludes in his note on Emin.[140] Novikov's work was an indispensable source of information for all interested in Russian literature; it was a product of painstaking and patriotic endeavor. Despite its polemical nature for the time it was published,[141] it is generally a compilatory and uneven work. Karamzin introduced elements which it noticeably lacked: balanced criticism, historical awareness, stylistic commentary, although these are found alongside passages of sentimental expansiveness, completely contrary to the general conciseness of the notes. All Karamzin's authors are found in Novikov's dictionary, with the understandable omission of Boian and of two authors at different ends of the social scale—the Tsarevna Sofiia Alekseevna and the Cossack poet, Semen Klimovskii. Klimovskii's inclusion was polemical, as is evident from the closing exhortation: "Russian authors, who are here represented! Do not be ashamed to see him in your company";[142] it is also an indication of Karamzin's overcoming of his old prejudice against folk songs.[143] There are few points of contact between Novikov's dictionary and Karamzin's work, apart from inevitable dates and biographical details. The nearest Karamzin comes to an exclusive use of the earlier material is his note on Petr Buslaev.[144] Occasionally, however, Karamzin seems deliberately to dispute Novikov's fulsome tributes, especially to Trediakovskii and Sumarokov. Novikov's expressions of astonishment that Trediakovskii was able to achieve and innovate so much in his lifetime contrast with Karamzin's overt irony: "If willingness and application could replace talent, who would not have been surpassed by Trediakovskii in versifying and eloquence" and "he wrote a multitude of verses to prove that he . . . had no ability for writing."[145] Challenging Novikov's view, Karamzin finds Sumarokov's fables inferior to La Fontaine's and now consistent with his Shakespearean principles, dismisses his tragedies as flat and unconvincing: "He attempted to describe feelings rather than present characters in their aesthetic and moral truth."[146]

Karamzin's literary judgments are primarily linguistic and stylistic comments. Feofan Prokopovich's "language is impure and, one may say, unattractive"; Popov's style is "not always pure and pleasant" and Popovskii's "verse is better than his prose, which is quite lucid but insufficiently smooth."[147] Lomonosov is praised as the first reformer of the Russian language and "the first to discover in it elegance, strength, and harmony";[148] Karamzin believed that his genius was best revealed in his odes, for he lacked the imaginative power to be an epic poet. He concludes with a criticism of Lomonosov's prose in the terms Kamenev recorded.

In his note on Antiokh Kantemir Karamzin suggests that "dividing our language into epochs, we must begin the first with

Kantemir, the second with Lomonosov, the third with the Slavo-Russian translations of Elagin and his numerous imitators, and the fourth with our time, in which attractiveness of language was achieved."[149] It was a periodization which became in effect the signal for Karamzin's contemporaries to identify the new epoch with the name of Karamzin himself. Already in the 1790's there was recognition for Karamzin's organizational skill and initiative and for what was instantly felt to be a "new style." Podshivalov, who had remained close to Karamzin since the days of the Friendly Learned Society, quoted with approval examples from Karamzin's work in a style manual he published in 1796;[150] in 1799 Ivan Heym listed four of Karamzin's publications as providing examples of usage in his Russian-French-German dictionary.[151] Derzhavin and Kheraskov immediately and generously paid tribute to him and were as willing to contribute to his publications as he was eager to solicit their collaboration. Although at the turn of the century, Kheraskov was known in Moscow literary circles as "the elder states-man" (starosta) of Russian literature and Karamzin as "the lieu-tenant" or "foreman" (desiatnik),[152] the authority clearly lay with Karamzin. It was Karamzin whom young authors, such as Kame-nev, Ivanov, and V. A. Polenov, came to see and write about.[153] In the opening decades of the nineteenth century the authority of leading authors, such as Zhukovskii, Dmitriev, Batiushkov, and Viazemskii, rather than the eulogies of epigones like Shalikov and N. Ivanchin-Pisarev, established the concept of the Karamzin pe-riod of Russian literature, but it gained currency not by default or lack of opposition. Even before Admiral Shishkov published his notorious attacks on Karamzin, beginning in 1803 with his *Deliber-ation on the Old and New Styles of the Russian Language [Ras-suzhdenie o drevnem i novom sloge rossiiskogo iazyka]* and extend-ing far beyond questions of style and language, which led to the eventual formation of the two warring camps of the Beseda and Arzamas, writers beginning with Krylov and Klushin had satirized his views and language with a persistence that acknowledged his significance. The most interesting and substantial criticism came from Andrei Turgenev, the eldest son of I. P. Turgenev and an intimate friend of Zhukovskii, who delivered a speech in March 1801, to the Friendly Literary Society (Druzheskoe literaturnoe obshchestvo), in which he recognized, but regretted, a Karamzin period. "Karamzin has made an epoch in our literature and in spite of our Russian character and climate and suchlike . . . He has inclined us too much toward mildness and softness." Turgenev finds Karamzin "more harmful than useful to our literature," precisely because "he writes so beautifully in his chosen field." He believed that Karamzinism, with its cult of minor forms and soft sentimentality, had come prematurely to Russia, which was in need of a second Lomonosov, and not a Karamzin.[154]

Although Turgenev's criticism aptly characterized certain features of Karamzin's work, it was an over-simplification of what he had achieved in the 1790's; it ignored the variety and quality of his work, his integrity as an author, his contribution to Russian literature as a stylist, critic, translator, journalist, and organizer—aspects which were appreciated by many contemporaries to a greater or lesser degree. His work from *Aglaia* to his two pantheons illustrates a long period of stress and crisis in Karamzin's life, of fluctuation between optimism and despair. Although many of his youthful "castles in the air" were destroyed, he had regained a belief in enlightenment and progress which allowed him to take advantage of the opportunities "the beautiful beginning of Alexander's days" was to bring and to weather further disappointments, both public and private. His steady stream of publications testify to his enterprise and energy, but also to economic necessity. His increasing financial needs and his ability to live by his pen and keep his independence point to the transition from literature as a pastime for gentlemen to a dignified profession.

SIX

Karamzin's Verse
and *Aonides*
1796-1799

The Pantheon of Foreign Literature apart, Karamzin's major undertaking in the second half of the 1790's was a poetic almanac, for which he proposed to act as editor and arbiter of good taste. It was conceived in the autumn of 1795, when he explained his project to Dmitriev: "For the past five days I have been occupied with a new plan—to publish in the New Year a Russian Almanach des Muses, in a small format, on Dutch paper, etc. . . . Let us begin —and others in time will take the responsibility for its continuation. Let us open a stage to Russian poets, where they might show themselves without shame to the public. Let us drive away all monsters but summon all who have talent! If we gather little that is *good*, we will publish the *passable*; but we will refuse what is base, impure, and grotesque. Thus each year we could publish a small book of verse—and our ladies would not be ashamed to carry it in their pockets."[1] Originally entitled "Our Muses in 1796" ["Nashi muzy v 1796 godu"],[2] the almanac appeared in August 1796, as *Aonides*.[3] Subsequent volumes appeared during Paul's reign in 1797 and 1799. They were a unique and important phenomenon at this period of Russian literature and provided, as Karamzin had hoped, a forum not only for the best poets of the day but also the promising beginners. By a tradition carried on from the *Moscow Journal*, each collection began with a poem by Kheraskov and all the major contributors to that journal—Derzhavin, Dmitriev, L'vov, Neledinskii-Meletskii, and Karamzin himself—were well represented. The second of the three volumes is of particular interest both for

172

Karamzin's important introduction and the variety and quality of the poetry. Dmitriev, who had refused to contribute to the first volume, sent over twenty poems for the second, which included several poems by Derzhavin, Kheraskov, and Vasilii Pushkin, as well as three by Murav'ev, including "To the Goddess of the Neva" ["K bogine Nevy"], to which Pushkin alludes in the opening chapter of *Eugene Onegin*. The third volume shows a considerable decline in quality, despite the inclusion of no less than twenty-seven poems by Karamzin himself; he was attracting fewer worthwhile poems at a time when he himself wrote that "it is impossible to write *fresh* verse without self-absorption, and something is preventing me from occupying myself continuously with my thoughts."[4] *Aonides* was a short-lived venture; contrary to Karamzin's expectation, no one took the responsibility for its continuation. But the poetic almanac enjoyed a vogue with the next generations of poets, and in 1823 *The New Aonides* [*Novye Aonidy*] was published under the editorship of S. E. Raich and others and included contributions from such as Pushkin, Baratynskii, Davydov, Viazemskii, and Fedor Glinka.

Karamzin enjoyed considerable popularity as a poet among his contemporaries. Derzhavin found his "Epistle to Women" "very, very good," although he was somewhat disturbed by the dubious morality of its final line;[5] it was this poem which "flew from hand to hand" among young Guards officers.[6] His ballad "Count Guarinos" ["Graf Gvarinos"] (1789 and published in 1792) was set to music and was heard sung in provincial towns, giving rise to an amusing error among scholars of the Spanish *romancero*.[7] Another of Karamzin's early ballads, "Raisa," entranced the young Belinskii[8] and Gogol' twice quotes, unflatteringly, Karamzin's poems to illustrate provincial tastes in poetry in the 1830's. It is not surprising that Shalikov and other devout Karamzin-worshippers found him "a most enchanting poet."[9] It is significant, however, that Zhukovskii omits Karamzin from his list of notable poets in his survey of Russian literature and although Pushkin considered Karamzin a better poet than Dmitriev, it is in context scant praise.[10] Nevertheless, Pushkin, not least among poets of the Golden Age, was influenced, particularly in his Lyceum verse, by certain linguistic and thematic aspects of Karamzin's poetry.[11] Posterity has relegated Karamzin to a generation of poets "interesting precisely for its attempts and strivings" and not for its attainments.[12] Karamzin was an accomplished *stikhotvorets* rather than a poet, a distinction he himself made about others but not about himself; as Lotman, the editor of the authoritative edition of Karamzin's verse, has suggested, "it is impossible to understand Karamzin the prose writer and ignore Karamzin the poet," but he concedes that "his poetic gift, perhaps, revealed itself with even greater force in his prose."[13] Karamzin introduced new themes to Russian poetry, brought a fresh approach to traditional subjects and genres, and experimented with form and meter. His verse in its variety and changes provides a commentary on his general artistic and ideological development and his pronouncements on the nature of poetry occupy an important place in his aesthetic theory.

Karamzin wrote verse throughout his career; his first poems appeared in *Children's Reading*, many more in the *Moscow Journal* and thereafter in *Aglaia, Aonides,* and the *Messenger of Europe.* Formally and thematically, they fall into two groups, which have as their chronological boundary the summer of 1793, the period of Karamzin's ideological and spiritual crisis.

A feature of Karamzin's early verse is the absence of rhyme. This in itself is not remarkable, for, as Lotman has pointed out, "from different standpoints Trediakovskii, Radishchev, L'vov and Bobrov criticized the use of rhyme. Almost all the poets at the end of the eighteenth and the beginning of the nineteenth century paid their tribute to unrhymed verse."[14] Its use by Karamzin is, however, distinctive, when considered in relation to his choice of meter and its persistence in his early poetry. Karamzin soon curtailed his active experiments in unrhymed verse but retained an affection for it much longer, as Kamenev recorded in 1800.[15] Dmitriev, who in matters of poetic technique was a much more conventional poet than Karamzin, was nevertheless clearly impressed by his friend's efforts and wrote to Pushkin in 1832 that "since Karamzin (in his early small poems) only Pushkin has made me read unrhymed verse and forget about rhyme."[16]

Karamzin's championing of unrhymed verse finds its closest parallel and commentary in the theories of the young poet in Radishchev's *Journey from Petersburg to Moscow,* who explained to the Traveler: "Ears which have grown accustomed to rhyme will long be a hindrance to a beneficial change in versification.

Since a similar ending to lines has been heard for a long time, the absence of rhyme will seem coarse, uneven, and unharmonious. Thus it will remain, as long as French is used in Russia more than other languages."[17] Karamzin's views on meter were also at this period close to Radishchev's. Radishchev criticized not only rhyme but the predominance of the iamb: "Parnassus is surrounded by iambs, and rhyme stands everywhere on guard."[18] He advocated the use of the dactyl and trochee, believing that the neglect of these measures in Russian poetry had been encouraged by Lomonosov's and Sumarokov's emphasis on the iamb as well as by Trediakovskii's unsatisfactory demonstration of the hexameter's qualities in his *Telimakhida*. In Moscow, Karamzin was attempting to practice what Radishchev was propounding in St. Petersburg; V. P. Semennikov has even advanced the engaging thesis that it was precisely Karamzin Radishchev had in mind in describing his "new-style poet" (novomodnyi stikhotvorets).[19]

In 1788, two years before the publication of Radishchev's *Journey*, Karamzin was advising Dmitriev, who was about to join the Russian campaign against Sweden: "If you yourself should think of extolling your great deeds and those of all our forces, then please sing in dactyls and trochees, Greek hexameters, and not in six-foot iambic lines, which are unsuited to epic poems and extremely wearying. Be our Homer, not Voltaire. Two dactyls and a trochee, two dactyls and a trochee. For example:

$$\overline{Tru}\breve{by}\ v\ \overline{po}/kho\breve{de}\ \overline{gre}/me\breve{li}/\ \overline{kri}\breve{ki}\ p\breve{o}/\ \overline{voz}d\breve{u}kh\breve{u}/mch\overline{ali}s'."^{20}$$

Later that year (November 17, 1788) he sent Dmitriev his poem "To D*" ("K D*"), to which he added the note: "Thus does a poor Moscow poet, now learning to spell out the Greek poets, dare to sing the praises of his friend in Greek meters."[21] When the poem first appeared in the *Moscow Journal*, its metrical scheme was printed above it.[22] Convinced of the novelty in Russian poetry of his chosen meters, Karamzin drew attention to them by a similar device on three other occasions in his journal;[23] in all probability it was a procedure imitated from Klopstock and Ramler—and to be repeated in Russia a decade later by Aleksandr Kh. Vostokov.[24] Karamzin used dactylo-trochaic measures eight times in all in the period 1787–93, experimenting with different combinations of dactyls and trochees, as shown below:

1] ‒◡◡‒◡◡‒◡◡‒◡   ("To D*," 1788)
   ‒◡◡‒◡◡‒

2] ‒◡◡‒◡◡‒◡◡‒◡   ("Autumn" ["Osen'," 1789])
   ‒◡◡◡‒◡

3] ‒◡◡‒◡◡‒◡◡‒◡   ("Recovery" ["Vyzdorovlenie," 1789])
   ‒◡◡‒

4] ‒◡◡‒◡◡‒◡◡‒◡◡‒◡   ("A Sigh" ["Vzdokh," 1789])
   ‒◡◡‒◡◡‒◡◡‒

5] ‒◡◡‒◡◡‒◡◡‒◡◡‒◡   ("The Sylph" ["Sil'fida," before
   ‒◡◡‒◡◡‒◡◡‒   1791])

6] ‒◡◡‒◡◡‒◡◡‒◡◡‒◡   ("To the Beauty" ["K prekrasnoi,"
   ‒◡◡‒◡◡‒◡◡‒◡◡‒◡   1791])
   ‒◡◡‒◡◡‒◡◡‒◡
   ‒◡◡‒◡◡‒◡◡‒◡

7] ‒◡◡‒◡◡‒◡◡‒◡   ("The Cemetery" ["Kladbishche,"
   ‒◡◡‒◡◡‒◡◡‒◡   1792])
   ‒◡◡‒◡◡‒

8] ‒◡◡‒◡◡‒◡◡‒◡   ("We are happy to work in the
   ‒◡◡‒◡◡‒◡◡‒   fields,"[25] ["Veselo v pole rabotat',"
                     1793]).

Several of Karamzin's variations (Nos. 2, 3, 5, 6, and 8) are essentially catalectic dactylic measures, for it is only in the final foot that a trochee appears; yet there is little doubt that Karamzin himself saw them as mixed meters. It is also noticeable that Karamzin never employed the hexameter, such as he had defined it in his letter to Dmitriev. Richard Burgi in his study of the Russian hexameter describes Karamzin's recommended line as "an unproductive and specifically Karamzinian innovation, which eliminates the free logaedic character of the hexameter, changing it in reality to two catalectic dactylic trimeters."[26] This is well illustrated by example 8, which, despite the division into two lines, is the nearest Karamzin came in practice to his own concept of the hexameter. Despite his claims to be an innovator, Karamzi himself was paradoxically inflexible and rigorous in his innovations; he had an academic interest in meter rather than a poetic flair and feeling for the interplay of meter and rhythm.

Although admitting in his dactylo-trochaic poems lines of different lengths, he did not pursue the possibilities in the alternation of dactyl and trochee in the way his German mentors had done.

Evidence of this is the poem "The Sylph," which is a close translation of Matthisson's song "Der Schmetterling."[27] The German original was written in accordance with the adaptation of the Sapphic stanza introduced by Klopstock, whereby variety was given to the successive lines of the quatrain by varying the position of the dactyl in an otherwise trochaic line (see Klopstock's "Die Deutsche Bibel").[28] The metrical scheme of "Der Schmetterling,"

$$- \smile \smile - \smile - \smile - \smile$$
$$- \smile - \smile \smile - \smile - \smile$$
$$- \smile - \smile - \smile \smile - \smile \smile$$
$$- \smile \smile - \smile$$

has been replaced by a catalectic dactylic tetrameter in Karamzin's version.

Karamzin's "We are happy to work in the fields" was his last experiment in mixed dactylo-trochaic measures; the eight poems in which he employed these meters represent 14.8 percent of the fifty-four poems he wrote before 1794.[29] After that date his only use of a ternary meter—if we exclude "Il'ia of Murom" (1794)—was in the song "To Lila" ["K Lile"] (1796).[30] This poem was not only the last example of Karamzin's use of unrhymed verse,[31] and completely unexpected at a time when he weas writing only regular rhymed iambic lines, but also the only time he attempted amphibrachs—an amphibrachic dimeter:

$$\breve{T}y \; pl\bar{a}ch\breve{e}sh' \; / \; L\breve{i}l\bar{e}t\breve{a}?$$

$$\breve{O}kh! \; pl\bar{a}k\breve{a}l \; / \; \breve{i} \; \bar{y}a$$

Thus the rejection of dactylo-trochaic measures was paralleled by the abandonment of unrhymed verse. All the dactylo-trochaic poems had been unrhymed, but there were eighteen other unrhymed poems in trochaic or iambic measures. Only "Il'ia of Murom" and "To Lila" were unrhymed in Karamzin's verse after 1793. The twenty-six examples of unrhymed verse represent 48.1 percent of Karamzin's early verse, but far more revealing is that of a total of twenty-two poems written in the period 1787–90 only *two* were rhymed and one of these was merely a quatrain in a letter to Dmitriev. The decline of unrhymed verse in the second half of the early period (1791–93) is closely related to the similar decline in dactylo-trochaic measures.

A third feature of Karamzin's early verse which requires comment is his use of purely trochaic measures. Trochees had certainly been used by earlier eighteenth-century Russian poets, but far less frequently than iambs; Radishchev, it will be remembered, recommended the trochee as well as the dactyl. Karamzin did not reject trochaic measures as abruptly as he did dactylo-trochaic meters and unrhymed verse; he continued to use trochees throughout his career, but only on eight occasions after 1793, compared with twelve instances in the preceding period. It is interesting, however, that trochaic measures (all tetrameters) appear only three times before 1791 and are unrhymed, whereas there are nine instances in the period 1791–93 and all are rhymed—a marked contrast to the fate of dactylo-trochaic measures.

The contrast in general between the verse Karamzin wrote up to and after 1793 is remarkable. Dmitriev's partial explanation of the change was that unrhymed and regular verse was expected and demanded by the poetry-reading ladies of Moscow[32]—the obstacle of habit which Radishchev had foreseen. Karamzin's increasing concessions to conservative tradition brought his verse back to the iamb-beleaguered Parnassus that Radishchev had criticized. Clear evidence of Karamzin's rejection of his earlier theories and enthusiasms was the publication in the first volume of *Aonides* of his version of a passage from the sixth book of the *Iliad*, entitled "Hector and Andromache" ["Gektor i Andromakha"] (1795).[33] Radishchev's poet, commenting on Ermil Kostrov's translation of the first six books of the *Iliad* (1787), had expressed the wish that "Homer had not appeared in iambs in Russia, but in verse similar to his own—hexameters—and Kostrov, although not a poet but a translator, would have made an epoch in our prosody, accelerating the progress of poetry by a whole generation."[34] As if in support of such an opinion, Karamzin had translated for the *Moscow Journal* a biography of Klopstock, in which the iambic hexameter was condemned as "unbearably monotonous and wearying" and Klopstock was acclaimed for his skill in attempting the true Greek measure in German. Karamzin added a footnote to explain the difference between the true hexameter and its iambic form, the alexandrine.[35] Karamzin's translation in 1795 was not, however, in Greek hexameters but in rhymed alexandrines; Karamzin had followed without demur the translation by André Dacier, and his Homer remained the emasculated and genteel product of French sentimentalism.[36]

Despite his liking for trochaic and dactylo-trochaic meters in his early verse, Karamzin by no means avoided the iamb. Thirty-four, or 62.9 percent, of his poems before 1794 were iambic, but, like the trochaic poems, they show a decisive swing from lack of rhyme to rhyme in 1792. Rhymed iambics became the hallmark of his subsequent verse. He continued to use the tetrameter as his basic line, but he also made wide use of the hexameter and, to a lesser extent, the trimeter. The variety in his iambic verse was provided by a sharp increase in the number of heterogeneous poems, which gave up to three different line lengths within a single poem. There was likewise a new variety in the stanza forms he employed. Seventeen of the twenty-six poems he had written up to the end of 1791 were in quatrains, but this figure drops to a third of all the poems he composed in his career. There are instances of all stanza forms up to the twelve-line, with the single exception of the eleven-line stanza, and the vast majority of the variations occur after 1794.[37]

Karamzin's loss of interest in unrhymed verse and dactylo-trochaic measures and his increasing use of canonized iambic forms would seem to be connected with his ideological crisis and the resulting marked conservative tendencies in his philosophy. At the same time there occurs an undoubted, if not abrupt, shift in his literary allegiances: he became increasingly influenced by French literature and thought. Although retaining his love for German and English poets, he was affected stylistically and thematically by characteristic features of French salon poetry. The strong Anglo-German influences on Karamzin before his journey have already been demonstrated; nowhere in his early work is there a favorable reference to a French poet and he had provocatively excluded the French from his Parnassus in "Poetry." Prominent among his beloved English poets was Thomson, whose *Seasons* is in blank verse and contains the compliment to John Philips' "rhyme-unfetter'd verse" ("Autumn," l. 646).[38]

Karamzin noted as one of the outstanding features of contemporary German poetry its "Greek spirit." On arrival in Weimar in July 1789, he paid a visit to Herder, who read him a number of small poems by Goethe, including "Meine Göttin," about which he exclaimed: "That is completely in the Greek manner." Recording Herder's remarks, Karamzin explained: "Herder, Goethe, and others like them have appropriated the spirit of the ancient Greeks and have managed to bring even their language close to Greek, making it the richest and most suitable language for poetry; and thus neither the French nor the English have translations from the Greek to equal those with which the Germans have now enriched their literature."[39] It is pertinent to note that Goethe's "Meine Göttin" was unrhymed and in a mixed dactylo-trochaic meter, which was, however, used with a freedom and fluency the more restrained and regular Karamzin could never emulate. Karamzin had informed Dmitriev of his attempts to read Greek verse in the original, but, as he confessed elsewhere, he made little progress with the language.[40] Karamzin's attempt to introduce into Russian literature classical verse forms and meters thus arose not from his study and appreciation of Greek originals but from the practice of German poets like Goethe and Matthisson and under the influence of German critics like Herder.

Karamzin's experiments with unusual meters and unrhymed verse were accompanied—from about 1789—by the introduction of far from classical subject matter. His essays in the ballad, his treatment of "melancholy" autumn, and his attitude to nature and God are consonant with themes current in European preromantic literature, particularly German and English. There is in his early poetry a general, pervasive influence of motifs from Ossian, Young, and Thomson, but Karamzin's reliance on German sources is more specific and demonstrable. N. D. Chechulin, believing that "the influence of the lyric poetry of German poets of the *Sturm und Drang* period, particularly that of Goethe, was reflected in the lyrics of Karamzin more than in the lyrics of any other Russian poet,"[41] went on to make several questionable parallels between poems by Karamzin and Goethe. There are, however, more obvious adaptations and imitations of German originals in Karamzin's verse, particularly in the period 1789–92. Karamzin, interesting himself in the historical ballad, based his "Count Guarinos" on Friedrich J. Bertuch's German version of the original sixteenth-century Spanish *romance*.[42] His "Cemetery" is an adaptation of Ludwig T. Kozegarten's "Des Grabes Furchtbarkeit und Lieblichkeit."[43] Also in 1792 Karamzin published his "Song of Peace" ["Pesn' mira"], which was modeled to some extent on Schiller's "An die Freude,"[44] and followed this with an imitation of Magnus-Gottfried Lichtwer's "Die seltsame Menschen," entitled "The Strange People."

To these is to be added his translation of Matthisson's "Die Sch-metterling"; the virtues he detected in Matthisson's songs—"tender meekness, lively feelings, purity of language"[45]—together with their meters, align them alongside the small poems of Goethe which he admired. Karamzin's other ballad from the *Moscow Journal,* "Raisa," subtitled "an ancient ballad" as opposed to the definition of "Count Guarinos" as "an ancient Spanish historical song," bears a strong thematic relationship to G. A. Bürger's "Des Pfarrers Tochter von Taubenhain,"[46] but characteristically, Karamzin re-moves the action into a Nordic setting, naming his heroine and hero Raisa and Kronid and providing a wild Ossianic backdrop.

There is a vigor and variety about the poetry in the *Moscow Journal* that Karamzin was never to regain, even though his later verse reveals his attainment of a smooth and polished diction, capa-ble of expressing nuances of feeling and meaning, but aimed pri-marily at the fair sex and the habitués of the salons. Viazemskii, who possessed a fine historical appreciation of Russian poetry, re-veals in his marginal comments to the 1848 edition of Karamzin's verse how impressed he was by the novelty of almost all Karamzin's poems in the journal.[47] There is little in Karamzin's later verse which recalls his former manner and interests. Only one poem, "Retirement" ["Otstavka"] (1796), which has a certain resem-blance to the opening of Schiller's "Resignation,"[48] testifies to his earlier predilection for German sources, but even here the French epigraph to the poem reveals the paramount French influence at this period.

Karamzin's concentration on German and English literature and the influence of the literary tastes of his close friends and teach-ers had led to a superficial and prejudiced acquaintance with French literature. During his foreign travels his attitude toward France was considerably modified; from that time dates his assiduous reading of French literature. In a letter from Geneva in November 1789, he wrote: "I am reading French authors, both new and old, in order to have a full understanding of French literature."[49] Although Karam-zin retained throughout his career his antipathy toward pseudo-classical drama, French literature increasingly provided sources for translation and imitation, apt quotations, and epigraphs.

This development is seen clearly in Karamzin's verse of the post-*Moscow Journal* period. He turned increasingly to poetic genres always cultivated by Dmitriev—the epigram and epitaph, the madrigal and sentimental love song. These were dominant in his verse particularly in the years 1795–99, when Karamzin sought distraction in the salons and at the balls and card parties of fashionable society. His "Inscriptions on a Statue of Cupid" ["Nadpisi na statuiu Kupidona"] (1798), "Impromptu for Two Young Ladies" ["Impromptu dvum molodym damam"] (1797), and "Inscription for a Lady's Snuff-box" ["Nadpis' k damskoi tabakerke"] (1797) are typical examples distinguishable from the work of contemporary poetasters only by the polish and control of language. Nevertheless, Karamzin was keen to promote the writing of such verse; he wished to encourage literary games in the salon and within the family. He himself provided examples of *bouts-rimés*, verses on set words, as well as of the intricate metrical pattern of the triolet.[50] Although such exercises had none of the rich possibilities of his early innovations, Karamzin thus continued to show his versatility as a versifier. Karamzin's light verse was roundly attacked by young poets such as Andrei Turgenev and particularly I. A. Ivanov, who was impressed by the anguish and nobility of the poems published in *Aglaia* and saw in his society poems an abject betrayal of his former self.[51] It was nonetheless such poetry which was influential at the beginning of the nineteenth century and a characteristic defense of its value came in Batiushkov's "Speech on the Influence of Light Poetry on Language" ["Rech' o vliianii legkoi poezii na iazyk"] (1816). Arguing that "poetry even in minor genres is a difficult art which demands all of one's life and spiritual endeavors," Batiushkov finds Karamzin's verse "full of feeling, a model of clarity and harmony of thought."[52]

The French orientation of much of Karamzin's society verse may be seen from such superficial evidence as the epigraphs to "Hope" ["Nadezhda"] (1796) and "Retirement," in the pretense that "To the Unfaithful One" ["K nevernoi"] (1796) was a "translation from the French" and in the setting of "Separation" ["Razluka"] (1797) to the air "J'entends dans la forêt." An interesting example of French influence may also be detected in "Il'ia of Murom."

"Il'ia of Murom," which Bolotov immediately noted as "a new kind of poem,"[53] appeared in the second volume of *Aglaia*. According to Pogodin, the poem became instantly popular and "everywhere people were soon reciting it by heart."[54] Its general historical importance and its uniqueness in Karamzin's verse lie in its relation to Russian folk literature and the choice of meter. Karamzin subtitled his poem "an heroic tale" (bogatyrskaia skazka) and added in subsequent editions a note on his meter: "I will say as regards the meter that it is completely Russian. Almost all our old songs are composed in this type of verse."[55] He was overstating his case. The meter had previously been largely restricted to eighteenth-century soldiers' songs, although both Sumarokov and Popov had used it to a limited extent.[56] It is usually termed a four-foot trochaic line with a dactyllic clausula, although it has also been called an epic trochaic tetrameter because of the occasional stress on the final syllable.[57] The meter soon became popular and was widely imitated, principally by Kheraskov in his "Tale-Spinning" ["Bakhar' iana"] (1802);[58] it influenced Radishchev's "Bova" (published in 1807) and Pushkin's unfinished "Bova" (1814), as well as possibly N. A. L'vov's "Dobrynia" (begun in 1794, published in 1804),[59] where Karamzin's meter is used in conjunction with other folk measures. Karamzin's meter became mistakenly identified with the Old Russian epic meter, although Karamzin's note refers it back to popular song and not to the *bylina*. It was Vostokov, who had praised "the attractiveness of its style" and "the novelty of its meter,"[60] who finally emphasized the distinction in his "Essay on Russian Prosody" ["Opyt o russkoi stikhoslozhenii"] (first published in a separate edition in 1817), describing the meter as a lyric or *pesennyi* measure, which was "too short and monotonous for large narrative compositions."[61] Karamzin's innovation was to use a song measure for a subject seemingly borrowed from a *bylina*; Vostokov's strictures curtailed such further experiments.

Karamzin attempted to create a poem which fused motifs from Russian folk literature with European literary traditions. He addressed his work to an ideal public of sensitive ladies and men of taste and willingly and consciously abused the true spirit of his Russian source. His poem is the companion in verse to "Natalia, the Boyar's Daughter": not only does his wish to relate a story such as heard "from my late nannies" recall his "story, heard by me in the region of shadows in the kingdom of imagination from my grandfather's grandmother," but his intention to use "an ancient style" (slog drevnosti) parallels his story's "ancient coloring." Karamzin selected certain formulas from folk poetry, such as "softer than yellow way" (miagche vosku beloiarogo), which were easily absorbed into the general sentimental lexicon of the poem.[62] Karamzin's hero, Il'ia, is not the sturdy *bogatyr'* we recognize on the later paintings of Vasnetsov but a sylphlike sentimental hero, with a sensitive soul, responsive to nature and God's goodness: "He resembles fair May: / Red roses and lilies / bloom on his face. / He resembles the tender myrtle: / slender, straight and stately." The heroine is a worthy mate for Il'ia, "a peerless beauty, / a collection of all the graces, / a rarity of attractive female charms." Karamzin displays his sentimental manner in the intimate digression, the confession that a poet's pen cannot rival a painter's brush, typical eighteenth-century eroticism, such as found in a Fragonard painting or a Wieland novel, and the protestations of a simplicity which is wholly literary: "The knight had not read Gessner; / but having a tender heart, / he admired the beauty of the day."

Karamzin was intent on creating a Russian poem in the style of Ariosto or La Fontaine—suggested in the combination of a "Russian" subtitle and the epigraph from La Fontaine. To some degree he had already been anticipated by Bogdanovich, whose *Dushen'ka* (1783) attempts the russification of a story already treated by Apuleius and La Fontaine. A basic and important difference between the two poems is Karamzin's turning to true Russian sources —to the story of a Russian folk hero, as recounted in Chulkov's *Russian Tales*. Karamzin's theoretical understanding of such a verse tale is in his essay on Bogdanovich in the *Messenger of Europe*, where his remarks are directly applicable to his own poem: "*Dushen'ka* is a light game of the imagination, based solely on the rules of tender taste; and for them there is no Aristotle. In such a work all is correct which is amusing and gay, wittily devised, well-expressed."[63] It was in the tradition of Bogdanovich and Karamzin that Pushkin wrote *Ruslan and Ludmila*. Pushkin's poem is connected with Karamzin's not merely through names like Chernomor and themes like the sleeping maiden but also by the bantering tone, the autobiographical detail and the aphoristic turn of phrase. Karamzin's defense of Pushkin's poem for its "liveliness, lightness, wit, taste" against Dmitriev's criticism is totally in character.[64]

In addition to its importance as a work of literature, "Il'ia of Murom" is significant as an ideological document and takes its place in the series of epistles, odes, and expository poems which Karamzin wrote before and predominantly after 1793. It is a series which begins with two poems published in the *Moscow Journal* in 1792, which present the literary and the sociopolitical aspects of his philosophy. "Poetry" initiates a sequence of literary program poems which continues through "Il'ia of Murom," "Epistle to Women" (in part), "To a Poor Poet" ["K bednomu poetu"] (1796), "Gifts" ["Darovaniia"] (1796) and "Proteus, or a Poet's Contradictions" ["Protei, ili nesoglasiia stikhotvortsa"] (1798). "To Mercy," on the other hand, is the first of a series of "civic" poems in Karamzin's work, which is traceable through the odes to Paul (1796) and Alexander (1801) to the two literary works of his "historical" period, "The Warriors' Song" ["Pesn' voinov"] (1806) and "The Liberation of Europe and the Glory of Alexander I" ["Osvobozhdenie Evropy i slava Aleksandra I"] (1814). Although there is a clear line of demarcation between these two groups, there is a third series, concerned primarily with questions of philosophy, which blurs the boundaries and reflects thereby the essential unity of Karamzin's world view. Such poems include the epistles to Dmitriev and Pleshcheev (1794), "Solomon's Practical Wisdom" ["Opytnaia Solomonova mudrost'"] (1796), "Melancholy" ["Melankholiia"] (1800), "To Emiliia" ["K Emilii"] (1802), "Hymn to Fools" ["Gimn gluptsam"] (1802), and "To Virtue" ["K dobrodeteli"] (1802). It is pertinent to note that two of these poems, "Solomon's Practical Wisdom" and "Melancholy," are both derived from French sources: the first is a free adaptation of Voltaire's "Précis de l'Ecclésiaste" and the second is based on a passage in Jacques Delille's "L'Imagination."

"With him there was born in Russia the poetry of feeling, love of nature, tender nuances of thought and impressions: in a word, poetry, intimate, heartfelt. In it for the first time there was reflected not simply the external setting but communicated a confession of what the heart felt, loved, concealed and nourished within itself."[65] Viazemskii's characterization of Karamzin's poetry was echoed by Rozanov, who saw Russian eighteenth-century poetry as a development from "impersonal poetry to the confession of the heart." Karamzin's poetry is an important and harmonious part of all his strongly personal work in prose and does not thereby reveal, as is the case with other writers, an unknown and new personality. It may, however, be read as a self-contained diary of his life and like most diaries intended for immediate or ultimate publication, it does not show the whole man or the whole truth.

In broad outline his poetry traces his spiritual development from the days of his pessimism and unsure quest for self-knowledge to an assertive sense of his talent and skill as an innovator, from a period of philosophical and even artistic crisis to the cautious, resigned position of his maturity, reflected not only in the content but also in the form of his poetry. His renunciation of poetry coincides with his marriage in 1801. The happiness he feels in marriage is not the stuff of poetry: "No, my dear! the love of man and wife is so sacred, / That it must be concealed from impure eyes; / Its heart —a holy temple, its witness—God, not society; / Its happiness—a friend, not Phoebus, the friend of society and hypocrisy: / In its modesty it does not love versifying."[66] "To Emiliia" is a fascinating document not merely because Karamzin essentially appraises the significance and value of the numerous love poems he wrote in the late 1790's but because it draws heavily on his unpublished essay of 1797, "Quelques idées sur l'amour." If this poem brings to a close Karamzin's love poetry, "To Virtue," written later in the same year, is his final poetic homage to "you, who was / In my eyes always charming, / To my soul always dear / And to my heart since childhood known!"[67] It is again a poem of retrospection and appraisal, composed at a time of acute anguish following the death of his wife. In all these characteristics it looks back to the epistles to Dmitriev and Pleshcheev; together they are part of a tradition of poems, particularly in evidence in Catherine's reign, by strongly independent and individual poets, sustained by their dedication to Virtue in periods of ideological crisis (cf. Sumarokov's "On the Love of Virtue" ["O liublenii dobrodeteli," 1768] and Derzhavin's "On Moderation" ["Na umerennost'," 1792]).[68] Karamzin's poems, their intimate qualities notwithstanding, are linked with other poems that are of a distinctly public nature.

The persistence of the civic tradition in Karamzin's verse has been obscured by its seeming opposition to Karamzin's orientation on minor genres, which Andrei Turgenev attacked as the exclusive characteristic of the Karamzin period. It is nonetheless consistent with his intentions to write prose panegyrics to Peter I and Lomonosov and his later published panegyric to Catherine. Karamzin's position would seem to be justified—at least in his own eyes, by his independence as a writer, free to praise, to assume the mantle of the concerned citizen and poet-tribune, or to be silent. It was a position he obviously respected in Derzhavin in contradistinction to such "pocket poets" as Vasilii Petrov. Thus his refusal to sing praises to Catherine because of his "quiet lyre" is first and foremost a political gesture, an indication of his disapproval for Catherine's ignoring the previous year his appeal in a major key, the ode "To Mercy." Nevertheless, his "Reply to My Friend" is also an expression of his view of the ode as a generally insincere genre and its practitioners as pitiful flatterers, which runs through a number of his poems. In "Il'ia of Murom" he describes how "I have seen our knights, / our versifying rhymesters, / drunk with singing odes, / climb the Pindaric peaks, / lose their footing and plunge down."[69] In "To a Poor Poet" he berates ". . . Versifiers, / Tyrants of the ear, pseudo-Orpheuses, / Whose muses lie in odes / With clumsy, pompous words."[70] In addition to these satirical shafts, Karamzin wrote a number of short poems, which reveal once more an aspect of his work which contradicts his general aesthetic position. During his years with freemasons and again toward the end of the 1790's he expresses an antipathy toward satire and even toward literary criticism, but in the *Moscow Journal* and subsequent publications he is prepared to defend his position by criticism, satire, and parody. In the *Moscow Journal* he wrote a prose fable entitled "The Nightingale and the Crow" ["Solovei i vorona"], in which he, the nightingale, is opposed to the raucous and envious crow;[71] this was followed in 1793 by a verse fable, "The Nightingale, the Jackdaws and the Crows" ["Solovei, galki i vorony"], again attacking the poets who "alas, attack people's hearing mercilessly."[72] The nightingale appears in a later fable, "The Screech-Owls and the Nightingale, or Enlightenment" ["Filiny i solovei, ili prosveshchenie"] (1803), where the attack is directed against the enemies of enlightenment.[73] Karamzin parodied feeble poets and playwrights in his "Verses from De Masures to I. I. Dmitriev" ["Stikhi ot De Maziura k I. I. Dmitrievu"] (1794) and "To the Imitator of Shakespeare" ["K Shekspirovu podrazhateliu"] (1797).[74] These poems take their place in a general broadside against the opponents of enlightenment and "the new poetry," for which Dmitriev is usually accorded pride of place for such satires as his "Hymn to Rapture" ["Gimn vostorgu"] (1792) and "Strange Doctrine" ["Chuzhoi tolk"] (1794).[75] Satire and parody played an important role in the disputes between the Karamzinists and Shishkovites in the first two decades of the nineteenth century.[76]

"Poetry," representing Karamzin's early positive views on the nature of poetry and the poet, would seem to indicate by its publication in one of the later issues of the *Moscow Journal* its continuing validity as a program. It is upheld in that journal by a number of statements in original works and carefully chosen translations. To his translation of Meister's biography of Klopstock he adds a footnote on the nature of lyric poetry, the essence of which is found in a "high soaring of thoughts, together with warmth of feeling . . . Our poets generally seek in odes the empty thunder of words — seek and find it."[77] A footnote to a subsequent article from Bouterwek clearly defines Karamzin's demands on the poet: "Mankind and nature are the two great subjects of poetry. He, only he can be a poet who penetrates mankind and nature with his gaze deeper than other men, who finds there beauties hidden from the gaze of others."[78] As Vishnevskaia has rightly insisted,[79] Bouterwek's work is completely in harmony with Karamzin's views. It propounds the view of the "poet-genius" (tvorcheskii dukh) who is able to give noble and moving expression to sentiments and feelings; he possesses "a sensitive heart" and "a fiery imagination" to express the truth which evades the "poet-impostor" (poet-samozvanets), "who lies against nature and the human heart," producing lifeless, unconvincing works. Poetry by its very absorption with nature and man is beautiful and hence moral; thus it does not need to moralize. Although God obviously reveals himself through nature, Bouterwek is not concerned with poetry as homage to the Creator, and he stresses that "we do not know heaven, but we know the earth."[80] This shift is noticeable, if not absolute, in Karamzin. In "Poetry" the first poem is described as "a tender hymn of praise to God";[81] in Karamzin's essay of 1793, "About the Sciences," he advances the view that "the first poetic work was no other than the outpouring of a quietly grieving heart; that is to say, the first poetry was elegiac."[82]

It is in the introduction to the second volume of *Aonides* (1797) that Karamzin gives the most lucid exposition of his later views on poetry.[83] Karamzin continues his attack against bad poets, but it is now on two fronts. Not only does he criticize "excessive pomposity" but also "frequently mawkish tearfulness." Believing that "poetry consists not in the inflated description of terrible scenes in nature but in the liveliness of thoughts and feelings," Karamzin characterizes his true poet as "the slave" and not "the tyrant" of his imagination; he describes what he knows and feels, such as "the first impressions of love, friendship, the tender beauties of nature." Great and lofty themes are not a unique source of inspiration for the poet, who "finds the poetic side to the most ordinary things." Karamzin puts the opposition in a typical aphorism: "The intelligent line lodges itself in the memory, the loud line is soon forgotten." In order to move his reader, the poet should not merely talk about tears or describe grief in general and hackneyed terms, but seek their causes and supply the striking and effective detail: "these features, these details and this, so to speak, personality assure us of the truth of what is being described and frequently deceive; but such deception is the triumph of art." Karamzin's criticism of the epigones of sentimentalism is anticipated in Vasilii Pushkin's "Epistle to I. I. D[mitriev]" ["Poslanie k I. I. Dmitrievu"], published in the first volume of *Aonides*.[84] Pushkin ridicules "All our poetasters / Who desire fame for their tearful lyre" and parodies their themes and attitudes: elegies, love plaints, moonlight and owls, tears and burials—and their punctuation: "Here a mass of exclamation marks and dots will appear!" Although such criticism might seem to apply to the youthful Karamzin, Pushkin defends "our Sterne," "the sweet and tender -in," and also excludes Dmitriev, Derzhavin, and Kheraskov as poets who imitated great models but were able to be great themselves. It is clear that there was emerging an inner group of "sons of Apollo" who indulged in mutual compliments and were raised above the mediocrity of both their opponents and their followers.[85]

Karamzin's basic ideas in *Aonides* are reiterated and developed in the series of important program poems of the mid-1790's. In his "Epistle to Women" Karamzin combines his demand for the subtle rendering of emotional and psychological states with a sentimentalist's typical homage to woman and her beneficient influence on literature and society; he insists that his reason for becoming a writer was "In a pure style, comprehensible to the heart, / To depict for you the nuances / Of happy and unhappy passions, / Both mild and terrible; / So that you might say: / 'He is truly sweet and faithfully translates / All that is obscure in our hearts into clear language; / He finds words for delicate feelings.' "[86] The concern with "the picture of the moral world" is emphasized in "Gifts" and the poet *"Depicts hearts for the eyes* / With his living brush: / The ebb and flow of passionate desires, / Their shadings, benefit, sweet poison; / The bright paradise, the heaven of beautiful souls, / The harm of vice and the hell of malice."[87] In "Proteus" Karamzin defends the poet's right to change constantly in mood and attitude and sees his only obligation in the recording of these changes: "These contradictions should not be held against / The favorites of the tender muses; their task is to express / The nuances of different feelings, not to harmonize ideas; / Their task is not to resolve, but to move and amuse."[88] It is in accord with such preferences that the sentimentalist's favorite mood is melancholy, that "most tender transition / From grief and longing to the delights of enjoyment! / As yet there is no gaiety but no longer is there torment."[89]

The poet's interest in "every aspect of nature"[90] parallels his absorption in the world of emotions, but whereas his desire to describe psychological states and nuances in sentiments suggests an advance toward a complex and profound portrayal of character, his depiction of nature—as opposed to his historically important interest in the natural world—is pale and conventional. The early fluctuations in Karamzin's attitude toward nature have been described in the first chapter: although Karamzin could write in 1787 to Lavater that "art always cedes to nature and a copy is always worse than the original,"[91] his friend, Petrov, was to ask him the same year "how can a person who finds no attraction in the original itself still acquire a taste for belles-lettres and the artificial imitation of beautiful nature?"[92] He came genuinely to love nature for itself, but writes in 1796: "And frequently the charm in an imitation / Is more appealing to us than in nature itself: / A wood, a flower, which have been described / Are even more pleasing to the eye,"[93] and he admits that without the descriptive poetry of St. Lambert, Thomson, Delille, and Kleist nature would be less attractive. In a footnote to this passage he comments that "all the charms of the fine arts are no other than the imitation of nature; but the copy is sometimes better than the original, at least it makes it more absorbing for us: we have the pleasure of comparing." In practice, the poets Karamzin admires do not so much allow him to compare as dictate to him his vision of nature. Although the idea of Karamzin as a nature poet seems to impress itself, in fact very little of his poetry is concerned with the depiction of nature. Nature is present in a number of poems as a soothing background for the troubled poet or occasionally provides a contrast to his moods, but it is nature almost without the individual detail, a lacquered nature, certainly nearer to the picturesque English garden than the French, full of bosky groves, winding rivers, and feathered friends. "The Volga" (1793) is almost a unique nature poem in Karamzin's work, but again perhaps the nearest to Thomson's manner, not least in the juxtaposition of a local detail—the sturgeon—with the periphrastic "damp element."[94]

A similarly ambivalent position is apparent in Karamzin's view of art as deception. In the sense in which it is advocated in the introduction to *Aonides* it is a deception based on careful observation and the convincing detail and is opposed thereby to the pomposity and falsity of the ode writer's rhetoric. Both the theory of art as imitation of beautiful nature and of poetry as "un mensonge perpétuel, qui a tous les caractères de la verité"[95] originate for Karamzin with Batteux, but in Karamzin's insistence on *"Lie, Untruth, the appearance of truth,"*[96] solely in his poetry after 1793, the ideological implications are obvious. In "To a Poor Poet" the poet is counseled: "My friend! Reality is poor: / Play in your soul with dreams,/ Otherwise life will be boring." In a world where "By an impenetrable mist / Truth is concealed from us," the poet is free to spin his attractive fictions: "whoever is able to invent pleasantly, / In verse or prose—he is fortunate! / It is necessary only that it be probable. / What is a poet? A skillful liar: / To him the glory and the crown!"[97] The realities of life have shattered the poet's fond illusions; he is unable to discover truth and he abandons the real world for his imaginative world, concerned only to make "le beau idéal" "vraisemblable."

Both Karamzin's poetic theory and practice point to that eclecticism which is a basic feature of his general literary and philosophical position. In his early poetry there are themes and attitudes which are truly preromantic and even in his later work the poet's absorption in his own subjective world points to the individualism of the Romantics. He campaigns for Shakespeare but is nevertheless strongly influenced by such critics as Batteux and Bouterwek.[98] Essentially in his poetry of the later 1790's he reveals himself to be an "Augustan" poet, if this term may be introduced into a Russian context without excessive qualification and confusion. The term suggests itself not merely by his predilection for Pope, particularly evident at this period, or for Thomson, but by his general philosophy of life and art, the balance which he attempts to achieve between reason and sentiment, his concern for language and the establishment of poetic diction. If satire and criticism are taken as a characteristic aspect of the Augustan poet, there is much in Karamzin's poetry to support this, as has been shown earlier. It may be argued that the suggested influence of French poetry on the later Karamzin in no way contradicts the use of "Augustan," for the "gold" of such poets as Thomson and Pope was immediately accessible to the French and free from the "dross" they found in Milton, Young, or Shakespeare.

Karamzin was intent on encouraging poets to write with true feeling and taste, but also on insisting that they write correctly and smoothly. His attention to exactness of expression, correct word-stress and rhyme is in evidence in his footnotes to N. L'vov's poem in the *Moscow Journal* and to the work of a young poet in the *Messenger of Europe*.[99] His letters to Dmitriev in the 1790's are a continuous discussion of the appropriateness of expressions and the aesthetic connotations of words;[100] his suggestions were almost invariably accepted by Dmitriev, even if occasionally they are an amusing anticipation of Turgenev's purist corrections of the poetry of Fet and Tiutchev.

Both as poetic theorist and practicing poet Karamzin was influential in his time. Although his wide knowledge, his intelligence, his taste, even his revered sensibility did not in themselves make him a poet, they were the guarantee of the interest and often the potential of what he attempted. The realization of the potential was the achievement of the next generation of poets. Viazemskii suggested that Karamzin's accolade for poetry was "c'est beau comme de la prose"[101] and in some of his marginal comments indicated an exactness of expression in Karamzin's verse which was essentially prosaic.[102] It was in prose that Karamzin wrote his best poetry; as early as August 1791, Derzhavin noted: "Sing, nightingale!—and in prose / You are heard [Karamzi]n."[103]

The *Messenger of Europe*

1802~1803

IN FEBRUARY 1801, Karamzin wrote to his brother, Vasilii, that he desired the advent of spring and nothing more;[1] spring came and brought much more. In March Paul was assassinated and Alexander came to the throne, and Karamzin in the ode on his accession wrote: "Hearts are ready to breathe in You: / Our spirit is revived by hope. / Thus does the appearance of sweet spring / Bring with it oblivion / Of all the dark horrors of winter."[2] After the gloom of Paul's reign Karamzin not unexpectedly experienced the wave of optimism which swept through Russia. F. F. Vigel' described how "everyone felt a kind of moral expansion, looks became kinder, the walk bolder, the breathing freer";[3] Grech sought to characterize the change by reference to Karamzin's own sentiments: "It is impossible to describe the astonishment, joy, enthusiasm, aroused by what was in fact an unfortunate, loathsome event [Paul's murder]. Russia breathed freely. No one thought of pretending any more. Karamzin justly remarked in his memoir on the state of Russia: 'Who was more unfortunate than Paul! Tears at his death were shed only within his family.' Not only in words but in writing, in print, particularly in poems, people expressed their joyful feelings of release from his tyranny."[4]

Karamzin's optimism was further sustained by personal and literary events. In April he married Elisaveta Ivanovna Protasova, the sister of Anastasia Ivanovna Pleshcheeva, his "unique, incomparable friend," the object for so long of a typical sentimental cult of the married woman;[5] "Emiliia" henceforth assumed the position in his work previously occupied by "Aglaia-Nanina." Also in April new or withheld editions of his works began to appear; there was a reprinting of the first two volumes of *Aonides* and a third edition of *Aglaia* and of *My Trifles,* bearing the date and indication of the second edition, but with the discreet omission of Karamzin's ode to Paul. In July the fifth volume of *Letters* was released, together with a reprinting of the earlier volumes, and finally in December the sixth and last volume appeared. The end of 1801 saw the first folder of *The Pantheon of Russian Authors,* which continued into 1802, when the second edition of the *Moscow Journal* was started. Thus his first journal again became available at the same time as he was editing his new *Messenger of Europe.* Following the relaxation of the censorship on Alexander's accession, the Moscow publishers courted Karamzin as the most popular and potentially profitable author in Russia. Richter was soon spreading through Europe details of the unheard-of sums for a Russian author which Karamzin received for his *Historical Panegyric to Catherine II* and the *Messenger of Europe.*[6]

The *Messenger of Europe* is the focal point of Karamzin's thought and work at the beginning of Alexander's reign; it is the culmination of his pioneering work for Russian literature and his swan song before his entry into "the temple of History."[7] His reputation and influence throughout Alexander's reign were challenged but not destroyed, although only with the publication of the first eight volumes of his *History of the Russian State* in 1818 did he again occupy the literary limelight. The experiences of the decade between the *Moscow Journal* and the *Messenger of Europe* had modified his approach to journalism; in the earlier journal he had been preeminently a man of letters; to this role he now added those of an historian and a political publicist. His propaganda for enlightenment took on a new, strongly nationalistic coloring. Karamzin was both the editor and chief contributor of the *Messenger of Europe;* he left his stamp on every aspect of its contents and presentation as indelibly as he had done on his earlier journal. Karamzin himself was perhaps not fully aware to what degree he assumed his new role as public tribune; in the foreword to the first issue (as well as in an article at the end of 1802) he emphasizes his concern for literature and enlightenment and expresses the hope that the political section for "the sake of Europe will not be very rich and interesting."[8] The journal is divided into two parts: "Literature and Miscellany" and "Politics," but politics dominate the journal not only in the form of European news but also as open discussion of Russia's internal reforms. "Literature and Miscellany" brings to a close Karamzin's work as a poet, translator, story writer and reformer of the Russian literary language; "Politics" concentrates his earlier scattered ideas and remarks on historical, political, and social questions into a comprehensive system and points to the future development of his career.

In certain respects the literary section continues the traditions of the *Moscow Journal*. Of the original five features Karamzin planned for his earlier journal, three—Russian works in verse and prose, translations, and interesting anecdotes—remain; a fourth—critical reviews of Russian books—is continued with severe limitations in its scope and, consequently, in its interest, and the fifth—drama criticism—is completely rejected. The literary works Karamzin chose to translate lack the interest and variety of those in the *Moscow Journal*. He turned once more to Mme. de Genlis, whose religiosity, moralizing, and attacks on "false" philosophers pervade a series of stories appearing from part 2 of the journal. Characteristic of the prevailing tastes of the day is the translation of a tale by August Lafontaine, who rivaled Genlis, Marmontel, and Kotzebue in popularity with the Russian reading public. English, French, and German journals provided Karamzin with a wealth of Eastern allegories, moral fables, and news snippets of a literary nature. Despite the orientation on foreign literature, which Karamzin himself indicates in an editorial at the end of 1802, original contributions from Karamzin and his friends provide the main literary interest in the journal. Ivan Dmitriev, now living in retirement in Moscow and collaborating closely with Karamzin, regularly contributed poems; there are also poems by Derzhavin, Kheraskov, and Neledinskii-Meletskii, but the one poem of particular note is Vasilii Zhukovskii's version of Gray's *Elegy*.[9] Karamzin's own verse, which includes the "Hymn to Fools," "Melancholy," and "To Virtue," forms a distinctive and important coda to his work as a poet, but it is his prose rather than his verse which marks a final significant stage in his creative work. "A Knight of Our Time," "Martha the Mayoress," "My Confession," and "The Sensitive and the Cold" reveal his search for new themes and narrative techniques.

Karamzin's unwillingness to continue his drama and book reviews was rooted in his changed attitude toward literary criticism.

In the opening "Letter to the Editor," which he wrote himself, Karamzin formulates his new position: "But does criticism really teach one how to write? Do not models and examples act more strongly? And have not talents everywhere preceded learned and stern judgement? La critique est aisée, et l'art est difficile! Write whoever is able to write well: that is the best criticism of bad books!"[10] At the end of 1802 he is insisting: "As far as the criticism of new Russian books is concerned, we do not consider it a true requirement of our literature (not to mention the unpleasantness of dealing with the easily injured vanity of people). It is more useful for an author to be judged than to judge. Good criticism is the luxury of literature; it is born of great riches, and as yet we are not Croesuses. It is better to add to the general *estate* than to be concerned with its evaluation."[11] Karamzin was now in direct opposition to the standpoint he had adopted in the *Moscow Journal* in the dispute between Podshivalov and Tumanskii over the value of criticism. Clear evidence of his *volte-face* is the exclusion of the exchanges between Tumanskii and Podshivalov from the second edition of that journal. But Karamzin's change of heart came equally from his new patriotic fervor and his conviction that young Russian authors were to be encouraged rather than condemned: "We are not aristocrats in literature: we do not look at names but at works, and we are sincerely glad to help the emergence of young authors."

The change in emphasis in Karamzin's attitude did not bring an absolute renunciation of criticism. Although, as Makogonenko has demonstrated,[12] he tended to substitute for the review the leading article, in which he propounded criticism of a general rather than specific nature, Karamzin states: "We make no promise that sometimes we will not discuss old and new Russian books; it is merely that we do not accept a definite obligation to be critics." The criticism in the *Messenger of Europe*, unlike that in the *Moscow Journal*, is occasional and unsystematic, but nonetheless of considerable extent and importance. Karamzin exercised restraint when reviewing Russian works, but was outspoken with foreign literature. Karamzin reviewed recent foreign, predominantly French, works, which were not yet available in Moscow, such as J. J. Barthélemy's *Voyage en Italie*, Mme. de Staël's *Delphine*, and Chateaubriand's *Génie du Christianisme*. Karamzin's attack on Chateaubriand's work is heavily ironical—and both the technique and tone are reminiscent of his review of Nikolev's *Spoilt Darling* in the *Moscow Journal*: "We cannot imagine anything more foolish than this nonsense. Such is the way some of the new French authors write. I assure readers that my new translation is as faithful as any in the world."[13] Foreign works in Russian translation were also reviewed. Karamzin was particularly enthusiastic about N. I. Strakhov's translation of Barthélemy's *Voyage du jeune Anacharsis*, which he considered one of the outstanding works of the eighteenth century,[14] and he praised the "zealous patriotism" of H. Storch, whose historical survey of Russian trade was being translated from German.[15] The third of such reviews—of a translation of E. F. Lantier's *Voyages d'Antenor* [*Antenorovy puteshestviia po Gretsii i Azii* (Moscow, 1802)], is particularly interesting for its similarity to Karamzin's earlier reviews of translated works; it is even introduced under the heading "Criticism" and reveals his old techniques at every turn. An examination of the book's contents is followed by close attention to the quality of the translation. Nevertheless, aware that a review of this nature contradicted his new position, Karamzin was at pains to minimize the effect of his criticism: "But isn't such criticism carping? We are not to blame if we find here no very important mistakes; and thus discovering from our unsuccessful attempt at criticism that the translator has taken measures to ensure against criticism, we close the Russian Antenor."[16]

These reviews apart, the main criticism in the *Messenger* is contained in two major articles, one by Dmitriev and the other by Karamzin. Dmitriev's "On Russian Comedies" ["O russkikh komediiakh"] is the only dramatic criticism in the journal: it advances a concept of genteel comedy in opposition to coarse naturalism and attacks the vogue for vulgar farce and comedy.[17] Karamzin's article is devoted to the life and work of Ippolit Bogdanovich, whose death in 1802 occasioned a flood of inept epitaphs in the *Messenger*.[18] "On Bogdanovich and His Works" ["O Bogdanoviche i ego sochineniiakh"] is a notable milestone in the history of Russian literary criticism.[19] Karamzin attempts to trace Bogdanovich's development as an author, to analyze his main work, *Dushen'ka*, and to compare it with La Fontaine's *Les Amours de Psyché et de Cupidon*, which was its model. Uniting an exposition of certain systematic theories on the nature and obligations of art, a wide knowledge of his subject, and an ability to write in a lucid and engaging style, Karamzin was obviously at the same time serving his basic thesis in the *Messenger*—applaud, rather than condemn, things Russian—and thereby modifying his true assessment of Bogdanovich's worth. In 1800 Kamenev had heard Karamzin criticizing Bogdanovich's work, particularly certain lines from his translation of Voltaire's poem on the Lisbon earthquake,[20] although by 1803 he could write: "Bogdanovich translated [the poem] so successfully that many lines match the beauty and strength of the French." In addition, Karamzin tends to re-create Bogdanovich in his own sentimentalist image and basic facts from Bogdanovich's biography serve as a starting point for an exposition of Karamzin's views on the joys of artistic creation, on the requirements for a peaceful life, or even on the undesirability of stern criticism. On the other hand, Karamzin's comparison of the relative values of prose and verse on the basis of concrete examples and his assessment of Bogdanovich's contribution to Russian literature are objective and historically important.

A further interesting aspect of literary criticism in the journal are translated articles which accord with Karamzin's opposition to the excesses of lachrymose sentimentalism, already apparent in his foreword to the second volume of *Aonides*. He translates a letter about a projected ten-volume history of tears, which reduces to the absurd the use of tears for all occasions and at all epochs.[21] A translated review of Delille's latest poetry criticizes its monotony, affectation, and emotionalism.[22] These translations are closely connected with Karamzin's self-criticism in "My Confession," which had appeared at the end of 1802.

Karamzin's desire to review Russian literature more indulgently than he had done in the 1790's and to relate its development to post-Petrine Russia's advance toward enlightenment was already evident in the *Pantheon of Russian Authors*, which although conceived in Paul's reign, is preeminently in the spirit of Alexander's. Karamzin in fact reviews his *Pantheon* in *Messenger* and prints in full his notes of Prokopovich, Trediakovskii, and Lomonosov. These are prefaced by his attempt at a new periodization of eighteenth-century Russian literature: "Feofan and Kantemir comprise this first epoch: this is followed by Lomonosov and Sumarokov; the third must be termed the reign of Catherine the Great, already rich in the number of authors; and we are still awaiting the fourth."[23] Karamzin was engaged not only in formulating an apology for earlier Russian literature but in directing Russia's immediate literary development. The fourth period was to be the reign of Alexander, which he describes in his program for the *Messenger* as a time "when the sciences and arts by their rapid progress promise even greater successes; when talents, in free peace and ease, can devote themselves to all subjects which are useful and dear to the soul; when in the present intellectual climate, literature should have a greater influence than ever before on morality and happiness."[24] Despite the fact that there was still a lack of talent and taste in Russian authors, he believed that "in Russia literature can be even more useful than in other lands: feeling is newer and fresher in us; the beautiful therefore acts more strongly on the heart and bears greater fruit."[25]

Karamzin had clearly rejected his view of literature as private consolation for the poet and his friends, to which he had been driven by adverse conditions in Russia and Europe. His path to a utilitarian and patriotic view of art was both logical and predictable. The disillusionment he had suffered from events in France bolstered his patriotic feeling and suggested the important role that Russia might play in European affairs. The task of literature was therefore not only to consolidate Russia's eminence in the eyes of Europe but also to inspire pride in Russians: "It is nearer and dearer for Russian talent to praise what is Russian in this happy time, when the Monarch and Providence itself call us to true glory. Russians must be taught to respect what is their own; they must be shown how it can become the subject for an artist's inspiration and for the strong effects of art on the heart. Not only the historian and the poet, but also the painter and the sculptor are organs of patriotism."[26]

Pursuing this aim in another essay, "On Love of One's Country and National Pride" ["O liubvi k otechestvu i narodnoi gordosti"], he exaggerates the importance of certain (unspecified) works of Russian literature: "The successes of our literature . . . show the great ability of Russians. Have we not long known what style in verse and prose is?—and we can in certain respects already compare ourselves with foreigners. Already in the sixteenth century in France Montaigne was philosophizing and writing—is it any wonder that in general they write better than we do? On the other hand, isn't it a wonder that some of our works can be placed alongside the best of theirs both for the painting of ideas as well as for nuances of style? Let us at least be just, dear compatriots, and feel the value of our own."[27] He follows this with an eulogy of the Russian language: "Our language is expressive not only for lofty rhetoric, for loud, colorful poetry but also for tender simplicity, for the sounds of the heart, and sensibility. It is richer in harmony than French and more able to render tones in the outpouring of the soul; it offers more *analogous* words, i.e., in accord with the action being expressed—an advantage enjoyed only by root languages. Our misfortune is that we all wish to speak French and do not think of perfecting our own language: is it surprising that we are thus unable to express in it certain subtleties in conversation?"[28]

Karamzin reiterated these views in an important essay directly concerned with the problems of Russian literature and language, "Why Are There Few Writers of Talent in Russia?" ["Ot chego v Rossii malo avtorskikh talantov?"]. In his analysis of literary backwardness in Russia, Karamzin seeks the causes "not in the climate, but in the circumstances of Russian civic life."[29] He demands application and study from the aspiring writer and an ability to understand and use language. In contrast to the previous essay, Karamzin is now concerned with realities rather than possibilities. Thus the comparative immaturity of the Russian language is acknowledged as well as the lack of inspiring models in most literary genres. He sees the normal solution to the problem of the development of a language in the spoken word, but stresses that society women, the usual source for attractive language, spoke only French. He does not consider, however, going beyond polite society to the Russian-speaking classes, for this would be to bypass the gentry whose enlightenment and advancement were his political concerns. Consequently, his solution is intellectual and artificial. It relies on the example of fully developed European languages and the potentialities within the Russian language that a man of talent or genius might reveal: "What is there left for an author to do? Invent and devise expressions, sense the best choice of words, give to the old a certain new sense, present them in a new combination, but so skillfully as to deceive readers and conceal from them the unusualness of the expression."[30] These are the principles Karamzin followed consistently, founded on his view that "the French write as they speak, and Russians still have to speak on many subjects in the way a talented man will write."[31]

Karamzin's concern with national needs and virtues in matters of language and literature do not necessarily bring him into conflict with the basic tenets of his earlier cosmopolitanism. The *Messenger* reveals his tendency to point out the failings and inadequacies of other literatures, particularly of contemporary English literature,[32] but Karamzin was far from renouncing his love of great writers and thinkers, essential to his understanding of enlightenment. His theoretical admiration for the true cosmopolitan mind is upheld in a translation he made of Herder's "Gespräch über eine unsichtbar-sichtbare Gesellschaft" (1793). The desired society, unlike Freemasonry, is one "which is not secret, not hidden from the light, but working openly, not with ceremonies and symbols, but with lucid words and deeds, not confined to two or three nations, but everywhere where there is true enlightenment."[33] Above national prejudices and petty strife, the society would draw its inspiration from the world of books and a love of humanity. "In conversation with Homer, Plato, Xenophon, Tacitus, Bacon, Fénelon, I do not think of what state they belonged to, what class they were from, and what temples they prayed in."[34]

Retaining his love of such ideals, Karamzin stresses the nobility of patriotism. Truly great writers, for instance, are shown to be great patriots; Klopstock "attempted to shame his pitiful fellow citizens and ceaselessly praised love for one's country in a land where for several decades the nation had respected only what was foreign."[35] Karamzin was sensitive to the negative connotations of the word "cosmopolitan" and contrasted sham cosmopolitan with the inspiring example of Peter the Great: "He was a Russian in his soul and a patriot; and those gentlemen anglomaniacs or gallomaniacs wish to call themselves cosmopolitans. Only we ordinary people cannot soar with our minds above *base* patriotism; we stand on the earth, Russian earth; we look at the world not through the spectacles of systematic philosophers but with our own natural eyesight."[36]

Peter is central to Karamzin's concept of Russian enlightenment; his reforms mark the beginning of Russia's accelerated advance toward equality with the West and his example, according to Karamzin's thesis, inspired Catherine and Alexander. Reviewing a poem by André Chénier on enlightenment, Karamzin pointedly adds the footnote: "And Peter the Great?" to Chénier's tribute to Frederick the Great as the supreme national enlightener.[37] At the same time Karamzin's interest in pre-Petrine Russia increased, and he attempts to show how deep the roots of Russian culture and history are. As yet he chooses to see no conflict between Peter's revolutionary methods and Russian traditions, for Russian history provides a further boost to Russian national pride and self-awareness: "I do not trust that love for country which despises its chronicles or is not interested in them: we must know the present; we should be informed about the past."[38]

Karamzin's interest in history was becoming his major preoccupation; already in 1801, he saw clearly his future career as an historian, as his first ode to Alexander shows. During his editorship of the *Messenger* he takes the opportunity to share the fruits of his study with his readers, hereby serving both his personal interests and the wider aims of the journal.

"Natalia, the Boyar's Daughter," "The Bird of Paradise," the opening pages of "Poor Liza," as well as the unfinished poem "Il'ia of Murom," show Karamzin's willingness to use (or abuse) Russian history and legend; but "Martha the Mayoress" is his first true historical tale. In December 1802, the month before he published "Martha," he gives what might be regarded as the theoretical as well as the patriotic justification for such attempts. His essay, "On the Incidents and Characters in Russian History, Which May Provide Subjects for the Arts" ["O sluchaiakh i kharakterakh v rossiiskoi istorii, kotorye mogut byt' predmetom khudozhestv"], is primarily concerned with possible subjects for painting, but Karamzin's suggestions are directed at all creative artists. Closely linked with this article and with the fictional re-creation of Martha is another essay by Karamzin, entitled "Information on Martha the Mayoress from the Life of St. Zosima" ["Izvestiie o Marfe Posadnitse, vziatoe iz zhitiia Zosimy"] (June 1803). Apart from the new information it gives on Martha's character, the essay is a call to "a skilled pen" to "represent for us a gallery of Russian women, famed in history or deserving of this honor."[39] His list of such women essentially continues the earlier one containing suggestions for suitable subjects for painting. Karamzin was possibly prompted once more by foreign example; Mme. de Genlis, in an article translated by Karamzin, had written: "Most of all I would like to represent with my brush the most famous women in history, their main traits and virtues, their lives."[40]

As a result of his historical studies Karamzin came to acknowledge the importance of preserving folk songs and proverbs. He says with approval of Bogdanovich that "he published Russian proverbs in which were preserved the valuable remains of our forefathers' thought, their true conceptions about good and their wise rules for life."[41] Karamzin himself printed a Yakut folk song which "depicts with simplicity and life the attachment of this good-natured people to animals, which are indeed worthy of man's gratitude."[42] Karamzin sees the need to collect all manner of historical anecdotes and legends; indeed, this is a patriotic duty: "How good it would be to collect all Russian legends which are related either to history or old customs! I would praise the Russian who would undertake to travel round some of the regions of our fatherland with such an intention."[43] He regrets that the oral accounts of old people who remembered Peter the Great, Anne, and Elizabeth had not been copied down and religiously preserved.[44] He himself recorded an alleged meeting with an old couple, who had been married more than eighty years; his old peasant is made to utter a string of proverbs and near-proverbs—obviously indicative of antique wisdom—in a typically stylized sentimental style.[45]

Karamzin was anxious not only to preserve information about the past but also to have recorded in print all the glorious deeds of the present for the edification of posterity: "We are to blame for having as yet no collection of true anecdotes about Russian national virtue which would disarm all misanthropes, I would not include in such a collection anything fictional or untrue—nor anything exaggerated: truth by itself is attractive."[46] There is a tendency to find Russian equivalents for anything the West could offer and English example in all things *pro bono patriae* seems to present a particular challenge to Russian patriotism. The third article in the opening number of the *Messenger* tells of an English scheme to erect a monument to the country's past glories and victories,[47] and a footnote to a later translation records the dedication of a monument in Westminster Abbey by a "grateful King and Country" to a fallen soldier.[48] Karamzin formulates the need for such information about Russia to be recorded in the first story of Russian "Good Deeds" ["Blagodeianie"] to be printed in the *Messenger*: "Acts of philanthropy are an adornment of their age and country. Whenever and wherever men act virtuously, every sensitive heart rejoices; but the nearer the philanthropist is to us the greater our pleasure. If a Russian touches me with his magnanimity, then I rejoice as a man and still more as a son of Russia. A patriot who loves virtue in all lands worships it in his own country; it is the greatest service to the state, and its example is not only consoling but useful in civil relations, since it has a salutary influence on general morals."[49] He ends by inviting "all patriots, all friends of mankind, to send him information about events that are consoling for the feeling heart."[50] Soon stories of unsung Russian virtues were being printed in increasing numbers in the *Messenger*. The honesty of the Russian peasant was extolled together with the generosity of the gentry.[51]

If Karamzin collected proverbs, folk songs, anecdotes of the past and present out of a belief in their patriotic and historical value, he also contributed historical articles which were the fruit of careful research and documentation. He brought to his essays a high degree of literary art, attempting to make Russian history living and real for his readers. In a sense, he was the first accomplished popularizer of Russian history. He presents examples from earlier Russian history for a recent Moscow earthquake, informs his readers of the historical associations of places and buildings in and around Moscow, explains the origin and function of the Secret Chancellery, and analyzes the causes of the Moscow revolt of 1648.[52] Karamzin was seemingly intent on shaming his fellow Russians for their ignorance of Russia's past and at the same time preparing the way for his future career as an historian. His historical essays refer to the rudimentary state of Russian historiography, the limitations of the chronicles, and the prejudices of foreign travelers; he corrects mistakes made by his immediate predecessors, V. N. Tatishchev and M. M. Shcherbatov, attacks foreigners like Levesque for writing ill-informed works on the history of Russia, and regrets that the Professor of Russian History in the Russian Academy had been a foreigner. He believes that "because we have no respectable history, the great and wondrous deeds of our forefathers are little known to us; but there is sufficient for an eloquent pen":[53] Karamzin saw, and rightly, that pen as his.[54] His comments on the tasks facing the historian anticipate features of his yet unwritten history: on the one hand, there is his strong interest in character and on the other, the yardstick of virtue and morality. He translated the views of other historians on the writing of history and in the early volumes of his own work he was obviously aware of Antoine Thomas's belief that "an historian should not describe in detail those events which cannot be described dramatically; i.e., divided into *statement, development* and *conclusion*. Otherwise such descriptions will be tedious and can only interest contemporaries, who have sympathy for them because of their involvement."[55] Making a distinction between historians and chroniclers, Karamzin declares that "our chroniclers are not Tacituses: they did not judge tsars; they related not all their deeds, only the most brilliant—military successes, evidence of religious devotion, etc.":[56] it was precisely because he detected elements of both types of writer in him that Pushkin was to term Karamzin "our first historian and last chronicler."[57]

Combining the moral and emotional aspects of enlightenment and patriotism with a specific interest in social and political institutions is Karamzin's concern for Russian advances in education. He regarded education as an internal, patriotic matter and was heavily sarcastic of foreign attempts to criticize or influence Russian methods. In "An Aberration" ["Strannost' "] he ridiculed a Frenchman's scheme to set up a school near Paris, where among other subjects young Russians would be taught their native language; Karamzin insisted on the need for Russians to be brought up and educated in Russia: "We know that everyone should grow up in his homeland and early become accustomed to its climate, habits, character of its people, way of life, and government; we know that in Russia alone it is possible to become a good Russian—and for our national happiness neither the French nor the English are necessary to us."[58] In "My Confession" he criticized the sort of gentry education that could lead to contempt for one's country.[59] He was therefore very ready to support all measures to improve educational facilities within Russia. Karamzin had praised Catherine for her national schools, the importance of which he emphasized again in his *Historical Panegyric to Catherine II*[60] and when Alexander introduced a number of educational reforms, Karamzin heralded them with a series of essays in the *Messenger*.[61]

In his role as an enlightened patriot Karamzin agitated for the replacing of foreign tutors by Russians for "there will never be perfect moral education until we have good Russian teachers, who alone are able to instill the feelings and principles of a good Russian into a young heart."[62] His fervor for the cause of enlightenment

made him condemn ignorance as "antipatriotic, even a sign of opposition to the Tsar" for "it hinders every enactment of the ruler's
benevolent intentions at every step, stops it, removes the strength
from great and wise laws, encourages abuses, injustices and in a
word, does not allow the state to enjoy its general internal prosperity which alone deserves to be the aim of a truly great, that is to say
virtuous, monarch."[63]

Karamzin in the *Messenger* assumed the role of apologist of
the Russian gentry—a role which allowed him to criticize, indulgently, existing abuses within that class in the name of its ideal
function and character. He believed that "the gentry is the soul and
noble image of the whole nation. I love to imagine the Russian
gentry not only with a sword in its hands, not only with the scales
of Themis, but also with the laurels of Apollo as well as with the
symbols of the goddess of agriculture."[64] Although he recognized
that a learned member of the gentry was a rarity in any country and
that teachers would have to be found from among the lower
classes,[65] he was soon proudly publishing details about the first
"gentleman-professor" in Russia—Grigorii Glinka of Derpt University.[66] Such events gave force to his thesis that "excellent knowledge is necessary to affirm the illustrious rights of the gentry."[67]

Turning to the central critical question of the relationship between master and serf, Karamzin saw enlightenment leading to a
decrease in arbitrary power: "Those loathsome tyrants, comfortingly for the good heart few in number, who forget that, for a true
member of the gentry, to be a good master is to be the father of
one's subjects, could no longer act in darkness."[68] He expands this
view in what is perhaps the most optimistic and idyllic essay he
wrote for his journal—"Pleasing Prospects, Hopes and Desires of
the Present Time": "Enlightenment destroys the abuse of a master's power, which even according to our existing laws is not tyrannical and unlimited. A member of the Russian gentry gives necessary land to his peasants; he is their protector in civil affairs and
their helper in accidental or natural disasters: these are his duties!
For this he demands from them half the working days in a week:
this is his right!"[69] Given just masters and such an understanding of
his position, the peasant was to be content with his lot and serve
his country as his station in life allowed. Enlightenment, Karamzin
argues, allowed the peasant to see the justice of his position; edu-

cated European peasants who "bless their modest lot in civil society, consider themselves not its victims but beneficiaries like other classes, all of which must work, if in different ways, for their own and their country's benefit."[70]

In his defense of the Russian social system Karamzin was consciously reacting against what he considered were ill-informed attacks and criticism from foreigners;[71] his most open defense of serfdom, "The Letter of a Country Dweller" ["Pis'mo sel'skogo zhitelia"], rejects foreign travelers' explanation of the laziness of the Russian peasant as a consequence of the evils of slavery. Karamzin saw the serfs as "lazy by nature, habit, and ignorance of the advantages of industry."[72] In addition, they had an incorrigible weakness for drinking, the bête noire to which Karamzin pointed in any discussion of emancipation without enlightenment.[73] Karamzin was heavily critical of the study-bound scholar's pipe dreams, the systematic philosopher's theories, which ignored realities;[74] faithful to his gospel of the middle way, Karamzin saw change coming gradually, unhurriedly: "Time moves forward the reason of nations, but quietly and slowly: woe to the lawgiver who flies ahead! The wise man goes step by step, looking around him. God sees whether I love mankind and the Russian people; whether I am prejudiced, whether I worship the loathsome idol of self-interest— but for the true prosperity of our peasants I wish only that they have good masters and the means to enlightenment, which alone will make possible all that is good."[75] Karamzin was firmly opposed to immediate emancipation. He was unable to envisage freeing the peasants without land—and this he considered at that time impracticable; equally he believed that without some degree of education and awareness of the many problems facing them, the peasants would abuse their liberty with idleness and drink. His caution was apt to be interpreted as reactionary by a generation of eager young reformers, his defense of serfdom as a preference for slavery over freedom.[76]

Karamzin's defense of gentry supremacy and serfdom is one aspect of a comprehensive statement on the type of government and society he envisaged for Russia. It is based on certain beliefs fundamental even to his early writings, but modified by his experiences, both public and private, during the reigns of Catherine and Paul. Karamzin's writings in the first years of Alexander's reign reveal him to be a consummate political publicist. He greeted Alexander's accession as he had Paul's—with an ode. He wrote a further ode for Alexander's coronation and by the end of 1801, he had completed for publication his *Historical Panegyric to Catherine II*. There is little doubt that Karamzin wished to impress Alexander from the outset by his sincerity, patriotism, and erudition. He sent copies of all these three works for Alexander with covering letters to D. P. Troshchinskii.[77] For his pains he received two signet rings and a snuffbox encrusted with diamonds, which were "not very sparkling,"[78] as the only sign of imperial interest. The three works outline Karamzin's demands on the young tsar and anticipate the main arguments of the *Messenger of Europe*. The burden of his odes is the need for a code of civil laws which would ensure the freedom of the individual and define the responsibilities of the citizen.[79] There is no suggestion that the law is *above* the monarch, for he is supreme and answerable only to God; nevertheless, fear of history's judgement is an incentive for a monarch to be virtuous: "To tyrants my scroll is frightening; / To good monarchs it is kind."[80]

Karamzin's panegyric to Catherine was an attempt to veil his demands on the new reign under praise for certain aspects of Catherine's; Karamzin was prompted to this stratagem by promises contained in Alexander's first manifesto: "Accepting the throne, We accept the responsibility of governing the nation entrusted to Us by God according to the laws and heart of Our most august grandmother, the Empress Catherine the Great."[81] Karamzin's allegedly historical survey of Catherine's achievements is a fantasy of what might have been; he elected to forget the reasons for his limited praise during her reign and portray Catherine in an ideal light. She became an indispensable part of his scheme of Russian development, which linked her name with those of Peter the Great and Alexander. For his new tasks of civic oratory Karamzin used all the devices and pathos of his sentimental style, as a contemporary satirist clearly recognized.[82]

Following a short introduction, in which he drew attention to the "immortal pages" of Montesquieu's *Esprit des lois*, a work of immense importance for both Catherine's and his own political concepts, Karamzin reviewed Catherine's achievements under the three heads of victories, lawgiving, and institutions. The result, however, is essentially an outline of Karamzin's own political and social views, to be illustrated not only from the pages of the *Messenger* but from such later writings as the *Memoir on Ancient and Modern Russia* [*Zapiska o drevnei i novoi Rossii*] (1811), "The Opinion of a Russian Citizen" ["Mnenie russkogo grazhdanina"] (1819), and "Thoughts on True Freedom" ["Mysli ob istinnoi svobode"] (1826). Karamzin justifies Catherine's wars as necessary for Russia's security, attacks "impudent and malicious Poland,"[83] and when praising Catherine's wise choice of military leaders, carefully omits to mention Potemkin—possibly a survival of the old masonic antipathy toward him.[84] The third section, where Karamzin extols such institutions as the Academy of Arts, the National Schools, the Orphans' Home, and even the wise censorship,[85] is the Russian response to the social institutions which Karamzin considered to be one of England's glories. It is, however, the discussion of Catherine the lawgiver that is most revealing for Karamzin's views on systems of government and the relationship of individual and state. Karamzin portrays Catherine as favoring comprehensive laws and opposed to all arbitrary power, "since She knew that personal security is the first blessing of a man and that without it our life is an eternal torturing worry amidst all the other forms of happiness and enjoyment. This mild spirit in government, proof of Her love and respect for mankind, was to be the main characteristic of Her decrees."[86] Karamzin dwells at length on Catherine's arguments in favor of autocracy contained in her *Nakaz* and attempts to illustrate their justice by examples: he points to the sorry failure of contemporary France to rule itself and its need of a "Corsican soldier" to save itself from utter collapse. Simultaneously with his support for autocracy Karamzin reaffirms his love of the great Republicans of history. Although he had himself rejected the possibility of realizing the ideal republic in the modern world,[87] he admired the republican virtues. Nevertheless, the demands on the individual in a republic are too high and loss of civic virtue brings the downfall of a republic: "Either people have to be angels or every complex form of government based on the action of different wills becomes eternal dissension and the people become the unhappy instrument of a few ambitious men, who sacrifice their country for their own personal benefit."[88]

The idea of autocracy as the time-hallowed and only fitting

form of government for Russia is propounded by Karamzin throughout the *Messenger*. Whenever possible, Karamzin praises Alexander as the wise autocrat and connects Russia's imminent glory with his personal rule and example.[89] He is particularly anxious that false courtiers or advisers should not blind Alexander to his true obligations to his country or attempt to impinge upon his power. In his first ode Karamzin speaks of these "sly flatterers";[90] in his essay on the Moscow revolt of 1648 he paints the picture of a good tsar, a "little father" to his people but prevented from helping them by the machinations of his favorites.[91] As distinct from their position Karamzin's is that of a loyal well-intentioned patriot, one of the "unhypocritical friends of good / Able to speak the truth."[92] The picture emerges of a Russia ruled by a wise autocrat, beneath whom the gentry, the ever-increasing bourgeoisie and the peasantry perform their duties loyally and virtuously, respecting the contribution of every member of society to the general prosperity and content with their position: for the rejected western models of republics and constitutional monarchies Karamzin substitutes his own autocratic Arcadia.

Behind Karamzin's persuasive and insistent arguments in favor of what Pushkin was to call the "necessity of autocracy / And the charms of the knout"[93] stood a fear of upheaval, of tyranny by one man or many, or more specifically, the spectre of the French Revolution which had haunted and influenced his thought for more than a decade: "The Revolution has elucidated ideas: we have seen that the civil order is holy even in its most local or chance defects, that authority is not tyranny for nations but protection from tyranny, that when it shatters the beneficent aegis, a people becomes the victim of terrible disasters which are incomparably more evil than all the usual abuses of authority, that even Turkish rule is better than anarchy, which is always the consequence of state conflict, that all the bold theories of the mind, which from the study wishes to prescribe new laws for the moral and political world, must remain in books, together with other more or less curious products of wit, that the institutions of antiquity have a magical force, which cannot be replaced by any force of intellect, that only time and the good will of legal government should correct the imperfections in civil societies, and that with this trust in the action of time and the wisdom of authorities, we private citizens must live peacefully, obey willingly, and perform all possible good around us."[94] He admits that all the outstanding minds of the day had desired "great changes and novelties in the constitution of societies," but they had learnt that "revolution was the abuse of freedom."[95] To provide an example of a great European mind, seduced by the French Revolution and eventually rejecting it, Karamzin chose to translate an article on Klopstock by Archenholz. Its relevance is obvious from the reference to Klopstock which Karamzin makes in the first edition of "To Women." In a footnote to the line: "The most famous authors, / Plato's friends, immortal singers," he mentions Klopstock's interest in his writings.[96] In nineteenth-century editions of the poem Karamzin omitted the footnote and substituted: "And Phoebus's friends" for "Plato's friends," thus concealing a juxtaposition of the poet and the utopian dreamer, characteristic of his work in the early 1790's.[97] Not only is the central passage an apology for Karamzin's own attitude to the Revolution but the article as a whole echoes many of Karamzin's ideas on both patriotism and literary work: "Klopstock, like all true philanthropists and all people of unusual intelligence, who are not egoists but friends of the general good, was a friend of the French Revolution, when it seemed a beneficial change in human destiny in France. Together with others he hoped that a strong and enlightened nation could be its own wise lawgiver: at that time much appeared captivating, especially from afar. Above all, his humane heart was enraptured by the famous decree of the National Assembly that France would forever reject wars of aggression— a decree made in the dawn of this great event but soon mocked and forgotten by the new rulers of France. But this passionate love for the new freedom of the French gradually died as a result of subsequent events and finally disappeared completely during the terrors of the Convention."[98] To some extent the same function is served by an earlier translated article on Lavater, who had died in 1801. In one particularly interesting footnote Karamzin refers to later letters from Lavater, which have not been discovered, and quotes his view on the French Revolution: "Lavater was in the beginning enthusiastic about the French Revolution, as were all the Swiss; but he soon changed his opinion. When I was still in Geneva, he wrote to one of my acquaintances there that the Revolution was the work of men and not of Providence, as he had earlier believed. In his last letter to me he says: 'Great deeds are being done, but even greater ones are being prepared; you will not understand me, but with time you will.' "[99] Finally, Karamzin places himself among such disillusioned enthusiasts in the fifth stanza of his ode "To Virtue," published at the end of 1802.[100]

Karamzin's desire to exorcise the French influence is apparent from the very first number of the *Messenger*. In addition to a translation entitled "A History of the French Revolution, Selected from Latin Authors" ["Istoriia frantsuzskoi revoliutsii, izbrannaia iz latinskikh pisatelei"], in which the horrors and excesses of each stage of the Revolution are illustrated by quotations from Tacitus, Sallust and others;[101] the piece "Alcibiades to Pericles" ["Al'tsibiad k Periklu"] is full of obvious allusions to the pseudo wisdom of the revolutionary leaders.[102] A third article, "Ladies' Wigs" ["Zhenskiye pariki"], links the fashion for wigs with the "unfortunate victims" of the Revolution;[103] Karamzin in an original essay, "On the Light Dress of Fashionable Beauties" ["O legkoi odezhde modnykh krasavits XIX veka"], published three months later in April 1802, attacks Russian women for imitating the shameless French women, "who danced contredanses on the graves of their parents, husbands, and lovers!"[104]

Karamzin sighed for the civilization of prerevolutionary days; he was anxious to record all that suggested the return of gentle morals and amiability. Translated articles such as "On Habit" ["O privychke"] and "On Politeness and Bon Ton" ["Ob uchtivosti i khoroshem tone"],[105] together with remarks about the "bad taste of *the nouveaux riches*" and the wish to see "social subtleties" reintroduced,[106] recall Karamzin's aphorism from 1793 that "politeness, affability, is the flower of society" and stress his constant desire to encourage such qualities among the Russian gentry.

Articles about French personalities and life in Paris, as well as more general works from French sources, fill a considerable part of the "Literature and Miscellany" section of the *Messenger*. Not unexpectedly, the political fortunes of France occupy a prominent place in the journal's "Politics" section. It is this section which truly justifies the journal's title by informing the Russian public of the internal affairs of European countries. It was not, however, merely a process of translating interesting articles from the foreign press; Karamzin was involved in European events but was equally intent on using foreign material to comment on Russia's internal problems. To this aim Karamzin often re-edited or freely translated foreign originals, so that external authority seemingly supported opinions he had expressed elsewhere or felt unable to voice openly. It is a technique which has been convincingly demonstrated by Lotman with reference to translated articles on widely differing topics.[107]

Karamzin began his political commentaries with a detailed survey of a decade of upheaval in Europe, in which he stresses the desire of all countries for prolonged peace and stable government. His attention was directed above all to France, and particularly to Napoleon. It is Napoleon who dominates the *Messenger* both as a personality and as the key to European peace. In this opening essay Karamzin characterizes him as "a new Caesar, a new Clovis" and observes that "the dangerous and foolish Jacobin principles, which brought the rest of Europe to arms against the Republic, have disappeared in their own homeland, and France, despite the name and a few republican forms of government, is now in fact nothing other than a true monarchy."[108]

It was, among other things, the realization of Napoleon's autocratic designs that led to a change in Paul's attitude to France; Alexander, although carefully wooed by the English government, was also well disposed toward Napoleon. Karamzin was therefore reflecting the official line, and indeed Karamzin's attitudes to Napoleon reflect the numerous changes in Russian opinion toward him in the years 1800–1812. Nevertheless, Napoleon's restitution of the monarchy in all but name seemed to support Karamzin's thesis of the one, and one only, historically justified form of government for a country. Every issue of the *Messenger* contains references to Napoleon and during the two years of Karamzin's editorship, over thirty articles deal directly with him and his actions. Napoleon meets Karamzin's demands on a Great Man, such as he had set out in his *Historical Panegyric to Catherine II*: "They decide the fate of mankind, determine its path; with inexplicable force they draw millions of people to some aim designed by Providence; they create and destroy kingdoms; they form epochs, of which all others are but the consequence; in a sense, they form a chain in the immensity of centuries, stretching their hands one to another, and their life is the history of peoples."[109] Napoleon possessed what Montaigne had called "un peu de folie,"[110] without which nothing great was achieved in life, for "fundamental rationalism was never a merit in heroes of ambition."[111] Although Karamzin sees Napoleon as a great general and leader of men, he also detects certain human weaknesses in him which deny him the accolade of great *and* virtuous. "By killing the monster of the Revolution, he has earned the eternal gratitude of France and even of Europe. In this respect we shall always thank him willingly as a great doctor, who has cured heads of a dangerous giddiness. We shall regret that he had not the legislative wisdom of Solon and the pure virtue of Lycurgus who, having formed Sparta, banished himself forever from his homeland! That is an heroic action before which all the Lodis and Marengos of the world disappear! After two thousand seven hundred years it still fires the mind and a good youth reading the life of Lycurgus weeps in rapture . . . Evidently it is far easier to be a skillful general and a cunning politician than to be a great, that is to say, heroically virtuous man."[112] Despite the blemishes, Karamzin was ready to acclaim Napoleon, especially when he re-established the authority of the church or helped the advancement of enlightenment.[113]

Karamzin followed closely French legislative decrees as well as France's sponsoring of the constitution mania which affected in particular Switzerland and Italy. In 1802 he expresses the wish that independence be restored to the Swiss for "republican freedom and independence belong to Switzerland as much as her granite and snow-covered mountains: man does not destroy the works of nature."[114] Therefore, when the Landammann Alois Reding organized a secessionist movement among the small Swiss cantons, Karamzin was enraged by this rejection of history. "It is a pity that such cruel and ambitious men influence the fate of that good but simple people, who lived for so many centuries in happy union with the large cantons, and who now, following the promptings of one malicious egoist, demand partition."[115] The strife that followed in Switzerland caused him to reiterate his view that without national virtue a Republic was doomed: "That is why a monarchy is far more happy and reliable; it does not put excessive demands on its citizens and can raise itself from a degree of morality at which republics would fall."[116] Karamzin's hostility toward Reding continued from issue to issue, but in March 1803, he translated a German article, in which Reding was praised as a selfless and dedicated patriot.[117] This is essentially an illustration of Karamzin's desire to present an objective picture of European events, although his own point of view was clearly stated in his "News and Comment" ["Izvestiia i zamechaniia"] column. Karamzin also made use of German material for "external" criticism of both France and Germany. Certain German journalists were strongly pro-English and delighted in revealing the "hypocrisies" of French policy;[118] Karamzin himself found satisfaction in playing off the French press against its English counterpart, pointing out their readiness to abuse and libel their opponents.[119]

Karamzin's interest in English affairs is the counterbalance to his absorption with Napoleon; he himself made the revealing opposition that "in the one we are curious to know about national affairs and in the other, the actions of Consul Bonaparte."[120] His interest is primarily in English patriotism, in social institutions rather than political forms. He tends to point out that the much-vaunted English political system, especially Parliament and democratic elections, were not so ideal or worthy of imitation. In an amusing account of an English election Karamzin quotes Rousseau's remark that this was the only time Englishmen enjoyed true freedom, but warns that "these elections may be called merely a ceremony: the ministers control them unseen, in agreement with the best people in each district."[121]

Karamzin's political commentary in the *Messenger* coincided with a brief period of peace in Europe. The first number announced the imminent meeting at Amiens, but the last issues were filled with apprehension lest hostilities be resumed. As Napoleon prepared to invade England, Karamzin was led to wonder whether victory for France or England would be the better outcome for Europe; admiration for Napoleon conflicts with his love of England: "England abuses its dominance at sea, but who would wish the French to conquer this most fortunate country in the world, where wise laws reign and the citizens prosper."[122] Yet it is important to note that the prospects of a new European conflict did not plunge Karamzin into despair and anguish—as the events of the Terror and the revolutionary wars had done. The reason behind his comparative equanimity was his patriotic faith in Russia and his new independence of Europe. His confidence was founded not only on Russia's internal strength and identity, given to it by the accession of Alexander, but also on its European mission and influence. "It can despise the usual tricks of diplomacy and, elected by Fate, can, it seems, be a true intermediary between nations."[123] He proudly records that Russia's intervention into German affairs made it "an object of universal respect, universal trust," that the Corfu islanders had welcomed Russian help and that even England acknowledged Russia's might.[124]

THE *Messenger of Europe* offered the Russian public a rich variety of reading matter, but it is a journal dominated by the personality and interests of one man, given unity both by his style and by the persistence of certain themes and ideas. Compared with the *Moscow Journal,* the *Messenger* is preeminently a political rather than a literary journal; Karamzin's desire for cultural enlightenment is linked with his propaganda for a particular social and political system, within which his ideals could be realized. The journal was the messenger of European affairs to the degree that European experience could demonstrate, negatively or positively, a course for Russian development; it is essentially the testament of a man who had learnt and taken much from western culture but who now felt the tide to be turning and wished to encourage Russians to an awareness of their greatness and potential.

The *Messenger of Europe* occupies a distinguished place in the history of Russian journalism as "the patriarch of Russian journals,"[125] the first of the *tolstye zhurnaly* (thick journals), and its importance was immediately recognized by Karamzin's contemporaries. It was initially published in six hundred copies but was so successful that the first number was republished and the monthly printing doubled to twelve hundred copies. Zhukovskii saw its significance in the fact that Karamzin "a tourné l'attention sur les objets politiques et a beaucoup influé sur la pensée. . . . Il donne de l'attrait à la pensée par le charme du style,"[126] but perhaps the most impressive tribute came from an opponent, the Shishkovite and Decembrist Kiukhel'beker, who wrote in exile: "It must be admitted that for its time this journal is extremely good; and even today it would not occupy the last place among our publications by the attractiveness of its articles and almost the first place by its language."[127] In June 1832, he noted: "They have brought me two volumes of Karamzin's *Messenger* and two of his successors'. What a difference! One must be just to Karamzin that as a journalist he was a master of his craft."[128]

EIGHT

INTO THE TEMPLE OF HISTORY

The year 1803 was the watershed in Karamzin's career. For twenty years and particularly since 1791 he had published a steady stream of works which allowed the reading public to follow developments in his style, interests, and thought; before him lay a similar period in time, when removed from public view, he quietly devoted himself to historical research and scholarship. This was a period to be marked by one publishing event: the first eight volumes of his history in 1818. His retirement from active literary work was astutely timed; it came when his reputation was at its height and his position in the Russian literary hierarchy unchallenged. Karamzin, who had lived happily most of his life under the influence of western literature and thought, was distinctly proud of his growing reputation abroad; when he asked Murav'ev, at that time Curator of Moscow University, to petition the tsar for the position of historiographer, he characterized himself as "a man, who has aided the development of language and taste, earned the flattering attention of the Russian public, and whose trifles, published in the different languages of Europe, have brought good reviews from famous foreign authors."[1] In a subsequent letter he acknowledged his debt to Richter whose "translations have made me known in Germany, England, and France,"[2] translations which he had reviewed in a series of notices in the *Messenger*.[3] A curious aspect of his English reputation is that he became known solely by his early works—his *Letters* and sentimental stories, despite Richter's numerous translations from the *Messenger*. He gained prominence later for his history, but again this was never translated into English. Translations of two essays from the *Messenger* did appear in English, but without acknowledgment of Karamzin's authorship.[4]

In 1803 the first edition of Karamzin's collected work began to appear (completed in 1804) and for the next two decades his work in different editions and collections provided the Russian public with its staple reading matter. The spread of his works even to the most remote provinces of Russia is illustrated in the reminiscences of two prominent nineteenth-century historians: Pogodin recalls finding in 1813 a copy of *Letters* in the home of his grandmother, a Saltykov serf,[5] and Kliuchevskii mentions that *Aglaia* was one of the first books read by him as a child in a region "where a non-church book was a great rarity."[6] Karamzin had become "a classic" in his lifetime; the only evidence of his continued existence as an author was provided by two poems, the interest of which lies in their political and patriotic sentiments rather than in any literary quality. "The Warriors' Song" (1806) combines scorn for "the haughty Gaul" Napoleon with a reminder of Russia's proud military heritage;[7] "The Liberation of Europe and the Glory of Alexander I" (1814) is an exultant ode to Russia's contribution to European security and an attempt to draw edifying political lessons from the rule of the French tyrant and the contemporary history of France.[8] Statements such as "Nations! submit to authority; / Do not be tempted by false freedom" and "The new is dangerous in governments, / And anarchy is terrible" are the only *published* evidence in these years of Karamzin's deepening political conservatism, expressed more cogently and systematically in writings of a private and restricted nature.

In December 1803, Karamzin wrote that he was obliged to say farewell to his public "for a long time, and in a certain sense forever. History removes us from our contemporaries."[9] In a strict literary sense he was correct, but his study of history and absorption in the past only heightened his appreciation of contemporary events and figures. Evidence of this is his *Memoir on Ancient and Modern Russia,* which was written in 1810–11 with the active encouragement of the Grand Duchess Catherine Pavlovna and presented by her to the Emperor Alexander at Tver' in 1811.[10] It is a document of great political significance, known to many people but available to few; extracts were published by Pushkin in the *Contemporary* [*Sovremennik*] in 1837, but the work was not published in its entirety in Russia until 1870. In it Karamzin gave expression to the growing conservative dissatisfaction with the reforms advanced particularly by M. M. Speranskii in the opening years of Alexander's reign; dedicated to the thesis that "Russia was founded by victories and monocracy, she perished from the division of authority, and was saved by wise autocracy,"[11] Karamzin looks to contemporary events with a caution inspired by his historical deliberations. Faithful to his belief in the exacting demands of civic and private virtue and exhibiting a greater deference to tradition, Karamzin adopts a harsher attitude toward Peter's reforming zeal as well as toward Catherine's moral laxity.[12] His basic political beliefs, however, remain consistent with views already in his *Messenger of Europe.*

From a literary-philosophical point of view the album Karamzin presented to Catherine Pavlovna on her name day, November 24, 1811, is of greater interest.[13] N. Lyzhin, its editor, suggested that the album "was probably compiled . . . with the intention of presenting philosophical proofs in favor of the principles, which he had drawn in the *Memoir* from the long past and recent fortunes of Russia,"[14] but it occupies in its own right a logical place in Karamzin's literary work. Although the album as such is closely linked with the *Memoir* ideologically and chronologically, the materials which it includes were garnered predominantly during the reign of Paul. The album is both the complement and continuation of *The Pantheon of Foreign Literature*, although Russian writers are represented with selections from Derzhavin, Dmitriev, and Karamzin himself. Quotations from Buffon, Montaigne, and Pompignan which Karamzin had copied into his notebooks in 1797 are included in the album, together with Karamzin's poem "Peace and Glory" ["Pokoi i slava"], which was first published in the second volume of *Aonides* in that year. Karamzin's selections from Cicero, "Thoughts on God," which opened the first volume of *The Pantheon* in 1798, a long quotation from Metastasio, whom Karamzin was reading assiduously in 1797, as shown by quotations in his notebook and a reference in a letter to Dmitriev,[15] and an equally long quotation from Pope's "Essay on Man," which had influenced Karamzin's *Dialogue on Happiness*, also appear in the album. Other assembled literary authorities—Goethe, Milton, and Rousseau—had long been among Karamzin's favorite authors, but it is his manipulation of quotations from Rousseau which is particularly characteristic and revealing.

The album comprises twenty-five sections, mostly of a quotation or quotations from a single author; they illustrate Karamzin's basic views on patriotism, religion, the nature of man, forms of government, the obligations of rulers and ruled, the essence of virtue, married life, and friendship. The author whose authority is advanced more than any other is Rousseau; quotations from his work appear in no less than seven sections. However, these extracts which have the form of harmonious and consistent quotations are skillfully constructed from various originals, including *Émile, La Nouvelle Héloïse, Le Contrat Social, Le Gouvernement de Pologne,* and *L'Economie politique.* As Lyzhin has pointed out, the quotations "taken together with what precedes and follows them sometimes lead to conclusions which are completely different from those to which Karamzin adapted them."[16] Karamzin was once again recreating his own Rousseau and masking what he considered were errors and fallacies in the Genevan's thinking.

The album was a private expression of Karamzin's literary and philosophical views; his last public statement on Russian culture and enlightenment was his speech to the Russian Academy on December 5, 1818.[17] True to his position in the *Messenger of Europe,* Karamzin reiterates his call for moderate and understanding criticism, for encouragement of young and immature talents, who may be discouraged by uncharitable and biased attacks. He attempts to strike a balance between respect for Russian cultural traditions and imitation of western attainments. Although he looks back with pride to the *Igor' Tale* and regrets the loss of the songs of Boian, he emphasizes that Russia must keep in line with the age, that "posterity will look not for the beauties of the *Igor' Tale* or the beauties of the *Odyssey* in our creations, but only for those in keeping with the present state of human capabilities." A feature of Russia's development is its "unusual speed: we are maturing not by centuries, but by decades" and he predicts with foresight that "the age of Pericles and Augustus" is imminent for Russian literature. In his speech Karamzin gives the clearest statement of his understanding of "national" literature, elaborating both his general theoretical comments in the *Moscow Journal* and their specific Russian application in the *Messenger of Europe.* He points to the finality of the intellectual rupture between ancient and modern Russians, which was brought about, for better or worse, by the reforms of Peter the Great: "We do not wish to imitate foreigners, but we write as they write, because we live as they live, read what they read, have the same examples of wit and taste, participate in the

universal mutual rapprochement of nations which is a consequence
of their very enlightenment." He believes that "the particular beauties" which distinguish a *national* literature are secondary in importance to "general beauties," which are eternal. His aphorism "It is
good to write for Russians: it is even better to write for all men"
is a slight but significant rewording of his earlier view that "everything *national* is nothing before the human."[18] He then suggests
that Peter was nevertheless unable to change everything that was
truly and basically Russian and that "although it is sometimes impossible to distinguish a Russian from a Briton, we can always
distinguish Russians from Britons: in *the many* is revealed *the national*." Applying this to literature, he finds "the sounds of a Russian heart, the play of a Russian mind in the works of our literature,
which become more evident as it develops."

   In the opening section of his speech Karamzin dwells on the
great achievement of the Academy in producing a dictionary, which
he considered unrivaled in Europe. Compliments to the Academy
are quickly followed by advice as to its future obligations: "Your
main task was and will be the *systematic formulation* of the language: but its immediate *enrichment* depends on the advancement
of society and of literature, on the gifts of writers—and gifts come
only from fate and nature. Words are not invented by academies:
they are born together with ideas or in the use of language or in
talented works—as a happy inspiration. These new words, which
embody ideas, enter the language independently, adorn and enrich
it, without any scholarly legislation on our part: we do not give, but
receive. The very rules of a language are not invented, but exist already in it: we must only discover or demonstrate them." Karamzin
was intent on justifying his own artistic and linguistic practice in
his enemies' stronghold. The polemical nature of Karamzin's remarks is to be appreciated particularly in the context of the fierce
arguments that raged in the period between the end of Karamzin's
editorship of the *Messenger of Europe* and the publication of his
History. In the *Messenger of Europe* Karamzin had included certain materials which indicate his close attention to the Academy's
concern with a Russian grammar and dictionary. In October 1803,
he published a letter from Fonvizin to a friend, in which plans for
a dictionary were discussed, and indicated clearly his own views in
a number of footnotes.[19] Karamzin's own article, "A Great Man of

Russian Grammar" ["Velikii muzh russkoi grammatiki"] was super-
ficially an amusing sketch of his old friend, the academician and
grammarian Barsov, but its polemical application was instantly
recognized: Metropolitan Evgenii wrote to Count Dmitrii Khvostov that "the Russian Academy's grammar has been hissed in the
Messenger of Europe."[20] It was precisely in 1803 that the antago-
nisms between the adherents of the "old" and "new" languages
were brought into the open with the publication in St. Petersburg
of Shishkov's *Dissertation on the Old and New Style of the Russian Language.* Karamzin himself took no further part in the dispute until his 1818 speech, but his work was energetically defended
by his supporters and friends, who in 1816 formed the society
known as Arzamas in opposition to the Shishkov Gathering of the
Lovers of Russian Literature (Beseda liubitelei rossiiskoi slovesnosti). In the years 1803–20 both factions published books, pam-
phlets, and articles, which reveal that from the very beginning the
arguments were not confined to problems of literature and language
but extended to social and political questions.[21] The polemics about
"the new style" *were* about the nature and transformation of the
Russian language, the relation of the written, literary language to
the spoken but reflected the deeper problems of national identity
in literature and social mores, of Russia's place in Europe, of tradition and change. Karamzin stood for progress, reform, enlightenment and continued to fill this role for the liberals until the publication of his history. He was a symbol of change, almost despite
himself and the fact that the change in him was perceptibly from
"new" to "old" in political and even in linguistic terms. It is interesting to note that Karamzin himself was elected a member of the
Beseda, to which his friend Dmitriev, who was also an academician,
belonged. Whatever the motives behind this election, it is symbolic
of a certain linguistic rapprochement between Karamzin and Shishkov. Vigel' notes in his memoirs: "Whatever might be said, the
Beseda, although perhaps not established from the most praiseworthy motives, was in my opinion useful in many ways. Firstly,
Shishkov's attacks made Karamzin somewhat circumspect; he indicated ways of making his historical style more elevated and dignified; he could do no more but Karamzin with his wonderful
intelligence and talent did not disregard them."[22] Grech saw the
publication of the history as bringing the linguistic disputes finally

to an end by demonstrating that "Karamzin had no intention of rejecting the characteristics and beauties of the church language but simply because of the character of his earlier work had not considered it necessary to use them."[23] This is not to suggest that Karamzin abandoned his earlier linguistic principles but his style acquired a new richness and resonance in his history. His preoccupation with language throughout his "historical" period is evident in his revisions of his earlier works in successive collected editions in the nineteenth century as well as his interesting editing and polishing of the collected works of his friend and benefactor, the late M. N. Murav'ev, in 1810.[24]

Karamzin's belated election to the Russian Academy was finally brought about by the publication of the first eight volumes of his history. In less than a month the first edition of three thousand copies was sold out and the Russian public was engrossed in discovering its past, recreated by the "magic pen" of its most eminent author. If in the preceding two decades Karamzin had been considered a progressive force in Russian life and letters, the publication of his history with its dedication to Alexander and the apologia of autocracy in its introduction inevitably alienated many of the young liberals, particularly future Decembrists, such as Nikita Murav'ev and M. F. Orlov. Despite the bitingly negative analysis of the history which Murav'ev composed,[25] the fact that he showed his paper to Karamzin and received the historiographer's blessing to circulate it illustrates both the respect Karamzin commanded and his encouragement of intellectual debate and free expression of opinions, however antithetical to his own. The moral and intellectual dignity and independence of Karamzin's position were to be fully appreciated by Pushkin, who was the author of one of the earliest and most incisive epigrams on Karamzin's history. In the year of Karamzin's death Pushkin looked back to the reception accorded the first volumes of the history and recalled how "the young Jacobins were indignant; a few scattered deliberations in favor of autocracy, eloquently refuted by the true relation of events, seemed to them the height of barbarity and servility." He himself now considered the work "not only the creation of a great writer but also the accomplishment of an honest man."[26]

Karamzin's history was not simply the fruit of twelve years' historical research;[27] it was the climax of his whole career as a writer.

His history was an event both in Russian literature and Russian historiography, admired for its erudition and disposition and accumulation of materials but equally for its style, its dramatic relation of incidents, and vividness of characterization.[28] It became a rich source of "national subjects" for Decembrist and conservative writers alike. Subsequent volumes continued to be read eagerly by the public. Volume 9, which appeared in 1821 and extracts from which Karamzin had read to enthralled audiences in St. Petersburg, was devoted to the reign of Ivan the Terrible. Karamzin's strong moral condemnation of Ivan's tyranny in the second part of his reign brought a change of attitude in the young liberals, which is seen most clearly in the remarks of Kondratii Ryleev: "I do not know which to marvel at more, the tyranny of Ivan or the talent of our Tacitus."[29] Karamzin's strictures on Ivan and subsequently on Boris Godunov (in volume 11) are, nonetheless, completely in keeping with his lifelong belief that rulers are required to follow the paths of virtue even more than private citizens and with the remark casually included in his speech to the Academy that "even the power of autocrats has its limits."[30] Karamzin did not succeed in finishing what Belinskii called his "epic poem in the eighteenth-century manner,"[31] a description echoed by later critics; volume 12 remained uncompleted at his death. In this respect, it joined the series of Karamzin's earlier unfinished works in prose and verse, beginning with "Liodor" and ending with "A Knight of Our Time."

Pushkin's recognition of Karamzin's integrity as man and author was echoed, almost regularly at twenty-year intervals, by other great Russian writers. In 1846 Gogol' termed Karamzin "an unusual phenomenon," a man who "was the first to show that it is worth sacrificing everything for the vocation of a writer, that a writer can be independent in Russia, and that if he is consumed by a love of good, apparent in all his organism and in all his deeds, then he is able to say everything."[32] In 1866 Tiutchev characterized him as "Able, without bending his head / Before the charms of the throne, / To be to the end the friend of the Tsar / And a loyal citizen of Russia."[33] Such opinions have an authority which removes them from the general cult of Karamzin by his friends after his death as well as from the official canonization of the history, fostered by S. S. Uvarov;[34] they point to the complexity of Karamzin's relationship with Alexander over the period 1811–25.

Karamzin's self-appointed role as critic of his reign, his reforms, his favorites in the *Memoir on Ancient and Modern Russia*
could not but bring about a cooling in Alexander's attitude toward
his historiographer; despite their subsequent reconciliation, there
were always occasions when the Tsar must have felt that Karamzin
assumed too readily the mantle of Clio. One of the reasons for the
protracted printing of his history was Karamzin's reluctance to pay
a courtesy call to Alexander's powerful favorite, Count Arakcheev;
once this was done, an audience with Alexander followed. Karamzin's *Unpublished Works and Correspondence* present the graphic
raw material of Karamzin's tribulations in St. Petersburg as well
as containing the series of documents which pinpoint the climactic
moments in his relations with Alexander after 1816.[35] Of particular
interest is his "Opinion of a Russian Citizen," which he read to
Alexander on October 17, 1819, at Tsarskoe Selo and in which he
spoke out against the Tsar's intention to make Poland an independent kingdom.[36] It is followed by an appendix, "For Posterity" ["Dlia
potomstva"], dated December 29, 1819, in which he records his
conversation with the Tsar and his apprehension that their friendship was at an end. Tiutchev's description of Karamzin as a man
who did not bow his head to the Tsar is borne out by his words:
"Sire, Vous avez beaucoup d'amour-propre... Je ne crains rien. Nous
sommes tous égaux devant Dieu."[37] A further note, dating from
four days after the Decembrist uprising, relates that the Tsar continued to tolerate Karamzin: "He was always patient, mild, in-
explicably kind; he did not seek my advice, listened, however,
although, for the most part, did not follow it."[38] Karamzin then
enumerates the subjects on which he spoke out: "I did not keep
silent about taxes in peacetime, the foolish G[ur'ev] financial system, the terrible military settlements, the strange choice of certain
of the highest dignitaries, the Ministry of Enlightenment or darken-
ing, the need to reduce the army, which was fighting only against
Russia,—about the false repair of roads, which was so burdensome
for the people,—finally about the need to have precise laws, civil
and state."[39] Thus to the end of his life Karamzin did not betray
his position as a responsible citizen; he spoke from conviction and
"there was no flattery on his tongue." Although in many respects
their careers and talents are so different, Karamzin stands near to
his old friend, Derzhavin, in his willingness to speak his mind to

tsars; although he did not accept high public office, he exercised an influence and possessed a sense of commitment which escaped, for all his official position, his old friend of long-standing, the pale Dmitriev.

BELINSKII was perhaps the first critic, chronologically and intellectually, who was able to provide a more or less objective assessment of Karamzin's place in the history of Russian literature and enlightenment. Although he did not devote a separate study to Karamzin as he did to Derzhavin and Krylov, he referred to him constantly throughout his career, and in particular in the first two of his series of articles on the work of Pushkin. Belinskii makes a contrast between two types of writers, between those who have an immediate influence on their contemporaries but whose value ultimately proves to be essentially historical and those who are in advance of their time, who speak to, and are recognized by, future generations.[40] Belinskii, strongly rejecting Karamzin's value for his own [Belinskii's] generation, relegates him to the first category; he, nonetheless, insists on the concept of a "Karamzin period" in Russian literature, following the "Lomonosov period" and in turn succeeded by the "Pushkin period": "Karamzin marks with his name an epoch in our literature; his influence on his contemporaries was so great and strong that the whole period of our literature from the 1790's to the 1820's may be called with justice the Karamzin period."[41] Karamzin's claims to such a distinction, according to Belinskii's scattered remarks, may be summarized as follows: he was not simply a reformer, but an initiator and creator in all aspects of his activity; in reforming the literary language he introduced a wealth of new concepts and ideas; in this connection, his Gallomania was a positive force for "it revived our literature"—it brought Russian literature in line with contemporary European literature and his translations from Mme. de Genlis and Marmontel were as important in this respect as his own short stories; he was the first "educated man of letters" (obrazovannyi literator) in Russia and in this role rather than as a poet or scholar he recognized and met the needs of the Russian public. The superficiality of much of his writings was indeed a strength in the pervailing condition of Russian culture; finally, "he created a Russian reading public, which did not previously exist," for he inspired it with the wish to read—and to read Russian works.[42] For all the perceptiveness of his judgments, Belinskii minimizes the extent and variety of Karamzin's achievement. If for Belinskii's generation he had lost his appeal, there was much in his work and in his thought which attracted and continues to attract other than literary historians.

It was as a translator that Karamzin made his first real contribution to Russian letters. Although many of the translations he produced fit easily into the general catalogue of works published by the Novikov presses, his version of *Julius Caesar*, with its appraisal of Shakespeare's genius which so enthused a Belinskii, unaware of Karamzin's authorship, is a landmark in Russian acquaintance with the work of the English playwright. Of his early original work, his long poem "Poetry" is significant for its distinctive literary allegiances and suggestive ideas on the nature of poetry. Both the introduction to *Julius Caesar* and "Poetry" were ahead of their time in Russia in certain respects and, moreover, their influence was artificially restricted since copies of the first were burnt and Karamzin himself withdrew the second from his collected works.

During his years with the Friendly Learned Society Karamzin acquired the literary tastes and interests which received their distinctive and influential development in his work after his return from his European travels. The *Moscow Journal* revealed from the beginning Karamzin's considerable abilities as a journalist. He produced a journal comparable in presentation and content with the European models he so admired, one unequaled in Russian eighteenth-century journalism; he introduced as a basic feature informed criticism of Russian and foreign works and plays; he published carefully written and selected translations from western originals on a wide range of subjects; he mustered contributions from the leading poets of the day and provided in his own *Letters of a Russian Traveler* and in stories such as "Poor Liza" and "Natalia, the Boyar's Daughter" examples of accomplished Russian prose writing, which caught the imagination of the public and ensured the success of sentimentalism as a literary vogue in Russia. Not least, the *Moscow Journal* heralded a stylistic revolution. Without the carefully wrought embroidery of what became known as the "new style," the emotional finesse and nuance on which sentimentalism relied could not have been realized. The spirit of Karamzin's journal is enlightened, humane, idealistic, and independent. Without attacking the system, he spoke out strongly against injustice and arbitrary action; he was a true child of the Enlightenment in his attacks on obscurantism, intolerance, war, in his optimism in the future of mankind, in the ability of good to prevail over evil, in his attempts to stress the rights of the individual, the classless beauty of human dignity and virtue.

The qualities of the *Moscow Journal* are fully reproduced in *Letters of a Russian Traveler. Letters* was far more than the mirror of the author's soul; it was a rich and important source of information on the history, culture, and life of western Europe, conveyed in an original and entertaining way by the first Russian to publish an account of travels, made "sa plume à la main." Karamzin successfully combined the attitudes of a sentimental traveler with the attentiveness of a young Russian, bent on learning from the West. Often superficial in Belinskii's eyes, he, nevertheless, attempted a serious formulation of the differences he detected in the character and way of life of Germans, Swiss, French, and English and an appreciation of the significance of each country's cultural and social heritage.

Despite the overall length of the work, *Letters* by its very epistolary nature presents comparatively small pen-pictures of incidents, scenes, people, monuments, works of art; Karamzin's short stories are similarly carefully worked miniatures. In the space of a few pages, Karamzin was able to construct often deceptively simple plots, create effective characters, and modulate subtly the responses of his readers. He was a conscious and skilled innovator, providing Russian literature with distinctive prototypes of stories popular in European literature. Despite persistent sentimental features and techniques, his range was considerable and there is a distinct development from the story with few characters and minimal plot toward the major form of the novel. He reveals increasing objectivity and depth in his treatment of character and in the manipulation of his narrative method. His stories were the most important and influential part of his literary work.

Karamzin's standing as a poet is markedly inferior to that as a prose writer, but even here his contribution was original and considerable. He experimented with new meters, introduced new genres and themes into Russian poetry. Both as a practitioner and theorist, he influenced the development of Russian light verse at the beginning of the nineteenth century. Likewise his conception of *Aonides* as a Russian *Almanach des Muses* parallels his attempts to emulate the West in other spheres of his literary activity.

The *Messenger of Europe* is in every respect a fitting climax to the period of Karamzin's work and thought examined in this study. Anticipating on the one hand his subsequent career as a historian and self-appointed adviser to the Tsar and on the other bringing to a close his work as essayist, poet, and writer of prose fiction, it gave Russia a new standard in journalism. By its division into "Politics" and "Literature" and by the importance and quality of the material included under these heads, the *Messenger* became the worthy initiator of the tradition of the "thick journals"; under different editors, the *Messenger* itself was to continue for thirty years. As the title suggests, Karamzin's journal was indeed the "messenger of Europe"; in an editorial at the end of 1802 Karamzin wrote: "In keeping with its title, [the *Messenger*] will contain the main European news in both literature and politics: all that seems to us interesting, well written and is published in France, England, Germany . . . Thus the best European authors will be in a sense our *collaborators* for the pleasure of the Russian public; it only remains for us to present their thoughts as best we can. Not many people receive foreign journals, but many wish to know what and how they write in Europe: the *Messenger* can satisfy this curiosity, and at the same time with some benefit for language and taste."[43] Despite Karamzin's more pronounced patriotic sentiments in the *Messenger of Europe*, when he looked on the West no longer as a pupil, but as an equal, conscious of his own achievement as well as of Russia's potential, all his work is united by its European quality.

The *Messenger of Europe* is a title equally applicable in the field of literature and philosophy to all Karamzin's publications in the 1790's. The *Moscow Journal, Letters of a Russian Traveler*, the "Miscellany" section in the *Moscow News*, the translations of Genlis and Marmontel, *The Pantheon of Foreign Literature* all proclaim Karamzin's sympathies, his wide knowledge of English, French, and German literatures. The majority of his public read French, but his harmonious, attractive Russian translations provided an alternative to French as the language in which to read if not French originals, then English, German, or Italian works. He introduced new names and works to the Russian public, and in the reign of Paul, when the import of foreign works was severely restricted, his *Pantheon of Foreign Literature* was an important source of new reading. Galakhov with reason, if with some exaggeration, called Karamzin "the first Russian European";[44] one might equally adopt for him the title Pushkin used to characterize himself—"the Minister of Foreign Affairs" in the field of Russian literature.[45]

Karamzin's "Europeanness" was ideologically important. Despite the change from his early, enthusiastic cosmopolitanism to a more conservative and nationalist position, Karamzin's independence in cultural matters, his unwillingness to abandon western authors out of political considerations, his conviction about the shared cultural heritage of Europe and Russia made his position in the 1790's a liberal one. He was never a radical thinker, but he was an enlightened and cultured man of letters. He continued to write and publish through a period of reaction, and it is the evidence of works *published* between 1791 and 1803, where he discusses obliquely or openly his own personal crisis and his attitudes toward European events, where his contribution and dedication to Russian literature are so apparent, that fully justifies the recognition of a "Karamzin period" in Russian literature.

Checklist of Original and Translated Reviews in the

MOSCOW JOURNAL

NOTES / SELECTED BIBLIOGRAPHY / INDEX

CHECKLIST OF ORIGINAL AND TRANSLATED
REVIEWS IN THE *MOSCOW JOURNAL*

KARAMZIN's reviews in the *Moscow Journal* represent one of the least known and least accessible parts of his literary legacy. Few libraries outside the Soviet Union possess sets of the *Moscow Journal* in either its first or second editions and Karamzin's collected works excluded his reviews entirely. A selection of the original reviews was eventually published by Lev Polivanov in his valuable anthology, *Izbrannye sochineniia N. M. Karamzina*, 1 (Moscow, 1884), 395–420, and more recently was included in the two-volume Soviet *Izbrannye sochineniia*, 2 (Moscow-Leningrad, 1964), 82–119. The checklist which follows has been compiled to illustrate the breadth of Karamzin's interests and his unprecedented activity as a reviewer at a time when reviewing in Russia was virtually an unknown and unpracticed art. It demonstrates Karamzin's consistent interest in contemporary European literature, which he also popularized by translation and in *Letters of a Russian Traveler*; at the same time it shows his concern for the state of Russian literature and enlightenment.

Karamzin's often meager bibliographical information has been checked and amplified by reference to English, French, German, and Russian bibliographies and contemporary journals. The list includes all titles included in the four sections: "About Russian Books" (RB), "About Foreign Books" (FB), "Moscow Theatre" (MT), and "Paris Theatres" (PT). However, no difference is made between those works which received extensive reviews and those which were simply listed.

1791

JANUARY G. E. Lessing, *Emilia Galotti*, translated from the German by N. M. Karamzin (Moscow, 1788). [MT]

M. M. Kheraskov, *Kadm i Garmoniia drevnee povestvovanie*, 2 pts. (Moscow, 1789). [RB]

F. Le Vaillant, *Voyage dans l'intérieur de l'Afrique par le Cap de Bonne Espérance, dans les années 1780,*

235

1781, 1782, 1784, and 1785, 2 vols. (Paris, 1790).   [FB]
[Original review by S. R. N. Chamfort in the *Mercure de France.*]

FEBRUARY

Paris Theatres (June–mid-August 1790)
[Translated from N. E. Framéry's "Les Spectacles" section in the *Mercure de France.*]

a) N. F. Guillard, *Louis IX.* Music by J. B. Le Moine.
[PT]

b) P.-F.-N. Fabre d'Églantine, *Le Présomptueux, ou l'Heureux imaginaire.*   [PT]

c) J.-C. B. Dejaure, *Les Époux réunis,* adapted from *Der deutsche Hausvater* by O. Gemmingen-Hornberg.   [PT]

J.-F. Collin d'Harleville, *L'Optimiste, ou l'Homme toujours content,* in the Russian version: *Optimist, ili chelovek vsem dovol'nyi.*   [MT]

G. L. L. de Buffon, *Histoire naturelle,* translated by S. Rumovskii and I. Lepekhin: *Vseobshchaia i chastnaia estestvennaia istoriia grafa de Biuffona,* pt. 1 (Spb., 1789).   [RB]

G. E. Groddeck, *Uber die Vergleichung der alten besonders griechischen mit der deutschen und neuern Litteratur* (Berlin, 1789).   [FB]
[From an original review in *Allgemeine deutsche Bibliothek,* 90 (1790).]

MARCH

J. C. Brandes, *Der Graf von Olsbach,* in a Russian version.   [MT]

Thomas More, *Utopia,* translated from French version as: *Filosofa Rafaila Gitlode stranstvovanie v Novom Svete i opisanie liubopytstva dostoinykh primechanii i blagorazumnykh ustanovlenii zhizni miroliubivago naroda ostrova Utopii* (Spb., 1790).   [RB]

Richard Hole, *Arthur; or, the Northern Enchantment. A Poetical Romance,* 7 bks. (London, 1790).   [FB]

John Howard, *An Account of the principal Lazarettos in Europe: with various Papers, relative to the Plague: together with further Observations on Some Foreign Prisons and Hospitals, and additional Remarks on the present State of those in Great Britain and Ireland* (London, 1791).   [FB]

APRIL   Paris Theatres (August–December 1790)
a) G. Saulnier, *La Divinité du sauvage, ou le Portrait.* Music by S. Champein.   [PT]
b) P. F. Desfontaines, *Le Tombeau de Desilles.*   [PT]
c) J. Fievee, *Les Rigueurs du cloître.* Music by H. M. Berton.   [PT]
d) F.-B. Hoffmann, *Euphrosine, ou le Tyran corrigé.* Music by E. N. Méhul.   [PT]
e) P. F. Desfontaines, *Ver-Vert*, adapted from the poem by J.-B. Gresset. Music by N. Dalayrac.   [PT]
f) J.-C. B. Dejaure, *Le Nouveau d'Assas.* Music by H. M. Berton.   [PT]
g) [Anon.], *Adèle et Didier.*   [PT]

K. D. von Dittersdorf, *Apotheker und Doktor*, in the Russian version by F. Rozanov: *Aptekar' i Doktor* (1788).   [MT]

P. P. Ostrogorskii, *Featr chrezvychainykh proizshestii iztekaiushchago veka, otkryt i predstavlen ocham sveta v sleduiushchikh sozertsaniiakh: Prokazy ezuitov i frantsiskanskikh monakhin'; Strannoe prikliuchenie odnogo markiza pri tselovanii papskago tuflia; Uzhasnaia konchina odnogo aglichanina; Gibel'naia uchast' docheri frantsuzskago kuptsa; Zlost' sviashchennika; Nevinno poveshennyi, poluchivshii zhizn'; Brodiashchee mnimoe prividenie po nocham; Posramlennoe legkoverie uchenykh; Unichizhennaia gordynia gishpantsa na Rusi; Razvrat uchitelia frantsuza; Plody kovarstva; Khrabrost' Rossa; Posramlenie nevezhdy, i proch.* (Spb., 1790).   [RB]

Kort historia om den kongl. Gustavianska familien. i fran . . . Gustaf den förste, intil . . . Gustaf III (Stockholm, 1786), translated by K. Merlin: *Kratkaia istoriia korolevskoi shvedskoi familii imianuemoi Gusta-vov, nachinaishchaiasia ot Korolia Gustava III* (Moscow, 1790). [RB]

U. Bräker, *Lebensgeschichte und natürliche Abentheuer eines armen Mannes von Tockenburg* (Zurich, 1789). [FB]
[From an original review in *Allgemeine deutsche Biblio-thek*, 92 (1791).]

MAY

Mémoires de M. Goldoni pour servir à l'histoire de sa vie, et à celle de son Théâtre, 3 vols. (Paris, 1787). [FB]

Romantische Gemälde der Vorwelt (Leipzig, 1789). [FB]
[From an original review in *Allgemeine deutsche Biblio-thek*.]

Jonathan Swift, *Miscellaneous Pieces in Prose and Verse* (London, 1789). [FB]

Voltaire, *Henriade*, translated by A. I. Golitsyn: *Gen-riada, geroicheskaia poema g. Voltera* (Moscow, 1790). [FB]

JUNE

Paris Theatres (completion of April review)
a)   J. Patrat, *Le Point d'honneur.* [PT]

A. F. Kotzebue, *Menschenhass und Reue*, translated by A. F. Malinovskii: *Nenavist' k liudiam i raskaianie* (Moscow, 1796). [MT]

L. Ariosto, *Orlando Furioso*, translated from French version into Russian by P. S. Molchanov: *Neistovyi Roland, geroicheskaia poema g. Ariosta*, pt. 1 (Moscow, 1791). [RB]

K. P. Moritz, *Götterlehre oder mythologische Dichtun-gen der Alten* (Berlin, 1791). [FB]

Pollingrove Robinson, *Cometilla; or, Views of Nature*, vol. 1 (London, 1789). [FB]

L. Langlès, trans., *Fables et contes indiens* (Paris, 1790).

[FB]

JULY

P. Corneille, *Le Cid*, translated and adapted by Ia. B. Kniazhnin: *Sid tragediia Petra Korneliia* (Spb., 1775).

[MT]

J. J. Barthélemy, *Voyage du jeune Anacharsis en Grèce, vers le milieu du quatrième siècle avant l'ère vulgaire*, 7 vols. (Paris, 1788).   [FB]
[Original review in *Allgemeine Literatur-Zeitung* (Jena, 1789).]

AUGUST

William Coxe, *Sketches of the natural, civil, and political state of Swisserland*, translated from the French version into Russian by V. Raevskii: *Opyt nyniashnago estestvennago, grazhdanskago i politicheskago sostoianiia Shveitsarii*, 2 pts. (Moscow, 1791).   [RB]

SEPTEMBER

Paris Theatres (in 1791)
a) C. Harny, *La Liberté conquise, ou le Despotisme renversé*.   [PT]
b) C.-M.-L.-E. Carbon de Flins, *Le Mari directeur, ou le Déménagement du couvent*.   [PT]
c) J.-F. Collin d'Harleville, *Monsieur de Crac dans son petit castel*.   [PT]
d) J.-N. Bouilly, *J.-J. Rousseau à ses derniers moments*.
                                                          [PT]
e) E. G. F. de Favières, *Paul et Virginie*, adapted from the story by J. H. Bernardin de Saint-Pierre. Music by Kreutzer.   [PT]
f) P.-F.-N. Fabre d'Eglantine, *Le Convalescent de qualité, ou l'Aristocrate*.   [PT]

Samuel Richardson, *Clarissa*, translated from French version into Russian by N. P. Osipov and P. Kil'diushevskii: *Dostopamiatnaia zhizn' devitsy Klarissy Garlov, istinnaia povest'*, pt. 1 (Spb., 1791).   [RB]

K. G. Langer (Carl Heinrich), *Polnyi geograficheskii leksikon, soderzhashchii v sebe po azbuchnomu poriadku podrobnoe opisanie vsekh chastei sveta, iz noveishikh i dostoverneishikh izvestii,* pts. 1–2 (Moscow, 1791). [RB]

NOVEMBER   N. P. Nikolev, *Baloven', ili ob zaklad proigrannaia neve-sta.*   [MT]

G. E. Lessing, *Miss Sara Sampson,* in Russian version by V. A. Levshin.   [MT]

DECEMBER   Paris Theatres (1791)
     a)   J. M. Boutet de Monvel, *Les Victimes cloîtrées.* [PT]
     b)   A. V. Arnault, *Marius à Minturnes.*   [PT]
     c)   C. S. Favart, *La Vengeance du bailli.*   [PT]
     d)   J. E. B. Dejaure, *L'Ombre de Mirabeau.*   [PT]

Memoires de la vie privée de Benjamin Franklin, écrits par lui-même, et addressés à son fils (Paris, 1791).   [FB]

P. Manuel, *La Police de Paris dévoilée,* 2 vols. (Paris, 1791).   [FB]
[Reviewed in the *Mercure de France* (July 1791).]

James Bruce, *Travels to discover the source of the Nile, in the years 1768 to 1773,* 5 vols. (Edinburgh, 1790). [FB]

1792

JANUARY   *Traur, komediia v odnom deistvii, perevedennaia s fran-tsuzskogo iazyka.* (Ia. B. Kniazhnin's *Traur, ili uteshen-naia vdova?*)   [MT]

C. F. Volney, *Les Ruines, ou Méditations sur les Révolutions des Empires* (Paris, 1791).   [FB]

L.-S. Mercier, *De J.-J. Rousseau, considéré comme l'un des premiers auteurs de la Révolution* (Paris, 1791). [FB]

MARCH   Paris Theatres (end of 1791)
a) J. M. Boutet de Monvel, *Philippe et Georgette.*
       Music by N. Dalayrac.   [PT]
b) [Anon.], *J.-J. Rousseau sur l'île de St. Pierre.* [PT]

J. P. Florian, *Gonzalve de Cordoue, ou Grenade reconquise,* 2 vols. (Paris, 1791).   [FB]
[Original review in the *Mercure de France* (January
1792).]

APRIL   F. J. Bertuch, *Elfriede,* in Russian translation: *El'frida*
(Spb., 1780).   [MT]

MAY   N. P. Osipov, *Virgilieva Eneida, vyvorochennaia na
iznanku,* pt. 1 (Spb., 1791).   [RB]

Paris Theatres (1792)
a) J.-F. Collin d'Harleville, *Le Vieux célibataire.* [PT]

F. Sayers, *Dramatik Sketches of the Ancient Northern
Mithology* (London, 1791).   [FB]

JULY   K. P. Moritz, *Reisen eines Deutschen in Italien,* pt. 1
(Berlin, 1792).   [FB]

AUGUST   C. H. Spiess, *Das Ehrenwort,* freely translated into Russian by A. F. Malinovskii: *Chestnoe slovo* (Moscow,
1793).   [MT]
[This review was not by Karamzin but by a friend, M*.]

G. R. Derzhavin, *Videnie Murzy,* translated into German by A. F. Kotzebue: *Der Traum des Mursa* (Spb.,
1792).   [FB]

Thomas Holcroft, *Anna St. Ives,* 7 vols. (London, 1792).
                                                       [FB]

SEPTEMBER   J. W. von Goethe, *Neue Schriften,* 1 (Berlin, 1792). [FB]

G. R. Derzhavin, *Felitsa*, translated into German by
A. F. Kotzebue: *Felizens Bild* (Spb., 1792).   [FB]

K. G. Langer, *Ruchnoi rossiiskii slovar' s nemetskim i
frantsuzskim perevodami* (Moscow, 1792).   [RB]

L.-S. Mercier, *Fictions morales*, 3 vols. (Paris, 1792).
[FB]

C. M. Wieland, *Geheime Geschichte des Philosophen
Peregrinus Proteus*, 2 vols. (Berlin, 1791).   [FB]

G. Sale, trans., *The Koran, commonly called the Alcoran
of Mohammed* (London, 1734), translated into Russian
by A. Kolmakov: *Al-Koran Magomedov . . . i so priso-
vokupleniem obstoiatel'nago i podrodnago opisaniia
zhizni lzhepropoka Maromeda, sochinennago slavnym
doktorom Prido*, 2 pts. (Spb., 1792).   [RB]
[The Life of Mohammed was translated by P. S. And-
reev.]

NOTES

Introduction

[1] *Panteon rossiiskikh avtorov*, 1 (Moscow, 1801) [frontispiece].
[2] Marc Raeff, *Origins of the Russian Intelligentsia: The Eighteenth-Century Nobility* (New York, 1966), p. 109.
[3] V. O. Kliuchevskii, *Ocherki i rechi* (Moscow, 1915), p. 270.
[4] G. Makogonenko, *Nikolai Novikov i russkoe prosveshchenie XVIII veka* (Moscow-Leningrad, 1951), p. 507.
[5] On the activities of the society, see V. P. Semennikov, *Sobranie staraiushcheesia o perevode inostrannykh knig, uchrezhdennoe Ekaterinoi II. 1768–1783* (Spb., 1913).
[6] On Kheraskov, see A. Vlasto, "M. M. Heraskov: A Study in the Intellectual Life of the Age of Catherine the Great," Ph.D. dissertation, Cambridge University, 1952.
[7] *Polnoe sobranie vsekh sochinenii, v stikakh i proze . . . Aleksandra Petrovicha Sumarokova*. Sobrany i izdany . . . Nikolaem Novikovym, 1 (Moscow, 1781) [frontispiece].
[8] N. I. Novikov, *Izbrannye sochineniia* (Moscow-Leningrad, 1951), pp. 350–51.
[9] Cf. G. N. Pospelov, "U istokov russkogo sentimentalizma," *Vestnik Moskovskogo Universiteta*, No. 1 (1948), pp. 3–27; K. A. Nazaretskaia, "Ob istokakh russkogo sentimentalizma," *Uchenye zapiski Kazanskogo gos. universiteta*, 123, No. 8 (1963), 3–34; K. A. Nazaretskaia, "Poeziia i proza v moskovskikh zhurnalakh 60-kh godov XVIII (K voprosu o formirovanii sentimentalizma)," ibid., 124, No. 5 (1964), 3–25.
[10] See particularly Gr. Gukovskii, *Ocherki po istorii russkoi literatury i obshchestvennoi mysli XVIII veka* (Leningrad, 1938), pp. 235–98.
[11] Henry M. Nebel, Jr., *N. M. Karamzin: A Russian Sentimentalist* (The Hague-Paris, 1967), pp. 50–83, 177–79.
[12] V. V. Vinogradov, *Problema avtorstva i teoriia stilei* (Moscow, 1961), p. 239.

1 The Formative Years (1766–1790)

[1] *Vestnik Evropy*, 10 (July 1803), 121.
[2] *Sochineniia Karamzina*, 3 vols. (Spb., 1848), 2:549. (This is the basic edition used in this study and cited hereafter as *Sochineniia*.)

3   N. S. Tikhonravov, "Professor I. M. Shaden," *Sochineniia*, 3, part. 1 (Moscow, 1898), 44–59.

4   *Perepiska Karamzina s Lafaterom* (Spb., 1893), p. 4.

5   *Sochineniia*, 2:120.

6   Ibid., p. 773.

7   A. V. Starchevskii, *Nikolai Mikhailovich Karamzin* (Spb., 1849), p. 14.

8   A. D. Galakhov, "Karamzin (Materialy dlia opredeleniia ego literaturnoi deiatel'nosti)," *Sovremennik*, 37, No. 1 (1853), 16–26.

9   *Sochineniia*, 2:115.

10 *Pis'ma N. M. Karamzina k I. I. Dmitrievu* (Spb., 1866), pp. 463–64.

11 I. I. Dmitriev, "Vzgliad na moiu zhizn'," *Sochineniia*, 2 (Spb., 1895), 24.

12 N. Grech, *Chteniia o russkom iazyke*, 2 (Spb., 1840), 121.

13 *Perepiska Karamzina s Lafaterom*, p. 6.

14 Dmitriev, *Sochineniia*, 2:25–26.

15 Ibid., p. 25; *Pis'ma k Dmitrievu*, p. 351.

16 *Russkii arkhiv* (1863), p. 887.

17 Ibid., pp. 889–90.

18 A. N. Pypin, *Russkoe masonstvo XVIII veka i pervaia chetvert' XIX v.* (Petrograd, 1916), p. 516.

19 Dmitriev, *Sochineniia*, 2:25–26.

20 I. V. Lopukhin, "Zapiski," *Russkii arkhiv*, No. 1 (1884), p. 16.

21 Dmitriev, *Sochineniia*, 2:26.

22 E. Solov'ev, *N. M. Karamzin: ego zhizn' i nauchno-literaturnaia deiatel'-nost'* (Spb., 1894), p. 15.

23 *Perepiska s Lafaterom*, p. 20.

24 "O knizhnoi torgovle i liubvi ko chteniiu v Rossii," *Sochineniia*, 3: 545–46.

25 Cf. "Poslednie snosheniia Karamzina s N. I. Novikovym," *Russkii arkhiv*, 3, No. 11 (1890), 367–75; M. N. Longinov, *Novikov i moskovskie martinisty* (Moscow, 1867), p. 383.

26 "Zapiska o N. I. Novikove," *Neizdannye sochineniia i perepiska Nikolaia Mikhailovicha Karamzina*, 1 (Spb., 1862), 225–26.

27 E. I. Tarasov, *K istorii russkogo obshchestva vtoroi poloviny XVIII veka (Mason I. P. Turgenev)* (Spb., 1914), p. 20.

28 Ibid., p. 22.

29 Iu. Lotman, " 'Sochuvstvennik' A. N. Radishcheva A. M. Kutuzov i ego pis'ma k I. P. Turgenevu," *Trudy po russkoi i slavianskoi filologii*, 6, *Uchenye zapiski Tartuskogo gosudarstvennogo universiteta*, vypusk 139 (1963), p. 321.

30 Ibid., p. 299.

31 Karamzin recommended the translation of *Messias* as "faithful and lucid." *Sochineniia*, 2:127.

32 E. I. Tarasov, *K istorii masonstva v Rossii (Zabytyi rozenkreitser A. M. Kutuzov)* (Spb., 1910).

33 Cf. G. Makogonenko, *Nikolai Novikov i russkoe prosveshchenie XVIII*

veka (Moscow-Leningrad, 1951), pp. 339 ff.; P. Brang, "A. M. Kutuzov als Vermittler des oesteuropäischen Sentimentalismus in Russland," *Zeitschrift für slavische Philologie*, 30, 1 (1962), 44–57.

34 Published in *Moskovskoe ezhemesiachnoe izdanie*. See Makogonenko, *Novikov*, p. 444.
35 *Uchenye zapiski Tartuskogo universiteta*, vypusk 139 (1963), p. 322.
36 Iu. M. Lotman, "Evoliutsiia mirovozzreniia Karamzina (1789–1803)," *Uchenye zapiski Tartuskogo universiteta*, vypusk 51 (1957), pp. 123–24.
37 K. S. Serbinovich, "Nikolai Mikhailovich Karamzin: vospominaniia," *Russkaia starina*, 11, No. 10 (1874), 242.
38 N. Vtorov, "Gavrila Petrovich Kamenev," *Vchera i segodnia*, 1 (1845), 58.
39 *Sochineniia*, 3:362.
40 Ibid., p. 361.
41 Cf. *Russkii arkhiv* (1863), p. 891, and *Perepiska Karamzina s Lafaterom*, p. 16.
42 Cf. V. Kliuchevskii, "Vospominanie o N. I. Novikove i ego vremeni," *Ocherki i rechi* (Moscow, 1915), p. 270 and E. G. Plimak, "Masonskaia reaktsiia protiv materializma v Rossii," *Voprosy filosofii*, No. 2 (1957), p. 56.
43 S. P. Shevyrev, *Istoriia Imperatorskogo Moskovskogo Universiteta* (Moscow, 1855), p. 235.
44 *Russkii arkhiv* (1863), p. 893.
45 Ibid., p. 894.
46 *Detskoe chtenie dlia serdtsa i razuma*, 2 (1785), 136–37. (Possible linguistic evidence of Petrov's authorship is his use of *balsamnyi zapakh* [as opposed to Karamzin's and others' *bal'zamicheskii zapakh*] both here and in a later piece, ibid., p. 118; 20 [1789], 171.)
47 Ibid., 6 (1786), 179–80.
48 *Sochineniia*, 3:362.
49 *Polnoe sobranie sochinenii g-na Gesnera*, 4 parts (Moscow, 1802–3), 1: 279–91.
50 Ibid., 1:v.
51 *Detskoe chtenie*, 17 (1789), 200.
52 *O proiskhozhdenii zla, poema velikogo Gallera* (Moscow, 1786), p. 11.
53 *Dereviannaia noga, shveitsarskaia idiliia gos Gesnera* (Spb., 1783), p. 7. Cf. Salomon Gessner, *Schriften*, 2 (Zurich, 1778), 94.
54 Cf. *Moskovskii zhurnal*, 4 (1791), 65 and *Sochineniia*, 2:192.
55 A. Kross, "Raznovidnosti idilii v tvorchestve Karamzina," *XVIII vek*, 8 (Leningrad, 1969), 211–28.
56 Cf. *Moskovskii zhurnal*, 4, 278–86, and Gessner, *Schriften*, 2:70–74.
57 *Sochineniia*, 2:648; 3:586.
58 *O proiskhozhdenii zla*, p. 26.
59 Ibid., p. 49.
60 *Perepiska Karamzina s Lafaterom*, p. 44.
61 *Detskoe chtenie*, 18:3–53; 19:165–202.

62 *Sochineniia,* 2:433, 3:455.

63 *Perepiska Karamzina s Lafaterom,* pp. 38, 40.

64 *O proiskhozhdenii zla,* p. 70.

65 Ibid., pp. 11, 43, 45–46.

66 Ibid., pp. 5–6.

67 P. Pekarskii, "O knigakh, pechatannykh v tipografii N. I. Novikova, i ob izdanii Karamzina: Besedy s Bogom," *Pis'ma k Dmitrievu,* pp. 470–71.

68 See *British Museum General Catalogue of Printed Books,* 232 (London, 1964), 90–94.

69 L. B. Svetlov, *Izdatel'skaia deiatel'nost' Novikova* (Leningrad, 1946), p. 63.

70 V. I. Rezanov, *Iz razyskanii o sochineniiakh V. A. Zhukovskogo,* 1 (Spb., 1906), 24.

71 *Pis'ma k Dmitrievu,* pp. 469–70, 472.

72 Dmitriev, *Sochineniia,* 2:27.

73 Cf. Rezanov, pp. 27–30.

74 N. S. Tikhonravov, "V. A. Zhukovskii," *Sochineniia,* 3, part. 1 (Moscow, 1898), 404.

75 Christopher C. Sturm, *Reflections on the Works of God in Nature and Providence, for Every Day of the Year,* tran. Adam Clarke (New York, 1824), p. iii.

76 *Detskoe chtenie,* 1 (1785), 4.

77 E. P. Privalova gives Petrov as the translator of *Betrachtungen,* without indication of source, in "O sotrudnikakh zhurnala *Detskoe chtenie dlia serdtsa i razuma,*" *Russkaia literatura XVIII veka: Epokha klassitsizma: XVIII vek,* 6 (Moscow-Leningrad, 1964), 259.

78 S. Smirnov, "Tsenzurnaia vedomost' 1786–1788 godov," *Osmnadtsatyi vek,* 1, 2nd ed. (Moscow, 1869), 496–97.

79 See Petrov's references to Karamzin's Shakespeare projects: letters of May 20 and June 11, 1785, *Russkii arkhiv* (1863), pp. 887, 889.

80 *Zhizn' i smert' Richarda III korolia anglinskogo, tragediia g. Shakespera* (Spb., 1787). Translated in 1783.

81 See D. M. Lang, "Sumarokov's *Hamlet:* A Misjudged Russian Tragedy of the Eighteenth Century," *Modern Language Review,* 43 (1948), 67–72.

82 Quoted in Mary Gertrude Cushing, *Pierre Le Tourneur* (New York, 1908), p. 196. In her chapter, "The Translator of Shakespeare" (pp. 154–252), Cushing provides a thorough examination of Le Tourneur's views and translation and of the literary disputes.

83 Sumarokov's article on Beaumarchais' *Eugénie* and Voltaire's letter to Sumarokov were printed at the beginning of *Dimitrii Samozvanets, tragediia Aleksandra Sumarokova* (Spb., 1771).

84 *Iulii Tsezar', tragediia Villiama Shekespira* (Moscow, 1787), pp. 3–6.

85 See M. N. Rozanov, *Poet perioda "burnykh stremlenii" Iakob Lents, ego zhizn' i proizvedeniia* (Moscow, 1901), pp. 450–92.

86 *Iulii Tsezar',* p. 21.

87 *Les Nuits d'Young* (Marseilles, 1770), p. lxvii.

[88] *Iulii Tsezar'*, pp. 40, 47, 21.

[89] V. G. Belinskii, *Polnoe sobranie sochinenii*, 2 (Moscow, 1953), 266.

[90] Letter of August 1, 1787, *Russkii arkhiv* (1863), pp. 892–93.

[91] *Sochineniia*, 2:578.

[92] Ibid., pp. 732, 747–48.

[93] Letter of June 22, 1793; *Pis'ma k Dmitrievu*, p. 39.

[94] *Russkii arkhiv* (1863), p. 893.

[95] *Emiliia Galotti, tragediia v 5 deistviiakh, sochinennaia* G. Lessingom (Moscow, 1788), p. 3.

[96] Ibid.

[97] *Moskovskii zhurnal*, 1 (Jan. 1791), 71.

[98] *The Works of Mr. James Thomson*, 1 (London, 1803), 162.

[99] *Detskoe chtenie*, 12 (1787), 201.

[100] See R. Pascal, *Shakespeare in Germany, 1740–1815* (Cambridge, Eng., 1937), p. 5. Cf. *Sochineniia*, 2:321, 417, 472–74.

[101] *Moskovskii zhurnal*, 4 (Nov. 1791), 244.

[102] A. V. Predtechenskii, "Obshchestvenno-politicheskie vzgliady Karamzina v 1790-kh godakh," *Problema Prosveshcheniia i russkaia literatura XVIII veka* (Moscow-Leningrad, 1961), p. 69.

[103] Quoted in Rezanov, *Iz razyskanii o V. A. Zhukovskom*, 1:25, fn. Cf. *Unterhaltungen mit Gott in den Abenstunden*, 1 (Reutlingen, 1813), 57–59.

[104] M. N. Pogodin, *Nikolai Mikhailovich Karamzin, po ego sochineniiam, pis'mam i otzyvam sovremennikov*, 1 (Spb., 1866), 48.

[105] *Detskoe chtenie*, 1 (1785), 3–8.

[106] Gr. Gukovskii, *Ocherki po istorii russkoi literatury i obshchestvennoi mysli XVIII* (Leningrad, 1938), p. 304.

[107] See E. P. Privalova, "*Detskoe chtenie dlia serdtsa i razuma* v otsenke chitatelei i kritiki," *Rol' i znachenie literatury XVIII veka v istorii russkoi kul'tury: XVIII vek*, 7 (Moscow-Leningrad, 1966), 254–60.

[108] E. P. Privalova, "O sotrudnikakh zhurnala *Detskoe chtenie dlia serdtsa i razuma*," *XVIII vek*, 6:258–68.

[109] Cf. "Perepiska ottsa s synom o derevenskoi zhizni," *Detskoe chtenie*, 2:112–25, 129–42, 145–70; "Razgovor o povinovenii, kakoe deti dolzhny okazat' svoim roditeliam," ibid., 4:97–119; "Povest' o Seleme i Ksamire," ibid. 1:8–42.

[110] Ibid., 4:27.

[111] Cf. "Razgovor," *Detskoe chtenie*, 7:158–59.

[112] Ibid., 4:190–92.

[113] Ibid., 4:24.

[114] Ibid., 1:40.

[115] Ibid., 3:130–31.

[116] "Nedovol'nyi svoim sostoianiem," *Detskoe chtenie*, 1:183–91.

[117] See Violet Wyndham, *Madame de Genlis* (London, 1958), pp. 80–103.

[118] Mme. de Genlis, *Les Veillées du château*, 1 (Paris, 1798), xxi.

[119] Ibid., p. 128.

120 *Detskoe chtenie,* 9:157.
121 V. V. Sipovskii, N. M. *Karamzin, avtor "Pisem russkogo puteshestven-nika"* (Spb., 1899), p. 125.
122 *Les Veillées du château,* 1:xiv.
123 I.I. Dmitriev, *Sochineniia,* 2:26.
124 *Detskoe chtenie,* 15 (1788), 27–94.
125 *Sovremennik,* 42, No. 11 (1853) otdel iii, 54.
126 *Detskoe chtenie,* 15:96.
127 "O sotrudnikakh zhurnala *Detskoe chtenie dlia serdtsa i razuma,*" XVIII *vek,* 6:262.
128 The arguments for this attribution are given in my article "Karamzin's First Short Story?" which is awaiting publication.
129 *Sochineniia,* 3:363.
130 *Detskoe chtenie,* 15:37–38.
131 Ibid., pp. 179–204.
132 See the analysis of "Moia ispoved' " in chapter 4 of this volume.
133 *Detskoe chtenie,* 17:44–48.
134 Cf. *Sochineniia,* 3:474–75. Compare also the passage on Baron Bliefeld (*Detskoe chtenie,* 17:47–48) with *Letters of a Russian Traveler* (*Sochineniia,* 2:685).
135 *Detskoe chtenie,* 18:21, 31; 19:185, 186.
136 Ibid., 18:65–77, 81–92, 97–107, 113–40, 145–50.
137 Ibid., p. 150.
138 Ibid., pp. 161–75.
139 Karamzin inserts a rapturous tribute to Young in his translation of Thomson's "Summer," *Detskoe chtenie,* 10 (1787), 205.
140 See E. P. Privalova, "O sotrudnikakh zhurnala *Detskoe chtenie dlia serdtsa i razuma,*" XVIII *vek,* 6:267–68.
141 *Detskoe chtenie,* 18:141–44, 151–58; 19:138–44.
142 *Perepiska Karamzina s Lafaterom,* p. 20.
143 N. M. Karamzin, *Polnoe sobranie stikhotvorenii,* ed. Iu. M. Lotman (Moscow-Leningrad, 1966), pp. 69–70.
144 *Pis'ma k Dmitrievu,* p. 7. Cf. *Russkii arkhiv* (1863), pp. 884–85.
145 *Polnoe sobranie stikhotvorenii,* pp. 58–63.
146 Cf. G. A. Vishnevskaia, "Iz istorii russkogo romantizma (literaturno-teoreticheskie suzhdeniia N. M. Karamzina 1787–1792 gg.)." *Uchenye zapiski Kazanskogo universiteta,* 124, No. 5 (1964), 39–40; Henry Nebel, Jr., N. M. *Karamzin: A Russian Sentimentalist* (The Hague-Paris, 1967), pp. 87–88.
147 Rozanov, *Poet perioda "burnykh stremlenii" Iakob Lents,* pp. 488–89.
148 Cf. Trediakovskii's "Epistola ot rossiiskoi poezii k Apollinu," *Izbrannye proizvedeniia* (Moscow-Leningrad, 1963), pp. 390–95.
149 *Neizdannye sochineniia i perepiska,* pp. 223–24.
150 *Russkii arkhiv* (1866), p. 1756. Petrov's letters, edited by Karamzin, were eventually published in *Pamiatnik otechestvennykh muz* (Spb., 1827), pp. 10–24.

[151] Quoted in Pogodin, *Karamzin*, 1:68.
[152] G. P. Shtorm, "Novoe o Pushkine i Karamzine," *Izvestiia Akademii Nauk SSSR, Otdelenie literatury i iazyka*, 19, No. 2 (1960), 150.
[153] Ibid.
[154] *Sochineniia*, 3:364.

2 The *Moscow Journal* (1791–1792)

[1] G. P. Shtorm, "Novoe o Pushkine i Karamzine," *Izvestiia Akademii Nauk SSSR, Otdelenie literatury i iazyka*, 19, No. 2 (1960), 151.
[2] Ia. L. Barskov, *Perepiska moskovskikh masonov XVIII-go veka* (Petrograd, 1915), p. 30.
[3] *Sochineniia Karamzina*, 2 (Spb., 1848), 4.
[4] *Sochineniia*, 3:364.
[5] Barskov, p. 2.
[6] Ibid., p. 29.
[7] Ibid., p. 6.
[8] Printed in full in M. N. Pogodin *Nikolai Mikhailovich Karamzin*, 1 (Spb., 1866), 170–72.
[9] *Perepiska Karamzina s Lafaterom* (Spb., 1893), p. 58.
[10] Barskov, p. 109.
[11] Ibid., pp. 49, 55, 58, 70, 86–87, 89, 94–95, 99–100, 106.
[12] Ibid., pp. 70–73.
[13] Ibid., p. 49.
[14] L. B. Svetlov, " 'Obshchestvo liubitelei rossiiskoi uchenosti' pri Moskovskom universitete," *Istoricheskii arkhiv*, 5 (1950), 305.
[15] Letter to I. I. Shuvalov, September 3, 1789. *Istoricheskii arkhiv*, 5 (1950), 320.
[16] Karamzin's complex relations with the masons are analyzed at length in V. V. Vinogradov, *Problema avtorstva i teoriia stilei* (Moscow, 1961), pp. 246–323.
[17] *Moskovskii zhurnal*, 1 (Jan. 1791), 5.
[18] Cf. his praise of Kheraskov in a letter to Lavater (*Perepiska Karamzina s Lafaterom*, p. 20) and in *Letters* (*Sochineniia*, 2:128). See R. D. Keil, "Ergänzungen zu russischen Dichter-Kommentaren (Lomonosov und Karamzin)," *Zeitschrift für slavische Philologie*, 30 (1962), 380–83.
[19] Karamzin hailed Derzhavin as "the first Russian poet" in his announcement; Derzhavin paid his famous tribute to Karamzin's prose style in the final lines of his poem, "Progulka v Sarskom Sele" (*Moskovskii zhurnal*, 3 [Aug. 1791], 127); Karamzin dedicated his translation of Ossian's "Songs of Selma" to Derzhavin in the same number, ibid., p. 134.
[20] *Perepiska Karamzina s Lafaterom*, p. 20.
[21] *Vchera i segodnia*, 1 (1845), 58.
[22] V. V. Sipovskii, *Ocherki iz istorii russkogo romana*, 1, part 1 (Spb., 1909), 43. Sipovskii's figures require some modification in the light of

subsequent bibliographical research, but Karamzin's contribution would not be significantly undercut.

23 Cf. *Pis'ma N. M. Karamzina I. I. Dmitrievu* (Spb., 1866), pp. 17, 19.
24 *Moskovskii zhurnal*, 5 (Jan. 1792), 137–48.
25 Ibid., 5 (Feb. 1792), 278.
26 Ibid., p. 281.
27 N. I. Novikov, *Izbrannye sochineniia* (Moscow-Leningrad, 1951), p. 726.
28 Ibid., p. 275.
29 M. A. Dmitriev, *Melochi iz zapasa moei pamiati*, 2nd ed. (Moscow, 1869), pp. 31–32.
30 Barskov, p. 95.
31 *Zritel'*, 2 (June 1792), 158–59.
32 *Moskovskii zhurnal*, 1 (Jan. 1791), 80–101.
33 Ibid., pp. 102–3.
34 Ibid., 5 (March 1792), 401. Cf. *Mercure de France* (Jan. 1792), p. 19.
35 Ibid., 2 (June 1791), 322.
36 *Severnyi vestnik*, 3, No. 8 (1804), 144–45.
37 Kheraskov's preface is printed in full in Sipovskii, *Iz istorii russkogo romana i povesti*, 1 (Spb., 1903), 221–23.
38 Cf. Pogodin, *Karamzin*, 1:37.
39 *Rassuzhdenie o geroicheskoi poeme, i o prevoskhodstve stikhotvoreniia Telemaka* (Moscow, 1787).
40 *Uchenye zapiski Tartuskogo gos. universiteta*, vypusk 139 (1963), p. 316.
41 *Moskovskii zhurnal*, 1 (Jan. 1791), 84–89.
42 *Moskovskii zhurnal*, 2 (May 1791), 24; 3 (Aug. 1791), 221–22; 1 (March 1791), 359–63.
43 Ibid., 2 (June 1791), 311.
44 Ibid., 2 (Feb. 1791), 253.
45 E. Erämetsä, *A Study of the Word "Sentimental" and of other Linguistic Characteristics of Eighteenth-Century Sentimentalism in England* (Helsinki, 1951), p. 126.
46 *Moskovskii zhurnal*, 6 (May 1792), 205.
47 Ibid., pp. 207–8.
48 *Sochineniia*, 2:745, 762.
49 *Moskovskii zhurnal*, 4 (Oct. 1791), 108–9.
50 *Detskoe chtenie dlia serdtsa i razuma*, 12 (1787), 200.
51 *Moskovskii zhurnal*, 1 (Jan. 1791), 71.
52 *Sochineniia*, 2:749.
53 Ibid.
54 *Moskovskii zhurnal*, 6 (May 1792), 215.
55 Ibid., 7 (Aug. 1792), 256–57.
56 Ibid., 2nd ed. (1803), p. 261. For a more detailed account of Karamzin's views on English literature see A. G. Cross, "Karamzin and England," *Slavonic and East European Review*, 43, No. 100 (1964), 91–114.

57 *Sochineniia*, 2:84.
58 *Moskovskii zhurnal*, 2 (April 1791), 85.
59 Ibid., p. 95.
60 The books and plays reviewed by Karamzin are listed in a special appendix.
61 *Moskovskii zhurnal*, 3 (July 1791), 84–97.
62 Ibid., p. 88.
63 Ibid., 1 (Jan. 1791), 76–77.
64 *Detskoe chtenie*, 12 (1787), 201.
65 "Afinskaia zhizn'," *Sochineniia*, 3:420.
66 *Moskovskii zhurnal*, 6 (April 1792), 102–3.
67 *Pis'ma k Dmitrievu*, p. 26.
68 *Moskovskii zhurnal*, 7 (July 1792), 254.
69 *Sochineniia*, 3:548.
70 *Moskovskii zhurnal*, 2 (June 1791), 306.
71 Ibid., 2 (April 1791), 23.
72 *Sochineniia*, 2:72–73.
73 *Moskovskii zhurnal*, 2 (June 1791), 253–76.
74 Cf. his review of *Emilia Galotti*: 1 (Jan. 1791), 77.
75 A. A. Grigor'ev, *Sochineniia*, 1 (Spb., 1876), 497.
76 *Moskovskii zhurnal*, 1 (Feb. 1791), 234–35.
77 Ibid., pp. 230–31.
78 *Sochineniia*, 2:417.
79 Ibid., p. 472.
80 Ibid., p. 480.
81 Ibid.
82 *Moskovskii zhurnal*, 2 (April 1791), 77–78.
83 *Sochineniia*, 2:732.
84 Ibid., p. 748.
85 Ibid., pp. 83–84.
86 *Moskovskii zhurnal*, 1 (March 1791), 357.
87 Ibid.
88 Ibid., 1 (Nov. 1791), 233.
89 Ibid., p. 244.
90 Ibid., 2 (May 1791), 205–6.
91 Ibid., 2 (June 1791), 311; 4 (Oct. 1791), 112.
92 Ibid., 4 (Oct. 1791), 115.
93 *Pis'ma k Dmitrievu*, pp. 20, 28, 37.
94 *Moskovskii zhurnal*, 2 (May 1791), 215.
95 Ibid., 4 (Oct. 1791), 110.
96 Ibid., 2 (May 1791), 215.
97 *Pis'ma k Dmitrievu*, p. 23.
98 *Moskovskii zhurnal*, 2 (May 1791), 216.
99 Ibid., 1 (Feb. 1791), 241–42.
100 Ibid., 3 (Aug. 1791), 217–18. Cf. 1 (March 1791), 365; 4 (Oct. 1791), 110.

[101] Ibid., 1 (March 1791), 365. Cf. 3 (Aug. 1791), 221–23.

[102] *Bibliograficheskie zapiski*, No. 19 (1858), p. 587.

[103] K. A. Grot, *N. M. Karamzin i F. N. Glinka. Materialy k biografiiam russkikh pisatelei* (Spb., 1903), p. 9.

[104] *Vchera i segodnia*, 1 (1845), 51–52.

[105] *Moskovskii zhurnal*, 4 (Nov. 1791), 247.

[106] See Karamzin's footnotes to the first and third stories, *Moskovskii zhurnal*, 1 (March 1791), 281, and 3 (Sept. 1791), 241.

[107] Ibid., 8 (Oct.–Nov. 1792), 159.

[108] Ibid., 7 (July 1792), 66–99; 7 (Sept. 1792), 282–321; 8 (Oct.–Nov. 1792), 70–76.

[109] Ibid., 4 (Oct. 1791), 13–32.

[110] Ibid., 2 (April 1791), 51.

[111] Ibid., 5 (Feb. 1792), 233–34.

[112] *Rossiiskii magazin*, 1 (Nov. 1792), 198–207.

[113] *Moskovskii zhurnal*, 1 (Feb. 1791), 249.

[114] Ibid., 6 (May 1792), 125.

[115] Ibid., 8 (Oct.–Nov. 1792), 125.

[116] *Sochineniia*, 2:122.

[117] *Moskovskii zhurnal*, 1 (Jan. 1791), 5.

[118] Ibid., 1 (Feb. 1791), 194.

[119] *Sochineniia*, 2:119.

[120] *Moskovskii zhurnal*, 6 (Sept. 1792), 321–43.

[121] Ibid., 6 (May 1792), 167–76.

[122] Ibid., 2 (June 1791), 277–80. (Probably by way of Herder's edition of 1786.)

[123] Ibid., 1 (Feb. 1791), 229.

[124] Ibid., 1 (Jan. 1791), 114–15.

[125] The real author was J. A. Eberhard (1739–1809). See Hans Rothe, *N. M. Karamzins europäische Reise* (Berlin, 1968), p. 123.

[126] *Moskovskii zhurnal*, 3 (Aug. 1791), 150–64.

[127] Ibid., 6(April 1792), 65–73. See Vinogradov, *Problema avtorstva i teoriia stilei*, pp. 264–323.

[128] *Russkii arkhiv* (1866), p. 1761.

[129] *Sochineniia*, 2:133–37.

[130] *Moskovskii zhurnal*, 4 (Nov. 1791), 205–35, 325–42; 5 (Jan. 1792), 57–83, 234–71.

[131] *Sochineniia*, 2:137.

[132] *Moskovskii zhurnal*, 1 (March 1791), 281.

[133] Ibid., 5 (Jan. 1792), 12–15. See Vinogradov, *Problema avtorstva i teoriia stilei*, pp. 324–38.

[134] *Bibliograf*, No. 9 (1885), pp. 37–38.

[135] A. A. Grigor'ev, *Sochineniia*, 1 (Spb., 1876), 609–11.

[136] *Sochineniia*, 2:72.

[137] Barskov, *Perepiska moskovskikh masonov*, p. 86.

[138] *Moskovskii zhurnal*, 1 (Feb. 1791), list of subscribers for January.

[139] *Sochineniia*, 2:126. R* could possibly refer to A. K. Rubanovskii, the close friend of Kutuzov and Radishchev, who settled in Moscow in the 1780's.

[140] N. M. Karamzin, *Polnoe sobranie stikhotvorenii* (Moscow-Leningrad), p. 111.

[141] *Russkii arkhiv* (1866), p. 1762.

[142] *Moskovskii zhurnal*, 6 (May 1792), 208.

[143] P. A. Viazemskii, *Polnoe sobranie sochinenii*, 1 (Spb., 1878), 321.

[144] Pogodin, *Karamzin*, 1:168.

[145] Barskov, *Perepiska moskovskikh masonov*, p. 99.

[146] *Moskovskii zhurnal*, 3 (Sept. 1791), 327.

[147] Quoted in K. L. Wood, "The French Theatre in the XVIIIth Century According to Some Contemporary English Travellers," *Revue de littérature comparée*, 12 (1932), 614–15.

[148] *Moskovskii zhurnal*, 4 (Dec. 1792), 342; 2 (April 1791), 71.

[149] Ibid., 1 (Feb. 1791), 203.

[150] Ibid., 5 (Jan. 1792), 150–51.

[151] *Uchenye zapiski Tartuskogo gos. universiteta*, vypusk 51 (1951), p. 130.

[152] *Moskovskii zhurnal*, 2 (Sept. 1791), 328–29.

[153] Pogodin, *Karamzin*, 1:375.

[154] Karamzin seems to acknowledge his gratitude to Barsov by publishing his "Svod bytii rossiiskikh," a work out of keeping in language and content with the rest of the journal: *Moskovskii zhurnal*, 7 (Sept. 1792), 346–58.

[155] *Sochineniia*, 2:515.

[156] V. A. Zhukovskii, "Neizdannyi konspekt po istorii russkoi literatury," *Trudy otdela novoi russkoi literatury*, 1 (1948), 299.

[157] These remarks appeared without acknowledgment in William Tooke, *The Life of Catharine II*, 3, 3rd ed. (London, 1799), 403. This was the first mention in English of a work by Karamzin, which preceded the first instance of his name.

[158] *Moskovskii zhurnal*, 4 (Nov. 1791), 246–47.

[159] *Arzamas i arzamasskie protokoly* (Leningrad, 1931), p. 240.

3 Letters of a Russian Traveler (1791–1801)

[1] See T. Roboli, "Literatura puteshestvii," *Russkaia proza* (Leningrad, 1926), pp. 42–73.

[2] An exhaustive analysis of these aspects is provided in V. V. Sipovskii, *Nikolai Mikhailovich Karamzin, avtor "Pisem russkogo puteshestvennika,"* (Spb., 1899), pp. 148–237.

[3] This is calculated according to the pagination of the Smirdin edition; the missing pages are 460–66, 493–651. References in the text of this chapter are to this edition, which for many reasons has to be used with caution.

[4] Karamzin supervised five distinct editions in his lifetime: the final three

were in his collected works of 1803–4, 1814, and 1820. The first two are most important for ideological changes, although the third has particular linguistic interest: Karamzin compared the two earlier editions and in some cases opted for the original version.

5 *Pis'ma russkogo puteshestvennika*, 1 (Moscow, 1797), p. v–vi.

6 Ibid., p. v. Cf. announcement in *Moscow News*.

7 *Moskovskii zhurnal*, 3 (Aug. 1791), 220.

8 V. G. Belinskii, *Polnoe sobranie sochinenii*, 7 (Moscow, 1955), 135.

9 *Pis'ma russkogo puteshestvennika*, 1 (1797), vi–vii.

10 Ibid., p. vi.

11 *Spectateur du Nord*, 4 (Oct. 1797), 58.

12 *Opyt Trudov Vol'nogo Rossiiskogo Sobraniia*, 2 (1775), 105–45.

13 *Priiatnoe i poleznoe preprovozhdenie vremeni*, 4 (1794), 56 ff.

14 Translated extracts from these works and Demidov's are included in my "18th Century England through Russian Eyes," in preparation. On eighteenth-century Russian travelers, see K. V. Sivkov, *Puteshestviia russkikh liudei za granitsu v XVIII veke* (Spb., 1914).

15 See Sipovskii, *Karamzin, avtor "Pisem russkogo puteshestvennika,"* pp. 327–31.

16 *Pis'ma N. M. Karamzina k I. I. Dmitrievu* (Spb., 1866), pp. 7, 8.

17 See I. Glebov, "Dva nabliudatelia evropeiskoi zhizni. (Pis'ma iz-za granitsy Fonvizina i Karamzina)," *Nabliudatel'*, No. 6 (1898), pp. 74–94.

18 *Spectateur du Nord*, 4 (1797), 59–60.

19 *The Man of Feeling* (New York, 1958), p. 36. Cf. pp. 3, 29–30, 35. Fielding's Parson Adams in *Joseph Andrews* expresses similar views.

20 Cf. "I am a Russian; I have read *Anacharsis*; I am able to delight in the creations of great and immortal talents": *Sochineniia*, 2:509.

21 *Spectateur du Nord*, 4:59–60.

22 Jean-Jacques Rousseau, *Les Confessions*, 3 (Paris, 1926), 137.

23 *Moskovskii zhurnal*, 1 (March 1791), 298.

24 Baggesen left an account of his travels which provides many interesting parallels with Karamzin's work. See K. Tiander, *"Labirint* Baggesena i *Pis'ma russkogo puteshestvennika* Karamzina," *Datsko-russkie issledovaniia*, 1 (Spb., 1912), 1–82.

25 *Spectateur du Nord*, 4:65.

26 *Vestnik Evropy*, 9 (May 1803), 56.

27 The controversy aligned Poussin, Raphael, and Caracci on one side and Rubens, Titian, Correggio, and Watteau on the other.

28 See R. Michéa, "Le 'Plaisir des Tombeaux' au XVIIIᵉ siècle," *Revue de littérature comparée*, 18 (1938), 287–311.

29 Quoted in *The Portable Romantic Reader*, ed. H. E. Hugo (New York, 1960), p. 341.

30 J. W. von Goethe, *The Sorrows of Young Werther, and Selected Writings*, trans. C. Hutter (New York, 1962), p. 83.

31 Laurence Sterne, *A Sentimental Journey* (London, 1960), p. 125.

[32] *Bibliograf*, No. 9 (1885), p. 38.
[33] *N. M. Karamzin i F. N. Glinka* (Spb., 1903), p. 4.
[34] S. N. Glinka, *Zapiski* (Spb., 1895), p. 77.
[35] Ibid., p. 99.
[36] N. I. Grech, *Zapiski o moei zhizni* (Moscow-Leningrad, 1930), p. 168.
[37] In a letter to Dmitriev in 1821 concerning S. E. Raich's translation of Virgil's *Georgics*, Shishkov argued that no great writer had ever used dashes, for they added nothing to clarity of thought or strength of expression: *Russkii arkhiv* (1866), pp. 1620–21.
[38] The work is not mentioned in the article by V. I. Kuleshov, "Iz istorii russko-nemetskikh literaturnykh sviazei ('Vestnik Evropy' N. M. Karamzina i 'Russische Miszellen' I. G. Rikhtera)," *Slavianskaia filologiia*, 5 (Moscow, 1963), 436–51.
[39] *Annual Register, or General Repository of History, Politics, and Literature for the Year 1799* (London, 1800), p. 278.
[40] *Monthly Magazine; or British Register*, 10 (Aug.–Dec. 1800), 51–52.
[41] *German Museum, or Monthly Repository of the Literature of Germany, the North and the Continent in general*, 2 (Aug. 1800), 104–6 ("Flor [sic] Silin"); 2 (Sept. 1800), 211–24 ("Julia"); 3 (Jan. 1801), 30–38 ("Poor Lise").
[42] Ibid., 2 (Aug. 1800), 107.
[43] *Anti-Jacobin Review and Magazine, or, Monthly Political and Literary Censor*, 11 (1802), 500–506.
[44] *Travels from Moscow, through Prussia, Germany, Switzerland, France, and England*, 3 vols. (London, 1803). On Feldborg see *Dansk Biografisk Leksikon*, 6 (Copenhagen, 1935), 624; on his translations of Karamzin see A. G. Cross, "Karamzin and England," *Slavonic and East European Review*, 43, No. 100 (1964), 110–12.
[45] *Edinburgh Review*, 3 (January 1804), 321–28. Brougham's authorship has been established in *The Wellesley Index to Victorian Periodicals*, ed. Walter E. Houghton, 1 (Toronto, 1966), 434.
[46] *Anti-Jacobin*, 18 (1804), 483–84.
[47] Ibid., 17 (1804), 23–37.
[48] *Monthly Review or Literary Journal*, 44 (1804), 262–72; *Annual Review, and History of Literature*, 2 (1804), 97–100; *Annual Register, or General Repository . . . for the Year 1803* (1804), pp. 301–2.
[49] *The Pantheon of the Age or, Memoirs of 3000 contemporary public characters British and Foreign, of all ranks and professions*, 2, 2nd ed. (London, 1825), 451.

4 Sentimental Fiction (1789–1803)

[1] *Vestnik Evropy*, 7 (Feb. 1803), 231.
[2] *Pis'ma N. M. Karamzina k I. I. Dmitrievu* (Spb., 1866), p. 106.
[3] *Vchera i segodnia*, 1 (1845), 42; N. Belozerskaia, *Vasilii Trofimovich Narezhnyi*, 2nd ed. (Spb., 1896), pp. 4–5. The pond is noted on the

map of Moscow in Baedeker's *Russland* (Leipzig, 1904), facing p. 237, sq. E7.

[4] Iu. M. Lotman, " 'Bednaia Liza' Karamzina v pereskaze krest'ianina," *Uchenye zapiski Tartuskogo universiteta*, vypusk 98 (1960), p. 310.

[5] *Aglaia*, 2 (Moscow, 1795), 7.

[6] *Vestnik Evropy*, 10 (July 1803), 121.

[7] "The Recluse," which I have attributed to Karamzin, is omitted.

[8] The years are publication dates. All the stories, with the exception of "Eugene and Julia" and "Liodor" are reprinted in *Sochineniia Karamzina*, 3 (Spb., 1848). Quotations in the basic analysis of a story are not footnoted.

[9] *Contes moraux*, 5 (Paris, 1820), 303. Cf. *Novye Marmontelevy povesti*, 1 (Moscow, 1822), 231: "Bednaia Luiza, proshchaiasia so mnoi, skazala, chto ona brositsia v vodu."

[10] *Sochineniia* 2:732. Cf. the suicide scene in Karamzin's "Sofiia."

[11] Ibid., p. 679.

[12] Ibid., p. 642. Milon's conduct after the death of the heroine also directly parallels Erast's.

[13] N. N. Bulich, *Biograficheskii ocherk N. M. Karamzina i razvitie ego literaturnoi deiatel'nosti* (Kazan', 1866), p. 108.

[14] V. V. Sipovskii, *Ocherki iz istorii russkogo romana*, 1, part. 1 (Spb., 1909), 213.

[15] *Priiatnoe i poleznoe preprovozhdenie vremeni*, 7 (1795), 100.

[16] *Les Veillées du château*, 1 (Paris, 1798), 83; 2:377. Cf. *Detskoe chtenie dlia serdtsa i razuma*, 9 (1787), 105; 14 (1788), 78.

[17] *Contes moraux*, 4:24, 67. Cf. *Novye Marmontelevy povesti*, 1:84, 126.

[18] V. V. Sipovskii, *Iz istorii russkogo romana i povesti*, 1 (Spb., 1903), 224, 226.

[19] "Rostovskoe ozero," *Priiatnoe i poleznoe preprovozhdenie vremeni*, 6 (1795), 310.

[20] Compare the characterization of Liza's father who "was quite a well-off peasant, because he loved to work, ploughed the earth well and always led a sober life."

[21] *Contes moraux*, 4:23. Cf. *Novye Marmontelevy povesti*, 1:82–83.

[22] Karamzin's idealized portraits of the peasantry are paralleled by certain paintings of Aleksei Venetsianov (1780–1840), completed in the 1820's, which emphasize the poetic side of the peasant's work and eschew all suggestion of hardship, toil, or coarseness.

[23] See the imitations of Karamzin's piece listed in Sipovskii, *Ocherki*, 1, part 2 (Spb., 1910), 734–43.

[24] Quoted in *Istoriia russkoi literatury v trekh tomakh*, 1 (Moscow, 1958), 482.

[25] Sipovskii, *Ocherki*, 1, part 2, 318–19.

[26] *Moskovskii zhurnal*, 8 (Oct.–Nov. 1792), 23. In later editions the reference to Wall's story was omitted.

[27] Christopher C. Sturm, *Reflections on the Works of God in Nature and Providence* (New York, 1824), p. 277.

28 *Sochineniia*, 2:221–22.

29 Cf. *Contes moraux*, 4:266–67 and 5:240 with *Novye Marmontelevy povesti*, 2:6, 180.

30 *Moskovskii zhurnal*, 5 (March 1792), 315.

31 Sipovskii, *Ocherki*, 1, part 2, 730–31.

32 Cf. particularly P. Brang, " 'Natal'ja bojarskaja doč' und Tatjana Larina," *Zeitschrift für slavische Philologie*, 27 (1959), 348–62.

33 *Russkii arkhiv* (1863), p. 897; *Pis'ma k Dmitrievu*, p. 31.

34 *Moskovskii zhurnal*, 6 (July 1792), 57.

35 P. N. Sakulin, *Russkaia literatura*, 2 (Moscow, 1929), 305.

36 *Bibliograf*, Nos. 9–10 (1885), p. 37.

37 *Russkaia starina*, 96 (1898), p. 36.

38 Sipovskii, *Ocherki*, 1, part 2, 520–24.

39 Although Karamzin's "Ossianism" is generally independent of Goethe's influence, it is interesting that he translated for the *Moscow Journal* "The Songs of Selma," which Werther himself "translated."

40 *Sochineniia*, 2:767.

41 Ibid., pp. 464–65.

42 *Sochineniia*, 2:786.

43 The references to the rosemary, the translation of Sierra Morena as *black* mountain, *Detskoe chtenie*, 11 (1787), 99–100.

44 See B. M. Eikhenbaum, *Skvoz' literaturu* (Leningrad, 1924), p. 48.

45 L. V. Krestova, "Povest' N. M. Karamzina 'Sierra Morena,' " *Rol' i znachenie literatury XVIII veka v istorii russkoi kul'tury: XVIII vek*, 7 (Moscow-Leningrad, 1966), 261–66.

46 *Sochineniia*, 3:411.

47 *Sochineniia*, 3:442–43.

48 Ibid., 2:150.

49 See my article "N. M. Karamzin and Barthélemy's *Voyage du jeune Anacharsis*," *Modern Language Review*, 61 (1966), 469–72.

50 N. M. Karamzin, *Polnoe sobranie stikhotvorenii* (Moscow-Leningrad, 1966), pp. 89–90, 135.

51 *Sochineniia*, 2:81.

52 Karamzin obviously does not employ the term; in fact, all the pieces discussed are without any indications of genre, except "The Country-side" ("a fragment").

53 Cf. *Sochineniia*, 2:142.

54 *Moskovskii zhurnal*, 3 (1791), 201. This footnote was omitted from the second edition of the journal.

55 L. B. Krestova, "Drevnerusskaia povest' kak odin iz istochnikov povestei N. M. Karamzina 'Raiskaia ptichka,' 'Ostrov Borngol'm,' 'Marfa Posadnitsa,' " *Issledovaniia i materialy po drevnerusskoi literature* (Moscow, 1961), pp. 193–226.

56 Robert T. Clarke, Jr., *Herder, His Life and Thought* (Berkeley and Los Angeles, 1955), pp. 348–49.

57 *Sochineniia*, 2:141.

58 *Moskovski zhurnal*, 1 (1791), 349–51.

[59] *Contes moraux*, 2:267. Cf. *Novye Marmontelevy povesti*, 2:49.

[60] *Spectateur du Nord*, 1 (1797), 183.

[61] The complete review is given in Sipovskii, *Iz istorii russkogo romana i povesti*, 1:242.

[62] Cf. P. Brang, *Studien zu Theorie und Praxis der russischen Erzählung 1770–1811* (Wiesbaden, 1960), pp. 171 ff.

[63] Sipovskii, *Ocherki*, 1, part 2, 494–96.

[64] U. Leman, "N. M. Karamzin i V. fon Vol'tsogen," *XVIII vek*, 7 (Moscow-Leningrad, 1966), 270.

[65] *Pis'ma k Dmitrievu*, p. 91.

[66] V. K. Kiukhel'beker, *Dnevnik* (Leningrad, 1929), p. 62.

[67] V. Shklovskii, *Teoriia prozy* (Moscow-Leningrad, 1925), p. 139.

[68] *Sochineniia*, 2:84.

[69] *Vestnik Evropy*, 10 (July 1803), 121.

[70] *Sochineniia*, 3:478–79.

[71] *Istoriia russkogo romana*, 1 (Moscow-Leningrad, 1962), 74.

[72] Cf. Z. Rozova, "*Novaia Eloiza* Russo i 'Natal'ia, boiarskaia doch'' Karamzina," *Russkaia literatura*, No. 4 (1966), pp. 149–53.

[73] R. V. Ivanov-Razumnik, "Istoriko-filosofskaia otsenka sentimentalizma," *Karamzin: zhizn' i tvorchestvo* (Spb.-Warsaw, 1911), p. 33.

[74] *Vestnik Evropy*, 4 (July 1802), 133.

[75] J.-J. Rousseau, *Julie ou La Nouvelle Héloise* (Paris, 1960), p. 476.

[76] *Sochineniia*, 2:304.

[77] J. W. von Goethe, *The Sorrows of Young Werther, and Selected Writings*, trans. C. Hutter (New York, 1962), p. 58.

[78] *Sochineniia*, 2:310.

[79] See F. Z. Kanunova, *Iz istorii russkoi povesti* (Tomsk, 1967), pp. 143, 153–56.

[80] Cf. *Letters of a Russian Traveler*: "Note that cold people are generally great egoists" (*Sochineniia*, 2:777–78) and in "A Knight of Our Time" the passage on "prudent egoists" (*Sochineniia*, 3:266).

[81] Cf. the opening letter of *Letters of a Russian Traveler* and A *Flower on the Grave of My Agathon: Sochineniia*, 2:2; 3:362–63.

[82] *Istoriia russkogo romana*, 1:82; R. V. Ivanov-Razumnik, "Istoriko-filosofskaia otsenka sentimentalizma," *Karamzin: zhizn' i tvorchestvo*, p. 32.

[83] *Sochineniia*, 3:489–91.

[84] Ibid., p. 519.

[85] *Istoriia russkogo romana*, 1:72.

[86] *Sochineniia*, 3:535.

[87] There is an interesting note on the tale in an unpublished manuscript by Matthew Guthrie, a Scots doctor in Russian service: "We have a pretty Epic Poem intitled *Marpha* of Novgorod by Caramishoff of Mosco with whos history he has, of course taken the Poetic licence, of making her a flaming Patriot, animated with the most pure & noble Motives & &, which can interest and captivate the reader."—Brit. Mus. Additional Mss. 14390, folio 314.

88 Cf. V. I. Fedorov, "Istoricheskaia povest' N. M. Karamzina 'Marfa Posadnitsa,'" *Uchenye zapiski Moskovskogo gorodskogo pedagogicheskogo instituta imeni V. P. Potemkina*, 57, No. 6 (1957), 109–29; P. A. Orlov, "Povest' N. M. Karamzina 'Marfa Posadnitsa,'" *Russkaia literatura*, No. 2 (1968), pp. 192–201.

89 See his letter to the *Spectateur du Nord* (1797), his biography of Boian in *The Pantheon of Russian Authors*, his *Historical Panegyric to Catherine II.*

90 N. I. Mordovchenko, *Russkaia kritika pervoi chetverti XIX veka* (Moscow-Leningrad, 1951), p. 53.

91 *Pis'ma k Dmitrievu*, p. 249. Cf. "I am a republican in my soul and so I shall die": N. M. Karamzin, *Pis'ma k kniaziu P. A. Viazemskomu 1810–1826* (Spb., 1897), p. 60.

92 Quoted in A. M. Skabichevskii, *Ocherki istorii russkoi tsenzury (1700–1863)* (Spb., 1894), p. 161.

93 For a penetrating analysis of the origins of the expression, see M. P. Alekseev, "Remarka Pushkina 'narod bezmolvstuet,'" *Russkaia literatura*, No. 2 (1967), pp. 36–58.

94 See P. A. Orlov, "'Bednaia Liza' Karamzina i sentimental'no-povestvovatel'naia literatura kontsa XVIII-nachala XIX v.," *Vestnik Moskovskogo universiteta*, No. 6 (1966), pp. 16–26.

95 V. Fedorov, *Liza, ili sledstviia gordosti i obol'shcheniia* (Spb., 1817); F. F. Ivanov, *Marfa Posadnitsa ili pokorenie Novagoroda* (Moscow, 1809). See I. A. Kriazhimskaia, "Tragediia F. F. Ivanova *Marfa Posadnitsa*," *Voprosy izucheniia russkoi literatury XI–XX vekov* (Moscow-Leningrad, 1958), pp. 71–75.

96 V. G. Belinskii, *Polnoe sobranie sochinenii*, 7 (Moscow, 1955), 135.

97 Henry M. Nebel, Jr., *N. M. Karamzin: A Russian Sentimentalist* (The Hague-Paris, 1967), p. 45.

98 F. Z. Kanunova, *Iz istorii russkoi povesti*, p. 176.

99 K. A. Grot, ed., *N. M. Karamzin i F. N. Glinka: Materialy k biografiiam russkikh pisatelei* (Spb., 1903), p. 4.

100 *Russkii arkhiv* (1866), p. 1727.

101 A. A. Feldborg, trans., *Tales from the Russian* (London, 1804), p. vii.

102 John Bowring, *Rossiiskaia Antologiia: Specimens of the Russian Poets*, 1, 2nd ed. (London, 1821), xv.

103 *Spectateur du Nord*, 1 (1797), 183.

104 *Vestnik Evropy*, 7 (Feb. 1803), 231.

105 *Sochineniia*, 2:517.

106 Ibid., 3:528.

107 R. D. Mayo, *The English Novel in the Magazines, 1740–1815* (Evanston, Ill., 1962), pp. 376–81.

108 Quotations from the complete text in Sipovskii, *Iz istorii russkogo romana i povesti*, 1:242–44.

109 See Karamzin's remarks in 1816 to Robert Pinkerton, an agent of the British Bible Society, *Literaturnyi vecher* (Moscow, 1844), pp. 11–12.

[110] A thorough analysis of all these changes is found in V. V. Vinogradov, "O stile Karamzina i ego razvitii," *Protsessy formirovaniia leksiki russkogo literaturnogo iazyka (Ot Kantemira do Karamzina)* (Moscow-Leningrad, 1966), pp. 237–58.

5   From *Aglaia* to *The Pantheon of Russian Authors* (1793–1801)

[1] *Pis'ma N. M. Karamzina k I. I. Dmitrievu* (Spb., 1866), p. 32.
[2] Ibid., p. 14.
[3] Ibid., p. 42. Cf. pp. 48, 57.
[4] Ibid., p. 46.
[5] Ibid., pp. 33, 43.
[6] G. R. Derzhavin, *Sochineniia*, 5 (Spb., 1869), 867.
[7] *Bibliograf*, No. 9 (1885), p. 38.
[8] K. A. Grot, ed., *N. M. Karamzin i F. N. Glinka: Materialy k biografiiam russkikh pisatelei* (Spb., 1903), pp. 3–4.
[9] *Vchera i segodnia*, 1 (1845), p. 52.
[10] *Moskovskii zhurnal*, 8 (Dec. 1792), 336.
[11] *Aglaia*, 1 (Moscow, 1794), 144.
[12] Ibid.
[13] Derzhavin, *Sochineniia*, 6:6.
[14] N. M. Karamzin, *Polnoe sobranie stikhotvorenii* (Moscow-Leningrad, 1966), pp. 117–18.
[15] Ibid., p. 121.
[16] Ibid., p. 128.
[17] *Sochineniia Karamzina*, 3 (Spb., 1848), 359.
[18] *Polnoe sobranie stikhotvorenii*, pp. 190–92.
[19] Ibid., p. 116.
[20] Ibid.
[21] *Sochineniia*, 3:373–403.
[22] *Sochineniia*, 2:633.
[23] Rousseau, *Les Confessions*, 2 (Paris, 1926), 173.
[24] Karamzin is here closely following Batteux, *Les Beaux arts réduits à un même principe* (nouvelle édition, Paris, 1747), p. 6. Batteux's chapter is entitled "Division et origine des arts," pp. 5 ff.
[25] *Sochineniia*, 3:370–72.
[26] *Detskoe chtenie*, 10 (1787), 51–52.
[27] *Perepiska Karamzina s Lafaterom* (Spb., 1893), p. 18. Cf. his appraisal of Herder, *Sochineniia*, 2:148.
[28] Erenburg's comment on Boris Pasternak is interesting in this connection: "There was in Pasternak something childlike. His definitions, which seemed naive, childish, were the definitions of a poet. He said about one author: 'Well, how *can* he be a good poet, when he is a bad man?' " I. Erenburg, *Liudi, gody, zhizn'* (Moscow, 1961), p. 419.
[29] M. N. Murav'ev, *Sochineniia*, 2 (Spb., 1847), 238.

[30] *Iulii Tsezar'* (Moscow, 1787), pp. 8, 71, 136.

[31] *O proiskhozhdenii zla* (Moscow, 1786), pp. 30, 56, et passim. Cf. V. V. Vinogradov, "Istoriia slova *iziashchnyi,*" *XVIII vek,* 7 (Moscow-Leningrad, 1966), 434–42.

[32] Anthony, Earl of Shaftesbury, *Characteristics of Men, Manners, Opinions, Times,* 1 (Indianapolis–New York, 1964), 104.

[33] In a letter of February 17, 1793, Karamzin writes to Dmitriev of the "left-overs" (ogarki i oborvyshi) of the *Moscow Journal,* which were probably utilized for *Aglaia.* See *Pis'ma k Dmitrievu,* p. 34.

[34] Cf. G. Makogonenko, "Literaturnaia positsiia Karamzina v XIX veke," *Russkaia literatura,* No. 1 (1962), p. 78–79.

[35] *Sochineniia,* 3:402. Louis XVI was executed on January 21, 1793.

[36] Ibid., 2:745.

[37] *Polnoe sobranie stikhotvorenii,* p. 135.

[38] *Sochineniia,* 3:371–72.

[39] *Polnoe sobranie stikhotvorenii,* p. 137.

[40] Ibid., p. 135.

[41] Ibid., p. 139.

[42] Ibid., p. 138.

[43] Ibid., p. 121. Dumont's statement brought another, curious response from Russia. Matthew Guthrie, who contributed numerous articles to the Edinburgh journal, *The Bee,* under the pseudonym of Arcticus, wrote "On the Most Striking and Curious Phenomena of Natural History," glorifying the wonders of the Creation and with the epigraph: "The Fool says in his heart 'there is no God,' / And none but a fool would say so."—*Bee,* 17 (1793), pp. 193–201.

[44] *Sochineniia,* 3:449.

[45] *Polnoe sobranie stikhotvorenii,* p. 150.

[46] *Pis'ma k Dmitrievu,* p. 69.

[47] *Les Confessions,* 3:273–75.

[48] *Sochineniia,* 3:436–45, 446–57.

[49] *Pis'ma S. I. G.,* 2 (Moscow, 1836), 268–69.

[50] A. D. Galakhov, *Istoriia russkoi slovesnosti drevnei i novoi,* 2, 2nd ed. (Spb., 1880), 49.

[51] Cf. Karamzin's praise for John Howard in the *Moscow Journal* and Platner's remarks on Franklin in *Letters* (*Sochineniia,* 2:123).

[52] *Moskvitianin,* bks. 1–2, No. 3 (1854), p. 45. All the items in "Miscellany" were republished in this journal by S. P. Shevyrev.

[53] *Bibliograf,* No. 9 (1885), p. 51.

[54] *Moskvitianin,* bk. 1, No. 6, p. 14.

[55] Ibid., p. 25.

[56] Ibid., p. 22.

[57] Ibid., bk. 2, No. 12, pp. 191–92.

[58] *Sochineniia,* 3:400.

[59] *Moskvitianin,* bk. 1, No. 7, p. 40.

[60] Ibid., bks. 1–2, No. 3, p. 63.

61 Ibid., bk. 1, No. 7, p. 39. (From Rousseau.)

62 Ibid., 1–2, No. 3, p. 56.

63 Ibid., p. 55; bk. 2, No. 6, p. 17.

64 *Muza*, 2 (1796), 78–87.

65 Ibid., pp. 184–91.

66 *Pis'ma k Dmitrievu*, p. 70.

67 *Polnoe sobranie stikhotvorenii*, pp. 118, 178.

68 *Aglaia*, 1 (1794), 71.

69 *Polnoe sobranie stikhotvorenii*, pp. 56–57.

70 *Pis'ma k Dmitrievu*, p. 50.

71 See G. V. Vernadskii, *Russkoe masonstvo v tsarstvovanie Ekateriny II* (Petrograd, 1917), pp. 230–39.

72 *Atenei*, 3 (1858), 195.

73 *Polnoe sobranie stikhotvorenii*, pp. 185–90.

74 *Russkii arkhiv* (1878), pp. 1323–24.

75 Ibid., p. 1326.

76 N. M. Karamzin, *Pis'ma k bratu ego, Vasiliiu Mikhailovichu Karamzinu* (Spb., 1894), pp. iii–iv.

77 *Spectataeur du Nord*, 4 (1797), 65. (This passage was omitted from the fifth volume of *Letters*, when published for the first time in 1801.)

78 *Pis'ma k Dmitrievu*, p. 99.

79 Ibid., pp. 103–4. (Karamzin is referring to the second edition of the first volume of *Aonides*, which appeared in Nov. 1798.)

80 M. N. Pogodin, *Karamzin*, 1 (Spb., 1866), 282–83.

81 *Pis'ma k Dmitrievu*, p. 75; *Polnoe sobranie stikhotvorenii*, p. 235.

82 *Sochineniia*, 3:477–503.

83 *Moskovskii zhurnal*, 3 (Aug. 1791), 155.

84 A. D. Galakhov, "Karamzin, kak optimist," *Otechestvennye zapiski*, 116, No. 1 (1858), 131–34.

85 *Sochineniia*, 3:327.

86 *Pis'ma k Dmitrievu*, pp. 74, 80, 81. Cf. pp. 90–91, 113, 117.

87 *Sochineniia*, 3:484.

88 *Neizdannye sochineniia i perepiska Nikolaia Mikhailovicha Karamzina*, 1 (Spb., 1862), pp. 198–204 (Montaigne, Pompignan, and Rousseau are named as sources; the quotations in Italian are almost certainly from Metastasio: see *Pis'ma k Dmitrievu*, p. 82.)

89 Ibid., pp. 201–2.

90 The testimony of Nikolai Turgenev, *Rossiia i russkie* (Moscow, 1915), p. 342. See Iu. M. Lotman, "Otrazhenie etiki i taktiki revoliutsonnoi bor'by v russkoi literature kontsa XVIII veka" *Trudy po russkoi i slavianskoi filologii*, 7, *Uchenye zapiski Tartuskogo gos. universiteta*, vypusk 167 (1965), pp. 30–31.

91 P. A. Viazemskii, *Zapisnye knizhki 1813–1848* (Moscow, 1963), p. 129.

92 *Polnoe sobranie stikhotvorenii*, p. 239.

93 *Sochineniia*, 2:511.

94 Ibid., 2:749.

95 *Neizdannye sochineniia i perepiska*, 1:203.

96 *Sochineniia*, p. 774. For Karamzin's attitude to Hume, see A. G. Cross, "Karamzin and England," *Slavonic and East European Review*, 43, No. 100 (1964), 106–8.

97 *Neizdannye sochineniia i perepiska*, 1:200–201.

98 *Pis'ma k Dmitrievu*, pp. 85–88. See Karamzin's commentary, p. 89.

99 *Sochineniia*, 2:583–86.

100 *Vchera i segodnia*, 1 (1845), 49.

101 Translated by De Boullier, who also addressed a tribute in verse to Karamzin, *Spectateur du Nord*, 1 (Feb. 1797), 183 ff.

102 *Pis'ma k Dmitrievu*, pp. 92–93, 98–99.

103 A translation of a speech by Demosthenes appeared in the *Messenger of Europe* (1803) and subsequently in the second edition of *The Pantheon*, 1 (Moscow, 1818), 11–40. This edition contains three times more material than the first edition; the additional translations appeared originally in either the *Moscow Journal* or the *Messenger*.

104 *Panteon innostrannoi slovesnosti*, 2, 2nd ed. (Moscow, 1818), 337–43.

105 Walter Allen, *The English Novel* (London, 1960), p. 102.

106 *Panteon*, 2:176.

107 George Channing in "New Morality" from the *Anti-Jacobin*. Quoted in R. C. Whitford, "Satire's view of sentimentalism in the Days of George the Third," *Journal of English and German Philology*, 18, No. 2 (1919), 166.

108 *Pis'ma k Dmitrievu*, p. 99.

109 *Panteon*, 2:195–96.

110 Ibid., 1:1–10.

111 Ibid., 2, 1st ed. (1798), 32.

112 Ibid., 1:18.

113 Ibid., 2:297.

114 Ibid., 2, 2nd ed., 303.

115 Ibid., 1:237–99, 79–92, 185.

116 Ibid., 2:306.

117 Ibid., 1:125–27.

118 Ibid., 1:93–110; 2, 1st ed., 73–92.

119 Ibid., 2, 2nd ed., 7–23, 62.

120 Ibid., p. 177.

121 Ibid., pp. 189–97, 267–91, 317, 337–43.

122 Ibid., pp. 319–32.

123 Ibid., 1:79, 85.

124 Ibid., pp. 111–24.

125 Omitted from the second and subsequent editions.

126 See I. Z. Serman, "Russkaia literatura XVIII veka i perevod," *Masterstvo perevoda*, 1962 (Moscow, 1963), pp. 366–71.

127 *Moskovskii telegraf*, 18 (1827), otdel 3, 75.

128 *Spectateur du Nord*, 4 (Oct. 1797), 53–71.

129 *Pis'ma k Dmitrievu*, p. 111.

[130] Ibid., p. 92.

[131] N. I. Mordovchenko, *Russkaia kritika pervoi chetverti XIX veka* (Moscow-Leningrad, 1959), p. 56.

[132] Murav'ev, *Sochinenia*, 1:71, 75, 79, 83, 86.

[133] I. I. Dmitriev, *Sochineniia*, 2 (Spb., 1895), 6, 7, 11.

[134] K. N. Batiushkov, *Sochineniia* (Moscow, 1955), pp. 308, 328, 330, 333, 335.

[135] *Vchera i segodnia*, 1 (1845), 50.

[136] *Polnoe sobranie stikhotvorenii*, p. 234.

[137] *Sochineniia*, 3:642.

[138] *Pis'ma k Dmitrievu*, p. 116.

[139] Ibid., p. 115.

[140] *Sochineniia*, 1:595.

[141] See I. F. Martynov, " 'Opyt istoricheskogo slovaria o rossiiskikh pisateliakh' N. I. Novikova i literaturnaia polemika 60–70kh godov XVIII veka," *Russkaia literatura*, No. 3 (1968), pp. 184–91.

[142] *Sochineniia*, 1:581.

[143] See *Pis'ma k Dmitrievu*, p. 30.

[144] Cf. *Sochineniia*, 1:582 and N. I. Novikov, *Izbrannye sochineniia* (Moscow-Leningrad), pp. 286–88.

[145] *Sochineniia*, 1:583–84. Cf. Novikov, pp. 354–57.

[146] *Sochineniia*, 1:593. Cf. Novikov, pp. 350–51.

[147] *Sochineniia*, 1:573, 599, 601.

[148] Ibid., p. 590.

[149] Ibid., p. 577.

[150] *Sokrashchennyi kurs rossiiskogo sloga, izdannyi Aleksandrom Skvortovym* (Moscow, 1796). Skvortsov was a pupil to whom Podshivalov dictated his course.

[151] *Novyi rossiisko-frantsuzsko-nemetskii slovar'*, 1 (Moscow, 1799), 505–6.

[152] *Vchera i segodnia*, 1 (1845), 44. The terms are attributed to I. P. Turgenev.

[153] "Pis'ma V. A. Polenova k I. I. Martynovu," *Russkii arkhiv* (1866), pp. 1763–65.

[154] A. Fomin, "Andrei Ivanovich Turgenev i Andrei Sergeevich Kaisarov," *Russkii bibliofil*, No. 1 (1902), pp. 26–30.

6   Karamzin's Verse and *Aonides* (1796–1799)

[1] *Pis'ma N. M. Karamzina k I. I. Dmitrievu* (Spb., 1866), p. 61.

[2] Ibid., p. 63.

[3] *Aonidy, ili sobranie raznykh novykh stikhotvorenii*, 1 (Moscow, 1796).

[4] *Pis'ma k Dmitrievu*, p. 102.

[5] G. R. Derzhavin, *Sochineniia*, 6 (Spb., 1869), 51.

[6] S. N. Glinka, *Zapiski* (Spb., 1895), p. 169.

[7] M. P. Alekseev, "K literaturnoi istorii odnogo iz romansov v 'Don-Kikhote,' " *Servantes. Stat'i i materialy* (Leningrad, 1948), pp. 113–23.

8 V. G. Belinskii, *Polnoe sobranie sochinenii*, 1 (Moscow, 1953), 251.

9 K. Sh[alikov], "O konchine Nikolaia Mikhailovicha Karamzina," *Damskii zhurnal*, 14, No. 12 (1826), 279.

10 A. S. Pushkin, *Polnoe sobranie sochinenii*, 13 (Moscow-Leningrad, 1937), 381.

11 See N. M. Danilov, *Pushkin i Karamzin* (Kazan', 1917); V. I. Butakova, "Karamzin i Pushkin (Neskol'ko sopostavlenii)," *Pushkin i ego sovremenniki*, 38 (1928), 127–35.

12 I. N. Rozanov, *Russkaia lirika*, I: *Ot poezii bezlichnoi k ispovedi serdtsa* (Moscow, 1914), p. 83.

13 N. M. Karamzin, *Polnoe sobranie stikhotvorenii* (Moscow, Leningrad, 1966), pp. 26, 51. Lotman's introductory essay is by far the most stimulating and profound analysis of Karamzin's attainments as a poet.

14 Ibid., p. 27.

15 *Vchera i segodnia*, 1 (1845), 50.

16 I. I. Dmitriev, *Sochineniia*, 1 (Spb., 1895), 302.

17 A. N. Radischev, *Puteshestvie iz Peterburga v Moskvu* (Moscow-Leningrad, 1961), p. 125.

18 Ibid.

19 V. P. Semennikov, *Radishchev: Ocherki i issledovaniia* (Moscow-Leningrad, 1923), pp. 451–52. It is not impossible that Radishchev knew, or knew of, Karamzin. His friend, Kutuzov, characterizes Karamzin as "the new poet" (novyi stikhotvorets) in a letter of 1788 to Ivan Turgenev: *Uchenye zapiski Tartuskogo gos. universiteta*, vypusk 139 (1963), p. 316. It was also recently established that Turgenev was acquainted with Radishchev: *Izvestiia Akademii Nauk SSSR, Otdelenie literatury i iazyka*, 19, No. 2 (1960), 151.

20 *Pis'ma k Dmitrievu*, p. 10.

21 Ibid., p. 13.

22 *Moskovskii zhurnal*, 2 (May 1791), 115.

23 Ibid. 1 (Feb.), 146; 3 (Aug.), 123; 4 (Oct.), 11.

24 Vostokov, *Stikhotvoreniia* (Moscow, 1935), pp. 130, 152.

25 *Polnoe sobranie stikhotvorenii*, pp. 64–65, 79, 80, 357, 364, 100, 114–15, 129–30.

26 Richard Burgi, *A History of the Russian Hexameter* (Hamden, Conn., 1954), p. 74.

27 Friedrich von Matthisson, *Gedichte* (Zurich, 1821), p. 72.

28 H. G. Atkins, *A History of German Versification* (London, 1923), pp. 249–50.

29 This total includes the six poems in the Dubia section but excludes the verses in Karamzin's translation from Weisse as well as the translation in *Letters of a Russian Traveler*.

30 *Polnoe sobranie stikhotvorenii*, pp. 227–30.

31 This is discounting the particular case of Karamzin's translation in unrhymed verse of Haydn's oratorio *Die Schöpfung*, published in 1801.

32 M. N. Pogodin, *Nikolai Mikhailovich Karamzin*, 1 (Spb., 1866), 246.

[33] *Polnoe sobranie stikhotvorenii,* pp. 165–69.

[34] Radishchev, *Puteshestvie,* p. 125.

[35] *Moskovskii zhurnal,* 6 (April 1792), 78.

[36] A. N. Egunov, *Gomer v russkikh perevodakh XVIII–XIX vekov* (Moscow-Leningrad, 1964), p. 121–24.

[37] Before 1794 there are single examples of three-, six-, seven-, eight-, and ten-line stanzas and two instances of a five-line stanza.

[38] It is interesting, however, that when Karamzin followed his prose translation of *The Seasons* by a metrical version of the inset story "Lavinia" in 1789, he chose unrhymed alexandrines rather than blank verse. Indeed, despite his admiration for Thomson, Milton, Pope, and Klopstock, he never once used blank verse, preferring to write unrhymed verse in combination with other meters.

[39] *Sochineniia Karamzina,* 2 (Spb., 1848), 142–43.

[40] Ibid., p. 44.

[41] N. D. Chechulin, *O stikhotvoreniiakh Karamzina* (Petrograd, 1917), p. 11.

[42] *Servantes: Stat'i i materialy,* p. 117.

[43] Pointed out by A. Ia. Kucherov, editor of N. Karamzin and I. Dmitriev, *Izbrannye stikhotvoreniia* (Leningrad, 1953), p. 468.

[44] *Polnoe sobranie stikhotvorenii,* pp. 106–8. See F. W. Neumann, "Karamzins Verhältnis zu Schiller," *Zeitschrift für slavische Philologie,* 9 (1932), 366–67.

[45] *Sochineniia,* 2:406.

[46] Henry M. Nebel, Jr., *N. M. Karamzin: A Russian Sentimentalist* (The Hague-Paris, 1967), pp. 106–7.

[47] See P. Sheremetev, *Karamzin v Ostaf'eve, 1881–1911* (Moscow, 1911), pp. 91–97.

[48] Pointed out by Lotman, *Polnoe sobranie stikhotvorenii,* p. 394.

[49] *Sochineniia,* 2:324–25.

[50] In a footnote to his "Triolet Alete" (1795) Karamzin explained the technique of this "versifying game." See *Polnoe sobranie stikhotvorenii,* p. 180.

[51] N. Belozerskaia, *Vasilii Trofimovich Narezhnyi,* 2nd ed. (Spb., 1896), p. 5.

[52] K. N. Batiushkov, *Sochineniia* (Moscow, 1955), pp. 382–83.

[53] *Bibliograf,* No. 9 (1885), p. 38.

[54] Pogodin, *Karamzin,* 1:242.

[55] *Polnoe sobranie stikhotvorenii,* p. 149.

[56] A. Astakhova, "Iz istorii i ritmiki khoreia," *Poetika,* 1 (Leningrad, 1926), 60.

[57] C. L. Drage, "Trochaic Metres in Early Russian Syllabo-Tonic Poetry," *Slavonic and East European Review,* 38, No. 91 (1960), 373. A. Astakhova discusses this phenomenon as a non-metric stress which does not destroy the line's basic rhythm. She also provides an interesting comparative table of stress distribution in this measure. See "Iz istorii i ritmiki khoreia," *Poetika,* 1:66.

58 *Bakhar'* implies a storyteller or garrulous person. In his introduction to the poem Kheraskov deliberates on the best meter to use: "Or in such a meter, / As rightly pleases / In the unfinished *Il'ia of Murom.*" M. M. Kheraskov, *Izbrannye proizvedeniia* (Leningrad, 1961), p. 243.
59 Karamzin asked Dmitriev in 1795 about L'vov's work on a folk epic. *Pis'ma k Dmitrievu*, p. 57.
60 *Sankt-Peterburgskii vestnik*, 2, No. 6 (1812), 285.
61 Vostokov, *Stikhotvoreniia*, p. 70.
62 See A. N. Sokolov, *Ocherki po istorii russkoi poemy XVIII veka i pervoi poloviny XIX veka* (Moscow, 1955), pp. 286–88.
63 *Sochineniia*, 1:618.
64 *Pis'ma k Dmitrievu*, p. 290.
65 P. A. Viazemskii, "Stikhotvoreniia Karamzina," *Polnoe sobranie sochinenii*, 7 (Spb., 1882), 150–51.
66 *Polnoe sobranie stikhotvorenii*, p. 291.
67 Ibid.
68 A. P. Sumarokov, *Izbrannye proizvedeniia* (Leningrad, 1957), pp. 92–94; G. R. Derzhavin, *Stikhotvoreniia* (Leningrad, 1957), pp. 191–93.
69 *Polnoe sobranie stikhotvorenii*, p. 150.
70 Ibid., p. 193.
71 *Moskovskii zhurnal*, 3 (Aug. 1791), 197–98.
72 *Polnoe sobranie stikhotvorenii*, p. 127.
73 Ibid., pp. 295–96.
74 Ibid., pp. 74, 240.
75 I. I. Dmitriev, *Polnoe sobranie stikhotvorenii* (Moscow-Leningrad, 1967), pp. 282–83, 113–16.
76 See *Epigramma i satira*, 1 (Moscow-Leningrad, 1931), 25–132.
77 *Moskovskii zhurnal*, 6 (May 1791), 80.
78 Ibid., 8 (Oct.-Nov. 1792), 125.
79 *Uchenye zapiski Kazanskogo universiteta*, 124, No. 5 (1964), 61–63.
80 *Moskovskii zhurnal*, 8:123–35.
81 *Polnoe sobranie stikhotvorenii*, p. 58.
82 *Sochineniia*, 3:380.
83 *Aonidy*, 2 (1797), v–xi.
84 Ibid., 1 (1796), 92–95.
85 At the dinner to celebrate the publication of *Aonides*, Karamzin spoke of the need to exclude poets who composed "limp and watery verse," whereupon Nikolev commented wryly: "What can be said about us? What sort of poets are we? But, Nikolai Mikhailovich, you should have spared yourself." S. N. Glinka, *Zapiski*, pp. 159–60.
86 *Polnoe sobranie stikhotvorenii*, p. 170.
87 Ibid., pp. 219–20.
88 Ibid., p. 250.
89 Ibid., p. 260.
90 Ibid., p. 219.
91 *Perepiska Karamzina s Lafaterom* (Spb., 1893), p. 18.
92 *Russkii arkhiv* (1863), p. 894.

[93] *Polnoe sobranie stikhotvorenii*, p. 219.

[94] Ibid., p. 119.

[95] Batteux, *Les Beaux arts réduits à un même principe*, p. 16. For the pleasure of comparing the original and its imitation, see also p. 17.

[96] *Polnoe sobranie stikhotvorenii*, p. 151.

[97] Ibid., pp. 193, 195.

[98] Two theorists specifically rejected by Batiushkov, when he sketched his plan for a history of Russian literature: "It is easy to prattle from the rostrum like Batteux and Bouterwek, but what is the use?" *Sochineniia*, p. 397.

[99] *Moskovskii zhurnal*, 6 (June 1792), 227–34; *Vestnik Evropy*, 4 (July 1802), 52–56.

[100] *Pis'ma k Dmitrievu*, pp. 39, 42–43, 50, 73.

[101] P. A. Viazemskii, *Polnoe sobranie sochinenii*, 7:149.

[102] *Karamzin v Ostaf'eve*, pp. 94–95.

[103] *Moskovskii zhurnal*, 3 (Aug. 1791), 127.

7   The *Messenger of Europe* (1802–1803)

[1] M. N. Pogodin, *Nikolai Mikhailovich Karamzin*, 1 (Spb., 1866), 323.

[2] N. M. Karamzin, *Polnoe sobranie stikhotvorenii* (Moscow-Leningrad, 1966), p. 261.

[3] F. F. Vigel', *Zapiski*, 1 (Moscow, 1928), 125.

[4] N. I. Grech, *Zapiski o moei zhizni* (Moscow-Leningrad, 1930), p. 190. Grech is referring to *Zapiska o novoi i drevnei Rossii* and goes on to quote the lines from the ode to Alexander given earlier.

[5] Cf. the very similar relations of Baggesen and his Selina and his continued friendship with her husband. K. Tiander, *Datsko-russkie issledovaniia*, 1 (Spb., 1912), 7.

[6] *Russische Miszellen*, 1, No. 1 (1803), 131–33. Cf. *Edinburgh Magazine*, NS 22 (August 1803), 147; *Scots Magazine*, 65 (1803), 550; *Monthly Magazine*, 16, part 2 (1803), 56.

[7] *Polnoe sobranie stikhotvorenii*, p. 270.

[8] *Vestnik Evropy*, 1 (Jan. 1802), 8.

[9] Ibid., 6 (Dec. 1802), 319–25.

[10] Ibid., 1 (Jan. 1802), 7.

[11] Ibid., 6 (Dec. 1802), 228–29. Karamzin's new views on criticism were embraced by Zhukovskii, who began editing the same journal in 1808: "Criticism and luxury are the daughters of wealth; but we are not yet Croesuses in literature!": ibid. (Jan. 1808), p. 9.

[12] G. P. Makogonenko, "Literaturnaia positsiia Karamzina v XIX veke," *Russkaia literatura*, No. 1 (1962), p. 90.

[13] *Vestnik Evropy*, 3 (June 1802), 244.

[14] Ibid., 10 (July 1803), 57–58.

[15] Ibid., 5 (Sept. 1802), 56.

[16] Ibid., 3 (May 1802), 146.

17 Ibid., 2 (April 1802), 232–36. Cf. Karamzin's remarks in 1793 to Dmitriev on Klushin's play *Laughter and Grief* [*Smekh i gore*], *Pis'ma N. M. Karamzin k I. I. Dmitrievu* (Spb., 1866), pp. 36–37.

18 The response was so great that Dmitriev wrote "An Epitaph on Epitaphs" ["Epitafiia Epitafiiam, sochinennaia odnim iz avtorov epitafii"], *Vestnik Evropy*, 9 (May 1803), 46. The standard may be judged from the fact that Karamzin was obliged to make two grammatical corrections in an epitaph of two lines!: ibid., 8 (March 1803), 140.

19 Ibid., 9 (May 1803), 3–18, 75–111.

20 *Vchera i segodnia*, 1 (1845), 50.

21 *Vestnik Evropy*, 9 (May 1803), 18–22.

22 Ibid., p. 65.

23 Ibid., 5 (Oct. 1802), 285. In his notes on Kantemir in the *Pantheon of Russian Authors* Karamzin had divided the eighteenth century into *four* periods.

24 *Vestnik Evropy*, 1 (Jan. 1802), 3–4.

25 Ibid., p. 5.

26 *Sochineniia Karamzina*, 3 (Spb., 1848), 551–52. Karamzin's major essays in the *Messenger* are included in the 1848 edition, to which reference is made whenever possible.

27 Ibid., p. 473.

28 Ibid., pp. 474–75.

29 Ibid., p. 527.

30 Ibid., p. 528.

31 Ibid., p. 529. The idea of "writing as one speaks" was taken up by adherents of Karamzin, such as Batiushkov, but had been expressed as early as 1778 by F. G. Karin, a follower of Sumarokov. V. I. Saitov, "Fedor Grigor'evich Karin. Odin iz maloizvestnykh pisatelei vtoroi poloviny XVIII veka," *Bibliograf*, No. 1 (1893), p. 16.

32 *Vestnik Evropy*, 2 (March, 1802), 56. Cf. *Sochineniia*, 2:749.

33 *Vestnik Evropy*, 6 (Nov. 1802), 124.

34 Ibid., p. 126.

35 Ibid., 9 (June 1803), 172.

36 Ibid., pp. 167–68. Cf. *Sochineniia*, 3:609.

37 *Vestnik Evropy*, 1 (Jan. 1802), 44.

38 *Sochineniia*, 3:552.

39 Ibid., 1:384.

40 *Vestnik Evropy*, 9 (June 1803), 201.

41 *Sochineniia*, 1:641.

42 *Vestnik Evropy*, 6 (Nov. 1802), p. 133. An analysis of Karamzin's changing attitude to folk literature is given by N. N. Trubitsyn, *O narodnoi poezii v obshchestvennom i literaturnom obikhode pervoi treti XIX veka* (Spb., 1912), pp. 328–32.

43 *Vestnik Evropy*, 10 (July 1803), 60–61.

44 *Sochineniia*, 1:424–25.

45 Ibid., p. 470.

[46] *Vestnik Evropy*, 3 (May 1802), 140.

[47] Ibid., 1 (Jan. 1802), 17–19.

[48] Ibid., p. 48.

[49] Ibid., 2 (March 1802), 52.

[50] Ibid., p. 55.

[51] Ibid., 8 (March 1803), 39–42; (April), 227–29, 298–301; 9 (May), 124–26; (June), 235, 291–94; 12 (Nov.), 268–75.

[52] See the series of essays in *Sochineniia*, 1:398–524.

[53] Ibid., p. 479.

[54] Karamzin had himself in mind at the end of his essay on Martha: "A *gallery of famous women* could be a highly attractive work if an author of talent and taste would present these characters with the lively colors of love for the fair sex and the homeland. Is it necessary to say who should be entrusted with such a work in our time?" *Sochineniia*, 1:387.

[55] *Vestnik Evropy*, 2 (March 1802), 134.

[56] *Sochineniia*, 1:424.

[57] A. S. Pushkin, *Polnoe sobranie sochinenii*, 11 (Moscow-Leningrad, 1949), 120.

[58] *Sochineniia*, 3:607. Cf. Karamzin's letter to A. I. Turgenev on the same subject in September 1816, ibid., p. 740.

[59] Ibid., pp. 505–7.

[60] Ibid., 1:361.

[61] Ibid., 3:340–59, 611–17.

[62] *Vestnik Evropy*, 2 (April 1802), 363.

[63] *Sochineniia*, 3:349.

[64] Ibid., p. 597.

[65] Ibid., pp. 343–44.

[66] *Vestnik Evropy*, 9 (June 1803), 197–99. Karamzin later printed part of Glinka's first work, "The Temple of Svetovid" ["Khram Svetovida"], a labored investigation into the gods of Slavic mythology, ibid., 10 (Aug. 1803), 173–86.

[67] *Sochineniia*, 3:616.

[68] Ibid., 1:339.

[69] Ibid., 3:591. See also p. 580.

[70] Ibid., p. 351.

[71] Ibid., pp. 350, 573–74.

[72] Ibid., p. 573.

[73] Ibid., p. 570; 1:406.

[74] In his *Historical Panegyric to Catherine II* Karamzin reveals clearly the distinction he made between philosophical theorizing and political expediency: "Even good in a philosophical sense may be harmful in politics, as soon as it is out of step with the civil state of a nation. A sad truth, but demonstrated by experience!" *Sochineniia*, 1:370.

[75] Ibid., 3:575.

[76] Cf. Pushkin's account of a conversation he had with Karamzin on this subject and Karamzin's violent rejection of the accusation, Pushkin, *Polnoe sobranie sochinenii*, 12:306.

[77] The letters are quoted in Pogodin, *Karamzin*, 1:322, 337.

[78] *Pis'ma k Dmitrievu*, p. 124.

[79] In a later essay Karamzin said "a full methodical collection of civil laws, clearly and wisely written" was Russia's most pressing need, *Sochineniia*, 3:592.

[80] Ibid., 1:209.

[81] Quoted from A. M. Skabichevskii, *Ocherki istorii russkoi tsenzury* (1700–1863) (Spb., 1892), p. 86.

[82] See *Russkaia starina*, 92 (Nov. 1897), 306.

[83] *Sochineniia*, 1:289. Karamzin's antipathy toward Poland also informs his "Opinion of a Russian Citizen."

[84] G. V. Vernadskii, *Russkoe masonstvo v tsarstvovanie Ekateriny II* (Petrograd, 1917), pp. 236–38.

[85] He stressed the need for censorship because reason might stray from truth; he had been quick to forget the excesses of censors under Catherine and Paul.

[86] *Sochineniia*, 1:303–4.

[87] True to the theories of Montesquieu and Rousseau on the suitability of a republic for a small country, Karamzin is able to defend Switzerland's system, *Sochineniia*, 1:313, 320.

[88] Ibid., pp. 312–13.

[89] Ibid., 3:345, 349, 357.

[90] Ibid., 1:202.

[91] Ibid., pp. 401–3. Cf. Karamzin's translation of an article giving a similar view of Louis XVI, *Vestnik Evropy*, 1 (January 1802), 18–28.

[92] *Sochineniia*, 1:203. Cf. the epigraph to his *Memoir on Ancient and Modern Russia*: "There is no flattery on my tongue."

[93] This epigram on Karamzin's *History* is not included in the Academy edition of Pushkin's work, but Pushkin's authorship of it is convincingly argued by B. V. Tomashevskii, *Pushkin. Issledovaniia i materialy*, 1 (Moscow-Leningrad, 1956), 208–15.

[94] *Sochineniia*, 3:585–86. See also 2:462–63.

[95] Ibid., 3:586, 587.

[96] *Aonidy*, 1 (Moscow, 1796), 248.

[97] *Polnoe sobranie stikhotvorenii*, p. 179. See Lotman's note, p. 392.

[98] *Vestnik Evropy*, 9 (June 1803), 175–76.

[99] Ibid., 2 (March 1802), 109–10. Cf. these final remarks with Karamzin's in his letter to the *Spectateur du Nord* (1797).

[100] *Polnoe sobranie stikhotvorenii*, p. 293.

[101] *Vestnik Evropy*, 1 (Jan. 1802), 20–37.

[102] Ibid., pp. 9–16.

[103] Ibid., pp. 38–40.

[104] Ibid., 2 (April 1802), 251.

[105] Ibid., 7 (Jan. 1803), 85–91; 11 (May 1803), 24–30.

[106] Ibid., 1 (Jan. 1802), p. 33.

[107] *Uchenye zapiski Tartuskogo gos. universiteta*, vypusk 51 (1957), pp. 150–55.

[108] *Sochineniia,* 1:530. Karamzin also translated a speech by Baron Nekker favoring monarchy over a republic, V*estnik Evropy,* 5 (Oct. 1802), 301–19.

[109] *Sochineniia,* 1:276–77. Cf. "Not the French people but Providence placed this astonishing man at such a degree of greatness," V*estnik Evropy,* 3 (June 1802), 270.

[110] Quoted by Karamzin in "The Sensitive and the Cold," *Sochineniia,* 3:620.

[111] Karamzin is referring here to Napoleon's plans to invade England. *Vestnik Evropy,* 10 (Aug. 1803), 230.

[112] *Sochineniia,* 1:552.

[113] *Vestnik Evropy,* 3 (May 1802), 77–94; 2 (April 1802), pp. 276–77.

[114] *Sochineniia,* 1:536.

[115] *Vestnik Evropy,* 5 (Sept. 1802), 157.

[116] Ibid., (Oct. 1802), 319–20.

[117] Ibid., 8 (March 1803), 146–54.

[118] Particularly Archenholz, whom Karamzin called in *Letters* "this well-known anglomaniac," *Sochineniia,* 2:691.

[119] *Vestnik Evropy,* 2 (April 1802), 386; 4 (Aug. 1802), 247; 6 (Nov. 1802), 165.

[120] Ibid., 4 (Aug. 1802), 329.

[121] Ibid., 4 (July 1802), 73.

[122] Ibid., 11 (Sept. 1802), 160.

[123] *Sochineniia,* 3:590.

[124] *Vestnik Evropy,* 5 (Oct. 1802), 232; 10 (Aug. 1803), 213–15, 232.

[125] A. A. Bestuzhev-Marlinskii, "Vzgliad na russkuiu slovesnost' v techenie 1823 goda," *Sobranie stikhotvorenii* (Leningrad, 1948), p. 174.

[126] V. A. Zhukovskii, "Neizdannyi konspekt po istorii russkoi literatury," *Trudy otdela novoi russkoi literatury,* 1 (Moscow-Leningrad, 1948), 299.

[127] V. K. Kiukhel'beker, *Dnevnik* (Leningrad, 1929), pp. 60–61.

[128] Ibid., pp. 64–65. Karamzin's immediate successors were P. Sumarokov, M. T. Kachenovskii, and Zhukovskii.

8 Into the Temple of History

[1] Letter of September 28, 1803, *Sochineniia Karamzina,* 3 (Spb., 1848), 681.

[2] Ibid., p. 685.

[3] *Vestnik Evropy,* 7 (Feb. 1803), 230–31; 10 (Aug. 1803), 195–98; 12 (Nov. 1803), 50.

[4] *Literary Panorama,* 1 (1807), 145–49; John Bowring, *Rossiiskaia Antologiia: Specimens of the Russian Poets,* 1, 2nd ed. (London, 1821), 212–29.

[5] Quoted by V. Shklovskii, *Chulkov i Levshin* (Leningrad, 1933), p. 32.

[6] V. Kliuchevskii, *Ocherki i rechi* (Moscow, 1915), p. 278.

7 N. M. Karamzin, *Polnoe sobranie stikhotvorenii* (Moscow-Leningrad, 1966), pp. 298–99. This poem was first published in the second edition of Karamzin's collected works in 1814.

8 Ibid., pp. 300–311. The poem was published separately in 1814 with a dedication to the citizens of Moscow.

9 *Sochineniia*, 3:685.

10 For a detailed analysis of the work and its historical and political significance, see Richard Pipes, *Karamzin's Memoir on Ancient and Modern Russia. A translation and analysis* (Cambridge, Mass., 1959). Cf. a recent Soviet view by A. V. Predtechenskii, *Ocherki obshchestvenno-politicheskoi istorii Rossii v pervoi chetverti XIX veka* (Moscow-Leningrad, 1957), pp. 271–89.

11 Pipes, p. 110.

12 Ibid., pp. 120–27, 130–34.

13 N. Lyzhin, "Al'bom N. M. Karamzina," *Letopisi russkoi literatury i drevnosti*, 1, bk. 2 (1859), 161–92.

14 N. Lyzhin, "Materialy dlia kharakteristiki Karamzina, kak prakticheskogo filosofa," (1859), 11.

15 *Pis'ma N. M. Karamzina k I. I. Dmitrievu* (Spb., 1866), p. 82.

16 *Letopisi russkoi literatury i drevnosti*, 2:12.

17 *Sochineniia*, 3:641–54. First published in *Syn otechestva*, 51 (1819), 3–22.

18 *Sochineniia*, 2:515.

19 *Vestnik Evropy*, 11 (Oct. 1803), 163–78.

20 S. I. Ponomarev, *Materialy dlia bibliografii literatury o N. M. Karamzine* (Spb., 1883), p. 23, n. 3.

21 The most lucid account of the controversy is given by N. I. Mordovchenko, *Russkaia kritika pervoi chetverti XIX veka* (Moscow-Leningrad, 1959), pp. 77–98. A typically idiosyncratic, but stimulating discussion is found in Shklovskii, *Chulkov i Levshin*, pp. 199–226.

22 Quoted by Shklovskii, *Chulkov i Levshin*, p. 200.

23 N. Grech, *Chteniia o russkom iazyke*, 1 (Spb., 1840), 158.

24 See V. D. Levin, "Karamzin, Batiushkov, Zhukovskii—redaktory sochinenii M. N. Murav'eva," *Problemy sovremennoi filologii* (Moscow, 1965), pp. 182–91.

25 Published in *Literaturnoe nasledstvo*, 59 (Moscow, 1954), pp. 569–84.

26 A. S. Pushkin, *Polnoe sobranie sochinenii*, 12 (Moscow-Leningrad, 1949), 306.

27 Karamzin had completed the first eight volumes by 1815, but he encountered numerous difficulties and delays with their printing.

28 For a discussion of the literary qualities of the history and of its impact on Russian society, see G. P. Makogonenko, "Literaturnaia positsiia Karamzina v XIX veke," *Russkaia literatura*, No. 1 (1962), pp. 99–106.

29 K. F. Ryleev, *Polnoe sobranie sochinenii* (Moscow-Leningrad, 1934), p. 454.

30 *Sochineniia*, 3:650.

[31] V. G. Belinskii, *Polnoe sobranie sochinenii*, 7 (Moscow-Leningrad, 1955), 135.

[32] N. V. Gogol', *Polnoe sobranie sochinenii*, 12 (Leningrad, 1952), 61.

[33] F. I. Tiutchev, *Polnoe sobranie stikhotvorenii* (Leningrad, 1957), p. 231.

[34] See J. Laurence Black, "History in Politics: Karamzin's *Istoriia* as an Ideological Catalyst in Russian Society," *Laurentian University Review*, 1, No. 2 (1968), 110–11. Professor Black is preparing a detailed study of Karamzin as an historian.

[35] This collection is unique among editions of Karamzin's work (excluding publications of his correspondence) by being based exclusively on surviving Karamzin manuscripts. All the manuscripts and papers dating from his Moscow period, with the exception of the 1797–98 notebooks, were lost, together with his extensive library, in the great fire of 1812.

[36] *Neizdannye sochineniia i perepiska Nikolaia Mikhailovicha Karamzina*, 1 (Spb., 1862), 3–8.

[37] Ibid., p. 9.

[38] Ibid., p. 10.

[39] Ibid., pp. 10–11.

[40] Belinskii, *Polnoe sobranie sochinenii*, 2 (1953), 164–65.

[41] Ibid., 1:70.

[42] Ibid., 7:139.

[43] *Vestnik Evropy*, 6 (Dec. 1802), 227.

[44] A. D. Galakhov, *Istoriia russkoi slovesnosti*, 2, 2nd ed. (Spb., 1880), 126.

[45] Pushkin, *Polnoe sobranie sochinenii*, 13:142.

SELECTED BIBLIOGRAPHY

IN 1883, S. I. Ponomarev published a one hundred and fifty-two page bibliography to mark the centenary of Karamzin's first published work. It remains the fullest record of work on or by Karamzin published during that period. Nevertheless, Ponomarev, who was working in difficult conditions away from the principal libraries of Moscow and St. Petersburg, in his turn made errors and overlooked sources. Ponomarev's bibliography was subsequently amplified and extended in the bibliographical work of Vengerov (1910) and Vladislavlev (1924) records later items on Karamzin, including those connected with the 150th anniversary of Karamzin's birth in 1916. The principal Soviet bibliographical works with reference to Karamzin have all appeared in the last five years. The *Svodnyi katalog russkoi knigi grazhdanskoi pechati XVIII veka* (1963–67) lists all the works printed in the eighteenth century which Karamzin wrote, edited, or participated in. Major editions of Karamzin's work and the principal secondary material are recorded in K. D. Muratova's *Istoriia russkoi literatury XIX veka* (1962). However, this should be used in conjunction with the companion guide to the eighteenth century, *Istoriia russkoi literatury XVIII veka* (1968), under the editorship of P. N. Berkov. The fact that Karamzin's career spans two centuries has resulted in this way in an unsatisfactory bibliographical division.

A definitive bibliography on Karamzin would require a separate volume; the present bibliography is selected: it includes works cited in this study and consulted in its preparation. It is nevertheless intended to provide a guide to the major writings on Karamzin in Russian and other languages, particularly in the twentieth century up to 1968. Recent descriptive and critical accounts of the state of Karamzin studies are to be found in my article, "Karamzin Studies: For the Bicentenary of the Birth of N. M. Karamzin (1766–1966)," J. G. Garrard's "Karamzin in Recent Soviet Criticism: A Review Article," J. L. Black's "The Soviets and the Anniversary of N. M. Karamzin," and in the introduction to Hans Rothe's study, which appeared when the present work was virtually complete.

The bibliography is divided into the following sections:
a) Editions of Karamzin's work
b) English translations
c) Letters

d) Contemporary Russian sources, including correspondence, memoirs, journals, and literary works

e) Secondary sources in Russian, up to 1917

f) Secondary sources in Russian, since 1917

g) Primary and secondary sources in languages, other than Russian

The arrangement in the first three sections is chronological and in the last four sections, alphabetical.

a) Editions of Karamzin's work

Dereviannaia noga. Sheitsarskaia idiliia Gos Gesnera. Spb., 1783. [Translation.]

O proiskhozhdenii zla, poema velikogo Gallera. Moscow, 1786. [Translation.]

Besedy s Bogom, ili razmyshleniia v utrennie chasy, na kazhdyi den' goda; Razmyshleniia o delakh bozhiikh v tsarstve prirody i provid!eniia, na kazhdyi den' goda; Razmyshleniia v vechernie chasy, na kazhdyi den' goda. Moscow, 1787–89. [Karamzin's participation limited to first volumes.]

Iulii Tsezar', tragediia Villiama Shekespira. Moscow, 1787. [Translation.]

Detskoe chtenie dlia serdtsa i razuma. 20 parts. Moscow, 1785–89. [Karamzin editor, 1787–89.]

Emiliia Galotti, tragediia v 5 deistviakh, sochinennaia g. Lessingom. Moscow, 1788. [Translation.]

Moskovskii zhurnal. 8 vols. Moscow, 1791–92. (2nd ed., Moscow, 1802–3.)

Moi bezdelki. 2 vols. Moscow, 1794. (2nd ed., Moscow, 1797.)

Aglaia. 2 vols. Moscow, 1794–95. (2nd ed., Moscow, 1796.)

Novye Marmontelevy povesti. 2 vols. Moscow, 1794–98. (3rd ed., Moscow, 1822.) [Translation.]

"Smes'." *Moskovskie vedomosti.* 1795. Reprinted in *Moskvitianin,* Nos. 3–4, 6, 7, 10, 11, 12. 1854.

Melina, sochinenie g-zhi Stal'. Moscow, 1795. [Translation.]

Iuliia. Moscow, 1796.

Muza, 1, 258–59; 2, 78–87, 184–91. Spb., 1796. [Translations.]

Aonidy, ili sobranie raznykh novykh stikhotvorenii. 3 vols. Moscow, 1796–99.

Razgovor o schastii. Moscow, 1797.

"Lettre au Spectateur sur la littérature russe." *Spectateur du Nord,* 4, 53–71. 1797.

Pis'ma russkogo puteshestvennika. 6 vols. Moscow, 1797–1801.

Panteon inostrannoi slovesnosti. 3 vols. Moscow, 1798. (2nd ed., Moscow, 1818.) [Translations.]

Panteon rossiiskikh avtorov. Part 1, 4 folders. Moscow, 1801–2.

Istoricheskoe pokhval'noe slovo Ekaterine II. Moscow, 1802.

Vestnik Evropy. 12 vols. Moscow, 1802–3.

Sochineniia Karamzina. 8 vols. Moscow, 1803–4. (2nd augmented ed., 9 vols., Moscow, 1814.)

Istoriia Gosudarstva Rossiiskogo. 12 vols. Spb., 1818–29. (2nd ed., vols. 1–8, 1818–19.)

Sochineniia Karamzina. 3 vols. Moscow, 1848.

"Al'bom N. M. Karamzina." *Letopisi russkoi literatury i drevnosti*, 1, book 2, sec. 2, 161–92. 1859.

Neizdannye sochineniia i perepiska Nikolaia Mikhailovicha Karamzina. Part 1. Spb., 1862.

Izbrannye sochineniia N. M. Karamzina, s biograficheskim ocherkom, vvodnymi zametkami, primechaniiami istoriko-literaturnymi, kriticheskimi i bibliograficheskimi, i alfavitnym ukazatelem L'va Polivanova. Part 1. Moscow, 1884.

Sochineniia Karamzina. Vol. 1 (*Stikhotvoreniia*). Petrograd, 1917.

A Memoir on Ancient and Modern Russia. The Russian Text. Cambridge, Mass., 1959.

Izbrannye sochineniia. 2 vols. Moscow-Leningrad, 1964.

Polnoe sobranie stikhotvorenii. Moscow-Leningrad, 1966.

b) English translations

German Magazine, or Monthly Repository of the Literature of Germany, the North and the Continent in General. Vols. 2–3. 1800–1801. [Three tales.]

H[awkins], Ann P., trans. *Karamzin's Julia.* Spb., 1803

[Feldborg, A. A., trans.] *Travels from Moscow through Prussia, Germany, Switzerland, France and England.* 3 vols. London, 1803.

Elrington, J. B., trans. *Russian Tales.* London, 1803. [Pirated edition of Feldborg's translations.]

[Feldborg, A. A., trans.] *Tales, from the Russian.* London, 1804.

Literary Panorama. Vol. 1. 1807 [Translation of *O knizhnoi torgovle i liubvi ko chteniiu v Rossii.*]

Bowring, John, trans. *Rossiiskaia Antologiia. Specimens of the Russian Poets.* 2 vols. London, 1821–23.

Jonas, Florence, trans. *Letters of a Russian Traveler, 1789–1790.* New York, 1957.

Pipes, Richard, trans. *Karamzin's Memoir on Ancient and Modern Russia, A Translation and Analysis.* Cambridge, Mass., 1959.

Segel, Harold B., ed. *The Literature of Eighteenth-Century Russia.* 2 vols. New York, 1967. [Stories and articles.]

Nebel, Henry M., Jr., trans. *Selected Prose of N. M. Karamzin.* Evanston, Ill. 1969. [Stories and articles.]

c) Letters

"Perepiska N. M. Karamzin s 1799 po 1826 god." *Atenei*, 4–5, Nos. 19–28. 1858. [Letters to his brother, V. M. Karamzin.]

"Perepiska N. M. Karamzina." *Bibliograficheskie zapiski*, No. 19. 1858. [Letters to P. M. and R. M. Kheraskov and S. I. Selivanovskii.]

Pis'ma N. M. Karamzina k A. F. Malinovskomu i pis'ma A. S. Griboedova k S. N. Begichevu. Moscow, 1860.

Pis'ma N. M. Karamzina k I. I. Dmitrievu. Spb., 1866.

Perepiska Karamzina s Lafaterom. Spb., 1893.

"N. M. Karamzin. Pis'ma k bratu ego, Vasiliiu Mikhailovichu Karamzinu." *Prilozhenie k protokolam Otdeleniia russkogo iazyka i slovesnosti Imperatorskoi Akademii Nauk.* 1894.

Pis'ma N. M. Karamzina k kniaziu P. A. Viazemskomu 1810–1826 (Iz Ostaf'evskogo arkhiva). Spb., 1897.

"Pis'ma N. M. Karamzina k A. I. Turgenevu (1806–1826)." *Russkaia starina*, Nos. 1–4. 1899.

d) Contemporary Russian sources, including correspondence, memoirs, journals, and literary works

Arzamas i arzamasskie protokoly. Leningrad, 1933.

Barskov, Ia. L. *Perepiska moskovskikh masonov XVIII-go veka 1780–1792.* Petrograd, 1915.

———. "Pis'ma A. M. Kutuzova." *Russkii istoricheskii zhurnal*, Nos. 1–2. 1917.

Batiushkov, K. N. *Sochineniia.* Moscow, 1955.

Bestuzhev-Marlinskii, A. A. *Sobranie stikhotvorenii.* Leningrad, 1948.

Bogdanovich, I. F. *Stikhotvoreniia i poemy.* Leningrad, 1957.

Bulgarin, F. V. "Vstrecha s Karamzinym. (Iz literaturnykh vospominanii.)" *Al'bom severnykh muz.* Spb., 1828.

Derzhavin, G. R. *Sochineniia.* 9 vols. Spb., 1864–83.

Dmitriev, I. I. *Sochineniia.* 2 vols. Spb., 1895.

———. "Pis'ma k kniaziu P. A. Viazemskomu 1810–1836." *Starina i novizna*, 2. 1898.

———. *Polnoe sobranie stikhotvorenii.* Leningrad, 1967.

Dmitriev, M. A. *Melochi iz zapasa moei pamiati.* 2nd ed. Moscow, 1869.

Ekaterina Pavlovna. *Pis'ma.* Tver', 1888.

Epigramma i satira. 2 vols. Moscow-Leningrad, 1931–32.

Fomin, A. "Andrei Ivanovich Turgenev i Andrei Sergeevich Kaisarov. Novye dannye o nikh po dokumentam arkhiva P. N. Turgeneva." *Russkii bibliofil*, No. 1. 1912.

[Gamaleia, S. I.]. *Pis'ma S.I.G.* 3 vols. 2nd ed. Moscow, 1836.

Geim, I. [Heym, J.]. *Novyi rossiisko-frantsuzsko-nemetskii slovar'.* 3 vols. Moscow, 1799–1801.

Glinka, S. N. *Zapiski.* Spb., 1895.

Gogol', N. V. *Polnoe sobranie sochinenii*, Vol. 12. Leningrad, 1952.

Gorchakov, N. "Beseda Karamzina, I. I. Dmitrieva, velikobritanskogo agenta Pinkertona u moskovskogo arkhiepiskopa Avgustina." *Literaturnyi vecher.* Moscow, 1844.

Grech, N. I. *Zapiski o moei zhizni.* Moscow-Leningrad, 1930.
Grot, K. A., ed. *N. M. Karamzin i F. N. Glinka. Materialy k biografiiam russkikh pisatelei.* Spb., 1903.
Guberti, N. "Andrei Timofeevich Bolotov, kak kritik i retsenzent literaturnykh proizvedenii." *Bibliograf,* Nos. 9–10. 1885.
Iroi-komicheskaia poema. Leningrad, 1933.
Izmailov, V. "Sochineniia Karamzina." *Patriot,* 3. 1804.
Kheraskov, M. M. *Izbrannye proizvedeniia.* Leningrad, 1961.
Kiukhel'beker, V. K. *Dnevnik.* Leningrad, 1929.
Longinov, M. N. "Pis'ma Aleksandra Andreevicha Petrova k Karamzinu." *Russkii arkhiv.* 1863.
———. "Neizdannye otryvki iz pisem A. A. Petrova k N. M. Karamzinu." *Russkii arkhiv.* 1866.
Lopukhin, I. V. "Zapiski." *Russkii arkhiv,* No. 1. 1884.
[Makarov, I. P.]. "Kritika na knigu pod nazvaniem: Rassuzhdenie o starom i novom sloge rossiiskogo iazyka." *Moskovskii Merkurii.* 1803.
M. [Makarov, M. N.]. "Literaturnye vospominaniia." *Otechestvennye zapiski,* 24, No. 67. 1825.
[Martynov, I.]. "Rassmotrenie vsekh retsenzii, pomeshchennykh v ezhemesiachnom izdanii pod nazvaniem: 'Moskovskii zhurnal,' izdannyy na 1797, 1799 god [sic]. N. M. Karamzinym." *Severnyi vestnik,* 3, No. 8. 1804.
Murav'ev, M. N. *Sochineniia.* 2 vols. Spb., 1847.
Novikov, N. I. *Izbrannye sochineniia.* Moscow-Leningrad, 1951.
[Podshivalov, V. S.]. *Sokrashehennyi kurs rossiiskogo sloga, izdannyi Aleksandrom Skvortsovym.* Moscow, 1796.
Pushkin, A. S. *Polnoe sobranie sochinenii.* 16 vols. Moscow-Leningrad, 1937–49.
Radishchev, A. N. *Puteshestvie iz Peterburga v Moskvu.* Moscow-Leningrad, 1961.
Ryleev, K. F. *Polnoe sobranie sochinenii.* Leningrad, 1934.
Sankt-Peterburgskii Merkurii. 4 parts. Spb., 1793.
Serbinovich, K. S. "N. M. Karamzin. Vospominaniia." *Russkaia starina,* 11, Nos. 9–10. 1874.
Sh., K. [Shalikov, P. I.] "O konchine N. M. Karamzina." *Damskii zhurnal,* 14, No. 12. 1826.
Shishkov, A. S. *Rassuzhdenie o starom i novom sloge rossiiskogo iazyka.* Spb., 1803.
Sumarokov, A. P. *Izbrannye proizvedeniia.* Leningrad, 1957.
Timkovskii, I., trans. *Polnoe sobranie sochinenii g-na Gesnera.* 4 vols. Moscow, 1802–3.
Tiutchev, F. I. *Polnoe sobranie stikhotvorenii.* Leningrad, 1957.
Trediakovskii, V. K. *Izbrannye proizvedeniia.* Moscow-Leningrad, 1963.
Tumanskii, F. "Izveshchenie o prelozhenii G. Kostrovym Ossianovykh tvorenii i primery drugkikh perevodov." *Rossiiskii magazin,* 1. 1792.
Viazemskii, P. A. *Polnoe sobranie sochinenii.* 12 vols. Spb., 1878–96.

————. *Zapisnye knizhki 1813–1848.* Moscow, 1963.
Vigel', F. F. *Zapiski.* 2 vols. Moscow, 1928.
Vostokov, [A. Kh.]. *Stikhotvorennia.* Leningrad, 1935.
Vtorov, N. "Gavrila Petrovich Kamenev." *Vchera i segodnia,* 1. 1845.
Zhikharev, S. P. *Zapiski sovremennika.* Moscow-Leningrad, 1955.
Zhukovskii, V. A. "Neizdannyi konspekt po istorii russkoi literatury." *Trudy Otdela novoi russkoi literatury Instituta literatury Akademii Nauk SSSR,* Vol. 1. Moscow-Leningrad, 1948.
Zritel'. 3 parts. Spb., 1792.
[NB, in addition, the journals *Russkii arkhiv* and *Russkaia starina*, particularly for the year 1866, contain many important contemporary materials.]

e)   Secondary sources in Russian, up to 1917

Anon. "Perevody v proze V. Zhukovskogo." *Moskovskii telegraf,* 18. 1827.
Anuchin, D. N. *Stoletie "Pisem russkogo puteshestvennika."* Moscow, 1891.
Apostolov, N. *Karamzin kak romanist-istorik.* Petrograd, 1916.
Ashevskii, S. " 'Pis'ma russkogo puteshestvennika' Karamzina v novom osveshchenii." *Obrazovanie,* Nos. 5–6. 1901.
Belinskii, V. G. *Polnoe sobranie sochinenii.* 13 vols. Moscow, 1953–59.
Belozerskaia, N. *Vasilii Trofimovich Narezhny.* 2nd ed. Spb., 1896.
Bestuzhev-Riumin, K. *Biografii i kharakteristiki.* Spb., 1882.
Biograficheskii slovar' professorov i prepodavatelei Imperatorskogo Moskovskogo Universiteta. 2 vols. Moscow, 1855.
Bulich, N. N. *Biograficheskii ocherk N. M. Karamzina i razvitie ego literaturnoi deiatel'nosti.* Kazan', 1866.
Buslaev, F. I. " 'Pis'ma russkogo puteshestvennika.' " *Moi dosugi,* 2. Moscow, 1896.
Chechulin, N. D. *O stikhotvoreniiakh Karamzina.* Petrograd, 1917.
Danilov, N. M. *Pushkin i Karamzin.* Kazan', 1917.
Davydov, I. I. *Vzgliad na Istoriiu Gosudarstva Rossiiskogo Karamzina, so storony khudozhestvennoi.* Spb., 1855.
Galakhov, A. D. "Karamzin (Materialy dlia opredeleniia ego literaturnoi deiatel'nosti)." *Sovremennik,* 37, No. 1, 1853; 42, No. 11. 1853.
————. "Karamzin kak optimist." *Otechestvennye zapiski,* 116, No. 1, 1858.
————. "Biograficheskie i literaturnye zametki o Karamzine po povodu novykh materialov dlia ego biografii i deiatel'nosti." *Zhurnal Ministerstva Narodnogo Prosveshcheniia,* 133, No. 1. 1867.
————. *Istoriia russkoi slovesnosti drevnei i novoi.* 3 vols. 2nd ed. Spb., 1880.
Glebov, I. "Dva nabliudatelia evropeiskoi zhizni. (Pis'ma iz-za granitsy Fonvizina i Karamzina.)" *Nabliudatel',* No. 6. 1898.
Grech, N. *Chteniia o russkom iazyke,* 1–2. Spb., 1840.

Grigor'ev, A. A. *Sochineniia*, 1. Spb., 1876.

Grot, Ia. K. *Trudy*, 2–3. Spb., 1899–1901.

Kizevetter, A. A. "N. M. Karamzin." *Russkii istoricheskii zhurnal*, Nos. 1–2. 1917.

Kliuchevskii, V. O. "Vospominaniia o N. I. Novikove i ego vremeni." *Ocherki i rechi.* Moscow, 1915.

Korf, M. A. *Zhizn' grafa Speranskogo.* 2 vols. Spb., 1861.

Kovalevskii, E. *Graf Bludov i ego vremia.* Spb., 1866.

Linnichenko, I. A. "Politicheskie vozzreniia N. M. Karamzina." *Golos minuvshego*, No. 1. 1859.

Longinov, M. N. *Novikov i moskovskie martinisty.* Moscow, 1867.

Lyzhin, N. "Materialy dlia kharakteristiki Karamzina, kak prakticheskogo filosofa." *Letopisi russkoi literatury i drevnosti*, 2. Moscow, 1859.

Mel'gunov, S. P. and Sidorov, N. P. *Masonstvo v ego proshlom i nastoiashchem.* 2 vols. Moscow, 1914–15.

Nezelenov, A. *Literaturnye napravleniia v Ekaterininskuiu epokhu.* Spb., 1889.

Pogodin, M. N. *Nikolai Mikhailovich Karamzin po ego sochineniiam, pis'mam i otzyvam sovremennikov.* 2 vols. Moscow, 1866.

Polinovskii, A. *Sentimentalizm i Karamzin, kak predstavitel' etogo napravleniia v russkoi literature.* Odessa, 1911.

Ponomarev, S. I. *Materialy dlia bibliografii literatury o N. M. Karamzine.* Spb., 1883.

Priluko-Prilutskii, N. G., ed. *Karamzin, zhizn' i tvorchestvo.* Spb.-Warsaw, 1911.

Pypin, A. N. *Obshchestvennoe dvizhenie pri Aleksandre I.* 4th ed. Spb., 1908.

———. *Russkoe masonstvo. XVIII i pervaia chetvert' XIX veka.* Petrograd, 1916.

Rezanov, V. I. *Iz razyskanii o sochineniiakh V. A. Zhukovskogo.* 2 vols. Spb., 1906–16.

Roginskii, L. "Karamzin kak poet." *Severnye zapiski*, No. 11. 1916.

Rozanov, I. N. *Russkaia lirika. I: Ot poezii bezlichnoi k ispovedi serdtsa.* Moscow, 1914.

Rozanov, M. N. *Poet perioda "burnykh stremlenii" Iakob Lents, ego zhizn' i proizvedeniia.* Moscow, 1901.

———. *Zh. Zh. Russo i literaturnoe dvizhenie kontsa XVIII i nachala XIX v.* Moscow, 1912.

Semennikov, V. P. *Sobranie staraiushcheesia o perevode inostrannykh knig, uchrezhdennoe Ekaterinoi II. 1768–1783.* Spb., 1913.

Sheremetev, P. *Karamzin v Ostaf'eve 1811–1911.* Moscow, 1911.

Shevyrev, S. P. *Istoriia Imperatorskogo Moskovskogo Universiteta.* Moscow, 1855.

Sipovskii, V. V. *N. M. Karamzin, avtor "Pisem russkogo puteshestvennika."* Spb., 1899.

——. *Iz istorii russkogo romana i povesti* (*Materialy po bibliografii istorii i teorii russkogo romana*). Vypusk 1: XVIII vek. Spb., 1903.

——. *Ocherki iz istorii russkogo romana.* Vypusk 1, 2 parts.: XVIII vek. Spb., 1909–10.

——. *Russkaia lirika.* Vypusk 1: XVIII vek. Petrograd, 1914.

Sivkov, K. V. *Puteshestviia russkikh liudei za granitsu v XVIII veke.* Spb., 1914.

Skabicheskii, A. M. *Ocherki istorii russkoi tsenzury* (1700–1863). Spb., 1894.

Smirnov, S. "Tsenzurnaia vedomost' 1786–1788 godov." *Osmnadtsatyy vek,* 1. Moscow, 1869.

Solov'ev, E. N. M. *Karamzin. Ego zhizn' i nauchno-literaturnaia deiatel'-nost'.* Spb., 1894.

Starchevskii, A. V. *Nikolai Mikhailovich Karamzin.* Spb., 1849.

Tarasov, E. I. *K istorii masonstva v Rossii. Zabytyi rozenkreitser A. M. Kutuzov.* Spb., 1910.

——. *K istorii russkogo obshchestva vtoroi poloviny XVIII stoletiia* (*Mason I. P. Turgenev*). Spb., 1914.

Tiander, K. "'Labirint' Baggesena i 'Pis'ma russkogo puteshestvennika' Karamzina." *Datsko-russkie issledovaniia,* 1. Spb., 1912.

Tikhonravov, N. S. *Sochineniia.* 3 vols. Moscow, 1898.

Trubitsyn, N. N. *O narodnoi poezii v obshchestvennom i literaturnom obikhode pervoi treti XIX veka.* Spb., 1912.

Vernadskii, G. V. *Russkoe masonstvo v tsarstvovanie Ekateriny II.* Petrograd, 1917.

Veselovskii, A. A. *Liubovnaia lirika XVIII veka.* Spb., 1909.

Veselovskii, A. N. *Etiudy i kharakteristiki.* 2nd ed. Moscow, 1903.

——. *Zapadnoe vlianie v novoi russkoi literature.* 5th ed. Moscow, 1916.

——. *Prosvetitel'nyi vek i Aleksandrovskaia pora.* Moscow, 1916.

Vsevolodskii-Gerngross, V. "N. M. Karamzin i teatry." *Russkii bibliofil,* No. 8. 1916.

f) Secondary sources in Russian, since 1917

Alekseev, M. P. "K literaturnoi istorii odnogo iz romansov v 'Don-Ki-khote.'" *Servantes. Stat'i i materialy.* Leningrad, 1948.

——. "Remarka Pushkina 'narod bezmolvstvuet.'" *Russkaia literatura,* No. 2. 1967.

Arzumanova, M. A. "Ob odnoi rasprostranennoi legende." *Vestnik Leningradskogo universiteta,* No. 2 (*Seriia istorii, iazyka i literatury*). 1964.

——. "Russkii sentimentalizm v kritike 90-kh godov XVIII v." *Russkaia literatura XVIII veka. Epokha klassitsizma. XVIII vek,* Vol. 6. Moscow-Leningrad, 1964.

——. "Iz istorii literaturnoi-obshchestvennoi bor'by 90-kh godov XVIII v. (N. P. Nikolev i N. M. Karamzin)." *Vestnik Leningradskogo universiteta,* No. 20 (*Seriia istorii, iazyka i literatury*). 1965.

Astakhova, A. "Iz istorii i ritmiki khoreia." *Poetica*, 1. Leningrad, 1926.
Babushkina, A. P. *Istoriia russkoi detskoi literatury*. Moscow, 1948.
Baikova, L. S. "Bessoiuzyne predlozheniia v iazyke N. M. Karamzina."
    Uchenye zapiski Tartuskogo gosudarstvennogo universiteta, vypusk
    132. 1963.
———. *Struktura i stilisticheskaia napravlennost' bessoiuznykh predlozhenii
    v iazyke N. M. Karamzina*. Tallin, 1967.
Beliaev, M. D. "Karamzin. Odno iz poslednikh pisem." *Raduga*. Petersburg,
    1922.
Berkov, P. N. *Istoriia russkoi zhurnalistiki XVIII veka*. Moscow-Leningrad,
    1952.
———. *Vvedenie v izuchenie istorii russkoi literatury XVIII veka*. Vol. 1.
    Leningrad, 1964.
——— and Makogonenko, G. P. "Zhizn' i tvorchestvo N. M. Karamzina."
    N. M. Karamzin. *Izbrannye sochineniia*, 1. Moscow, 1964.
Blagoi, D. D. "Pushkin i russkaia literatura XVIII veka." *Pushkin—rodo-
    nachal'nik novoi russkoi literatury*. Moscow-Leningrad, 1941.
———. *Istoriia russkoi literatury XVIII veka*. Moscow, 1946.
Brukhanskii, A. N. "M. N. Murav'ev i 'legkoe stikhotvorstvo.' " *XVIII vek*,
    Vol. 4. Moscow-Leningrad, 1959.
Butakova, V. I. "Karamzin i Pushkin (Neskol'ko sopostavlenii)." *Pushkin i
    ego sovremenniki*, 37. 1928.
Danilevskii, R. Iu. "Lessing v russkoi literature XVII veka." *Epokha Prosve-
    shcheniia*. Leningrad, 1967.
Efimov, A. I. "Frazeologicheskii sostav povesti Karamzina 'Natal'ia, boiar-
    skaia doch'.' " *Materialy i issledovaniia po istorii russkogo literatur-
    nogo iazyka*, Vol. 1. Moscow-Leningrad, 1949.
———. *Istoriia russkogo literaturnogo iazyka*. 3rd ed. Moscow, 1957.
Egunov, A. N. *Gomer v russkikh perevodakh XVIII–XIX vekov*. Moscow-
    Leningrad, 1964.
Eikhenbaum, B. "Karamzin." *Skvoz' literaturu*. Leningrad, 1924.
Fedorov, V. I. "Povest' N. M. Karamzina 'Natal'ia, boiarskaia doch'.' "
    *Uchenye zapiski Moskovskogo gorodskogo pedagogicheskogo insti-
    tuta*, 48, No. 5. 1955.
———. "Istoricheskaia povest' N. M. Karamzina 'Marfa Posadnitsa.' "
    *Uchenye zapiski Moskovskogo gorodskogo pedagogicheskogo insti-
    tuta*, 62, No. 6. 1957.
———. "K kharakteristike sotsial'no-politicheskikh vzgliadov N. M. Karam-
    zina." *Uchenye zapiski Moskovskogo gosudarstvennogo ped. instituta*.
    1963.
Gippius, V. V. " 'Vestnik Evropy' 1802–1830 godov." *Uchenye zapiski
    Leningradskogo universiteta, seriia filologicheskikh nauk*, No. 3.
    1939.
Gofman, M. L. "Poeziia Karamzina i Zhukovskogo." *Vozrozhdenie*, 57.
    1956.
Grasshoff, H. "Pervyi nemetskii perevod 'Bednoi Lizy' i ego avtor." *Russko-
    evropeiskie literaturnye sviazi*. Moscow-Leningrad, 1966.

Gudzii, N. K. *Frantsuzskaia burzhuaznaia revoliutsiia i russkaia literatura.* Moscow, 1944.

Gukovskii, G. A. *Russkaia poeziia XVIII veka.* Leningrad, 1927.

———. *Ocherki po istorii russkoi literatury i obshchestvennoi mysli XVIII veka.* Leningrad, 1938.

———. *Russkaia literatura XVIII veka.* Moscow, 1939.

———. "Karamzin." *Istoriia russkoi literatury,* Vol. 5. Moscow-Leningrad, 1941.

Iliushin, A. " 'Izbrannye sochineniia Karamzina.' " *Voprosy literatury,* No. 2. 1965.

Isakov, S. G. "Materialy po russkoi literature i kul'ture na stranitsakh nemetskoi pribaltiiskoi pechati nachala XIX v." *Uchenye zapiski Tartuskogo universiteta,* vypusk 184. 1966.

Istoriia russkogo romana, Vol. 1. Moscow-Leningrad, 1962.

Istoriia russkoi kritiki, Vol. 1. Moscow-Leningrad, 1958.

Istoriia russkoi literatury v trekh tomakh, Vol. 2. Moscow, 1958.

Ivanova, T. A. "Upotreblenie prichastii v rannikh proizvedeniia N. M. Karamzina." *Materialy i issledovaniia po istorii russkogo literaturnogo iazyka,* Vol. 1. Moscow-Leningrad, 1949.

Kanunova, F. Z. "Istoriko-literaturnoe znachenie povesti N. M. Karamzina. Stat'ia pervaia." *Uchenye zapiski Tomskogo gos. universiteta,* 45. 1963.

———. "Istoriko-literaturnoe znachenie povesti N. M. Karamzina. Stat'ia vtoraia." *Uchenye zapiski Tomskogo gos. universiteta,* 48. 1964.

———. " 'Natal'ia, boiarskaia doch' ' kak pervyi opyt istoricheskoi povesti N. M. Karamzina." *Uchenye zapiski Tomskogo gos. universiteta,* 48. 1964.

———. "K evoliutsii sentimentalizma N. M. Karamzina ('Marfa Posadnitsa')." *Uchenye zapiski Tomskogo gos. universiteta,* 50. 1965.

———. "Evoliutsiia sentimentalizma Karamzina ('Moia ispoved' ')." *XVIII vek,* Vol. 7. 1966.

———. *Iz istorii russkoi povesti (Istoriko-literaturnoe znachenie povestei N. M. Karamzina).* Tomsk, 1967.

Karlova, T. S. "Tolstoi i N. M. Karamzin." *Uchenye zapiski Gor'kovskogo universiteta,* 6, No. 77. 1966.

Kisliagina, L. G. "K voprosu o formirovanii mirovozzreniia N. M. Karamzina (1785–1789 gg)." *Vestnik Moskovskogo universiteta,* No. 3 (*Seriia istorii*). 1964.

Kochetkova, N. D. "Ideino-literaturnye positsii masonov 80–90kh godov XVIII v. i N. M. Karamzin." *XVIII vek,* Vol. 6. Moscow-Leningrad, 1964.

———. *N. M. Karamzin i russkaia poeziia kontsa 80-kh—pervoi poloviny 90-kh godov XVIII veka.* Avtoreferat. Leningrad, 1964.

———. "Karamzin." *V mire knig,* No. 10. 1966.

Komarov, A. I. "Zhurnaly N. M. Karamzina i ikh napravleniia." *Ocherki po istorii russkoi zhurnalistiki i kritiki,* Vol. 1. Leningrad, 1950.

Kovalevskaia, E. G. "Slavianizmy i russkaia leksika v proizvedeniiakh N. M. Karamzina." *Uchenye zapiski Leningradskogo pedagogicheskogo instituta*, 173. 1958.

———. "Inoiazichnaia leksika v proizvedeniiakh N. M. Karamzina." *Materialy i issledovaniia po leksike russkogo iazyka XVIII veka.* Moscow-Leningrad, 1965.

Krestova, L. V. "Drevnerusskaia povest' kak odin iz istochnikov povestei N. M. Karamzina 'Raiskaia ptichka,' 'Ostrov Borngol'm,' 'Marfa Posadnitsa.' Iz istorii rannego russkogo romantizma." *Issledovaniia i materialy po drevnerusskoi literature.* Moscow, 1961.

———. "Povest' N. M. Karamzina 'Sierra-Morena.'" *XVIII vek*, Vol. 7. Moscow-Leningrad, 1966.

———. "Romanicheskaia povest' N. M. Karamzina 'Natal'ia, boiarskaia doch'' i russkie semeinye predaniia XVII veka." *Drevnerusskaia literatura i ee sviazi s novym vremenem.* Moscow, 1967.

Kriazhimskaia, I. A. "Teatral'no-kriticheskie stat'i N. M. Karamzina v 'Moskovskom zhurnale.'" *XVIII vek*, Vol. 3. Moscow-Leningrad, 1958.

———. "Iz istorii russkoi teatral'noi kritiki kontsa XVIII—nachala XIX veka." *XVIII vek*, Vol. 4. Moscow-Leningrad, 1959.

Kucherov, A. Ia. "Frantsuzskaia revoliutsiia i russkaia literatura XVIII veka." *XVIII vek*, Vol. 1. Moscow-Leningrad, 1935.

———. "Esteticheskie vzgliady Karamzina." *Literaturnaia ucheba*, No. 3. 1936.

———. "Sentimental'naia povest' i literatura puteshestvii." *Istoriia russkoi literatury*, Vol. 5. Moscow-Leningrad, 1941.

———. "Poeziia Karamzina." N. M. Karamzin and I. I. Dmitriev, *Izbrannye stikhotvoreniia.* Leningrad, 1958.

Kulakova, L. I. "Esteticheskie vzgliady N. M. Karamzina." *XVIII vek*, Vol. 6. Moscow-Leningrad, 1964.

Kuleshov, V. I. "Iz istorii russko-nemetskikh literaturnykh sviazei ('Vestnik Evropy' N. M. Karamzina i 'Russische Miszellen' I. G. Rikhtera)." *Slavianskaia filologiia*, 5. 1963.

———. *Literaturnye sviazi Rossii i zapadnoi Evropy v XIX veke (pervaia polovina).* Moscow, 1965.

Lapiken, P. P. "Neologizmy Karamzina." *Novyi zhurnal*, No. 90. 1968.

Lebenko, I. Iu. "Pis'mo N. Karamzina k popechiteliu vilenskogo universiteta kniaziu A. Chartoryiskomu." *Russkaia literatura*, No. 2. 1967.

Leman, U. "N. M. Karamzin i V. fon Vol'tsogen." *XVIII vek*, Vol. 7. Moscow-Leningrad, 1966.

Levin, Iu. D. "Ob istoricheskoi evoliutsii printsipov perevoda." *Mezhdunarodnye sviazi russkoi literatury.* Moscow-Leningrad, 1963.

———. "Angliiskaia prosvetitel'skaia zhurnalistika v russkoi literature XVIII veka." *Epokha Prosveshcheniia.* Leningrad, 1967.

Levin, V. D. *Ocherk stilistiki russkogo literaturnogo iazyka kontsa XVIII—nachala XIX v. (Leksika).* Moscow, 1964.

Selected Bibliography

———. "Karamzin, Batiushkov, Zhukovskii—redaktory sochinenii M. N. Murav'eva." *Problemy sovremennoi filologii*. Moscow, 1965.

Liuter, A. "Russkie pisateli XVIII–XIX veka v nemetskikh perevodakh." *Vremennik Obshchestva druzei russkoi knigi*, 4. 1938.

Livanova, T. N. *Russkaia muzykal'naia kul'tura XVIII veka v ee sviaziakh s literaturoi, teatrom i bytom*. 2 vols. Moscow, 1952–53.

Lotman, Iu. M. "Evoliutsiia mirovozzreniia Karamzina (1789–1803)." *Uchenye zapiski Tartuskogo gos. universiteta*, vypusk 51. 1957.

———. "'Bednaia Liza' Karamzina v pereskaze krest'ianina." *Uchenye zapiski Tartuskogo gos. universiteta*, vypusk 98. 1960.

———. "Puti razvitiia russkoi prozy 1800–1810kh godov." *Uchenye zapiski Tartuskogo gos. universiteta*, vypusk 104. 1961.

———. "'Sochuvstvennik' A. N. Radishcheva A. M. Kutuzov i ego pis'ma k I. P. Turgenevu." *Uchenye zapiski Tartuskogo gos. universiteta*, vypusk 139. 1963.

———. "Otrazhenie etiki i taktiki revoliutsionnoi bor'by v russkoi literature kontsa XVIII veka." *Uchenye zapiski Tartuskogo gos. universiteta*, vypusk 167. 1965.

———. "Ob odnom chitatel'skom vospriiatii 'Bednoi Lizy' N. M. Karamzina. (K strukture massovogo soznaniia XVIII veka)." *XVIII vek*, Vol. 7. Moscow-Leningrad, 1966.

———. "Poeziia Karamzina" N. M. Karamzin *Polnoe sobranie stikhotvorenii*. Moscow-Leningrad, 1966.

———. "Russo i russkaia kul'tura XVIII veka." *Epokha Prosveshcheniia*. Moscow-Leningrad, 1967.

Makogonenko, G. P. *Nikolai Novikov i russkoe prosveshchenie XVIII veka*. Moscow-Leningrad, 1951.

———. *Radishchev i ego vremia*. Moscow, 1956.

———. "Russkoe prosveshchenie i literaturnye napravleniia XVIII veka." *Russkaia literatura*, No. 4. 1959.

———. "Byl li karamzinskii period v istorii russkoi literatury?" *Russkaia literatura*, No. 4. 1960.

———. *Denis Fonvizin*. Moscow-Leningrad, 1961.

———. "Literaturnaia positsiia Karamzina v XIX veke." *Russkaia literatura*, No. 1. 1962.

Martynov, I. F. "'Opyt istoricheskogo slovariia rossiiskikh pisateliakh' N. I. Novikova i literaturnaia polemika 60–70-kh godov XVIII veka." *Russkaia literatura*, No. 3. 1968.

Maslov, V. I. "Interes k Sternu v russkoi literature kontsa XVIII i nachala XIX vv." *Istoriko-literaturnyi sbornik, posviashchennyi V. I. Sreznevskomu*. Leningrad, 1924.

———. *Ossianizm Karamzina*. Priluki, 1928.

Medvedeva, I. N. "Zapiska Nikity Murav'eva 'Mysli ob Istorii Gosudarstva Rossiiskogo' N. M. Karamzina." *Literaturnoe nasledstvo*, 59. Moscow-Leningrad, 1954.

Mishin, M. P. "Neskol'ko spravok iz istorii leksiki russkogo literaturnogo iazyka. (K voprosu o neologizmakh N. M. Karamzina)." *Uchenye zapiski Permskogo ped. instituta*, No. 17. 1958.

Mordovchenko, N. I. *Russkaia kritika pervoi chetverti XIX veka.* Moscow-Leningrad, 1959.

Nazaretskaia, K. A. "Ob istokakh russkogo sentimentalizma." *Uchenye zapiski Kazanskogo gos. universiteta*, 123, No. 8. 1963.

————. "Poeziia i proza v moskovskikh zhurnalakh 60-kh godov XVIII v. (K voprosu o formirovanii sentimentalizma)." *Uchenye zapiski Kazanskogo gos. universiteta*, 124, No. 5. 1964.

Nechkina, M. V. "Dekabrist M. Orlov—kritik 'Istorii' N. M. Karamzina." *Literaturnoe nasledstvo*, Vol. 59. Moscow-Leningrad, 1954.

Orlov, P. A. "Ideinyi smysl povesti N. M. Karamzina 'Bednaia Liza.'" *Uchenye zapiski Riazanskogo gos. ped. instituta*, No. 10. 1955.

————. "Radishchev i sentimentalizm." *Uchenye zapiski Riazanskogo gos. ped. instituta*, No. 13. 1956.

————. "'Bednaia Liza' Karamzina i sentimental'no-povestvovatel'naia literatura kontsa XVIII–nachala XIX v." *Vestnik Moskovskogo universiteta*, No. 6 (Seriia filologii). 1966.

————. "Literaturnaia programma 'Moskovskogo zhurnala' Karamzina." *Nauchnye doklady vysshei shkoly. Filologicheskie nauki*, 1, No. 2. 1966.

————. "Povest' N. M. Karamzina 'Marfa Posadnitsa.'" *Russkaia literatura*, No. 2. 1968.

Orlov, Vl. *Russkie prosvetiteli 1790–1800-kh godov.* 2nd ed. Moscow, 1956.

Osorgin, M. "Moskovskoi zhurnal." *Vremennik Obshchestva druzei russkoi knigi*, 4. 1938.

Pigarev, K. V. *Russkaia literatura i izobrazitel'noe iskusstvo (XVIII-pervaia chetvert' XIX veka).* Moscow, 1966.

————. "Neosushchestvlennyi zamysel Karamzina." *XVIII vek*, Vol. 7. Moscow-Leningrad, 1966.

Piksanov, N. K. "'Bednaia Aniuta' Radishcheva i 'Bednaia Liza' Karamzina. K bor'be realizma s sentimentalizmom." *XVIII vek*, Vol. 3. Moscow-Leningrad, 1958.

Plimak, E. G. "Masonskaia reaktsiia protiv materializma v Rossii (70–90-e gody XVIII veka)." *Voprosy filosofii*, No. 2. 1957.

Plotnikov, I. P. "'Bednaia Liza' Karamzina, kak tipicheskoe proizvedenie sentimental'nogo stila." *Rodnoi iazyk v shkole*, No. 2. 1923.

Pospelov, G. P. "U istokov russkogo sentimentalizma." *Vestnik Moskovskogo universiteta*, No. 1. 1948.

Predtechenskii, A. V. *Ocherki obshchestvenno-politicheskoi istorii Rossii v pervoi chetverti XIX veka.* Moscow-Leningrad, 1957.

————. "Obshchestvenno-politicheskie vzgliady N. M. Karamzina v 1790-kh godakh." *Problemy russkogo prosveshcheniia v literature XVIII veka.* Moscow-Leningrad, 1961.

Privalova, E. P. *Russkaia detskaia literatura XVIII veka.* Moscow, 1957.

————. "O sotrudnikakh zhurnala 'Detskoe chtenie dlia serdtsa i razuma.' " *XVIII vek,* Vol. 6. Moscow-Leningrad, 1964.

————. " 'Detskoe chtenie dlia serdtsa i razuma' v otsenke chitatelei i kritiki." *XVIII vek,* Vol. 7. Moscow-Leningrad, 1966.

Pukhov, V. "Pervaia russkaia povest' o bednoi Lize." *Russkaia literatura,* No. 1. 1965.

Roboli, T. "Literatura 'Puteshestvii.' " *Russkaia proza.* Leningrad, 1926.

Rozova, Z. " 'Novaia Eloiza' Russo i 'Natali'a, boiarskaia doch' ' Karamzina." *Russkaia literatura,* No. 4. 1966.

Sakulin, P. N. *Russkaia literatura. Sotsiologo-sinteticheskii obzor literaturnykh stilei,* Vol. 2. Moscow, 1929.

Selivanov, K. "N. M. Karamzin." *Russkie pisateli v Srednem Povol'zhe.* Kuibyshev, 1941.

Semennikov, V. P. *Radishchev. Ocherki i issledovaniia.* Moscow-Leningrad, 1923.

Serman, I. "Russkaia literatura XVIII veka i perevod." *Masterstvo perevoda.* 1962. Moscow, 1963.

————. "Literaturnoe delo Karamzina." *Neva,* No. 12. 1966.

Shklovskii, V. *O teorii prozy.* Moscow-Leningrad, 1925.

————. *Chulkov i Levshin.* Leningrad, 1933.

Shtorm, G. P. "Novoe o Pushkine i Karamzine." *Izvestiia Akademii Nauk SSSR. Otdelenie literatury i iazyka,* 19, No. 2. 1960.

Shvedova, M. Iu. "Sootnoshenie imennykh i chlennykh form prilagatel'nykh pri predikativnom ikh upotreblenii v khudozhestvennoi proze Karamzina." *Materialy i issledovaniia po istorii russkogo literaturnogo iazyka,* Vol. 1. Moscow-Leningrad, 1949.

Skipina, K. "O chuvstvitel'noi povesti." *Russkaia proza.* Leningrad, 1926.

Sokolov, A. N. *Ocherki po istorii russkoi poemy XVIII veka i pervoi poloviny XIX veka.* Moscow, 1955.

Stepanov, V. P. " 'Byl li karamzinskii period v istorii russkoi literatury?' (Diskussiia v Institute russkoi literatury)." *Russkaia literatura,* No. 3. 1961.

————. "Dva iubileia." *Russkaia literatura,* No. 3. 1967.

Svetlov, L. B. *Izdatel'skaia deiatel'nost' N. I. Novikova.* Leningrad, 1946.

————. " 'Obshchestvo liubitelei rossiiskoi uchenosti' pri Moskovskom universitete." *Istoricheskii arkhiv,* 5. 1950.

Toibin, I. " 'Istoriia Gosudarstva Rossiiskogo' N. M. Karamzina v tvorcheskoi zhizni Pushkina." *Russkaia literatura,* No. 4. 1966.

Tomashevskii, B. V. "Epigrammy Pushkina na Karamzina." *Pushkin. Issledovaniia i materialy,* Vol. 1. Moscow-Leningrad, 1956.

————. *Stilistika i stikhoslozhenie.* Leningrad, 1959.

Tynianov, Iu. *Arkhaisty i novatory.* Leningrad, 1929.

Utkina, V. P. "Leksika rannikh povestei N. M. Karamzina." *Izvestiia Krymskogo ped. instituta,* 19. 1954.

Verkhovskaia, N. *Karamzin v Moskve i Podmoskov'e.* Moscow, 1968.

Vinogradov, B. "Al'bom I. I. Dmitrieva." *Don,* No. 6. 1957.

Vinogradov, V. V. "Iz nabliudenii nad iazykom i stilem I. I. Dmitrieva."
    Materialy i issledovaniia po istorii russkogo literaturnogo iazyka, Vol.
    1. Moscow-Leningrad, 1949.
———. *Problema avtorstva i teoriia stilei.* Moscow, 1961.
———. "Istoriia slova *iziashchnyi.*" *XVIII vek,* Vol. 7. Moscow-Leningrad,
    1966.
———. "O stile Karamzina i ego razvitii (Ispravleniia teksta povestei)."
    *Protsessy formirovaniia leksiki russkogo literaturnogo iazyka. (Ot
    Kantemira do Karamzina).* Moscow-Leningrad, 1966.
———. "Problemy stilistiki perevoda v poetike Karamzina." *Russko-evro-
    peiskie literaturnye sviazi.* Moscow-Leningrad, 1966.
Vishnevskaia, G. A. "Iz istorii russkogo romantizma (Literaturno-teoreti-
    cheskie suzhdeniia N. M. Karamzina na 1787–1792 gg.)." *Uchenye
    zapiski Kazanskogo universiteta,* 124, No. 5. 1964.
Vladimirova, N. A. "Iz nabliudenii nad semantikoi obshchestvenno-politi-
    cheskoi leksiki istoricheskikh trudov M. V. Lomonosova i N. M.
    Karamzina." *Ocherki po istorii russkogo iazyka i literatury XVIII
    veka (Lomonosovskie chteniia),* vypusk 1. Kazan', 1967.
Zaborov, P. R. "Ot klassitsizma k romantizmu." *Shekspir i russkaia kul'tura.*
    Moscow-Leningrad, 1965.
Zapadov, A. V. "N. M. Karamzin." *Russkaia proza XVIII veka,* Vol. 2.
    Moscow-Leningrad, 1950.
———. *Russkaia zhurnalistika XVIII veka.* Moscow, 1964.
Zhirmunskii, V. *Gete v russkoi literature.* Leningrad, 1937.
Zolotova, G. A. "Struktura slozhnogo sintaksicheskogo tselogo v Karam-
    zinskoi povesti." *Trudy Instituta iazykoznaniia,* 3. 1954.

g) Primary and secondary sources in languages other than Russian

ENGLISH

Allen, W. *The English Novel.* London, 1960.
*Annual Register, or General Repository of History, Politics, and Literature
    for the Year 1799.* London, 1800.
*Annual Register, or General Repository of History, Politics, and Literature
    for the Year 1803.* London, 1804.
Annual Review, and History of Literature, 2. London, 1804.
*Anti-Jacobin Review and Magazine, or, Monthly Political and Literary
    Censor,* 11. London, 1802.
Atkins, H. G. *A History of German Versification.* London, 1923.
The Bee, 17. Edinburgh, 1793.
Black, J. L. "The Soviets and the Anniversary of N. M. Karamzin." *New
    Review,* 8, No. 3. 1968.
———. "History in Politics: Karamzin's *Istoriia* as an Ideological Catalyst
    in Russian Society." *Laurentian University Review,* 1, No. 2. 1968.

Burgi, Richard. A *History of the Russian Hexameter*. Hamden, Conn., 1954.

Clarke, Robert T. *Herder, His Life and Thought*. Berkeley and Los Angeles, 1955.

Cross, A. G. "Karamzin and England." *Slavonic and East European Review*, 43, No. 100. 1964.

————. "N. M. Karamzin and Barthélemy's *Voyage du jeune Anacharsis*." *Modern Language Review*, 61. 1966.

————. "Karamzin Studies: For the Bicentenary of the Birth of N. M. Karamzin (1766–1966)." *Slavonic and East European Review*, 45, No. 104. 1967.

————. "Problems of Form and Literary Influence in the Poetry of Karamzin." *Slavic Review*, 27, No. 1. 1968.

————. "N. M. Karamzin's 'Messenger of Europe' (*Vestnik Yevropy*), 1802–1803." *Forum for Modern Language Studies*, 5, No. 1. 1969.

Cushing, Mary Gertrude. *Pierre Le Tourneur*. New York, 1908.

Dewey, Horace. "Sentimentalism in the Historical Writings of N. M. Karamzin." *American Contributions to the Fourth International Congress of Slavists*. The Hague, 1958.

Drage, C. L. "Trochaic Metres in Early Russian Syllabo-Tonic Poetry." *Slavonic and East European Review*, 38, No. 91. 1960.

Edinburgh Review, 3, No. 6. Edinburgh, 1804.

Erämetsa, E. *A Study of the Word "Sentimental" and of Other Linguistic Characteristics of Eighteenth Century Sentimentalism in England*. Helsinki, 1951.

Garrard, J. G. "Karamzin in Recent Soviet Criticism." *Slavic and East European Journal*, 11, No. 4. 1967.

Harrison, W. N. *M. Karamzin. Bednaia Liza*. Letchworth, 1963.

Hugo, H. E., ed. *The Portable Romantic Reader*. New York, 1960.

Lang, D. M. "Sumarokov's 'Hamlet.' A Misjudged Russian Tragedy of the Eighteenth Century." *Modern Language Review*, 43. 1948.

McGrew, R. E. "Notes on the Princely Role in Karamzin's *Istorija Gosudarstva Rossijskago*." *American Slavic and East European Review*, 18, No. 1. 1959.

Mackenzie, Henry. *The Man of Feeling*. New York, 1958.

Mayo, R. D. *The English Novel in the Magazines 1740–1818*. Evanston, Ill., 1962.

Monthly Magazine; or British Register, 10. 1800.

Monthly Review or Literary Journal, 44. 1804.

Nebel, Henry M., Jr. *N. M. Karamzin: A Russian Sentimentalist*. The Hague-Paris, 1967.

Pantheon of the Age or, Memoirs of 3000 contemporary public characters British and Foreign, of all ranks and professions, Vol. 2. 2nd ed. London, 1825.

Pascal, R. *Shakespeare in Germany, 1740–1815*. Cambridge, Eng., 1937.

————. *The German Sturm und Drang*. Manchester, 1953.

Pipes, Richard. "Karamzin's Conception of the Monarchy." *Harvard Slavic Studies*, 4. 1957.

Raeff, Marc. *Origins of the Russian Intelligentsia. The Eighteenth-Century Nobility.* New York, 1966.

Rogger, Hans. *National Consciousness in Eighteenth-Century Russia.* Cambridge, Mass., 1960.

Shaftesbury, Anthony, Earl of. *Characteristics of Men, Manners, Opinions, Times.* 2 vols. Indianapolis–New York, 1964.

Simmons, E. J. *English Literature and Culture in Russia* (1553–1840). Cambridge, Mass., 1935.

Smith, I. H. "The Concept 'Sensibilité' and the Enlightenment." *AUMLA*, No. 27. 1967.

Sterne, Laurence. *A Sentimental Journey. The Journal to Eliza.* London, 1960.

Stilman, Leon. "Introduction N. M. Karamzin," *Letters of a Russian Traveler, 1789–1790.* New York, 1957.

Thaden, Edward C. "The Beginnings of Romantic Nationalism in Russia." *American Slavic and East European Review*, 13. 1954.

Thomson, James. *Works.* 3 vols. London, 1803.

Tooke, William. *The Life of Catharine II.* 3 vols. 3rd ed. London, 1799.

Turner, C. E. "Studies in Russian Literature: VII Karamsin." *Fraser's Magazine*, NS16. 1877.

Vlasto, A. "M. M. Heraskov: A Study in the Intellectual Life of the Age of Catherine the Great." Ph.D. dissertation, Cambridge University, 1952.

Whitford, R. C. "Satire's View of Sentimentalism in the Days of George the Third." *Journal of English and Germanic Philology*, 18, No. 2. 1919.

Wood, K. L. "The French Theatre in the XVIIIth Century According to Some Contemporary English Travellers." *Revue de littérature comparée*, 12. 1932.

Wyndham, Violet. *Madame de Genlis.* London, 1958.

FRENCH

Bakounine, Tatiana. *Le Répertoire biographique des francs-maçons russes.* Brussels, 1940.

Barthélemy, J. J. *Voyage du jeune Anacharsis en Grèce, vers le milieu du IVᵉ siècle avant l'ère vulgaire.* 7 vols. 3rd ed. Paris, 1790.

Batteux, C. *Les Beaux arts réduits à un même principe.* Nouvelle édition. Paris, 1747.

Baye, Baron de. *À propos du bicentaire Karamzin et Jean-Jacques Rousseau.* Paris, 1912.

Ehrhard, M. V. A. *Zhukovski et le préromantisme russe.* Paris, 1938.

Genlis, Mme. de. *Les Veillées du château.* 3 vols. Paris, 1798.

Lirondelle, A. *Shakespeare en Russie, 1748–1840.* Paris, 1910.

Marmontel, J. F. *Contes moraux.* 5 vols. Paris, 1820.
Michéa, R. "Le 'Plaisir des tombeaux' au XVIIIᵉ siècle." *Revue de littérature comparée,* 18. Paris, 1938.
Rousseau, Jean-Jacques. *Les Confessions.* 3 vols. Paris, 1926.
———. *Julie, ou La Nouvelle Héloise.* Paris, 1960.
Tieghem, P. van. "Gessner et le rêve pastoral romantique." *Revue de littérature comparée,* 14. 1924.
———. *Le Préromantisme.* 3 vols. Paris, 1947.
Tourneur, P. Le, trans. *Les Nuits d'Young.* Nouvelle édition. Marseilles, 1770.
West, C. B. "La Théorie de la traduction au XVIIIᵉ siècle par rapport surtout aux traductions françaises d'ouvrages anglais." *Revue de littérature comparée,* 12. 1932.

GERMAN

Baechtold, R. *Karamzins Weg zur Geschichte.* Basel, 1946.
Bittner, K. "Herderische Gedanken in Karamzins Geschichtsschau." *Jahrbücher für Geschichte Osteuropas,* 7. 1959.
———. "Der Junge Nikolaj Michajlovič Karamzin und Deutschland." *Herder-Studien.* Würzburg, 1960.
Brang, P. " 'Natal'ja, bojarskaja dočʹ' " und Tatjana Larina." *Zeitschrift für slavische Philologie,* 27. 1959.
———. *Studien zu Theorie und Praxis der russischen Erzählung, 1770–1811.* Wiesbaden, 1960.
———. "A. M. Kutuzov als Vermittler des westeuropäischen Sentimentalismus in Russland." *Zeitschrift für slavische Philologie,* 30. 1962.
Čiževskij, D. "Zu den Neologismen Karamsins. Literarische Lesefrüchte." *Zeitschrift für slavische Philologie,* 19. 1947.
Gessner, Salomon. *Schriften.* 2 vols. Zurich, 1777–78.
Goethe, J. W. von. *The Sorrows of Young Werther, and Selected Writings.* Trans. C. Hutter. New York, 1962.
Grasshoff, H. "Zur Rolle des Sentimentalismus in der historischen Entwicklung der russischen und der westeuropäischen Literatur." *Zeitschrift für Slawistik,* 8. 1963.
Hüttl-Worth, G. *Die Bereicherung des russischen Wortschatzes im XVIII Jahrhundert.* Vienna, 1956.
———. "Zur russischen Lexik des 18. Jhs." *Zeitschrift für slavische Philologie,* 24. 1956.
Keil, R. D. "Ergänzungen zu russischen Dichter-Kommentaren (Lomonosov und Karamzin)." *Zeitschrift für slavische Philologie,* 30. 1962.
Matthisson, Friedrich von. *Gedichte.* Zurich, 1821.
Mitter, W. "Die Entwicklung der politischen Anschauungen Karamzins." *Forschungen zur ostoeuropäischen Geschichte,* 2. 1955.
Neumann, F. W. "Karamzin Verhältnis zu Schiller." *Zeitschrift für slavische Philologie,* 9. 1932.
———. *Geschichte der russische Ballade.* Koenigsberg and Berlin, 1937.

Pamp, F. "Charles Bonnet und Karamsin." *Revue de littérature comparée,* 30. 1956.

Richter, J. G. *Moskwa. Eine Skizze.* Leipzig, 1799.

———. *Russische Miszellen.* 9 pts. Leipzig, 1803–4.

Rothe, Hans. "Karamzinstudien I." *Zeitschrift für slavische Philologie,* 29. 1960.

———. "Karamzinstudien II." *Zeitschrift für slavische Philologie,* 30.

———. *N. M. Karamzins europäische Reise: Der Beginn des russischen Romans.* Berlin-Zürich, 1968.

Stiede, W. "Nikolai Michailovič Karamzin und Johann Philipp Krug." *Zeitschrift für slavische Philologie,* 3. 1928.

Sturm, C. C. *Reflections on the Works of God in Nature and Providence, for Every Day of the Year.* Trans. Adam Clarke. New York, 1824.

Tiede, J. F. *Unterhaltungen mit Gott in den Abendstunden.* 2 vols. Reutlingen, 1813.

Wedel, Erwin. "Radiščev und Karamzin." *Die Welt der Slaven,* 4. 1959.

———. "A. N. Radiščevs *Reise von Petersburg nach Moskau* und N. M. Karamzins *Reisebriefe eines Russen.*" *Die Welt der Slaven,* 4. 1959.

Winkel, Hans-Jürgen zum. "Ein Brief Karamzins an Wieland vom Jahre 1789." *Slawistische Studien.* Göttingen, 1963.

ITALIAN

Cronia, Arturo. "Un'ignota versione italiana della *Julija* di Karamzin." *Richerche slavistiche,* 13. 1965.

INDEX

Aesop, 1
Aglaia: "Flower on the Grave of My Agathon, A" ["Tsvetok na grob moego Agatona"], 7, 36, 146, 152; "Melodor to Philalet" [Melodor k Filaletu"], 117, 152–53, 154; "On the Sciences, Arts and Enlightenment" ["Nechto o naukakh, isskustvakh i prosveshchenii"], 146–48, 149, 150, 153, 155, 156, 188; "Philalet to Melodor" ["Filalet k Melodoru"], 151, 152–53, 154; "What is Necessary for an Author?" ["Chto nuzhno avtoru"], 148–50; mentioned, 60, 66, 67, 104, 113, 117, 118, 119, 121, 139, 144, 145–53, 155, 158, 163, 171, 174, 182, 194, 219
d'Alembert, J. le R., xv, 49
Alexander I, 5, 33, 61, 67, 156, 164, 168, 171, 184, 192, 194, 198, 199, 201, 202, 205, 207, 208, 210, 213, 216, 219, 225, 226
Alfred, King, 132
Allgemeine deutsche Bibliothek, 53
Almanach des Muses, 172, 230
Andreae, J. V., 58
Anna Ivanovna, Empress, 203
Annual Register, 93, 95
Annual Review, 95
Anti-Jacobin, 94, 95
Aonides [Aonidy], 142, 144, 158, 165, 172–73, 178, 188–89, 191, 194, 198, 220, 230
Arakcheev, Count A. A., 226
Archenholz, J. W., 211, 272
d'Argental, Comte, 16
d'Argenville, A. I.: *Abrégé de la vie des plus fameux peintres*, 84
Ariosto, Ludovico: *Orlando Furioso*, 53, 54; mentioned, 44, 46, 54, 194
Aristotle, 8
Arzamas, 170, 223

Augustus, 105, 221
Aurelius, Marcus, 132

Bacon, Francis, 32, 148, 155, 201
Bage, Richard: *Man As He Is*, 162; mentioned, 162, 164
Baggesen, Hans, 77, 94, 254
Bagrianskii, M. I., 36, 60
Baratynskii, E. A., 173
Barsov, A. A., 63, 223, 253
Barthélemy, Jean-Jacques: *Voyage du jeune Anacharsis*, 74, 118, 197, 254; *Voyage en Italie*, 196; mentioned, 55, 72, 74, 117–18, 196, 197
Batiushkov, K. N.: "Speech on the Influence of Light Poetry on Language" ["Rech' o vlianii legkoi poezii na iazyk"], 182; mentioned, 92, 166, 170, 182, 268, 269
Batteux, Charles: *Les Beaux arts réduits à un même principe*, 260; mentioned, 8, 19, 44, 150, 191, 192, 260
Baudelaire, Charles, 119
Baumgarten, A. G., 8
Bayle, Pierre, 59, 152, 154, 159
Beaumarchais, P. A. C. de: *Eugénie*, 246
Beketov, P. N., 168
Belinskii, V. G., 18–19, 69, 137, 173, 225, 227–28, 229
Berquin, A.: *Ami de l'adolescence*, 27
Bertuch, F. J.: *Elfriede*, 50; mentioned, 50, 180
Beseda, 170, 223
Bestuzhev-Marlinskii, A. A., 142
Bion, 31
Blackstone, William, xv
Bobrov, S. S., 39, 174
Bogdanovich, I. F.: *Dushen'ka*, 184, 197; mentioned, 167, 168, 184, 197–98, 203

295

Boian, 167, 168, 169, 221
Boileau: *Art poétique*, xvi; mentioned, xvi, 8, 19
Bolotov, A. T., 59–60, 89, 111, 144, 153
Bonnet, Charles: *La Contemplation de la nature*, 12, 27; mentioned, 12, 14, 27, 28, 29, 32, 72, 73, 74, 82, 146, 148, 149, 150, 154
de Bouilliers, 140
Bouterwek, F.: "Apollo, Erklärung einer alten Allegorie," 57; mentioned, 57, 188, 192
Bowring, Sir John, 140
Boydell, Thomas, 84
Boyle, Robert, 32
Bräker, U.: *Lebensgeschichte und natürliche Abenteuer eines armen Mannes von Tockenburg*, 48; mentioned, 48, 58
Brandes, J. C.: *Der Graf von Olsbach*, 53
Brang, P., 123
Brougham, Henry, 94
Bruce, James: *Travels to Discover the Source of the Nile*, 58
Buffon, G. L., 14, 22, 54, 141, 154, 165, 220
Bürger, G. A.: "Des Pfarrers Tochter von Taubenhain," 180
Burgi, Richard, 176
Büsching, A. F., 69
Buslaev, Petr, 169

Caesar, Gaius Julius, 213
Cagliostro, Count Alessandro di, 59
Campe, J. H.: *Kleine Kinderbibliothek*, 14
Catherine II: *Pot-Pourri* [*Vsiakaia Vsachina*], xiv; *Nakaz*, xiv, 209; mentioned, xiii–xv, 5, 21, 33, 35, 37, 39, 41, 61, 67, 93, 143, 144, 155, 156, 157, 158, 186, 187, 198, 201, 207, 209, 220
Cato, 136, 164
Catherine Pavlovna, Grand Duchess, 219, 220
Cervantes, Miguel de, 43, 99
Chamfort, S. R. N., 38
Chateaubriand: *Génie du Christianisme*, 196; mentioned, 86, 196–97
Charlemagne, 132
Chaucer, Geoffrey, 86
Chechulin, N. D., 180
Chénier, André, 201

Chénier, M. J.: *Charles IX*, 52
Chernyshevskii, N. G.: *What Is To Be Done* [*Chto delat'*], 123
Children's Reading for the Heart and Mind [*Detskoe chtenie dlia serdtsa i razuma*], 8–9, 12, 14, 20, 21–29, 39, 55, 56, 116, 174
Chulkov, M. D.: *The Mocker* [*Peresmeshnik*], 106, 184
Cicero: *De Natura Deorum*, 163; mentioned, 8, 162, 163, 165, 220
Clovis, 213
Codrus, 117
Coiffier, Henri, 96
Colbert, J. B., 82
Collin d'Harleville, J. F.: *L'Optimiste*, 51, 58
Condillac, E. B., 148
Copernicus, 82
Corneille, Pierre: *Cinna*, 49; *Le Cid*, 49; mentioned, xv, 16, 49, 52, 88, 154
Correggio, 83–84
Coxe, William: *Sketches of the natural, civil, and political state of Swisserland*, 45, 58, 68

Dacier, André, 178
Danton, G. J., 162
Dashkova, Princess E. K.: "The Journey of a Russian Noblewoman through Some English Provinces" ["Puteshestvie odnoi rossiiskoi znatnoi gospozhi, po nekotorym anglinskim provintsiiam"], 70
David, 30
Davydov, Denis, 173
Delille, Jacques: *L'Imagination*, 185; mentioned, 185, 190, 198
Delolme, J. L.: *Constitution d'Angleterre*, 82
Demidov, N. A.: *Journal of a Journey ...through Foreign Countries* [*Zhurnal puteshestviia... po nekotorym inostrannym gosudarstvam*], 69–70
Demosthenes, 134, 162, 263
Derzhavin, G. R.: "On Moderation" ["Na umerennost' "], 186; "A Walk at Tsarskoe Selo" ["Progulka v Sarskom Sele"], 249; mentioned, 35, 38, 39, 45, 62, 143, 144, 145, 167, 168, 170, 172, 173, 186, 187, 189, 192, 195, 220, 226, 227, 249
Descartes, René, 82, 148

Diderot, Denis, xv, 51
Dionysius of Halicarnassus, 8
Dittersdorf, K. D.: *Apotheker und Doktor*, 52
Dmitrevskii, I. A., 37, 39
Dmitriev, I. I.: *And My Trifles [I moi bezdelki]*, 145; "Hymn to Rapture" ["Gimn vostorgu"], 187; "Strange Doctrine" ["Chuzhoi tolk"], 188; "On Russian Comedies" ["O russkikh komediiakh"], 197; mentioned, 2–3, 4, 14, 19, 21, 25, 29, 30, 35, 38, 39, 54, 59, 68, 111, 125, 143, 145, 150, 151, 156, 158, 159, 160, 166, 167, 168, 170, 172, 173, 174, 175, 176, 177, 178, 180, 182, 184, 186, 187, 188, 189, 192, 194, 197, 220, 223, 227, 269
Dmitriev, M. A., 42
Dolgorukaia, Princess, 158
Don Quixote, 125, 144
Dorat, C.-J., 154
Ducis, J. F., 15, 16
Dumont, A., 151
Dupaty, C. M.: *Lettres sur l'Italie en 1785*, 68

Écouchard-Lebrun, P. D., 165
Edinburgh Review, 94, 95
Elagin, I. P., 170
Elizabeth Petrovna, Empress, xvi, 2, 114, 203
Emin, F. A.: *Letters of Ernst and Doravra [Pis'ma Ernesta i Doravry]*, 96; mentioned, 96, 168
Emin, N. F., 143
Engel, J. J.: *De Philosoph für die Welt*, 58; mentioned, 55, 58, 150
Erasmus, 86
Eschenburg, J. J., 17
Euripides, 31
Evgenii, Metropolitan, 223

Farmer, Henry, 18
Fauvel, 1
Feldborg, A. A., 94, 95
Fénelon, François: *Télémaque*, 9, 43, 44, 45, 46; mentioned, 9, 43, 44, 45, 46, 154, 201
Ferguson, Adam, 161
Fet, A. A., 192

Fielding, Henry: *Tom Jones*, 3, 69; *Joseph Andrews*, 43; mentioned, xv, 3, 43, 47, 69, 80, 99
Fiévée, J.: *Les Rigueurs du cloître*, 62
Florian, J. P. C. de: *Gonzalve de Cordoue, ou Grenade reconquise*, 44; *Valérie*, 56, 114; mentioned, 44, 55, 56, 114, 115, 140
Fontenelle, B. de B., 154
Fonvizin, D. I.: *The Minor [Nedorosl']*, 3; "Starodum, or the Friend of Honest People" ["Starodum, ili drug chestnykh liudei"], 70; travel letters, 70; mentioned, 3, 70, 167, 168, 222
Fragonard, 184
Framéry, N. E., 48
Franklin, Benjamin, 58, 82, 162, 165
Frederick the Great, 201
Friendly Learned Society, 4, 5, 21, 34, 37, 39, 152, 170, 228
Friendly Literary Society, 170
Fuseli, Henry, 84

Gagarina, Princess P. Iu., 158, 161
Galakhov, A. D., 25, 26, 152, 159, 231
Gameleia, S. I., 33
Garve, C., 55, 58
Gay, John: *Beggar's Opera*, 46
Gellert, F. C.: *Moralische Vorlesungen*, 2; mentioned, xv, 2, 6, 87, 88
Genlis, Stéphanie Félicité de: *Suite des Veillées du château*, 24; "Daphnis et Pandrose," 24, 26, 99; *Les Veillées du château*, 24–27, 104; *Nouveaux contes moraux et nouvelles historiques*, 26; "L'Histoire de la Duchesse de C," 26; "Alphonse et Dalinde," 99; "Eugénie et Léonce," 99, 100; "Olympie et Théophile," 99; "Églantine, ou l'indolente corrigée," 149; mentioned, 24–27, 28, 32, 56, 99, 100, 115, 140, 149, 195, 202, 227, 230
German Museum, 93–94
Gessner, Salomon: "Das Hölzerne Bein," 3, 9–10; "Der Sturm," 10–11, 118; mentioned, 3, 9–11, 12, 26, 28, 29, 71, 72, 75, 76, 85, 90, 102, 118, 119, 140, 148, 149, 184
Gibbon, Edward, 160, 161
Gillies, 161
Glinka, F. N., 33, 55, 89, 139, 144, 173
Glinka, G. A., 206, 270
Glinka, S. N., 89

Gluck, C. W.: *Orphée*, 83; mentioned, 83, 88, 100
Godunov, Tsar Boris, 225
Godwin, William, 162, 163, 164
Goethe, J. W. von: *Werther*, 87, 100, 101, 112, 116, 127, 257; "Meine Gottïn," 119, 179, 180; *Wilhelm Meisters Lehrjahre*, 155; mentioned, 17, 50, 55, 72, 87, 88, 89, 100, 101, 112, 116, 119, 127, 140, 155, 179, 180, 181, 220, 257
Gogol', N. V., xx, 115, 139, 173, 225
Golden Crown, masonic lodge, 4
Goldoni, C., xv, 58
Golenishchev-Kutuzov, P. I., 134
Gray, Thomas, 195
Grech, N. I., 32, 92, 193, 223
Griboedov, A. S., 121
Grigor'ev, A. A., 50
Groddeck, G. E.: *Uber die Vergleichung der alten besonders griechischen mit der deutschen und neuern Litteratur*, 57
Gukovskii, G. A., 22
Guthrie, Matthew, 258, 261

Haller, A. von: *Vom Ursprung des Übels*, 10, 11, 150; "Die Alpen," 76; mentioned, 10, 11–13, 15, 28, 32, 37, 71, 72, 75, 76, 148, 150
Hamilton, Gavin, 84
Handel, G. F.: *The Messiah*, 83; mentioned, 83
d'Harcourt, Comte, 85
Haydn, Joseph: *Die Schöpfung*, 83, 265; *Stabat Mater*, 83; mentioned, 83, 88, 265
Helvetius, C. A., 154
Henri IV, 82
Herder, J. G. von: *Wie die Alten den Tod gebildet*, 85; *Paramythien*, 120; "Gespräch über eine unsichtbar-sichtbare Gesellschaft," 201; mentioned, 17, 31, 55, 57, 72, 74, 85, 120, 179, 180, 201, 252
Heym, Ivan, 170
Holbein, H., 84
Holcroft, Thomas: *Anna St. Ives*, 47; mentioned, 47, 162
Homer, 28, 32, 45, 46, 57, 82, 117, 148, 175, 178, 201, 221
Horace, 8

Howard, John, 261
Hume, David, 8, 160, 161, 163

evlev, V. T., 17
Igor' Tale [*Slovo o polku Igoreve*], 133, 166, 221
Ivan IV, 225
Ivanov, I. A., 97, 170, 182
Ivanov-Razumnik, R. V., 127
Izmailov, A. E.: *Eugene; Or, The Fatal Consequences of Bad Upbringing and Company* [*Evgenii, ili Pagubnye sledstviia durnogo vospitaniia i soobshchestva*], 131
Izmailov, V. V., 104

Jommelli, Nicolò: *Miserere*, 83; mentioned, 83
Jung-Stilling, J. H.: *Jugend*, 125; mentioned, 48, 125

Kalidasa: *Sakuntala*, 57
Kamenev, G. P., 55, 97, 161, 168, 169, 170, 174, 198
Kant, Immanuel, 58, 63, 72, 74, 82, 113, 127
Kantemir, Antiokh, 169, 170, 198
Kanunova, F. Z., 138
Kapnist, V. V., 39
Karamzin, Mikhail Egorovich, 1, 3
Karamzin, Nikolai Mikhailovich, works of:
—miscellaneous: "Album for Grand Duchess Catherine Pavlovna," 220–21; *Dialogue on Happiness* [*Razgovor o schastii*], 125, 129, 159, 165, 220; *Historical Panegyric to Catherine II* [*Istoricheskoe pokhval 'noe slovo Ekaterine II*], 164, 194, 205, 208–9, 213; *History of the Russian State* [*Istoria Gosudarstva Rossiiskogo*], 132, 138, 155, 194, 222, 223–25; "Ideas for a Panegyric to Peter I" ["Mysli dlia pokhval'nogo slova Petru I"], 160; *Letters of a Russian Traveller* [*Pis'ma russkogo puteshestvennika*], 5, 19, 29, 35, 36, 38, 40, 50, 52, 55, 56, 59, 63, 66–95, 113, 115, 128, 130, 140, 144, 147, 158, 160, 161, 166, 194, 219, 228, 229, 230; "Lettre sur la littérature russe," 166–67; *Memoir on An-*

cient and Modern Russia [*Zapiska o drevnei i novoi Rossii*], 209, 219–20, 226, 271; *My Trifles* [*Moi bezdelki*], 130, 144, 145, 194; "Opinion of a Russian Citizen" ["Mnenie russkogo grazhdanina"], 209, 226; *Pantheon of Foreign Literature* [*Panteon inostrannoi slovesnosti*], 55, 162–66, 172, 220, 230, 231; *Pantheon of Russian Authors* [*Panteon rossiiskikh avtorov*], 168–70, 194, 198; "Quelques idées sur l'amour," 161, 186; "Speech to Russian Academy," 221–22; "Thoughts on True Freedom" ["Mysli ob istinnoi svobode"], 209 —poetry: "Alina," 102; "Anacreontic Verses for A* A* P*" ["Anakreonticheskie stikhi A* A* P*"], 30; "Autumn" ["Osen' "], 176; "Cemetery, The" ["Kladbishche"], 85, 176, 180; "Count Guarinos" ["Graf Gvarinos"], 173, 180, 181; "Epistle to A. A. Pleshcheev" ["Poslanie k A. A. Pleshcheevu"], 185, 186; "Epistle to Dmitriev" ["Poslanie k Dmitrievu"], 151, 185, 186; "Epistle to Women" ["Poslanie k zhenshchinam"], 155, 158, 173, 185, 189–90, 211; "Epitaph of the Caliph Abdul Rahman" ["Epitafiia Kalifa Abdula-Ramana"], 146; "Gifts" ["Darovaniia"], 185, 190; "Hope" ["Nadezhda"], 182; "Hector and Andromache" ["Gektor i Andromakha"], 178; "Hymn to Fools" ["Gimn gluptsam"], 185, 195; "Il'ia of Murom" ["Il'ia Muromets"], 84, 111, 176, 177, 182–84, 185, 187, 202; "Impromtu for Two Young Ladies" ["Impromptu dvum molodym damam"], 182; "Inscription for a Lady's Snuff-box" ["Napis' k damskoi tabakerke"], 182; "Inscription for the Grave of Bonnet" ["Nadgrobnaia nadpis' Bonnetu"], 146; "Inscription on a Statue of Cupid" ["Nadpisi na statuiu Kupidona"], 182; "Last Words of a Dying Man, The" ["Poslednie slova umiraiushchego"], 158–59; "Liberation of Europe and the Glory of Alexander I, The" ["Osvobozhdenie Evropy i slava Aleksandra I"], 185, 219; "Melancholy" ["Melankholiia"], 6, 185, 195; "Nightingale, the Jackdaws and the Crows, The" ["Solovei, galki i vorony"], 187; "Nightingale and the Crows, The" ["Solovei i

vorony"], 54; "Offering to the Muses, An" ["Prinoshenie Gratsiiam"], 146; "On the Death of Prince G. A. Khovanskii" ["Na smert' kniazia G. A. Khovanskogo"], 146; "Peace and Glory" ["Pokoi i slava"], 220; "Picture, A" ["Kartina"], 84; "Poetry" ["Poeziia"], 30–32, 38–39, 167, 185, 188, 228; "Proteus" ["Protei"], 121, 185, 190; "Raisa," 173, 181; "Recovery" ["Vyzdorovlenie"], 176; "Reply to My Friend, Who Wanted Me to Write an Ode to Catherine the Great" ["Otvet moemu prilateliu, kotoryi khotel, chtoby ia napisal pokhval'nuiu odu Velikoi Ekaterine"], 156, 187; "Retirement" ["Otstavka"], 181, 182; "Screech-Owls and the Nightingale, or Enlightenment, The" ["Filiny i solovei, ili prosveshchenie"], 187; "Separation" ["Razluka"], 182; "Solomon's Practical Wisdom" ["Opytnaia Solomonova mudrost' "], 185; "Song of Peace" ["Pesn' mira"], 180; "Song to God" ["Pesn' Bozhestvu"], 151; "Spring Feeling" [Vesennee chuvstvo"], 146; "Strange People, The" ["Strannye liudi"], 59, 180; "Sylph, The" ["Sil'fida"], 176, 177; "Tacitus" ["Tatsit"], 160; "To a Poor Poet" [K bednomu poetu"], 185, 187, 191; "To D*" ["K D*"], 175, 176; "To Emiliia" ["K Emilii"], 185, 186; "To Lila" ["K Lile"], 177; "To Lomonosov's Portrait" ["K portretu Lomonosova"], 168; "To Mercy" ["K Milosti"], 5, 61, 156, 164, 185, 186; "To Mishen'ka" ["Mishen'ke"], 5; "To Mr. D** on His Illness" ["Gospodinu D** na bolezn' ego"], 30; "To the Beauty" ["K prekrasnoi"], 176; "To the Imitator of Shakespeare" ["K Shekspirovu podrazhateliu"], 187; "To the Nightingale" ["K solov'iu"], 146; "To the Unfaithful One" ["K nevernoi"], 182; "To Virtue" ["K dobrodeteli"], 118, 185, 186, 195, 212; "Verses from De Masures to I. I. Dmitriev" ["Stikhi ot De Maziura k I. I. Dmitrievu"], 187; "Volga, The," 191; "Warriors' Song, The" ["Pesn' voinov"], 185, 219; "We are happy to work in the fields" ["Veselo v pole rabotat' "], 176, 177 —prose fiction: "Anecdote" ["Anekdot"], 99, 131–32; "Athenian Life"

Karamzin, Nikolai Mikhailovich (*Continued*)
["Afinskaia zhizn' "], 99, 113, 116–18, 137, 152; "Beautiful Princess and the Fortunate Dwarf, The" ["Prekrasnaia tsarevna i shchastlivyi karla"], 97, 98, 99, 106–7, 108, 109, 111, 121; "Bird of Paradise, The" ["Raiskaia ptichka"], 113, 119, 121, 202; "Countryside, The" ["Derevnia"], 15, 111, 119; "Dedication of the Grove, The" ["Posviashchenie kushchi"], 119, 121; "Deep Forest, The" ["Dremuchi les"], 97, 98, 99, 107, 133, 152; "Eugene and Julia" ["Evgenii i Iuliia"], 24, 28, 29, 40, 97, 98, 99–100, 112; "Frol Silin," 93, 96, 97, 98, 99, 104, 105, 118; "Innocence" ["Nevinnost' "], 113, 119, 121; "Island of Bornholm, The" ["Ostrov Borngol'm"], 98, 99, 111, 113–15, 118, 137; "Julia" ["Iuliia"], 25, 93, 99, 121–23, 137, 138, 140, 141, 144, 155, 156, 161; "Knight of Our Time, A" ["Rytsar' nashego vremeni"], 1, 98, 99, 108, 110, 111, 112, 118, 121, 123–26, 128, 129, 132, 137, 138, 140, 159, 195, 225; "Liodor," 60, 99, 108, 111–13, 115, 118, 137, 225; "Martha the Mayoress" ["Marfa-posadnitsa"], 97, 99, 108, 109, 132–37, 142, 195, 202, 258; "My Confession" ["Moia Ispoved' "], 99, 129–31, 132, 137, 138, 139, 195, 198, 205; "Natalia, the Boyar's Daughter" ["Natal'ia, boiarskaia doch' "], 40, 63, 98, 99, 106, 107–10, 111, 112, 121, 124, 132, 133, 137, 142, 144, 183, 184, 202, 228; "New Year, The" ["Novyi god"], 113, 119, 121; "Night" ["Noch' "], 60, 119–21; "Picture of Life, A" ["Kartina zhizni"], 124; "Poor Liza" ["Bednaia Liza"], 40, 47, 63, 66, 92, 93, 96, 97, 98, 99, 100–103, 104, 105, 107, 109, 110, 112, 113, 114, 118, 122, 132, 137, 138, 139, 142, 144, 202, 228; "Recluse, The" ["Pustynnik"], 25–27; "Sensitive and the Cold, The" ["Chuvstvitel'nyi i kholodnyi"], 99, 126–29, 137, 138, 152, 161, 195; "Sierra Morena," 98, 99, 111, 113, 115–16, 121; "Tender Friendship in a Lowly Estate" ["Nezhnost' druzhby v nizkom sostoianii"], 99, 103–5; "Walk, A" ["Progulka"], 28–29
—translations: "Conversation in the Elysian Fields between Maria Theresa and the Empress Elizabeth," 2–3; *Conversation with God* [*Besedy s Bogom*], 11, 13–15; *Emilia Galotti*, 19–21, 48; *Julius Caesar* [*Iulii Tsezar'*], 3, 8, 15–19, 31, 32, 48, 150, 228; *New Tales by Marmontel* [*Novye Marmontelevy povesti*], 98, 101, 105, 144; *Wooden Leg, The* [*Dereviannaia noga*], 2, 9–11, 18

Karamzin, Vasilii Mikhailovich, 13, 157, 193

Karin, F. G., 269

Kauffman, Angelica, 84

Kheraskov, M. M.: *The Rossiad* [*Rossiada*], xviii, 42; *Cadmus and Harmonia* [*Kadm i Garmoniia*], 42–46, 62; *Vladimir*, 46; *Tale-Spinning* [*Bakhar'iana*], 183, 267; mentioned, xvii–xix, 37, 38, 39, 42–46, 62, 90, 136, 145, 167, 170, 172, 173, 183, 189, 195, 249, 267

Khvostov, Count Dmitrii, 223

Kiukhel'beker, V. K., 124, 137, 216–17

Klaudius, C. A., 144

Kleist, E. von, 190

Klimovskii, Semen, 169

Klinger, F. M. von, 50

Kliucharev, F. P., 37, 39

Kliuchevskii, V. O., xiv, 219

Klopstock, F. G.: *Messias*, 6, 82, 244; "Willkommen silberner Mond," 99–100; "Die Deutsche Bibel," 177; mentioned, 6, 30, 31, 82, 89, 99, 175, 177, 178, 188, 201, 211, 244

Klushin, A. I., 42, 143, 170

Kniazhnin, Ia. B., 49, 89, 168

Kolokol 'nikov, V Ia., 33

Kostrov, E. I., 178

Kotzebue, A. von: *Menschenhass und Reue*, 50, 60; *Maria Salmon*, 56; "Wer hatte das geglaubt?" 155–56; mentioned, 50, 52, 55, 56, 60, 88, 155, 195

Kozegarten, L. T.: "Des Grabes Furchtbarkeit und Lieblichkeit," 180

Kramer, J. A., 72

Krylov, I. A., xv, 42, 64, 143, 170, 227

Kutuzov, A. M., 5, 6–7, 33, 34, 35, 36, 37, 42, 44, 60, 61, 62, 265

La Bruyère, 154

Lafontaine, August, 195

La Fontaine, Jean de: *Les Amours de*

Psyché et de Cupidon, 197; mentioned, 169, 185, 197
La Harpe, J. F. de, 19, 44
Lais, François, 83
Lantier, E. F.: *Voyages d'Antenor*, 197
La Place, Pierre Antoine de, 15, 16
La Rochefoucauld, 154
Lavater, J. K., 3, 5, 11, 12, 39, 45, 71, 72, 74, 77, 107, 113, 149, 190, 211–12
Lebrun, Charles, 84, 86, 88
Leibnitz, G. W. von, 11, 12, 58, 148, 159
Lenz, J. M. R.: *Ammerkungen übers Theater*, 16, 17; "Über die deutsche Dichtkunst," 32; "Etwas über Philotas Karakter," 146; mentioned, 16, 17, 32, 88, 146
Leonidas, 117
Lermontov, Iu. M., 97
Lessing, G. E.: *Emilia Galotti*, 19–20, 21, 38, 47, 49; *Miss Sara Sampson*, 20; *Wie die Alten den Tod gebildet*, 85; mentioned, 19–21, 32, 38, 41, 47, 48, 49, 51, 85
Le Tourneur, Pierre, 16, 18
Le Vaillant, François: *Voyage dans l'intérieur de l'Afrique*, 38; mentioned, 38, 42, 58, 59
Levesque, P.-C., 160, 204
Levshin, V. A., 20
Lewis, M. G.: *The Monk*, 116
Lichtwer, M. G.: "Die seltsame Menschen," 180; mentioned, 59, 180
Linnaeus, 82
Locke, John, 32, 128, 148
Lomonosov, M. V., xvi, xx, xxi, 40, 167, 168, 169, 170, 171, 175, 186, 198
Lopukhin, I. V., 4, 14, 36
Lotman, Iu. M., 6, 62, 118, 119, 174, 213
Louis XIV, 85
Lucan, 162, 165
L'vov, N. A.: "Dobrynia," 183; mentioned, 39, 172, 174, 183, 192
L'vov, P. Iu.: *Russian Pamela, The* [*Rossiiskaia Pamela*], 96, 104; *Roza and Liubim* [*Roza i Liubim*], 104; mentioned, 96, 103, 104
Lycurgus, 117, 214
Lyzhin, N., 220, 221

Mably, G. B. de: *Observations sur l'histoire de France*, 82; mentioned, xv, 82

Mackenzie, Henry: *The Man of Feeling*, 72, 87, 88; "The Story of La Roche," 163; mentioned, 72, 87, 88, 163
Macpherson, James. See Ossian
Maikov, V. I., 167, 168
Makogonenko, G. P., 196
Malesherbes, F., 154
Mandeville, Bernard: *The Bees*, 11
Marchesi, Luigi, 83
Maria Fedorovna, Dowager Empress, 111
Marmontel, J.-F.: "Il le fallait," 101; "L'heureux divorce," 123; mentioned, 55, 56, 72, 98, 101, 104, 105, 108, 115, 122, 123, 124, 140, 141, 144, 195, 227, 230
Martynov, I. I., 44
Mason, John, 5, 59
Matthisson, F. von: "Der Schmetterling," 177, 181; mentioned, 72, 177, 180, 181
Maudru, Jean-Baptiste, 90
Maury, J. S., 79
Meister, J. H., 55, 188
Melissino, I. I., 37
Mendelsohn, M., 41
Mercier, L.-S.: "Anecdote historique," 56; *De J. J. Rousseau*, 62; *Le Tableau de Paris*, 85; mentioned, 17, 55, 56, 62, 85
Mercure de France, 38, 44, 48, 56, 62
Merzliakov, A. G., 97
Messenger of Europe, The [*Vestnik Evropy*]: "Aberration, An" ["Strannost'"], 205; "Alcibiades to Pericles" ["Al'tsibiad k Periklu"] (translation), 212; "Great Man of Russian Grammar" ["Velikii muzh russkoi grammatiki"], 223; "Historical Reminiscences and Notes on the Way to the Monastery of the Holy Trinity" ["Istoricheskie vospominaniia i zamechaniia na puti k Troitse"], 114; "History of the French Revolution, Selected from Latin Authors" ["Istoriia frantsuzskoi revolutssi, izbrannaia iz latinskikh pisatelei"] (translation), 212; "Information on Martha the Mayoress from the Life of St. Zosima" ["Izvestie o Marfe Posadnitse, vziatoe iz zhitiia Zosimy"], 202; "Ladies' Wigs" ["Zhenskie pariki"] (translation), 212; "Letter of a Country Dweller" ["Pis'mo sel'skogo zhitelia"], 207; "On Bogdanovich and His Works" ["O Bogdanoviche i ego sochineniiakh"], 197–98; "On Habit"

Messenger of Europe (*Continued*)
["O privychke"] (translation), 212; "On Love for One's Country and National Pride" ["O liubvi k otechestvu i narodnoi gordosti"], 27, 199; "On Politeness and Bon Ton" ["Ob uchtivosti i khoreshem tone"] (translation), 212; "On the Incidents and Characters in Russian History, Which May Provide Subjects for the Arts" ["O sluchaiakh i kharakterakh v rossiiskoi istorii, kotorye mogut byt' predmetom khudozhestv"], 202; "On the Light Dress of Fashionable Beauties" ["O legkoi odezhde modnykh krasavits XIX veka"], 212; "Pleasing Prospects, Hopes and Desires of the Present Time" ["Priiatnye vidy, nadezhdy i zhelaniia nyneshnego vremeni"], 11, 206; "Thoughts on Solitude" ["Mysli ob uedinenii"], 131; "Why Are There Few Writers of Talent in Russia" ["Ot chego v Rossii malo avtorskikh talantov"], 200; mentioned, 27, 55, 67, 76, 78, 93, 123, 129, 130, 131, 134, 138, 139, 142, 146, 156, 174, 184, 192, 193–217, 220, 221, 222, 230

Metastasio, Pietro, 220
Michaelangelo, 83
Miller, G. F., 40
Milton, John, 31, 32, 192, 220
Mirabeau, H. G., 79
Miscellany [*Smes'*], 105
"Miscellany" ["Smes' "]: "Deliberations of a Philosopher, an Historian and a Citizen, The" ["Rassuzhdenie filosofa, istorika i grazhdanina"], 154–55; mentioned, 144, 153–55, 159, 163, 230
Moltke, Count A. D. G. von, 77
Montaigne, Michel de, 48, 127, 151, 199, 214, 220
Montesquieu, Charles de Secondat: *Esprit des lois*, 208; mentioned, xv, 82, 154, 164, 208, 271
Montgolfier, 142
Monthly Compositions for Profit and Entertainment [*Ezhemesiachnye sochineniia, k pol'ze i uveseleniiu sluzhashchie*], xvii–xviii, 40
Monthly Magazine, 93
Monthly Review, 95
Monvel, J. M. Boutet de: *Les Victimes cloîtrées*, 62
Mordovchenko, N. I., 134, 167
More, Sir Thomas: *Utopia*, 45, 55
Moritz, C. P.: *Magazin zur Erfahrungsseelenkunde*, 58; *Reisen eines Deutschen in England*, 68; *Anton Reiser*, 124, 125; mentioned, 55, 58, 68, 72, 124, 125
Moschus, 31
Moscow Journal [*Moskovskii zhurnal*]: "Country Festival and Wedding, A" ["Sel'skii prazdnik i svad'ba"], 77; "Nightingale and the Crow, The" [Solovei i vorona"], 187; "Palemon and Daphnis" ["Palemon i Dafnis"], 10–11, 62, 104; "Sofiia," 50–51, 60; "Suicide, A" ["Samoubiitsa"], 38; "Various Fragments" ["Raznye otryvki (Iz zapisok odnogo molodogo rossiianina)"], 59, 156; mentioned, 20, 31, 35–65, 66, 67, 68, 69, 72, 76, 83, 90, 93, 99, 105, 106, 108, 113, 114, 118, 120, 130, 139, 143, 144, 145, 146, 152, 153, 154, 156, 158, 167, 172, 174, 175, 178, 181, 185, 187, 192, 194, 195, 196, 197, 216, 221, 228, 229, 230
Moscow News [*Moskovskie vedomosti*], 13, 21, 37, 144, 153
Moses, 30
Murav'ev, M. N.: "Concept of Rhetoric, The," ["Poniatie ritoriki"], 149; "A Suburban Dweller" ["Obitatel' predmestiia"], 167; "To the Goddess of the Neva" [K bogine Nevy"], 173; mentioned, 34, 149, 150, 167, 173, 218, 224
Murav'ev, N. M., 224
Muse, The [*Muza*], 155–56

Napoleon I, 213–14, 215, 219, 272
Nartov, A. A., xviii
Neledinskii-Meletskii, Iu. A., 39, 172, 195
Nestor, 168
Nevzorov, M. I., 33
New Aonides [*Novye Aonidy*], 173
New London Magazine, 27
Newton, Sir Isaac, 30, 82, 148
Nicolai, C. F., 72, 73, 74
Nikolev, N. P.: *Spoilt Darling* [*Baloven'*], 48, 196; mentioned, 48, 53, 196, 267
Nikon, 133, 168
Novikov, N. I.: *St. Petersburg Scholarly News for 1777* [*Sankt-Peterburgskie uchenye vedomosti na 1777 god*], 40, 41; *Windbag* [*Pustomelia*], 41; *Drone*

[*Truten'*], 64; *Painter* [*Zhivopisets*], 64; *Attempt at an Historical Dictionary of Russian Authors* [*Opyt istoricheskogo slovaria o rossiiskikh pisateliakh*], 168–69; mentioned, xiv–xvi, xvii, 4–5, 14, 21, 22, 27, 32, 37, 40, 41–42, 44, 60, 61, 64, 152, 157, 168–69, 228
Numus, 132

Orlov, M. F., 224
Orpheus, 31, 187
Osipov, N. P.: *Virgil's Aeneid in Reverse* [*Virgilieva Eneida, vyvorochennaia na iznanku*], 42, 46, 61
Ossian: "Carthon," 57; "The Songs of Selma," 57, 257; mentioned, 28, 31, 47, 55, 56–57, 107, 112, 115, 140, 165, 166, 180, 181, 257
Ostrovskii, A. N., 109
Ovid, 31, 32
Ozeretskovskii, N. Ia., 89, 90

Paine, Tom, 162
Panin, Count P. I., 70
Pantheon of the Age, The, 95
Patriot, The: "A View of Stories or Tales" ["Vzgliad na povesti ili skazki"], 141; mentioned, 123
Paul I, 67, 156, 157, 158, 159, 160, 161, 163, 164, 168, 172, 184, 193, 194, 198, 207, 208, 213, 230
Pel'skii, P. A.: *My Odds and Ends* [*Moe Koe-chto*], 145
Pericles, 221
Perrault, Charles: "Riquet à la houpe," 106
Peter I, 82, 86, 157, 160, 186, 201, 202, 203, 208, 220, 221, 222
Peter III, xiii
Petrov, A. A., 3–4, 7–9, 15, 16, 19, 21, 22, 24, 30, 33, 34, 36, 38, 59, 61, 68, 90, 111, 128, 143, 145, 146, 152, 190, 245, 246, 248
Petrov, V. P., 187
Phalereus, Demetrius, 8
Phales, 151
Phidias, 86, 88, 117
Philips, John, 179
Piccini, Nicolò, 83
Pigalle, Jean-Baptiste, 85–86
Pindar, xvi, 168

Pittacus, 151
Platner, E. P., 57, 58, 61, 72, 261
Plato, 12, 82, 117, 151, 201, 211
Pleshcheev, Aleksandr Alekseevich, 185, 186
Pleshcheev, Aleksei Aleksandrovich, 35, 36, 37
Pleshcheeva, A. I., 36, 119, 150, 193
Pleshcheevs, 68, 142
Plutarch, 161, 162, 164
Podshivalov, V. S., 22, 29, 39, 41, 170, 196
Pogodin, M. N., 21, 62, 183, 219
Polenov, V. A., 170
Pomerantsev, V. P., 19, 49
Pompignan, J. J., 160, 220
Pope, Alexander: "Universal Prayer," 12, 29; *Essay on Man*, 159, 220; mentioned, 12, 29, 32, 58, 72, 89, 150, 159, 192, 220
Popov, M. I., 168, 169, 183
Popovskii, N. N., 168, 169
Potemkin, Prince G. A., 209
Poussin, Nicholas, 84, 85
Predtechenskii, A. V., 21
Privalova, E. P., 26
Prokopovich, Feofan, 169, 198
Prokopovich-Antonskii, A. A., 14, 15, 22
Protasova, E. I., 193
Prozorovskii, Prince A. A., 21, 60–61
Pugachev, E. I., xiv, 23
Pushkin, A. S.: *Eugene Onegin*, 110, 173; *Tales of Belkin*, 110; *Boris Godunov*, 135; *Mozart and Salieri*, 149; "Bova," 183; *Ruslan and Ludmila*, 184; *Sovremennik*, 219; mentioned, xx, xxi, 62, 110, 135, 137, 142, 149, 166, 173, 174, 183, 184, 205, 210, 219, 224, 225, 227, 231
Pushkin, V. L.: "Epistle to I. I. D(mitriev)" ["Poslanie k I. I. D(mitrievu)"], 189; mentioned, 173, 189

Quintilian, 8

Rabelais, François, 86
Racine, Jean: *Iphigénie*, 49; mentioned, xvi, xviii, 16, 49, 52, 79, 88, 154
Radcliffe, Anna, 113–14
Radishchev, A. N.: *Journey from Petersburg to Moscow* [*Puteshestvie iz Peterburga v Moskvu*], xv, 6, 174–75;

Radishchev, A. N. (*Continued*)
Life of Fedor Ushakov [*Zhitie Fedora Vasil 'evicha Ushakova*], 69; "Bova," 183; mentioned, xv, 6, 61, 69, 174–78, 265
Raich, S. E., 173, 255
Rambler, The, 27
Ramler, K. W., 8, 72, 74, 175
Ramsay, A. M., le Chevalier, 44
Raphael, 83, 84, 85
Reding, Alois, 214–15
Reeve, Clara, 113
Reitzer, J., 27
Rezanov, V. I., 185
Richardson, Samuel: *Clarissa*, 53, 54, 101; *Sir Charles Grandison*, 69, 101; *Pamela*, 97, 101; mentioned, 47, 53, 54, 69, 96, 97, 101
Richelieu, L.-F.-A., Duc de, 82
Richter, J. G., 93, 194, 218
Ridiger, Christian, 144
Riurik, 135
Robertson, William, 160, 161
Robespierre, M. F. de, 160
Rollin, Charles, 1
Romantische Gemälde de Vorwelt, 53
Rosa, Salvator, 84
Rostopchin, F. V.: *Prussian Journey* [*Puteshestvie po Prussii*], 70
Rousseau, J.-J.: *Les Confessions*, 75, 80, 125, 126, 130, 148, 152; *La Nouvelle Héloise*, 76, 89, 96, 122, 127, 221; *Émile*, 122, 157, 221; *Discours sur la question, proposée par l'Académie de Dijon...*, 147; *Le Contrat Social*, 221; *L'Économie politique*, 221; *Le Gouvernement de Pologne*, 221; mentioned, 23, 48, 59, 62, 63, 72, 75, 76, 80, 82, 83, 85, 87, 88, 89, 90, 96, 97, 122, 125, 126, 127, 130, 140, 145, 147–48, 152, 154, 157, 161, 165, 215, 220, 221, 271
Rousseau (singer), 83
Rozov, Ivan, 144
Rubanovskii, A. K., 253
Rubens, P. P., 84, 85
"Russian in England" ["Rossiianin v Anglii"], 70
Ryleev, K. F., 225
Rzhevskii, A. A., xviii

Saadi, 164
Saint-Evremond, 154
Saint-Lambert, J. F., de, 190

Saint-Pierre, Bernadin de, 154
Sakulin, P. N., 111
Sallust, 162, 212
Sandunov, N. N., 22
Saurin, B. J., 145
Saxe, Maurice, Maréchal de, 85
Sayers, F.: *Dramatic Sketches of the Ancient Northern Mythology*, 47
Schaden, J. M., 1, 2, 10
Schiller, F.: *Don Carlos*, 53; *Uber naive und sentimentalische Dichtung*, 117; *Die Horen*, 155; "An die Freude," 180; "Resignation," 181; mentioned, 50, 53, 55, 117, 123, 155, 180, 181
Schröpfer, J. G., 59
Schwartz, J. G., 4, 8, 14, 37
Scott, Walter, 138
Scudéry, Madeleine de, 157
Séchelles, Hérault de, 162
Selivanovskii, S. I., 55
Semennikov, V. P., 175
Serbinovich, K. S., 7, 125
Shaftesbury, Anthony Ashley Cooper: *Characteristics*, 150; mentioned, 11, 31, 32, 46, 59, 150, 152, 159
Shakespeare, William: *Julius Caesar*, 3, 8, 15–19, 146, 150; *Hamlet*, 15, 101; *King Lear*, 50; mentioned, 3, 4, 8, 15–19, 20, 21, 31, 32, 47, 48, 49, 50, 52, 53, 84, 101, 146, 150, 167, 169, 191, 228
Shalikov, P. I., 87, 170, 173
Shatrov, N. M., 145
Shcherbatov, Prince M. M., 204
Sheshkovskii, I. S., 61
Sheshkovskii, S. I., 61
Shishkov, A. S.: *Deliberation on the Old and New Styles of the Russian Language* [*Rassuzhdenie o drevnem i novom sloge rossiiskogo iazyka*], 170, 223; mentioned, 6, 92, 134, 170, 188, 216, 223, 255
Shklovskii, V. B., 124
Shtorm, G. P., 35
Sipovskii, V. V., 25, 40, 68, 106, 123
Smollet, Tobias: *Travels through France and Italy*, 70
Society for Translation of Foreign Books, xv
Society of Friends of Russian Scholarship, 37
Socrates, 106, 117, 164
Sofiia Alekseevna, Tsarevna, 169
Solon, 117
Sophocles, 31, 49, 50, 117

Spectateur du Nord, Le, 69, 70, 74, 78, 157, 161, 166

Spectator, The, 27

Spectator, The [Zritel'], 42, 64, 144

Speranski, M. M., 219

Spirits' Postbag [Pochta dukov], 64

Staël, Anne Louise Germaine, Mme. de: *Méline,* 144; *Delphine,* 196; mentioned, 144, 196

Sterne, Laurence: *Tristram Shandy,* 56; *A Sentimental Journey,* 56, 68, 70; mentioned, 55, 56, 68, 70, 72, 87, 88, 92, 108–9, 124, 133, 140, 189

Storch, H., 63, 197

"Story of Frol Skobeeve" ["Povest' o Frole Skobeeve"], 110

Strakhov, N. I., 197

Sturm, C. C.: *Betrachtungen über die Werke Gottes,* 13, 14, 106–7; *Unterhaltungen mit Gott...,* 13; 13–15, 22, 32, 106–7

Sumarokov, A. P.: *False Demetrius [Dimitrii Samozvanets],* xvii; *Hamlet [Gamlet],* 15–16; "On the Love of Virtue" ["O liublenii dobrodeteli"], 186; mentioned, xvi-xx passim, 15–16, 20, 90, 167, 168, 169, 175, 183, 186, 198

Swift, Jonathan, xv

Tacitus, 160, 162, 201, 205, 212, 225

Tarasov, E. I., 6

Tasso, Torquato: *Gerusalemme liberata,* 165

Tatishchev, V. N., 204

Teutsche Merkur, 27

Theocritus, 31

Thomas, Antoine, 140, 205

Thomson, James: "Hymn, A," 12, 28; "Winter," 20, 47, 49; *The Seasons,* 24, 28, 32, 86, 139, 179; "Summer," 32, 248; "Lavinia," 101; "Autumn," 179; mentioned, 12, 20, 24, 28, 29, 30, 31, 32, 37, 47, 49, 72, 84, 86, 87, 101, 119, 139, 140, 148, 179, 180, 190, 191, 192, 248

Thucydides, 160

Tiede, J. F.: *Unterhaltungen mit Gott...,* 13; mentioned, 13, 14, 21, 32

Tikhonravov, N. S., 14

Timkovskii, I. F., 9, 10

Tissot, S. A., 25

Tiutchev, F. I., 192, 225, 226

Todi, Maria, 83

Tolstoi, L. N., 129

Town and Country Magazine, 27

Trediakovskii, V. K.: *Tilemakhida,* 44, 175; mentioned, xvi, l, 44, 169, 174, 175, 198

Troshchinskii, D. P., 208

Trubetskoi, N. N., 33, 36, 42, 143

Tumanskii, F. O.: *On the Improbable Myths by the Greek Writer Palaephatus [Palefata grecheskogo pisatelia O neveroiatnykh skazaniakh],* 41; *Russian Storehouse [Rossiiskii magazin],* 57; mentioned, 41, 57, 143, 158, 196

Turgenev, Andrei, 97, 170–71, 182, 186

Turgenev, I. P., 4, 5–6, 44, 59, 143, 170, 265

Turgenev, I. S., 97, 119, 192

Universal Chronicle, 127

Ushakov, F. V., 69

Uvarov, S. S., 225

Vallière, Louise de la, 85

Vasnetsov, V. M., 184

Venetsianov, Aleksei, 256

Vernes, François, 55

Viazemskii, A. I., 157

Viazemskii, P. A., 62, 64, 160, 170, 173, 181, 185, 192

Vigel', F. F., 193, 223

Virgil, 31, 32, 105

Vishnevskaia, G. A., 188

Voeikov, A. F., 165

Volney, C. F.: *Les Ruines,* 62

Voltaire: "Le taureau blanc," 3; *Brutus,* 16; *La Mort de César,* 16, 17; *Henriade,* 45, 46, 54, 82; *Candide,* 46, 150; "Précis de l'Ecclésiaste," 185; mentioned, xv, 3, 4, 16–17, 19, 26, 45, 46, 49, 52, 54, 72, 73, 82, 140, 150, 175, 185, 198, 246

Vostokov, A. Kh.: "Essay on Russian Prosody" ["Opyt o russkom strikhoslozhenii"], 183; mentioned, 175, 183

Wall, Anton: *Bagatellen,* 106, 142, 145, 156; *mentioned,* 106, 123, 140, 142, 145, 156

Walpole, Horace, 113
Warens, Mme. de, 126
Weisse, C. F., 28, 29, 32, 72, 73
West, Benjamin, 84
Wieland, C. M.: *Die Abderiten*, 34; *Cordelia*, 56, 114; *Geschichte des Agathon*, 74, 117; *mentioned*, 27, 29, 34, 55, 56, 72, 74, 92, 114, 117, 184
Wolzogen, W. von, 123

Xenophon, 201

Young, Edward: *The Complaint, or Night Thoughts*, 3, 6; mentioned, 3, 6, 18, 28, 31, 72, 88, 90, 180, 192, 248

Zagoskin, M. N.: *The Seducer* [*Iskusitel'*], 60
Zeno, 151
Zeuxis, 117
Zhukovskii, V. A., 14, 62, 92, 165, 170, 173, 195, 216, 168

Date D

WITHDRAWN

APR 0